**Exploring the Transnational Neighbourhood:
Perspectives on Community-Building, Identity and Belonging**

Exploring the Transnational Neighbourhood

Perspectives on Community-Building, Identity and Belonging

Edited by
Stephan Ehrig, Britta C. Jung, and Gad Schaffer

LEUVEN UNIVERSITY PRESS

Published with the support of the KU Leuven Fund for Fair Open Access, the Irish Research Council under grant numbers GOIPD/2018/61 and GOIPD/2017/803, as well as the UCD Humanities Institute and the IMLR, University of London.

Published in 2022 by Leuven University Press / Presses Universitaires de Louvain / Universitaire Pers Leuven. Minderbroedersstraat 4, B-3000 Leuven (Belgium).

Selection and editorial matter © 2022, Stephan Ehrig, Britta C. Jung, and Gad Schaffer
Individual chapters © 2022, The respective authors

This book is published under a Creative Commons Attribution Non-Commercial Non-Derivative 4.0 Licence.

Attribution should include the following information:
Stephan Ehrig, Britta C. Jung, and Gad Schaffer (eds), *Exploring the Transnational Neighbourhood: Perspectives on Community-Building, Identity and Belonging*. Leuven: Leuven University Press, 2022. (CC BY-NC-ND 4.0)

Unless otherwise indicated all images are reproduced with the permission of the rightsholders acknowledged in captions and are expressly excluded from the CC BY-NC-ND 4.0 license covering the rest of this publication. Permission for reuse should be sought from the rights-holders.

ISBN 978 94 6270 348 3 (Paperback)
ISBN 978 94 6166 481 5 (ePDF)
ISBN 978 94 6166 482 2 (ePUB)
https://doi.org/10.11116/9789461664815
D/2022/1869/49
NUR: 612

Layout: Crius Group
Cover design: Daniel Benneworth-Gray
Cover illustration: LxsDos, "Sister Cities / Ciudades Hermanas" 2015 (Photography: Federico Villalba www.LxsDos.com)

Contents

Acknowledgements · 7

Exploring the Transnational Neighbourhood: An Introduction · 9
Stephan Ehrig, Britta C. Jung and Gad Schaffer

Challenging Accusations of Separatism: Transnational Neighbourhood and Vernacular Cosmopolitanism in Insa Sané's *Comédie urbaine* (2006–2017) · 35
Christina Horvath

SECTION I
VIRTUAL NEIGHBOURHOODS

"We will be ephemeral": Encounter, Community and Unsettled Cosmopolitanism in Senthuran Varatharajah's *Vor der Zunahme der Zeichen* (2016) · 69
Maria Roca Lizarazu

All Saints Catholic Church in Williamsburg, Brooklyn, NYC: From Religious Space to Transnational Territory of Multiterritorial Mexican Immigrants · 93
Emilio Maceda Rodríguez

Networking and Representing the Transnational Neighbourhood Online: The Linguistic Landscapes of Latin Americans in London's Seven Sisters · 115
Naomi Wells

SECTION II
OVERLAPPING NEIGHBOURHOODS

The Translocalisation of Place: Sectarian Neighbourhoods, Boundaries and Transgressive Practices in Anna Burns' Belfast · 139
Anne Fuchs

The Quiet Unification of a Divided City: Jerusalem's
Train-Track Park 161
Gad Schaffer

Ruins and Representation: Remembering Flushing Meadows-
Corona Park in Queens, New York City 195
Daniela Bohórquez Sheinin

The Materiality of the Wall(s): Mural Art and Counterspace
Appropriation in El Paso's Chihuahuita and El Segundo Barrio 219
Anna Marta Marini

SECTION III
NEGOTIATING STRANGENESS AND MOBILE NEIGHBOURHOODS

Transnational Neighbourhoods in Barbara Honigmann's *Das
überirdische Licht* (2008) and *Chronik meiner Straße* (2016) 245
Godela Weiss-Sussex

Territories of Otherness: Genoa's Prè Neighbourhood as
a Deviant Terrain and Exotic Counterspace in Ilja Leonard
Pfeijffer's *La Superba* (2013) 265
Britta C. Jung

"Your Allah can't see you here": Moscow's Subterranean
Spaces and Dissimulated Life in Svetlana Alexievich's *Vremya
sekond khend* (2013) 291
Emma Crowley

Transnational Neighbourhood and Theatrical Practices: The
Concept of Home, Negotiating Strangeness and Familiarity,
and the Experience of Migrant Communities in North Essex 315
Mary Mazzilli

About the Authors 337

Acknowledgements

The present volume was preceded by two events that were jointly organised by the Institute of Modern Languages Research (IMLR, University of London) and the UCD Humanities Institute that sought to shift the focus away from othering multicultural and multi-ethnic environments by exploring transcultural encounters in the urban neighbourhood from a grassroots perspective: a workshop on *Transnational and Translingual Urban Writing* at the IMLR in London in June 2018, which was followed by a larger, interdisciplinary conference on the *Transnational Neighbourhood* held at the UCD Humanities Institute in Dublin in September 2019.

The finished work would not have been possible without the wonderful support of various institutions and individuals whom we would like to thank.

First and foremost we are grateful to Anne Fuchs, Godela Weiss-Sussex and Maria Roca Lizarazu, for all their help and support setting up, organising and running the events, as well as their invaluable input to the publication proposal.

We also wish to thank all our contributors for their continuous and punctual work, and further thank those conference participants who were not able to contribute but left their mark on the overall approach of this book, in particular Gillian Jein (Newcastle) and Sandra Ponzanesi (Utrecht).

Our utmost gratitude, furthermore, goes to Valerie Norton and Ricki Schoen from the UCD Humanities Institute and the administrative staff at the IMLR who have flawlessly shouldered all administrative, financial and logistical matters behind the scenes.

In design and publishing matters, we would like to thank the artist duo LxsDos for allowing us to use their great mural as the book cover, and Mirjam Truwant from Leuven UP for all her exceptional support in creating this book.

Finally, we are very grateful to our funders. The research conducted in this publication was funded by the Irish Research Council under grant numbers GOIPD/2018/61 and GOIPD/2017/803, both of which also contributed to the Open Access fee. Furthermore, the volume was published with the generous support of the KU Leuven Fund for Fair Open Access, the UCD Humanities Institute and the IMLR.

acknowledgments

Exploring the Transnational Neighbourhood

An Introduction

STEPHAN EHRIG, BRITTA C. JUNG AND GAD SCHAFFER

The Russian philosopher and literary critic Mikhail Bakhtin once described the relationship between a place and the people inhabiting it as a dialogical matter, attesting a certain reciprocity between the two through which they affect and transform each other.[1] Given the fact that we are living in an age of unprecedented human mobility,[2] it hardly comes as a surprise that global mass migration deeply affects this very relationship. The reasons for today's human mobility are manifold and encompass the personal and professional choices of a globalised operating workforce, as well as warfare, persecution and economic destitution. Climate change is yet another factor causing the displacement of millions of people. The associated loss of home and the making of a new one, the challenge of integrating migrants and transmigrants,[3] and the conflicting notions of identity and belonging are perhaps some of the most acutely felt transcultural predicaments of the 20th and 21st century. This applies to migrants and transmigrants, as well as those remaining in their place of origin throughout their lives who feel the loss of life-long members of their community and/or are confronted with the newcomers. As a result, terms such as identity, nationalism, cosmopolitanism, multiculturalism, plurilingualism and globalisation, as well as colonialism and postcolonialism, play a central role in our media and in political discourse.

Geographically and socially closely defined, the urban neighbourhood in particular has come to occupy the public imagination as a litmus test of migration and how it affects local communities. Urban neighbourhoods with a high percentage of migrants have been both hailed as multicultural success stories and condemned as ethnic hotspots and ghettos. Whereas New York City's Williamsburg, Singapore's Holland Village, São Paulo's Liberdade, London's Brixton, Berlin's Kreuzberg and (more recently) Tallinn's Kalamaja have become known as trendy multi- and transcultural neighbourhoods characterised by creativity and a newly affluent cosmopolitan class, others seem indeed troubled by disenfranchisement, discord, social dislocation, crime and radicalisation, with Molenbeek in Brussels and the Clichy-sous-Bois banlieue in Paris being perhaps the most notorious (European) examples in recent years. Building on the controversial, albeit historically persistent stereotype of the criminal immigrant, which – in turn – is based on the premise that many immigrants lack financial resources and experience blocked pathways to social and economic mobility,[4] immigrant neighbourhoods such as Molenbeek and Clichy-sous-Bois have become increasingly suspicious to those outside. Labelled as "vessels of a set of social problems" (Wiard, Pereira),[5] "badlands" (Dikeç),[6] and "no-go zones"[7] (e.g. De Vries) in (inter)national news media, Molenbeek was seen as a breeding ground for Islamist terrorism after the bombings in Paris and Brussels in 2015 and 2016. Clichy-sous-Bois, on the other hand, gained notoriety during the highly mediatised 2005 riots that erupted after the death of two local teenage boys, Zyed Benna and Bouna Traoré, and the subsequent spread to other disadvantaged neighbourhoods throughout France, prompting a national state of emergency.[8] "Depending on the politics of observers," Gillian Jein remarks, "the events were interpreted as evidence of the threat these neighbourhoods posed to the [French] Republic, or as signs of the Republic's abandonment of its poorest and postcolonial populations."[9] Jein further notes that transnational neighbourhoods such as Clichy-sous-Bois are frequently depicted as an Other and "deviant terrain".[10] However, voices from within often emphasise different perceptions and have the potential to challenge and counter normative discourses of national membership, as Jein's example of acclaimed French 'photograffeur' JR illustrates.[11] In an act of grassroots reframing from within the neighbourhood, JR's complex 2017 mural *Chroniques de Clichy-Montfermeil* charted the 2005 riots by encompassing 750 portraits of the neighbourhood's ethnically diverse residents. This act of spatial and historical localisation, i.e. the incorporation of the neighbourhood's face(s) at a specific point in time, is then counteracted by the mural's stylised references to modern France's revolutionary founding myth. Specifically, it quotes the canonical revolution paintings by Jacques-Louis David, *Le Serment des Horaces* (Oath of the Horatii, 1786) and *Le Serment du Jeu de paume* (Tennis Court Oath, 1794), as well as Eugène Delacroix's *La Liberté guidant le peuple* (Liberty Leading the People, 1830). JR's work thus transgresses conventional concepts of French identity and belonging by presenting the Othered as an integral and diverse part of French society. His reading and mediatisation of the Clichy-sous-Bois riots powerfully illustrate what Mustafa Dikeç overserves with regard to the banlieues and – as this volume argues – other comparable urban neighbourhoods around the world, i.e. that "despite their negative stereotype as 'badlands', banlieues are also sites of political mobilization – or of 'insurgent citizenship' to use Holston's notion – with democratic aspirations, drawing on a vocabulary of justice, citizenship and equality."[12]

The public sphere is often used as a canvas for both political mobilisation as well as communal identity building. Accordingly, this simultaneity not only underpins JR's mural but is also, for example, echoed in the *Make Shift* project of the art duo LxsDos (consisting of the artist couple Ramon and Christian Cardenas), who work in the US–Mexican twin cities of El Paso and Ciudad Juárez, and whose 2015 mural *Sister Cities/Ciudades Hermanas* in El Paso's El Segundo Barrio adorns the cover of this volume. Historically part of a fluid borderland, the El Paso–Juárez transborder agglomeration – and particularly the disadvantaged neighbourhoods adjacent to the border – encompasses communities with a shared heritage and cultural identity divided by ever-hardening migration regimes.[13] With the support of local business and property owners, as well as local art councils and members of the community, LxsDos' attempts to "make art available to poor neighborhoods or people who don't have the opportunity to go to the city museum" and thereby to empower local "communit[ies]" and the "normal people" on the streets.[14] Accordingly, *Make Shift* plays on various local art traditions, iconographies and themes, but also colourfully and positively reappropriates the cultural hybridity of the border neighbourhoods that are often framed as "no-go" migrant areas.[15] In doing so, LxsDos' art is inherently political: through its location and artistic expression it transcends and renegotiates territorial and cultural borders and boundaries, celebrates the shared heritage and ingenuity of the people, and advocates for individual and communal sustainability. Yet the cities' and their neighbourhoods' shared heritage and local identity is by no means exclusionary. In fact, as an immigrant himself, Ramon Cardenas is part of a minority in the US but also in the US–Mexican borderland. Born and raised in the Philippines, Cardenas relates to the shared Spanish influences and to certain socio-economic and cultural similarities to his homeland within the local communities, particularly in the poorer sister city, Ciudad Juárez.[16]

Clichy-sous-Bois and El Segundo Barrio (and JR's and LxsDos' artistic engagement with their respective neighbourhoods) capture in a succinct manner Bakhtin's dictum of a certain reciprocity between a place and the people inhabiting it and the transformative power it often entails. Indeed, an ever-increasing body of research suggests that immigrant settlement in urban neighbourhoods, many of which still suffer from the population declines and economic disinvestment of the 1970s, has rejuvenated some of these places.[17] Although terms such as *banlieue, ghetto, favela, barrio, township* and *inner-city* are frequently associated with migration and ethnic minorities, and have become a shorthand for disenfranchisement, discord, social dislocation, crime and radicalisation, it is their rootedness in place and community and creative potential to renegotiate conflicting notions of identity and belonging that makes them particular – and often simply a matter of framing. After all, neighbourhoods such as Williamsburg, Liberdade, Brixton, Kreuzberg and Kalamaja already attest to the fact that they can – in the public imagination – be both: relatively closed and static as well as dynamic, innovative and transgressive.

What Is a Transnational Neighbourhood?

The present volume, hence, seeks to engage with – and reframe – neighbourhoods such as Clichy-sous-Bois, El Segundo Barrio and Williamsburg and explore the concept of the *Transnational Neighbourhood*. The volume was preceded by two events that were jointly organised by the Institute of Modern Languages Research (IMLR) and the UCD Humanities Institute and sought to shift the focus away from othering multicultural and multi-ethnic environments by exploring transcultural encounters in the urban neighbourhood from a grassroots perspective: a workshop on *Transnational and Translingual Urban Writing* at the IMLR in London in June 2018, which was followed by a larger, interdisciplinary conference on the *Transnational Neighbourhood* held at the UCD Humanities Institute in Dublin in September 2019. Both events led to the conclusion that analysing the social microcosms of urban neighbourhoods allows for a more nuanced discussion of transculturality as lived practice.

Thanks to its multi- and interdisciplinary nature, the volume examines the relationship and interplay between different societal discourses and national narratives within a decidedly broader inter- and transnational context. Reflecting on the epistemological flaws of approaching mnemonic phenomena that undercut the combination of territorial, ethnic and cultural collectivity, Astrid Erll explains that this entails "looking beyond established research assumptions, objects and methodologies."[18] Erll points to the "sheer plethora of shared *lieux de mémoire* that have emerged through travel, trade, war, and colonialism" as well as the "great internal heterogeneity of cultural remembering."[19] Similarly, Michael Rothberg and Dirk A. Moses have also drawn attention "to the palimpsestic overlays, the hybrid assemblages, the non-linear interactions and the fuzzy edges of group belonging."[20] Yet, on the other hand, Aleida Assmann rightly reminds us that within the realm of the transnational "we need to acknowledge some borders that continue to exist and are even resurrected by some communities."[21] Ann Rigney and Chiara de Cesari suggest that we must recognise "the significance of national frameworks alongside the potential of cultural production both to reinforce and to transcend them".[22]

We therefore propose to define the transnational neighbourhood as follows. In the transnational neighbourhood, transculturality is performed as lived practice, emerging around the simultaneity of three key focal points of spatiality, temporality and agency. We wish to frame the urban neighbourhood as local but not provincial; as a fluid space in which various temporal and spatial axes intersect; as the locus where diverse trans/cultural practices can engender togetherness as well as differences and conflict. As a translocality, as Brickell and Datta argue, the neighbourhood is a reinscribed place of "grounded transnationalism"

– a space where otherwise deterritorialised networks of transnational relations take shape through migrant agency.[23] It is a densely packed contact zone where disparate cultures meet in often highly asymmetrical relations, fostering processes of hybridisation, creolisation and neoculturation. The neighbourhood is open to the type of multi-scalar perspective that, according to Rigney and de Cesari, avoids entrapment in a binary discourse.[24] As the chapters in this volume demonstrate in their approaches to different neighbourhoods, transnational neighbourhoods comprise comparably condensed, often peripheral spaces and places. They can be both urban and rural, and are often multiterritorial, re-/deterritorialised places/spaces for transmigrants, in an artificial and partially even forced setting. As liminal, overlapping and entangled spheres, these neighbourhoods foster mobility across different 'scales' and are constantly translated or in translation. They are spaces/places that contain a simultaneity of temporalities, spatialities and agencies: they produce a constantly shifting local and cultural knowledge that emerges from repetitive spatial experience and an exposure to kaleidoscopic cultural and communicative mnemonic practices, both of which are grounded in everyday experiences; moreover, they are transnationally mediated through technology. Most importantly, these neighbourhoods foster a productive social and cultural friction in their *throwntogetherness*.[25]

The simultaneity of temporalities, spatialities and agencies can take different forms whose interpretation and analysis afford different methods. Thus, by using an interdisciplinary focus combining sociological, ethnographic, anthropological, literary and geographical foci, the chapters in this volume observe how this simultaneity is being culturally employed, explored and manifested throughout the different case studies.

Gathering case studies that cover a multitude of aspects, this volume draws on current debates on the translocal and transcultural turn in the humanities and social sciences, and builds on more recent explorations in urban studies that, individually and primarily, take a narrow disciplinary perspective towards sustainability, climate change resilience and social policy (urban planning, marketing, economics, law).[26] The volume's interdisciplinary nature sheds light on the question of transnationalisation from different disciplinary and interdisciplinary angles, combining a variety of research methods (including human geography, ethnography, and the interpretation of literary texts and the visual arts), and exploring it in the physical as well as the virtual, social and cultural world. The proposed sections differentiate the three different levels of discourse, i.e. the virtual, the physical (trans)local and the transnational-global, offering a first starting point for a future engagement with the concept.

Examining the multidimensional quality of the transnational neighbourhood, the contributors to this volume shift the perspective on migration away from nationalised and politicised discourses and explore the transnational and transcultural dynamics of global neighbourhoods as multifaceted environments whose own voices and perspectives are rarely represented and compared through urban cultural studies. As the topic of migration has become particularly contentious in national and international debates in recent years, the various contributions address one of the key questions of our time: how do people create the feeling of community within an exceedingly globalised context? By focusing on the neighbourhood as a central space of everyday lived experience, this volume explores practices of community-building alongside cultural, social and historical obstacles, in often overlapping geographical spaces and cultural settings, and virtually interconnected through the World Wide Web and social media.

Crucial as a background for the discussion of transnational neighbourhoods is their intertwined nature of space/place with social habitus on the one hand, and their multifaceted encoding of the built environment with cultural meaning on the other. The large body of theoretical work on urban space and spatial perceptions since the 1960s has been fundamental for understanding how urban neighbourhoods are being perceived through human minds. Urban space has been approached as psychologically mapped,[27] "imageable",[28] and as corporeally experienced atmospheres,[29] while the French Marxist tradition understands it as produced, appropriated through everyday life, shaped by power structures and habitus.[30] Martina Löw, in her influential study *The Sociology of Space* (2018) describes the construction and perception of urban space as a dialogical process of *spacing* and *operations of synthesis* in contexts which are defined by class, gender and milieu-specific schemes.[31] Although the 'spatial turn' has shaped much humanities research, little emphasis so far has been put on grassroots perspectives on the dimension of cultural difference. For the transcultural perception of an urban neighbourhood, this consequently means that, on top of that, several simultaneous, overlapping and even contradictory cross-cultural processes of spatial perception need to be added. These, then, provide meaningful transcultural experiences of the urban neighbourhood within a coexistence of parallel and intertwined temporalities, spatialities, and social and cultural agencies.

This very coexistence is defined by blurring and complicating the clear lines of migration, ethnicity and culture – hence we speak of *trans-* and not *inter-* or *multi-*national neighbourhoods. This very 'trans-ness' calls for both a new terminology and a new methodology. The new transnational neighbourhoods have been described and analysed as intersectional cultural hybrids (Bhabha), *thirdspaces* (Bhabha, Soja) and even transcultural heterotopias, whose kaleidoscopic semantic encoding of the urban neighbourhood creates new acculturated forms of culture, social life, and notions of identity and belonging.[32] In her seminal book *For Space* (2005), the geographer Doreen Massey rejects the idea of a historically grown place or neighbourhood as the source of a fixed identity within an ever-changing world. Instead, she understands space dynamically and pluralistically as a product of our daily "interactions, from the immensity of the global to the intimately tiny."[33] Or, put another way, as something that is created through chance encounters and what she calls *throwntogetherness*, i.e. the being "set [...] down next to an unexpected neighbour."[34] Accordingly, Massey perceives space "as the sphere of the possibility [...] in which distinct trajectories coexist; as the sphere [...] of coexisting heterogeneity." Space is, therefore, "always under construction" and it is constituted by social practices, evolving narratives, and inevitable (re-)negotiations.[35] And, as Anne Fuchs notes in her reading of Massey in this volume, this "relational politics of place" also makes the case for a "politics of connectivity" in response to globalisation.[36]

Moreover, the rise of the World Wide Web and the continuous digital connectivity as part of a drastically changed global mediascape have impacted on the way in which the experience of cultural identity, transmigration, but also displacement, is resignified and transformed by new digital affordances from different vantage points – allowing for the creation and sustenance of multiple social relations that link together and deterritorialise societies of origin and residence.[37] On a different level, this shift in highly diverse neighbourhoods, furthermore, has in many cases not found its way into political and planning policy decisions, impacting on a strong regime of social and spatial injustice that ignores the complexity of the sociocultural milieu (Soja, Harvey).[38]

Theoretical Diversity: Spatialities, Temporalities, Agencies

The volume's overall concept is interdisciplinary and comparative in nature, bringing together chapters featuring different methodological approaches whose overlappings best unfold when studied in combination. While the volume, as a whole, is structured around the meta-structural complexes of how the contemporary transnational neighbourhood is virtually constituted and interconnected ('Virtual Neighbourhoods'), how they often consist of several overlapping geographical and mnemonic layers ('Overlapping Neighbourhoods'), and how their mobile residents negotiate strangeness ('Negotiating Strangeness and Mobile Neighbourhoods'), the aspect of simultaneous and intersecting spatial, temporal and agency-related factors features throughout the chapters and requires a general discussion and exploration of the chapters' theoretical and methodological diversity.

Literary texts provide one major source and mode of expression for transnational neighbourhoods that will be analysed in this volume. Building on spatial practices to further explore translocal and transcultural dynamics within the spectrum of spatiality and temporalities impacting on agency, Anne Fuchs' chapter in this volume, 'The Translocalisation of Place: Sectarian Neighbourhoods, Boundaries and Transgressive Practices in Anna Burns' Belfast' analyses the topography of segregation and the performance of subjectivity through boundary crossing in Anna Burns' Booker Prize-winning novel *Milkman* (2018). The novel is set in a fictionalised version of a 1970s Belfast, i.e. a city ripe with sectarian strife and violence, but Fuchs argues that the novel's thematic and aesthetic features as well as its spatial focus of the working-class, Catholic neighbourhood echo the transnational urban reality and its literary depiction we have come to associate with the 21st century. She uses Talja Blokland's discussion of a neighbourhood as "a geographically circumscribed, built environment that people use practically and symbolically."[39] Blokland's definition points to three important features: firstly, a neighbourhood is a bounded place in a predominantly urban setting; secondly, neighbourhoods engender social relations through practices and rules; thirdly, neighbourhoods accrue symbolic meaning and capital which – depending on social and economic factors – can go up and down. As a locality within an urban setting, neighbourhoods require other adjacent neighbourhoods for their self-definition. Quoting Arjun Appadurai, neighbourhoods can appear as "simply a set of contexts, historically received, materially embedded, socially appropriate, naturally unproblematic."[40] This, in return, directly impacts on a sense of neighbourhood that is defined by constant migration and mobility. Fuchs employs Paul Watts' and Peer Smets' argument that, while in our own era of hypermobility neighbourhoods are "spatially fixed and determinate places", they are, however, "also simultaneously being constantly made and remade via flows of people as they circulate in and out of, within and around these residential locales."[41] Furthermore, Fuchs quotes Ulrike Hanna Meinhof's description of the contemporary city as a space of "negotiation and encounter between culturally diverse people", which is "in principle and practice disruptive of the often monocultural imaginary of the nation-state."[42] Finally, Fuchs suggests the useful term *elective belonging* for forms of residential attachment that are no longer rooted in and authorised by historical ties to a particular locality.[43]

In a similar vein, Maria Roca Lizarazu's literary chapter '"We will be ephemeral": Encounter, Community and Unsettled Cosmopolitanism in Senthuran Varatharajah's *Von der Zunahme der Zeichen* (2016)' examines how the dis-located, disembodied *non-place*[44] of the World Wide Web affects the possibility of witnessing, recounting and transmitting histories of flight and expulsion, while also exploring what kinds of connection and community might arise in their aftermath. Transposed to the virtual dimension of the internet, Roca Lizarazu suggests that the concept of the transnational neighbourhood implies a tangle of issues having to do with coexistence, on the one hand, and transnationalism and cosmopolitanism, on the other. In her reading, the transnational neighbourhood brings these various topics together, urging us to explore transnational convivialities and everyday cosmopolitanisms in a "densely packed contact zone".[45] Here, the transnational neighbourhood is a space of chance and fleeting encounters, unwanted proximities, a virtualised urban microcosm defined by everyday interactions and intermingling, inviting us to reconsider what the term 'transnational' actually means. Roca Lizarazu argues here that the notion of the transnational neighbourhood can usefully complement the prevailing focus in transnational studies on border-crossings, thus allows for an exploration of a transnationalism or "cosmopolitanism of connections".[46] Questions of strangeness and familiarity, of inside and outside are thus central to cosmopolitanism as well as to the transnational neighbourhood.

Spatialities and, specifically, cultural production of the perception and employment of spatial practices are the specific focus of different chapters in this volume, providing their own spatio-cultural definitions of the transnational neighbourhood. In her chapter 'Transnational Neighbourhoods in Barbara Honigmann's *Das überirdische Licht* (2008) and *Chronik meiner Straße* (2016)', Godela Weiss-Sussex analyses two autofictive texts by the German author of Jewish faith who lives in Strasbourg. Straddling various cultural identities as an author, Honigmann's autofictive texts focus on her experience as writer in residence in Manhattan and the multicultural world of the author's local neighbourhood in Strasbourg, and shows how the author-narrator establishes a balance between distance and belonging in these neighbourhoods, illustrating that the notion of belonging and familiarity is compatible with a notion of openness, constant mobility and change. Weiss-Sussex defines the concept of the urban neighbourhood in spatial and relational terms – as based on space, but without fixed or even describable borders, constantly changing over time, and constituted by social practice and encounters between different, at times even antagonistic, city dwellers: "localized everyday life".[47] Heterogeneity and fluidity are characteristics of all neighbourhoods understood in this way, but the transnational neighbourhoods investigated here bring these constitutive elements to the fore. She regards cultural production, and specifically writing, as an expression of deterritorialisation and of not-quite-belonging, and goes on to explore how literary writing can capture and support the idea of a successful, vibrant transnational neighbourhood. How can it reflect – and what possibilities does it have to reflect upon – the constantly shifting spatial and relational characteristics that make up these neighbourhoods? How can it provide a sense of the "productive social and cultural friction [of the] throwntogetherness"[48] that constitutes them, while resisting expectations of cohesion and notions of harmonisation? The texts in her case study both evoke and celebrate the freedom of the stranger in a new city; the deterritorialisation of the self is seen as a productive and energising force. Such a state is – by definition – transitory, and fittingly, all groups of belonging described in this text on New York are transitory, too; they are temporary, constituted with the awareness of their impermanence, and they are conscious of their heterogeneity.

On the other hand, Emilio Rodriguez Maceda's ethnographic study 'All Saints Catholic Church in Williamsburg, Brooklyn, NYC: From Religious Space to Transnational Territory of Multiterritorial Mexican Immigrants' takes a sociological-ethnographic approach and explores what happens when the same territory is appropriated by various social groups with different cultural, social, economic and political practices. In the church, the immigrant community is territorialised, deterritorialised and reterritorialised. The fact that different groups coexist in this same space, and that each one contributes its own characteristics at the time of territorialising it, makes this church a multiterritorial and transnational space, since the links that immigrants have built with their places of origin influence the activities that take place in the church. He uses the writing of Rogério Haesbaert who, critiquing the way in which the concept of deterritorialisation has been understood as destruction or abandonment of a territory, instead suggests that it should be thought of as a process where the territory is reconsidered, reterritorialised, and where at the same time multiple territorialities emerge simultaneously.[49] In this sense, deterritorialisation is not only seen as negative, but it also raises the positive meaning where not only the idea of destruction is present, but also the reconstruction and construction of new territories. These subaltern groups are territorialised in spaces where, usually, they do not have the concrete and definitive domination of the territory but can have a more symbolic and experiential appropriation of the space, as migrants are one of the groups that experience the appropriation of space based on multiple territorialities, since, when travelling through different territories, they accumulate experiences and feelings on their way. With this, migrants manage to develop multiterritoriality, where they have the possibility of having simultaneous experiences in different territories. In this context of migration, there are some migrants who manage to establish strong ties with other members of their community, even in different countries; other migrants develop the possibility of travelling through foreign territories, especially those who live in precarious conditions and are forced to enter or transit through territories that belong to others. They are very conscious that they belong to multiple spaces, and that they have appropriated those spaces, not only symbolically, but also physically. Haesbaert defines this as successive multiterritoriality, while Ulrich Beck describes this as topopolygamy, i.e. being married to several places at the same time.[50]

The downside to this development is a strong regime of social and spatial injustice, as Anna Marta Marini discusses in her chapter 'The Materiality of the

Wall(s): Mural Art and Counterspace Appropriation in El Paso's Chihuahuita and El Segundo Barrio', which brings in cultural studies and critically examines the street art and visual representation of a transnational community at the US–Mexican border. Marini traces the community's connection with both the border itself and the other side, embodied in the hybrid reproduction of Mexican traditions and iconography. Exploring Edward Soja's works, she argues that the necessity to fight for spatial justice evidences that space and its (re)arrangement are strictly related to the sociocultural milieu.[51] A differential development of urban planning and the implementation of unequal urban policies evidently have a role in (re)producing social injustice. The tentative counter-appropriation of the neighbourhood and the creation of spaces that represent the community allow the minority population to assume a position that is simultaneously marginalised by the dominant society and centred within the neighbourhood.

Gad Schaffer's chapter, 'The Quiet Unification of a Divided City: Jerusalem's Train-Track Park', adds then a human geographical perspective and takes a closer look at the redevelopment of a derelict railway track into a new urban park by the City of Jerusalem, which was inaugurated in 2012, examining how, over time, borders shape space and consequently influence people. In this case, the physical and mental borders of eight demographically diverse Jerusalem neighbourhoods are displayed. Segregated by socio-economic and ethno-religious differences as well as legal status, the park passes through the neighbourhoods in an attempt to transform them into an area of transnational movement and encounters between the neighbourhoods' residents, allowing for a quiet unification. Since sustainable development is commonly seen as the right way to promote development that simultaneously enhances social equality and protects the environment,[52] Schaffer's analysis focuses on one feature of sustainable development, i.e. the social aspect, in particular by examining whether the new park promotes environmental justice and whether it has created a process of gentrification, which is often associated with such new redevelopment projects.

Social and spatial practices between different neighbourhood communities are also played out in a simultaneity of different temporalities, both as mnemonic practices as well as cultural and semantic encodings that allow for different communities to coexist in the same space. In her literary chapter 'Territories of Otherness: Genoa's Prè Neighbourhood as a Deviant Terrain and Exotic Counterspace in Ilja Leonard Pfeijffer's *La Superba* (2013)', Britta C. Jung explores the Dutch author's depiction of Genoa and, particularly, its migrant neighbourhood Prè. She takes a lead from Massey's and Wendy Wolford's conclusion that we need to move beyond the social construction of space by also incorporating the spatial construction of the social, i.e. the extent to which the physical environment of a city or its neighbourhoods is, as Wolford puts it, "internalized, embodied, imagined, and remembered."[53] Employing the term 'spatial imaginaries', Wolford goes on to define the spatial construction of the social as "cognitive frameworks, both collective and individual, constituted through the lived experiences, perceptions, and conceptions of space itself".[54] Jung argues that Pfeijffer (re)charts the Mediterranean spatial imaginary by casting the port city of Genoa as a gateway to Europe and a migratory junction in both a spatial and a temporal sense. As a result, Genoa becomes a multiterritorial, geographically and socioculturally ambiguous non-European Other and a counterspace to northern European urbanity, with Prè the focal point of – or a valve for – the narrator's colonial gaze.

Similarly, Naomi Wells' linguistic chapter 'Networking and Representing the Transnational Neighbourhood Online: The Linguistic Landscapes of Latin Americans in London's Seven Sisters' delves into the ephemeral qualities of transcultural places and uses the example of commercial spaces in London neighbourhoods such as Seven Sisters to illustrate how Latin American communities construct and sustain a highly localised identity through a wider transnational network of online communications and spatial representations. Due to their associations with trajectories of mobility, transnational neighbourhoods may risk being perceived as inherently transitory and temporary spaces, and while in practice it may be true that all spaces are as Massey explains always in a process of "becoming",[55] such a fleeting spatial identity can pose a real risk to those who inhabit these spaces and leave them without the means by which to sustain their continued existence within them. This points to the contradictions of political discourses that both seek to demonise *ethnic enclaves* and *parallel lives*, while simultaneously fostering a system whereby it becomes necessary to adopt a single and unified 'ethnic' identity to gain visibility and recognition.[56]

Daniela Bohórquez Sheinin's anthropological chapter 'Ruins and Representation: Remembering Flushing Meadows–Corona Park in Queens, New York City', on the other hand, traces the shifting formations and understandings of the transnational neighbourhoods that surround Flushing Meadows–Corona Park in Queens, New York City. By exploring the shifting populations in the vicinity of the park following the World Fair in 1964–1965, the chapter frames it not only as a physical space for the convergence for generations of immigrants from around the world but also as memory, exploring spatial imaginaries in the context of overlapping temporalities attached to the same urban environment by different communities. While neighbourhood demographics have shifted over time, the physical environment has remained, suffused each day with multi-national and multi-ethnic meanings by its diverse occupants who refashioned the space in their neighbourhood's image. The transnational neighbourhood, from this lens, operates in different modes of identity formation for different populations. Discussing New York's Flushing Meadows–Corona Park in Queens, her interviews show that, for ethnic whites, the park has come to operate as a material buttress for memory, a touchstone for the specific transnational constellation of communities the park and its neighbourhoods once housed decades ago. For many first- and second-generation Latin American immigrants, however, Flushing Meadows–Corona Park became a material and symbolic marker of the present and the future, with all of the opportunities, anxieties, harmonies and contestations implied thereby.

Lastly, the many chapters in this volume explore whether cultural production – be it street art or a literary text – can be regarded as a direct form of expressing and performing agency within the transnational neighbourhood, as well as providing a congenial medium to capturing it. Emma Crowley's chapter '"Your Allah can't see you here": Moscow's Subterranean Spaces and Dissimulated Life in Svetlana Alexievich's *Vremya sekond khend* (2013)', for instance, examines how Alexievich's polyphonic representation of urban Moscow challenges the way the Soviet past and the post-Soviet neighbourhood are entwined, focalising the oft-forgotten imperialist legacies of Soviet modernity and the particular transnationalism that it has produced. Employing Bakhtin, Crowley analyses how *polyphonic storytelling* is one mimetic mode to encapsulate the simultaneity of spatial and social agency, arguing that the technique of counterpoint illuminates the relational quality of divergent and opposing voices, creating a dialogic structure that can reveal the distinct forces at play in the structure of a novel.[57] She suggests that such a composition can also invoke a paratactic style, which, borrowing from the literary critic Edward Said, places together words or phrases independently, in a neighbourly manner, as it were, without coordinating them or subordinating them through the use of conjunctions.[58] For Said, parataxis as a literary device invites comparison while maintaining an ambiguous distance from the meaning of relation. In Crowley's analysis, the transnational neighbourhood is not so much a space of connection as a stifled multiplicity in which barriers mark out linguistic, ethnic and economic differences.

In addition to representation, Christina Horvath's chapter 'Challenging Accusations of Separatism: Transnational Neighbourhood and Vernacular Cosmopolitanism in Insa Sané's *Comédie urbaine* (2006–2017)' provides a literary analysis of one of Europe's most well-known banlieues, Sarcelles, which is located in the northern outskirts of Paris and home to a substantial number of *pieds-noirs*,[59] Assyrians, Sephardic Jews, and Caribbeans. She shows that culture can counter negative preconceptions about multiculturalism. Instead of the often-evoked conflict, these neighbourhoods are liminal spaces or contact zones in which heterogeneous populations tend to negotiate their differences on a daily basis while producing a new, vernacular form of cosmopolitanism. In her chapter, she analyses how the transcultural neighbourhood as narrated in novels is used to challenge dystopian representations of French banlieues and dismantle the myths of separatism and ghettoisation by proposing a vernacular cosmopolitan vision of banlieues as contact zones in which, despite the frictions resulting from the residents' exposure to economic hardship and different forms of otherness, the ideal of *mixité sociale* [localised social diversity] is at least partially accomplished. The transnational neighbourhood, in this case, is represented as a translocal space in which the networking and negotiation of different belongings and allegiances is continually in progress. As opposed to the imagined harmony which characterises the republican ideal of *mixité sociale*, the banlieue of Sarcelles is depicted as a contact zone where tensions and frictions exist and require constant mitigation. Defined by Mary Louise Pratt as "social spaces where cultures meet, clash, and grapple with each other, often in contexts of highly asymmetrical relations of power, such as colonialism, slavery, or their aftermaths as they are lived out in many parts of the world today",[60] contact zones are territories in which the coexistence of different languages, religions, culinary traditions can be occasionally chaotic or conflictual. Raised in such a contact zone, Sarcellois youths learn to co-habit with the Other from an early age and acquire thereby a vernacular cosmopolitan orientation.

Mary Mazzilli's chapter 'Transnational Neighbourhood and Theatrical Practices: The Concept of Home, Negotiating Strangeness and Familiarity, and the Experience of Migrant Communities in North Essex', on the other hand, takes both a theoretical as well as a creative approach and introduces community theatre as a performative space that can transform strangeness into familiarity. Mazzilli's *Human Side of Migration* project has involved migrant communities from the North Essex region in a research process that informed the writing of her stage play *Priority Seating*. On a theoretical level, her investigation of the reality of migrants in North Essex as a transitional urban network moves away from the definition of transnational neighbourhood as the 'other', but implies interconnectivity among different migrant communities and between migrant communities and local non-migrant communities. Mazzilli analyses agency arising from the tension of strangeness/familiarity as connected to the migrant experience, the concept of home and their interrelations, and argues that these can be brought to the fore through the theatrical medium. In particular, Mazzilli focuses on the question of space and place, employed as an educational tool to affect young people's understanding of migration and home. She uses Sanja Bahun and Bojana Petric's works on the connection between home and community, who describe the "close interaction, indeed co-formation, of (the ideas of) home and community" and proposes the notion of home as an affect, which has capacity to be experienced as polycentric, thus, as attached to a point of origin as well as of destination. The emotional dimension of home and home-making considers home "as it interacts with human values and human rights in various communities".[61] Mazzilli applies this notion to the migrant experience and suggests that, in their building up a sense of home, while assimilating the host culture, this describes the potential for migrants to form multidimensional emotional ties not only with the host community. Furthermore, it also applies to the many communities in the host country and with communities in their country of origin, thus generating further and extended communities that live and develop beyond national boundaries and geographies. Thus, Mazzilli argues that transnational neighbourhoods imply connections between communities at the micro level of communities rather than at macro level of cultural and national systems, where a sense of home as affect is formed and informs much of the migrant experience. Working at a micro level, her theatre project further empowers this microcosm of interactions, creating a shared place, a common ground facilitating the polycentric and multidimensional discourses and interactions among communities.

Structure

Engaging critically with the transnational, translocal and transcultural turn, the present volume filters these debates through the lens of geography, ethnography and anthropology, as well as literary and cultural studies. It investigates, analyses and presents its findings through close readings of cultural phenomena that always reflect broader theoretical and socio-political issues, and thus establish a multidisciplinary conceptualisation for the transnational neighbourhood. Indeed, the volume is the first to establish the *transnational neighbourhood* as an innovative concept through which recent debates around transnationalism and transculturality can be approached. As such it is a key intervention in the areas of transnational and transcultural studies that allows for a range of fresh perspectives and enables us to move past dominant binaries (global/local, flows/frictions, borders/borderlessness, etc.).

The volume was conceived as an interdisciplinary and comparative whole that best communicates its transnational design when read as one piece, thus allowing the different case studies to intertwine their overlapping characteristics, while each individual chapter will mainly zoom into one specific urban neighbourhood and explore the concept of the transnational neighbourhood through a monodisciplinary lens. However, we alternatively envisioned that the volume can be used by readers choosing to read the introduction and then those chapters that concern phenomena, areas or disciplinary, theoretical and methodological approaches they are interested in.

The volume opens with a first introductory chapter (Horvath) that explores one of Europe's most well-known banlieues, Sarcelles, just north of Paris. Horvath's analysis of Insa Sané's cycle *Comédie urbaine* (2006–2017) shows how the novels subvert some of the prejudices which surround stigmatised banlieues in the French spatial imagination as hubs of delinquency, Islamic radicalisation, discrimination against women and hatred for the republican law and order, and instead explore different aspects of a transnational neighbourhood marked by ethnic and religious diversity, colonial legacies and the residents' ambiguous feelings about the French capital.

The volume's first section, 'Virtual Neighbourhoods', examines how the World Wide Web as a global information medium has transposed the notion of neighbourhood into a simulated or the virtual world throughout the World Wide Web. Since its inception in 1989, it has become an integral part of transnational communities, connecting people, territories, cultures and ideas, irrespective of their physical-geographical location. On the one hand, the dis-located and dis-embodied non-space of the internet allows for migrant encounters as a coping mechanism for the multiple layers of the migrant experience, while on the other hand it facilitates the multiterritorial simultaneous interconnectedness linking different geographical regions, as well as space mapping the different linguistic communities within geographical neighbourhoods. Furthermore, the continuous digitised connectivity as part of a drastically changed global mediascape impacts on the way in which the experience of cultural identity, migration, but also displacement, is resignified and transformed by new digital affordances from different vantage points.[62] Finally in this section, the volume critically engages with linguistic landscape studies, which have become a primary method in sociolinguistic research for investigating the multilingual makeup of specific neighbourhoods, with emplaced public signs often treated as indicators of a place's transnational or 'superdiverse' identity. However, whilst neighbourhoods are often conceptualised as physical, offline spaces, much of what we observe offline – including public signs – is connected to and/or premised on the online presence of these spaces.[63] These virtual neighbourhoods therefore challenge common perceptions of spatiality and placeness, and simultaneously foster new forms of agency and temporality.

The second section, 'Overlapping Neighbourhoods', explores the cultural, historical and mnemonic semantics of bordering neighbourhoods. These are characterised by a simultaneity of visible and invisible borders that demarcate a hybridity of social and historical layers of segregation, the neighbourhoods that are performed through social ethnic codes, cultural identity markers and different overlapping space-claiming practices. The chapters in this section explore the spatial-geographical overlapping of neighbourhoods inasmuch as they can both coincide and clash with temporal perceptions, appropriations, as well as spatial practices through transcultural users.

The third section, 'Negotiating Strangeness and Mobile Neighbourhoods', gathers polyphonic perspectives and strategies of the migrant experience by negotiating the correlating binaries of distance and belonging as well as familiarity and constant mobility while attempting to appropriate a place of one's own, build a new community, and create visibility within hegemonial and hierarchical social settings. Hence, the focus of the chapters in this final section is directed towards the agency of migrants putting their spatio-temporal experiences into transcultural practices, for which the transnational neighbourhood represents the central space of action and negotiation.

Bringing together these different disciplinary and interdisciplinary angles on the transnational neighbourhood, combining a variety of research methods and exploring it in the physical as well as the social and cultural world, this volume aims to make a contribution to transnational, transcultural and translocal neighbourhood studies by focusing on the neighbourhood as a central space of everyday lived experience and community-building alongside cultural, social and historical obstacles. With the 'Transnational Neighbourhood', the volume proposes a concept that lends itself to further exploration both in a theoretical sense as well as applied research. With the proposed sections differentiating the three different levels of discourse (i.e. the virtual, the physical (trans)local and the transnational-global) emerging around the simultaneity of three key focal points (spatiality, temporality and agency) we hope to offer a first starting point for a future engagement with the concept.

Notes

1. Bakhtin, Mikhail (1981b): Discourse in the Novel. *The Dialogic Imagination: Four Essays*, edited by Michael Holquist. Austin: University of Texas Press, 259–422.
2. In January 2020 the World Economic Forum estimated that 272 million people or 3.5% of the world's population were international migrants, tripling the number of people living in a country other than they were born in since 1970 and already surpassing some projections for 2050. Cf. Edmond, Charlotte (2020): Global Migration, by the Numbers: Who Migrates, Where They Go and Why, https://www.weforum.org/agenda/2020/01/iom-global-migration-report-international-migrants-2020/.
3. Generally speaking, the term 'transmigrant' refers to an emigrant passing through a country en route to another one where they will settle as an immigrant. Cf. e.g. Merriam Webster's definition. However, Nina Glick Schiller and others have come to use the term 'transmigrant' more specifically to describe mobile subjects that create and

sustain multiple social relations that link together their societies of origin and residence. These mobile subjects are viewed as transnational migrants or transmigrants to distinguish them from migrants and immigrants. Cf. Glick Schiller, Nina, Linda Basch, and Cristina Szanton Blanc (1995): From Immigrant to Transmigrant: Theorizing Transnational Migration. *Anthropological Quarterly* 68(1), 48–63; Basch, Linda G., Nina Glick Schiller, and Blanc Cristina Szanton Blanc (1994): *Nations Unbound: Transnational Projects, Postcolonial Predicaments, and Deterritorialized Nation-States.* London: Gordon and Breach.

4. Lee, Matthew T., Ramiro Martinez, and Richard Rosenfeld (2001): Does Immigration Increase Homicide? Negative Evidence from Three Border Cities. *The Sociological Quarterly* 42(4), 559–580; Adelman, Robert, Lesley Williams Reid, Gail Markle, Saskia Weiss, and Charles Jaret (2017): Urban Crime Rates and the Changing Face of Immigration: Evidence across Four Decades. *Journal of Ethnicity in Criminal Justice* 15(1), 52–77; cf. also Ferracuti, Franco (1968): European Migration and Crime. *Crime and Culture: Essays in Honor of Thorsten Sellin*, edited by Marvin E. Wolfgang. New York: John Wiley and Sons, 189–219; Waters, Tony (1999): *Crime and Immigrant Youth.* Thousand Oaks, CA: Sage.

5. Wiard, Victor and Fábio Henrique Pereira (2019): Bad Neighbourhoods in a Good City? Space, Place and Brussels' Online News. *Journalism Studies* 20(5), 649–674; Jein, Gillian (2021): Speculative Spaces in Grand Paris: Reading JR in Clichy-sous-Bois and Montfermeil. *Aesthetics of Gentrification: Seductive Spaces and Exclusive Communities in the Neoliberal City*, edited by Christoph Lindner and Gerard F. Sandoval. Amsterdam: Amsterdam University Press, 221–246.

6. Dikeç, Mustafa (2007): *Badlands of the Republic: Space, Politics and Urban Policy.* Hoboken, NJ: Blackwell.

7. Cf. e.g. De Vries, Karl (2015): Paris Attacks Prompt Fears France's Muslim 'No-Go' Zones Incubating Jihad. *Fox News.* https://www.foxnews.com/world/paris-attacks-prompt-fears-frances-muslim-no-go-zones-incubating-jihad (12 January)Accessed 4 August 2021.

8. Indeed, the 2005 riot in Clichy-sous-Bois follows in the tradition of banlieue revolts such as the 1990 (and 1992) riot in Lyon's Vaulx-en-Velin which – as a neighbourhood – remains a major reference point in debates around urban planning and banlieues. Cf. Dikeç (2007), 14.

9. Jein (2021), 222. Cf. also Koff, Harlan, and Dominique Duprez (2009): The 2005 Riots in France: The International Impact of Domestic Violence. *Journal of Ethnic and Migration Studies* 35(5), 713–730.

10. Jein, Gillian (2015): (De)Facing the Suburbs: Street Art and the Politics of Spatial Affect in the Paris Banlieues. *The DS Project: Image, Text, Space/Place, 1830–2015*, http://thedsproject.com/. Accessed 28 June 2021.

11. Jein (2021), 235ff. JR's self-descriptive term *photograffeur* is a portmanteau of *photographer* and *graffeur*, i.e. the French word for graffiti artist.
12. Dikeç (2007), 14f.
13. Indeed, until 1888, Ciudad Juárez was named El Paso del Norte and settlements north of the Rio Grande were named/defined in relation to the city.
14. Martinez, Freddy (2016): On the Streets of El Paso and Juarez, 'Sister Cities' Art Project Pays Tribute to Border Communities. *Remezcla* (7 July), https://remezcla.com/features/culture/interview-los-dos/. Accessed 18 August 2021.
15. Ibid.
16. The wall art and Mexican mural traditions in El Paso's south side, including the art of LxsDos, will be further explored by Anna Marta Marini in this volume and discussed in terms of an urban counterspace that gives voice to a sizable but by and large silenced ethno-linguistic minority in the US.
17. Alba, Richard D., Nancy A. Denton, Shu-yin J. Leung, and John R. Logan (1995): Neighborhood Change under Conditions of Mass Immigration. *International Migration Review* 29(3), 625–656; Winnick, Louis (1990): *New People in Old Neighborhoods: The Role of New Immigrants in Rejuvenating New York's Communities*. New York: Russell Sage.
18. Erll, Astrid (2011): Travelling Memory. *Parallax: Transcultural Memory* 17(4), 4–18, 9.
19. Ibid., 8.
20. Rothberg, Michael, and Dirk A. Moses (2014): A Dialogue on the Ethics and Politics of Transcultural Memory. *The Transcultural Turn: Interrogating Memory Between and Beyond Borders*, edited by Lucy Bond and Jessica Rapson. Berlin and Boston: De Gruyter, 29–38, 32.
21. Assmann, Aleida (2016): *Shadows of Trauma: Memory and the Politics of Postwar Identity*. New York: Fordham University Press, 68.
22. Rigney, Ann, and Chiara de Cesari (2014): Introduction. *Transnational Memory: Circulation, Articulation, Scales*, edited by Ann Rigney and Chiara de Cesari. Berlin and Boston: De Gruyter, 1–25, 4.
23. Brickell, Katherine and Ayona Datta, eds. (2011): *Translocal Geographies: Spaces, Places and Connections*. Farnham: Ashgate, 3.
24. De Cesari, Chiara, and Ann Rigney, eds. (2014): *Transnational Memory: Circulation, Articulation, Scales*. Berlin: De Gruyter.
25. Massey, Doreen (2005): *For Space*. Los Angeles and London: Sage.
26. To name a few: Wharf, Barney, and Santa Arias, eds. (2009): *The Spatial Turn. Interdisciplinary Perspectives*. London: Routledge; Györke, Ágnes, and Imola Bülgözdi, eds. (2020): *Geographies of Affect in Contemporary Literature and Visual Culture: Central Europe and the West*. Leiden: Brill; Rędzińska, Katarzyna, and Monika Piotrkowska (2020): Urban Planning and Design for Building Neighborhood Resilience to Climate Change. *Land* 9(10), 387, doi.org/10.3390/land9100387; Fladvad Nielsen, Brita, Dan-

iela Baer, and Carmel Lindkvist (2019): Identifying and Supporting Exploratory and Exploitative Models of Innovation in Municipal Urban Planning: Key Challenges from Seven Norwegian Energy Ambitious Neighborhood Pilots. *Technological Forecasting and Social Change* 142, 142–153; Zhang, Qi, Esther H.K. Yung, and Edwin H.W. Chan (2018): Towards Sustainable Neighborhoods: Challenges and Opportunities for Neighborhood Planning in Transitional Urban China. *Sustainability* 10(2), 406, doi.org/10.3390/su10020406; Silverman, Robert Mark (2014): Urban, Suburban, and Rural Contexts of School Districts and Neighborhood Revitalization Strategies: Rediscovering Equity in Education Policy and Urban Planning. *Leadership and Policy in Schools* 13(1), 3–27; Metzger, John T. (2000): Planned Abandonment: The Neighborhood Life-Cycle Theory and National Urban Policy. *Housing Policy Debate* 11(1), 7–40.
27. Cosgrove, Denis E. (1984): *Social Formation and Symbolic Landscape*. Madison: University of Wisconsin Press, 61ff.; Tuan, Yi Fu (1976/2001): *Space and Place: The Perspective of Experience*. Madison: University of Minnesota Press.
28. Lynch, Kevin (1960): *The Image of the City*. Boston: MIT Press.
29. Böhme, Gernot (2017): *The Aesthetics of Atmospheres*. London and New York: Routledge; Schmitz, Hermann (2016): *Atmosphären*. Freiburg i.Br.: Herder.
30. Bourdieu, Pierre (1991): On Symbolic Power. *Language and Power*. Cambridge: Harvard University Press; De Certeau, Michel (1984): *The Practice of Everyday Life*. Berkeley, Los Angeles and London: University of California Press; Lefebvre, Henri (1991): *The Production of Space*. Oxford: Blackwell; Foucault, Michel (1977): *Discipline and Punish: The Birth of the Prison*. New York: Random House.
31. Löw, Martina (2018): *The Sociology of Space*. New York: Palgrave Macmillan, 150f.; Also: Löw, Martina (2018): *Vom Raum aus die Stadt denken: Grundlagen einer raumtheoretischen Stadtsoziologie*. Bielefeld: Transcript; Steets, Silke (2015): *Der sinnhafte Aufbau der gebauten Welt: Eine Architektursoziologie*. Berlin: Suhrkamp.
32. Bhabha, Homi K. (1994/2004): *The Location of Culture*. London: Routledge; Bhabha, Homi K. (1990): The Third Space. *Identity: Community, Culture, Difference*, edited by J. Rutherford. London: Lawrence and Wishart, 207–221; Soja, Edward W. (2010): *Seeking Spatial Justice*. Minneapolis: University of Minnesota Press.
33. Massey (2005), 9.
34. Ibid., 151.
35. Ibid. Similarly Tim Cresswell and Peter Merriman observe that "spaces are not simply contexts; they are also actively produced by the act of moving. [...] Practices of mobility animate and co-produce spaces, places and landscapes." See Cresswell, Tim, and Peter Merriman (2013): Introduction. *Geographies of Mobilities: Practices, Places, Subjects*, edited by Tim Cresswell and Peter Merriman. Farnham: Ashgate, 1–15, 7.
36. Ibid., 181.

37. Ponzanesi, Sandra (2019): Migration and Mobility in a Digital Age: (Re)Mapping Connectivity and Belonging. *Television & New Media* 20(6), 547–557; cf. also Glick Schiller, Basch, and Szanton Blanc (1995).
38. Harvey, David (1973/2009): *Social Justice and the City*. Athens: Georgia University Press.
39. Blokland, Tanja (2003): *Urban Bonds*. Cambridge: Polity Press, 213.
40. Appadurai, Arjun (1996): The Production of Locality. *Modernity at Large: Cultural Dimensions of Globalization*. Minneapolis: Minneapolis University Press, 178–199, 185.
41. Watts, Paul, and Peer Smets (2014): Introduction. *Mobilities and Neighbourhood Belonging in Cities and Suburbs*, edited by Paul Watts and Peer Smets. Basingstoke: Palgrave Macmillan, 1–23, 5.
42. Meinhof, Ulrike Hanna (2011): Introducing Borders, Networks, Neighbourhoods: Conceptual Frames and Social Practices. *Negotiating Multicultural Europe: Borders, Networks, Neighbourhoods*, edited by Heidi Armbruster and Ulrike Hanna Meinhof. Basingstoke: Palgrave Macmillan, 1–25, 7.
43. Savage, Mike, Gaynor Bagnell, and Brian Longhurst (2005): The Limits of Local Attachment. Globalization and Belonging, edited by Mike Savage, Gaynor Bagnell, and Brian Longhurst. London: Sage, 29–55, 53.
44. Augé, Marc (1992): *Non-Places: Introduction to an Anthropology of Supermodernity*, translated by John Howe. London: Verso, 122.
45. Ehrig, Stephan, Britta C. Jung, and Maria Roca Lizarazu (2020): Conference Report: Exploring the Transnational Neighbourhood. Integration, Community and Co-Habitation. *Journal of Romance Studies* 20(1), 179–181, 179.
46. Calhoun, Craig (2017): A Cosmopolitanism of Connections. *Cosmopolitanisms*, edited by Bruce Robbins and Paul Lemos Horta. New York: New York University Press, 189–200, 195.
47. Hannerz, Ulf (1980): *Exploring the City: Enquiries Toward an Urban Anthropology*. New York: Columbia University Press, 99.
48. Ehrig, Jung, and Roca Lizarazu (2020), 181.
49. Haesbaert, Rogério (2011): *El mito de la desterritorialización: Del fin de los territorios a la multiterritorialidad*, translated by Marcelo Canossa. Mexico City: Siglo XXI; Haesbaert, Rogério (2013): Del mito de la desterritorialización a la multiterritorialidad. *Cultura y representaciones sociales* 8(15), 9–42.
50. Beck, Ulrich (1997/2015): *Was ist Globalisierung? Irrtümer des Globalismus – Antworten auf Globalisierung*. Frankfurt a.M. and Berlin: Suhrkamp.
51. Soja, Edward W. (1996): *Thirdspace: Journeys to Los Angeles and Other Real and Imagined Places*. Hoboken, NJ: Blackwell.
52. Campbell, Scott (1996): Green Cities, Growing Cities, Just Cities? Urban Planning and the Contradictions of Sustainable Development. *Journal of the American Planning Association* 62(3), 296–312.

53. Wolford, Wendy (2004): This Land Is Ours Now: Spatial Imaginaries and the Struggle for Land in Brazil. *Annals of the Association of American Geographers* 94(2), 409–424, 410.
54. Ibid.
55. Massey (2005), 21.
56. Amin, Ash (2002): Ethnicity and the Multicultural City: Living with Diversity. *Environment and Planning A: Economy and Space* 34(6), 959–980.
57. Bakhtin, Mikhail (1981a): *The Dialogic Imagination: Four Essays by M. M. Bakhtin*, translated by Caryl Emerson and Michael Holquist. Austin: University of Texas Press.
58. Said, Edward W. (2003): Introduction to the Fiftieth Anniversary Edition. *Mimesis: The Representation of Reality in Western Literature*, edited by Eric Auerbach, translated by W.R. Trask. Princeton: Princeton University Press.
59. The term *pieds-noirs* refers to persons of French and other European origin who were born in Algeria during the period of French rule from 1830 to 1962, the vast majority of whom departed for mainland France or Corsica after Algerian independence.
60. Pratt, Mary Louise (1992): *Imperial Eyes: Travel Writing and Transculturation*. London: Routledge, 2.
61. Bahun, Sanja, and Bojana Petric (2018): Homing in on Home. *Thinking Home: Interdisciplinary Dialogues,* edited by Sanja Bahun and Bojana Petric. London: Bloomsbury Academic, 2018, 14–22, 14.
62. Ponzanesi (2019).
63. Blommaert, Jan, and Ico Maly (2019): Invisible Lines in the Online-Offline Linguistic Landscape. *Tilburg Papers in Culture Studies* 223.

Works Cited

Adelman, Robert, Lesley Williams Reid, Gail Markle, Saskia Weiss, and Charles Jaret (2017): Urban Crime Rates and the Changing Face of Immigration: Evidence across Four Decades. *Journal of Ethnicity in Criminal Justice* 15(1), 52–77.

Alba, Richard D., Nancy A. Denton, Shu-yin J. Leung, and John R. Logan (1995): Neighborhood Change under Conditions of Mass Immigration. *International Migration Review* 29(3), 625–656.

Amin, Ash (2002): Ethnicity and the Multicultural City: Living with Diversity. *Environment and Planning A: Economy and Space* 34(6), 959–980.

Appadurai, Arjun (1996): The Production of Locality. *Modernity at Large: Cultural Dimensions of Globalization*. Minneapolis: Minneapolis University Press, 178–199.

Assmann, Aleida (2016): *Shadows of Trauma: Memory and the Politics of Postwar Identity*. New York: Fordham University Press.

Augé, Marc (1992): *Non-Places: Introduction to an Anthropology of Supermodernity*, translated by John Howe. London: Verso.
Bahun, Sanja, and Bojana Petric (2018): Homing in on Home. *Thinking Home: Interdisciplinary Dialogues*, edited by Sanja Bahun and Bojana Petric. London: Bloomsbury Academic, 2018, 14–22.
Bakhtin, Mikhail (1981a): *The Dialogic Imagination: Four Essays by M. M. Bakhtin*, translated by Caryl Emerson and Michael Holquist. Austin: University of Texas Press.
Bakhtin, Mikhail (1981b): Discourse in the Novel. *The Dialogic Imagination: Four Essays*, edited by Michael Holquist. Austin: University of Texas Press, 259–422.
Basch, Linda G., Nina Glick Schiller, and Blanc Cristina Szanton Blanc (1994): *Nations Unbound: Transnational Projects, Postcolonial Predicaments, and Deterritorialized Nation-States*. London: Gordon and Breach.
Beck, Ulrich (1997/2015): *Was ist Globalisierung? Irrtümer des Globalismus – Antworten auf Globalisierung*. Frankfurt a.M. and Berlin: Suhrkamp.
Bhabha, Homi K. (1990): The Third Space. *Identity: Community, Culture, Difference*, edited by J. Rutherford. London: Lawrence and Wishart, 207–221.
Bhabha, Homi K. (1994/2004): *The Location of Culture*. London: Routledge.
Blokland, Tanja (2003): *Urban Bonds*. Cambridge: Polity Press.
Blommaert, Jan, and Ico Maly (2019): Invisible Lines in the Online-Offline Linguistic Landscape. *Tilburg Papers in Culture Studies* 223.
Böhme, Gernot (2017): *The Aesthetics of Atmospheres*. London and New York: Routledge.
Bourdieu, Pierre (1991): On Symbolic Power. *Language and Power*. Cambridge, MA: Harvard University Press.
Brickell, Katherine, and Ayona Datta, eds. (2011): *Translocal Geographies: Spaces, Places and Connections*. Farnham: Ashgate.
Calhoun, Craig (2017): A Cosmopolitanism of Connections. *Cosmopolitanisms*, edited by Bruce Robbins and Paul Lemos Horta. New York: New York University Press, 189–200.
Campbell, Scott (1996): Green Cities, Growing Cities, Just Cities? Urban Planning and the Contradictions of Sustainable Development. *Journal of the American Planning Association* 62(3), 296–312.
Cosgrove, Denis E. (1984): *Social Formation and Symbolic Landscape*. Madison: University of Wisconsin Press.
Cresswell, Tim, and Peter Merriman (2013): Introduction. *Geographies of Mobilities: Practices, Places, Subjects*, edited by Tim Cresswell and Peter Merriman. Farnham: Ashgate, 1–15.
De Certeau, Michel (1984): *The Practice of Everyday Life*. Berkeley, Los Angeles and London: University of California Press.
De Cesari, Chiara, and Ann Rigney, eds. (2014): *Transnational Memory: Circulation, Articulation, Scales*. Berlin: De Gruyter.

De Vries, Karl (2015): Paris Attacks Prompt Fears France's Muslim 'No-Go' Zones Incubating Jihad. *Fox News* https://www.foxnews.com/world/paris-attacks-prompt-fears-frances-muslim-no-go-zones-incubating-jihad (12 January). Accessed 4 August 2021.

Dikeç, Mustafa (2007): *Badlands of the Republic: Space, Politics and Urban Policy.* Hoboken, NJ: Blackwell.

Edmond, Charlotte (2020): Global Migration, by the Numbers: Who Migrates, Where They Go and Why. https://www.weforum.org/agenda/2020/01/iom-global-migration-report-international-migrants-2020/. Accessed 4 August 2021.

Ehrig, Stephan, Britta C. Jung, and Maria Roca Lizarazu (2020): Conference Report: Exploring the Transnational Neighbourhood. Integration, Community and Co-Habitation. *Journal of Romance Studies* 20(1), 179–181.

Erll, Astrid (2011): Travelling Memory. *Parallax: Transcultural Memory* 17(4), 4–18.

Ferracuti, Franco (1968): European Migration and Crime. *Crime and Culture: Essays in Honor of Thorsten Sellin*, edited by Marvin E. Wolfgang. New York: John Wiley and Sons, 189–219.

Fladvad Nielsen, Brita, Daniela Baer, and Carmel Lindkvist (2019): Identifying and Supporting Exploratory and Exploitative Models of Innovation in Municipal Urban Planning: Key Challenges from Seven Norwegian Energy Ambitious Neighborhood Pilots. *Technological Forecasting and Social Change* 142, 142–153.

Foucault, Michel (1977): *Discipline and Punish: The Birth of the Prison.* New York: Random House.

Glick Schiller, Nina, Linda Basch, and Cristina Szanton Blanc (1995): From Immigrant to Transmigrant: Theorizing Transnational Migration. *Anthropological Quarterly* 68(1), 48–63.

Györke, Ágnes, and Imola Bülgözdi, eds. (2020): *Geographies of Affect in Contemporary Literature and Visual Culture: Central Europe and the West.* Leiden: Brill.

Haesbaert, Rogério (2011): *El mito de la desterritorialización: Del fin de los territorios a la multiterritorialidad*, translated by Marcelo Canossa. Mexico City: Siglo XXI.

Haesbaert, Rogério (2013): Del mito de la desterritorialización a la multiterritorialidad. *Cultura y representaciones sociales* 8(15), 9–42.

Hannerz, Ulf (1980): *Exploring the City: Enquiries Toward an Urban Anthropology.* New York: Columbia University Press.

Harvey, David (1973/2009): *Social Justice and the City.* Athens: Georgia University Press.

Jein, Gillian (2015): (De)Facing the Suburbs: Street Art and the Politics of Spatial Affect in the Paris Banlieues. *The DS Project: Image, Text, Space/Place, 1830–2015*, http://thedsproject.com/. Accessed 28 June 2021.

Jein, Gillian (2021): Speculative Spaces in Grand Paris: Reading JR in Clichy-sous-Bois and Montfermeil. *Aesthetics of Gentrification: Seductive Spaces and Exclusive Communities in the Neoliberal City*, edited by Christoph Lindner and Gerard F. Sandoval. Amsterdam: Amsterdam University Press, 221–246.

Koff, Harlan, and Dominique Duprez (2009): The 2005 Riots in France: The International Impact of Domestic Violence. *Journal of Ethnic and Migration Studies* 35(5), 713–730.

Lee, Matthew T., Ramiro Martinez, and Richard Rosenfeld (2001): Does Immigration Increase Homicide? Negative Evidence from Three Border Cities. *The Sociological Quarterly* 42(4), 559–580.

Martinez, Freddy (2016): On the Streets of El Paso and Juarez: 'Sister Cities' Art Project Pays Tribute to Border Communities. *Remezcla* (7 July), https://remezcla.com/features/culture/interview-los-dos/. Accessed 18 August 2021.

Massey, Doreen (2005): *For Space*. Los Angeles and London: Sage.

Metzger, John T. (2000): Planned Abandonment: The Neighborhood Life-Cycle Theory and National Urban Policy. *Housing Policy Debate* 11(1), 7–40.

Lefebvre, Henri (1991): *The Production of Space*. Oxford: Blackwell.

Löw, Martina (2018 a): *The Sociology of Space*. New York: Palgrave Macmillan.

Löw, Martina (2018 b): *Vom Raum aus die Stadt denken: Grundlagen einer raumtheoretischen Stadtsoziologie*. Bielefeld: Transcript.

Lynch, Kevin (1960): *The Image of the City*. Boston: MIT Press.

Meinhof, Ulrike Hanna (2011): Introducing Borders, Networks, Neighbourhoods: Conceptual Frames and Social Practices. *Negotiating Multicultural Europe: Borders, Networks, Neighbourhoods*, edited by Heidi Armbruster and Ulrike Hanna Meinhof. Basingstoke: Palgrave Macmillan, 1–25.

Pratt, Mary Louise (1992): *Imperial Eyes: Travel Writing and Transculturation*. London: Routledge.

Ponzanesi, Sandra (2019): Migration and Mobility in a Digital Age: (Re)Mapping Connectivity and Belonging. *Television & New Media* 20(6), 547–557.

Rędzińska, Katarzyna, and Monika Piotrkowska (2020): Urban Planning and Design for Building Neighborhood Resilience to Climate Change. *Land* 9(10), 387, doi.org/10.3390/land9100387.

Rigney, Ann, and Chiara de Cesari (2014): Introduction. *Transnational Memory: Circulation, Articulation, Scales*, edited by Ann Rigney and Chiara de Cesari. Berlin and Boston: De Gruyter, 1–25.

Rothberg, Michael, and Dirk A. Moses (2014): A Dialogue on the Ethics and Politics of Transcultural Memory. *The Transcultural Turn: Interrogating Memory Between and Beyond Borders*, edited by Lucy Bond and Jessica Rapson. Berlin and Boston: De Gruyter, 29–38.

Said, Edward W. (2003): Introduction to the Fiftieth Anniversary Edition. *Mimesis: The Representation of Reality in Western Literature*, edited by Eric Auerbach, translated by W.R. Trask. Princeton: Princeton University Press.

Savage, Mike, Gaynor Bagnell, and Brian Longhurst (2005): The Limits of Local Attachment. *Globalization and Belonging*, edited by Mike Savage, Gaynor Bagnell, and Brian Longhurst. London: Sage, 29–55.

Schmitz, Hermann (2016): *Atmosphären*. Freiburg i.Br.: Herder.
Silverman, Robert Mark (2014): Urban, Suburban, and Rural Contexts of School Districts and Neighborhood Revitalization Strategies: Rediscovering Equity in Education Policy and Urban Planning. *Leadership and Policy in Schools* 13(1), 3–27.
Soja, Edward W. (1996): *Thirdspace: Journeys to Los Angeles and Other Real and Imagined Places*. Hoboken, NJ: Blackwell.
Soja, Edward W. (2010): *Seeking Spatial Justice*. Minneapolis: University of Minnesota Press.
Steets, Silke (2015): *Der sinnhafte Aufbau der gebauten Welt: Eine Architektursoziologie*. Berlin: Suhrkamp.
Tuan, Yi Fu (1976/2001): *Space and Place: The Perspective of Experience*. Madison: University of Minnesota Press.
Vertovec, Steven (2009): *Transnationalism*. New York and Abingdon: Routledge.
Waters, Tony (1999): *Crime and Immigrant Youth*. Thousand Oaks, CA: Sage.
Watts, Paul, and Peer Smets (2014): Introduction. *Mobilities and Neighbourhood Belonging in Cities and Suburbs*, edited by Paul Watts and Peer Smets. Basingstoke: Palgrave Macmillan, 1–23.
Wharf, Barney, and Santa Arias, eds. (2009): *The Spatial Turn. Interdisciplinary Perspectives*. London: Routledge.
Wiard, Victor, and Fábio Henrique Pereira (2019): Bad Neighbourhoods in a Good City? Space, Place and Brussels' Online News. *Journalism Studies* 20(5), 649–674.
Winnick, Louis (1990): *New People in Old Neighborhoods: The Role of New Immigrants in Rejuvenating New York's Communities*. New York: Russell Sage.
Wolford, Wendy (2004): This Land Is Ours Now: Spatial Imaginaries and the Struggle for Land in Brazil. *Annals of the Association of American Geographers* 94(2), 409–424.
Zhang, Qi, Esther H.K. Yung, and Edwin H.W. Chan (2018): Towards Sustainable Neighborhoods: Challenges and Opportunities for Neighborhood Planning in Transitional Urban China. *Sustainability* 10(2), 406 doi.org/10.3390/su10020406.

Challenging Accusations of Separatism

Transnational Neighbourhood and
Vernacular Cosmopolitanism in Insa Sané's
Comédie urbaine (2006–2017)

CHRISTINA HORVATH

Abstract
In the volumes of his *Comédie urbaine* [Urban Comedy], a cycle of five novels often compared to Balzac's *Comédie humaine* [Human Comedy], Insa Sané undertakes to deconstruct some of the prejudices which surround stigmatised banlieues in the French spatial imagination. This chapter proposes to examine how in *Sarcelles-Dakar* (2006), *Gueule de bois* (2009), *Daddy est mort* (2010), *Du plomb dans le crâne* (2013) and *Les Cancres de Rousseau* (2017), the Franco-Senegalese novelist attempts to shift dominant perceptions of Sarcelles, a transnational neighbourhood situated in the northern outskirts of Paris, to demonstrate that banlieues like Sarcelles should be regarded as transnational contact zones in which a vernacular cosmopolitanism is elaborated, rather than "badlands of the Republic" (Dikeç) or ghettos plagued by separatism. This chapter relies on the concepts of global diasporas (Cohen), vernacular cosmopolitanism (Bhabha, Werbner), contact zones (Pratt) and translocalities (Appadurai, Sinatti) to argue that, by exploring the themes of ethnic and cultural diversity, the tensions between Paris proper and the city's underprivileged periphery, the memory of colonisation and the residents' ambiguous feelings towards normative definitions of Frenchness, Sané does more than just debunking clichés attached to the French banlieues. His *Comédie urbaine* replaces elitist definitions of cosmopolitanism with vernacular alternatives to demonstrate the necessity to reframe dominant narratives about banlieues in the public imagination as a way to confront the French Republic with its missed ideal of liberty, equality, and fraternity.

> La ville connaît toutes les langues de Babel, s'étend par-delà toutes les frontières ; elle a prié sur les rives du Gange, défié le temps au bord du Nil, bâti des projets narcissiques sur les flots du fleuve Niger.
>
> [The city knows all the languages of Babel, extends beyond all borders; it prayed on the banks of the Ganges, defied time on the banks of the Nile, built narcissistic projects on the waves of the Niger river.]
>
> Insa Sané, *Gueule de bois* (2017), 140

Introduction

On 2 October 2020, President Emmanuel Macron pronounced a fervent speech in Les Mureaux, a disadvantaged banlieue in Greater Paris, announcing a new law proposal designed to challenge Islamist separatism. The speech identified Islamist radicalisation, a social ill that has long been plaguing France's peripheral neighbourhoods, as a consequence of ghettoisation, unresolved traumas of the colonial past and previous laisser-faire urban policies having resulted in high concentrations of ethnic minority populations in France's suburban housing estates:

> We ourselves have built our own separatism. It's the separatism of our neighbourhoods, it's the ghettoization which our Republic – initially with the best intentions in the world – has allowed to occur [...] We have crowded people together often according to their origins, their social backgrounds. [...] In this way we have created neighbourhoods where the promise of the Republic has no longer been kept [...] Added to all this is the fact that we are a country with a colonial past and traumas it still hasn't resolved. [...] And so we see children of the Republic, sometimes from elsewhere, children or grandchildren of today's citizens of immigrant origin from the Maghreb and sub-Saharan Africa, revisiting their identity through a post-colonial or anti-colonial discourse.[1]

By adding a new term, *separatism*, to the republican vocabulary employed to depict banlieues as a threat to national security and unity, Macron's discourse has associated peripheral working-class neighbourhoods with social apartheid, as well as "a form of menacing exteriority".[2] The controversial anti-separatism law, which after a long debate was finally adopted by the French Parliament on 23 July 2021, has further reinforced the idea launched in a call published by 100 French intellectuals in *Le Figaro* on 19 March 2018, that Muslim religiosity and the concentration of postcolonial minorities in French banlieues are not only incompatible with the republican principles, above all that of *laïcité* [secularism], but also a menace to all sorts of freedom:

> Le nouveau totalitarisme islamiste cherche à gagner du terrain par tous les moyens et à passer pour une victime de l'intolérance. [...] aujourd'hui, c'est un apartheid d'un nouveau genre qui est proposé à la France, une ségrégation à l'envers grâce à laquelle les « dominés » préserveraient leur dignité en se mettant à l'abri des « dominants ».

> [The new Islamist totalitarianism seeks to gain ground by all means and to pass for a victim of intolerance. [...] Today, it is an apartheid of a new kind which is proposed to France, an inverted segregation which would help the 'dominated' would preserve their dignity by sheltering themselves from the 'dominants'.][3]

However, as the detractors of the law have objected, separatism is less likely to be promoted by the marginalised residents of the urban periphery, who are the victims of exclusion rather than its promoters, than by the elite classes who actively choose to live among themselves, for example by preventing the construction of social housing on their territory, as has been demonstrated by the economist Éric Maurin.[4]

Banlieues are mostly high-rise housing estates that were constructed in the outskirts of French cities in the 1950s and 1960s in response to the post-war housing crisis. They surround most of France's large and even medium-sized cities and have progressively become "synonymous with areas of acute social disadvantage containing dense concentrations of minority ethnic groups".[5] In the late 1970s, when a new government scheme was introduced to enable middle-class residents to become homeowners, the concentration of exogenous populations who could not afford to buy their own dwellings increased in the suburban housing estates.[6] Since then, several waves of urban policies have attempted to promote the ideal of the so-called *mixité sociale* [diversity], commonly understood as the co-habitation of different social classes in the same geographical areas, which has long been celebrated in France as a panacea to rebalance the demographic composition of disadvantaged neighbourhoods while also boosting levels of tolerance, dialogue and social harmony. Yet social scientists like Cyprian Avenel have demonstrated that rather than strengthening conviviality between different social classes, spatial proximity tends to exacerbate conflicts.[7] Therefore, if by *mixité sociale* we mean a genuine demographic diversity and not policies forcibly regrouping populations against their will while routinely severing their links of solidarity and undermining their self-reliance, then transnational banlieues can be regarded as the French neighbourhoods that come the closest to this ideal.

This chapter proposes to examine the emergence of a vernacular cosmopolitanism by looking at five novels published by Franco-Senegalese writer Insa Sané. Through the close reading of this multi-volume cycle set in Sarcelles, an iconic banlieue town situated in the Val d'Oise department north of Paris, I will attempt to demonstrate that France's transnational working-class banlieues are not the insulated ethnic and religious ghettos President Macron is reclaiming for the Republic. On the contrary, these neighbourhoods are liminal spaces or contact zones in which heterogeneous populations tend to negotiate their differences on a daily basis while producing a new, vernacular form of cosmopolitanism. This premise will be tested through the analysis of the novels *Sarcelles-Dakar* [Sarcelles-Dakar] (2006), *Gueule de bois* [Hangover] (2009), *Daddy est mort* [Daddy is Dead] (2010), *Du plomb dans le crâne* [Lead in the Skull] (2013) and *Les Cancres de Rousseau* [The Dunces of Rousseau] (2017).[8] The five volumes of Sané's *Comédie urbaine* [Urban Comedy] have often been compared to 19th-century novelist Honoré de Balzac's monumental *Comédie humaine* [Human Comedy], a fresco of 95 novels published over 26 years in which he depicted the different social and topographical strata of 19th-century French society. Insa Sané's novels were published between 2006 and 2017 by Sarbacane, an independent publishing house mainly targeting adolescent and young adult readers. The author, who was born in Senegal in 1974, arrived in France at the age of six and grew up in Sarcelles, where he continues to live. As an actor, slam and rap artist and novelist, he has attempted to depict contemporary life in the urban periphery from various angles.

Located 16.3 kilometres from the centre of Paris, Sarcelles is a sub-prefecture of the Val d'Oise department. According to the 2017 census, 33.4% of the city's 58,811 inhabitants were born outside France.[9] In 2005, 66% of local youth under 18 were of immigrant origin, while the city's website takes pride in more than a hundred nationalities living together. Home to various ethnic and religious communities, including Sephardic Jews, Algerians, Moroccans, Assyrians, Chaldeans and Caribbean French, the city has a poverty rate of 34%, and in 2017 22.3% of the 17–64-year-old age group was unemployed, whereas the national unemployment rate was only 9.4%.[10] Sarcelles has also been permanently etched in the French public imagination as the local turf of the iconic rap group Ministère AMER. The city's reputation suffered a particular stain when its name was used to coin the neologism *sarcellite,* which, since 1964, has been used to refer to the pathological condition affecting homemakers in France's first high-rise housing estates.[11] This term has not only resulted in a dystopian imagery attached to Sarcelles but also contributed to a growing scepticism towards collective housing, which helped re-bolster faith in a freer real estate market and the single-family home:

The discourse of *sarcellite* medicalised a liberal-individualistic critique that argued social-capital investment in collectivist residential property incubated human neurosis. As a rhetorical device, therefore, *sarcellite* contributed to demarcating the geographical lines of spatial inclusion and exclusion in the Fifth French Republic.[12]

Concerned with policies of spatial inclusion and exclusion in contemporary France, this chapter will explore transculturalism at neighbourhood level in Sané's *Comédie urbaine*, examining this literary representation of Sarcelles as a social microcosm in which characters of various origins co-habit and interact. I will analyse how the transcultural neighbourhood is used in the novels to challenge dystopian representations of French banlieues and dismantle the myths of separatism and ghettoisation by proposing a vernacular cosmopolitan vision of French banlieues as contact zones in which, despite the frictions resulting from the residents' exposure to economic hardship and different forms of otherness, the ideal of *mixité sociale* is at least partially accomplished. To demonstrate this, I will first examine how the novels' topography, in particular boundary crossing at local, regional and international levels, helps establish a microcosmos which revolves around Sarcelles but communicates with Paris proper and different parts of the world. The second section will explore how family bonds, intragenerational links and neighbourhood ties are used to create cohesion between the characters and volumes of the *Comédie urbaine* while promoting alternative interpretations of history based on postcolonial and neighbourhood memory. The third section will look at the transnational neighbourhood not as a homogeneous, diasporic space but as a contact zone in which ethnically and culturally heterogeneous groups and individuals interact. Finally, the conclusion will highlight how the novels' generic, stylistic and narrative diversity enable Sané to translate the transnational neighbourhood's heterogeneity into a literary representation.

Topography and Boundary Crossing in the Novels

Sarcelles, the surrounding banlieues and Paris proper constitute the core settings of Sané's *Comédie urbaine*. Like in 19th-century novels by Zola or Balzac, the city is occasionally personified as a hostile, carnivorous monster that attracts and destroys characters like Éléonore, a Franco-Congolese prostitute and drug addict, and her son Daddy,[13] a thug, who is assassinated in *Daddy est mort*. In most of the novels, however, the French capital and its outskirts are endowed with a detailed topography and depicted in a realist fashion as the ordinary settings of everyday life. The protagonists are mostly youths raised in and around Sarcelles who share their time between Paris and its banlieues. They go to school or university, relax in bars in the Saint-Michel or Bastille areas, like le Mirage or l'Iguane, and eat out in restaurants like Chez Éléonore in Enghien-les-Bains. They meet with friends, family members and business partners near the Porte de la Chapelle, Porte d'Orléans, Voltaire, Flandre or Crimée métro stations, or at the railway stations of Gare du Nord, Gare de l'Est or Gare Saint-Lazare. They hang out at Sarcelles' highest peak called Colline Blanche, or in an informal subterranean venue known as the Underground, but also travel to Parisian working-class neighbourhoods like la Place des Fêtes, la Villette or la Goutte d'Or. Some of them commute between their homes and their workplace, like Farrel, who has a summer job at the Citroën plant at Aulnay, or Farah, who works at the Malik market in Clignancourt.

Like the "divided Paris, the battlefield between old wealth and ambitious petty bourgeois youth"[14] in Balzac's *Comédie humaine*, the urban topography in Sané's novels also mirrors the characters' spatial and social mobility through addresses and trajectories that correspond to their social status and aspirations. Sarcelles is depicted in the novels as the local turf where most of the characters were raised, but as grown-ups some of them choose to settle in Paris, like Éléonore, Tierno, Djiraël, Alassane or Daddy. Rather than appearing in the novels in isolation, Sarcelles is surrounded by other municipalities like Saint-Brice, Groslay, Montmagny, Villetanneuse, Stains and Villiers-le-Bel. These towns are home to various secondary characters and act as the markers of their ascending or descending social trajectories. Most of these towns are situated along the railway line connecting Sarcelles to Paris, with the notable exceptions of Luzarches, an affluent neighbourhood located in the far north of the Val d'Oise department where Prince's banker lives, or Boigneville, situated in the Essonne department.

Greater Paris is represented in the novels as a mosaic of high-rise housing estates, affluent towns endowed with a lake and a casino like Enghien-les-Bains, and modest garden suburbs like the one in Villiers-le-Bel where the economics teacher, Monsieur Fèvre lives: "On n'a pas idée de construire autant de pavillons sur une si grande étendue ! Fallait en remercier tous ces architectes addicts à la beuh qui, dans la fin des années 80, avaient décidé que la misère serait plus acceptable à l'horizontale qu'à la verticale" [Who would have thought of building so many detached houses over such a large area! We had to thank all these architects addicted to weed who, in the late 80s, had decided that poverty would be more acceptable horizontally than vertically] (LCdR, 239). The novels' spatial stratification allows Sané to defy simplifying binaries such as rich/poor, central/peripheral, working class/middle class, or monocultural/multicultural, which play a crucial role in the construction of a dominant discourse depicting banlieues as homogeneous entities where separatism is promoted. It also undermines the idea of a radical separation between banlieues and Paris proper in the public imagination, showing that residents like the protagonist Djiraël and his friends cross the city's boundaries on a regular basis to buy clothes, study in the Beaubourg library, eat out or go to the cinema.

Although the Sarcellois characters' circulation between Paris and the banlieues seems fluid, it is occasionally impeded by obstacles including the cost of public transport, racial profiling practised at nightclubs and identity checks imposed by the police on non-white youths disembarking from the suburban trains arriving in Paris. The absence of trains past midnight and the unwillingness of taxi drivers to take minority-ethnic passengers to peripheral destinations are additional hindrances which discourage youths from Sarcelles to go out in Paris at night. Djiraël makes a bitter experience of these barriers when he accompanies Tatiana and her middle-class friends to a fashionable Parisian nightclub only to find himself rejected at the entrance and subsequently "enfermé dehors" [locked out], like the protagonists of Matthieu Kassovitz's cult film, *La Haine*:

> Il était minuit trente. Impossible de choper un train, à cette heure. […] J'ai eu beau à tendre la pouce, les taxis parisiens ne prennent pas les négros, de surcroît lorsqu'ils crèchent dans le ghetto. […] Paris est ignoble, la nuit. […] J'aurais pu aller dormir chez mon cousin Youba qui habitait dans le 19e, mais il aurait fallu expliquer pourquoi je me retrouvais en galère à une heure tardive et il n'en était pas question.
>
> [It was half past midnight. Impossible to catch a train at this hour. […] No matter how much I stretched my thumb, Parisian taxis don't pick up niggas, especially when they live in the ghetto. […] Paris is despicable at night. […] I could have gone to sleep with my cousin Youba who lived in the 19th, but it would have been necessary to explain why I was having a hard time at a late hour and that was out of the question.] (LCdR, 120)

As this extract indicates, the novels' young protagonists are acutely aware of their spatial disadvantage and stigmatisation as non-white banlieue residents. Djiraël complains that Sarcelles, a city of 60,000 inhabitants, only has a library the size of a small apartment and that attending central Paris libraries requires strategies such as dividing larger groups into smaller ones to avoid police attention or reselling old schoolbooks at inflated rates to be able to afford the commute. However, even if he and his friends occasionally refer to their quartier as a ghetto, their impression of Sarcelles remains predominantly positive, mainly because their feeling of belonging overwrites the external blemishes attached to the town. In *Sarcelles-Dakar*, Djiraël explains his attachment to Sarcelles by both his intimate knowledge of the town's topography and stories and his own notoriety among the residents:

Tout en marchant, je songeais que cette ville m'avait marqué de son empreinte. Il me semblait ne rien connaître aussi bien que ses rues, ses trottoirs, ses murs, ses tags, ses graffitis, ses tours, ses quartiers, son marché aux puces et ses terrains de sport. Aucune de ses légendes, de ses petites histoires et aucun de ses faits divers n'avait de secrets pour moi. Alors que la plupart des gens vivaient dans l'anonymat, Sarcelles avait fait de moi un des personnages principaux de son histoire. On se connaissait depuis si longtemps qu'il était impossible de distinguer le prisonnier du geôlier. Les bandes des villes voisines n'aventuraient que très rarement à Sarcelles et de mon côté, je dois admettre qu'il m'arrivait d'avoir peur de m'éloigner de ma ville.

[As I walked, I thought that this city had left its mark on me. I seemed to know nothing as well as its streets, sidewalks, walls, tags, graffiti, towers, neighbourhoods, flea market and sports grounds. None of its legends, its little stories, and none of its news items held any secrets from me. While most people lived in anonymity, Sarcelles had made me one of the main characters in its story. We had known each other for so long that it was impossible to tell the prisoner from the jailer. Bands from neighbouring towns rarely ventured into Sarcelles and on my side, I have to admit that I was sometimes afraid to stray from my town.] (SD, 38f.)

Boundary crossing in the novels is not restricted to the characters' routine commute between their banlieue towns to Paris. Residential and social mobility allow characters to durably establish themselves on the better side of the *boulevard périphérique* in Paris, i.e. the high-speed ring road around Paris proper. Previously, their parents' migratory trajectories involved transcending national borders. Djiraël's parents arrived in France from Senegal, Daddy's grandfather from Congo, Farrel's and Farah's parents from Algeria, those of Samir and Sonia from Morocco, the families of Sonny, Freddy and Zulu from the French Caribbean. Raised in France, the children of postcolonial immigrants have constructed complex identities in which French citizenship, neighbourhood belonging, and culture of origins have equally important parts. The characters' double belonging to their country of origin and the French banlieue, rather than mainstream France, is an important foundation of their identity. This is exemplified by the case of Djiraël, a native speaker of Diola born in Senegal, who identifies as both a Sarcellois and a Senegalese. Nevertheless, in Dakar he is considered a Francenabé, that is "[u]n petit Sénégalais de France qui vient ici avec plein de billets" [a little Senegalese from France who comes here with lots of banknotes] (SD, 66). Unlike Djiraël, who is only a temporary visitor in Senegal, Farrel hopes to permanently settle in Algeria and open a crêperie on the beach of Bejaïa with his friend Freddy. Originally from the French Caribbean, Freddy belongs to those rare, uprooted residents in his neighbourhood who have no home country to return to for the summer vacations:

> Ses parents étaient arrivés des Antilles avant sa naissance pour ne jamais y retourner. L'été, quand Farrel partait en Algérie, Samir au Maroc, et les autres jeunes du quartier aux quatre coins du globe, lui tenait les murs du quartier tout seul. Il rêvait de connaître, avec Farrel, les montagnes de Kabylie, les plages de Bejaïa, le mont Yema Gouraya; ou, en compagnie de Samir, les promenades d'Agadir, les chaînes de l'Atlas, les souks de Marrakesh, les dunes du Sahara.
>
> [His parents had arrived from the West Indies before his birth never to return. In the summer, when Farrel went to Algeria, Samir to Morocco, and other neighbourhood youth to places around the world, he had the neighbourhood walls to him alone. He dreamed of seeing, with Farrel, the mountains of Kabylia, the beaches of Bejaïa, Mount Yema Gouraya; or, in the company of Samir, the walks of Agadir, the chains of the Atlas, the souks of Marrakesh, the dunes of the Sahara.] (GdB, 54f.)

Freddy's parents, who cut the ties with their native island, are an exception in the novels where most transcultural families see immigration as a series of return trips rather than a single one-way journey to France. This attitude is exemplified by Djiraël's father, a bookseller deeply committed to supporting the local community in his village of origin. He spends extended periods of time in Senegal building a school, founding a library, and dedicating most of his modest earnings to helping others rather than to purchasing a better car or buying fashionable clothes for his children. Djiraël, who initially resents his absences and reproaches him neglecting his own family while helping strangers, only realises the impact of his father's charitable work during his funeral in Senegal.

> Ils se sont présentés et nous ont dit ce que mon père avait fait pour eux. L'un avait pu inscrire son enfant dans une école grâce à mon père, un autre avait réussi à envoyer sa fille dans un bon hôpital avec l'argent que mon père lui avait donné, un dernier avait été sauvé de la famine par mon vieux à la suite d'une mauvaise récolte. [...] J'étais perplexe et, il fallait bien l'avouer, fier de mon père. J'avais l'impression d'être un de ces petits garçons qu'on trouve dans les comics Marvel, qui découvre que son père a des super-pouvoirs après l'avoir pris pour un loser.
>
> [They introduced themselves and told us what my father had done for them. One had been able to enrol his child in a school thanks to my father, another had managed to send his daughter to a good hospital with the money that my father had given her, a last one had been saved from starvation by my old man following a

bad harvest. [...] I was perplexed and, I must admit, proud of my father. I felt like one of those little boys you find in Marvel comics, who finds out his father has superpowers after mistaking him for a loser.] (SD, 98)

Djiraël's immersion in Senegal helps him reconcile with his deceased father but also triggers a confrontation between the Western ideals of consumerism and individualism and the traditional Senegalese values of self-sacrifice and solidarity. His father's commitment to the community is echoed by the loyalty of Kadiom, whose spirit Djiraël encounters in the forest where he is sent to wait for a message from his father. Kadiom, a young hunter who was killed by the French colonial army during World War I, is not only a messenger who transmits Djiraël the blessing of his deceased father. He is also a challenger of the Eurocentric assumption that individualism stands for modernity while African traditions hinder progress and prevent the Senegalese from "entering history", as President Nicolas Sarkozy termed it in his infamous speech at the University of Dakar in 2007.[15] Kadiom, who prefers to die at the hands of French soldiers rather than to break his oath of non-violence by joining the army, exposes the brutishness of the French colonial rule. His sacrifice echoes the father's subordination of personal interests to community welfare and reveals the selfishness of Western modernity. Acting as a mediator between the estranged father and son, the mother Abi encourages her son Djiraël to adopt Senegalese moral standards instead of following the "law of the street" which is popular amongst hypermasculine banlieue youths:

> Depuis ma rencontre avec Kadiom, quelque chose avait changé, je me sentais plus léger. Une semaine auparavant, ma mère avait dit que ce que je découvrirais au Sénégal, aucune école ne pourrait me l'enseigner. Je comprenais enfin ce qu'elle voulait dire. J'avais grandi en France, où tout était rationalisé. [...] Mon enfance, bercée par la rue, m'avait appris que le naïf avait très peu de chances de survivre. Alors, sur ces bases, la magie n'avait aucune valeur [...] Les contes, c'était pour les enfants, et la foi pour les faibles [...] Comme Kadiom et comme mon père, je devais décider de ce que serait mon existence.
>
> [Since my encounter with Kadiom, something had changed, I felt lighter. A week before, my mother had said that what I would discover in Senegal, no school could teach me. I finally understood what she meant. I had grown up in France, where everything was streamlined [...] My childhood, lulled by the streets, had taught me that the naive had very little chance of surviving. So, on that basis, magic had no value [...] Tales were for children, and faith for the weak [...] Like Kadiom and like my father, I had to decide what my existence would be like.] (SD, 173)

Although the novels' centre is Sarcelles, their microcosmos is connected to the world in multiple ways, including international travel and the characters' keen interest in global events. These offer new perspectives from which domination and marginalisation can be interpreted. A school trip to Brazil is suggested by Djiraël to study "the co-habitation of communities in emerging countries" (LCdR, 95). Characters follow the 2008 election in the United States because the international comparison allows them to better understand the connection between domination and blackness. Comparisons of France with other countries help them develop links with an *imagined community* (Anderson), which would be best described as a "global ghetto" with which all excluded populations in the world can identify.[16] This imagined community is on display in *Gueule de bois* when an excited multicultural crowd gathers in a Parisian bar to watch how a "métis [est] élu à 5000 bornes d'ici" [a mixed-race person is elected 5000 kilometres from here] (GdB, 118):

> Ils étaient tous là, Blancs, Noirs, Magrébins, Asiatiques, fils et filles de riches ou de déshérités, croyants ou athées, debout à fixer les écrans, silencieux comme avaient dû être le peuple de Moïse face à la Terre promise. Ils n'étaient plus des Français, des Africains, des Occidentaux ou de Tiers-mondistes, mais des enfants du monde, aussi différents qu'unis par le même espoir. La même attente. Tous rêvaient d'un ailleurs, ici et partout, d'un demain, maintenant et toujours ; d'une civilisation heureuse bâtie sur les cendres d'une cité de Babel.

> [They were all there, Whites, Blacks, North Africans, Asians, sons and daughters of the rich or the underprivileged, believers or atheists, standing staring at the screens, silent as the people of Moses must have been facing the Promised Land. They were no longer Frenchmen, Africans, Westerners or Third World natives, but children of the world, as different as they were united by the same hope. The same expectation. Everyone dreamed of somewhere else, here, and everywhere, of a tomorrow, now and always; of a happy civilisation built on the ashes of a city of Babel.] (GdB, 127)

In the next section, I will examine how this transition from a local Sarcellois identity to a global awareness of postcolonial oppression symbolised by the global ghetto takes place in the novels.

From a Local Banlieue Identity to the 'Global Ghetto'

The microcosmos of the *Comédie urbaine* is held together by three types of relationships between the characters: family bonds, intragenerational links and neighbourhood ties. The set of recurrent characters is primarily connected by Djiraël, the narrator of *Les Cancres de Rousseau* (2017) and *Sarcelles-Dakar* (2006). Set in 1995 and 1994, respectively, the two novels deal with his coming of age during his final year at high school and first year at university. *Daddy est mort* (2010), also set in 1995, narrates the death of Bruno Ekonga, one of Djiraël's childhood friends. The plot of *Du plomb dans le crâne* (2013) represents the 2005 banlieue uprisings through the adventures of Alassane, Djiraël's younger brother, and Sonny Cisko, a notorious thug from Villiers-le-Bel. Finally, *Gueule de bois* (2009) is set against the backdrop of Barack Obama's victory at the 2008 US elections, followed by his fictitious assassination. It introduces a new set of new teenage characters, Sonia, Farrel, Freddy and Samir, and gives the main role to the detectives Lait de Vache and Tonton Black Jacket, who appeared as secondary characters in *Du plomb dans le crâne*, *Daddy est mort* and *Gueule de bois*. All novels feature Djiraël and his siblings, Tierno, Alassane, Moussa and Saly, their mother Abi, and his cousin Youba. Other recurrent characters include Djiraël's group of high school friends, Rania, Doumam, Armand, Sacha and Jazz, the protagonists of *Les Cancres de Rousseau*, as well as his other friends Bruno Ekonga, aka Daddy, and Sébastien, aka Zulu. It appears from this short synopsis that family genealogy, generational links and neighbourhood ties not only instil coherence between the volumes but also offer a range of narrative opportunities to depict Sarcelles as a transnational neighbourhood. But how do these links contribute to establishing a *translocal*[17] banlieue identity which is simultaneously local and global?

Kinship links are vertical relationships that tie together different generations in the same family. They introduce genealogies rooted in migration and different colonial and postcolonial experiences which are transmitted from parents and grandparents to their children and grandchildren. Djiraël's parents are both Senegalese but belong to two different ethnic groups: "Les ancêtres de mon père venaient de l'empire du Mali, et ils se sont établis sur le territoire des ancêtres de ma mère, en Casamance. Le métissage existe également parmi les Noirs" [My father's ancestors came from the Mali Empire, and they settled in the territory of my mother's ancestors, in Casamance. Miscegenation also exists among blacks] (LCdR, 286). His cousins, Jean-Michel Jacques, aka Youba, and his brothers Moktar and Marko are half-Senegalese, half-Haitian. Bruno Ekonga, aka Daddy, is the illegitimate child of Éléonore, a Congolese described as "le diamant arraché au ventre du Congo et exposé avec insolence derrière une vitrine de la Place

Vendôme" [the diamond torn from the belly of the Congo and exposed with insolence behind a window in the Place Vendôme] (DEM, 155). Her father, Mr Left Punch, arrived in France from Kinshasa to achieve a career as a boxer but gave up the sport after accidentally killing an adversary. Sébastien, aka Zulu, and Sonny Cisko, aka Prince, are both of French Caribbean descent. Prince is the son of the light-skinned Fanny, who had been repeatedly raped by various male members of her adoptive family until she was married to the youngest son and sent to Paris. The mixed-race Tatiana, one of Djiraël's early love interests, connects two histories of victimhood since her father is black and her mother is a descendant of Holocaust survivors. Arjun Appadurai and Carol Breckenridge affirm that transnational migrants "always leave a trail of collective memory about another place and time and create new maps of desire and of attachment".[18] The memories accumulated by the characters' families evoke suffering provoked by enslavement, colonisation, Jewish deportations, genocides and neo-colonial exploitation. These personal stories contribute to the novels' critical stance towards Western domination and help question the official history that is taught at French schools.

A common feature of most families represented in the novels is the absence of the father. Young characters tend to grow up without knowing their genitors, like Jazz, whose father left; Youba, whose parents divorced; Rania, who was adopted; Prince, who helped his mother kill his violent father; Daddy, who was raised by his grandfather; and even Djiraël, who suffers from his father's extended absences in Senegal, followed by his early death. In most families, due to the father's absence, memories are lost or eroded and only fragments are transmitted. As Katelyn Knox observes,[19] the high number of family traumas and cases of questioned paternity in the novels triggers not only an unquenchable thirst for recognition in the hypermasculine young male characters but it also highlights their troubled, problematic belonging. Knox, who qualifies these mostly black or mixed-race male characters as Afropeans, relies on Achille Mbembe's and Anne Bocandé's definition of Afropean identity as a "quête de reconnaissance de la part d'un père inconnu" [quest for recognition from an unknown father].[20] Yet Djiraël, who in a heated debate reminds his father that he is not only not French but due to his blackness also remains a second-class citizen no matter how well he performs at school, sees his own identity less as a combination of European and African elements than a transnational experience of blackness that is reminiscent of the 'Black Atlantic'. Introduced by Paul Gilroy,[21] who demonstrated the validity of 'race' as an analytical category in presenting the 'Atlantic' as a discrete geopolitical unit in the modern capitalist world-system, the Black Atlantic posits the transnational diasporic black experience against cultural nationalisms such as the French one. In recent years, the colour-blindness of the French Republic has attracted much criticism from both French and foreign observers.[22] As the continuous reflection in the novels about race, ethnicity and social status suggests, blackness today in France remains an important factor of a social determinism that is difficult or impossible to counteract. As Djiraël puts it: "C'est la colonisation qui a fait de nous autres des *Noirs*. Être noir, c'est pas une revendication, c'est une injustice! Une malédiction! [...] Être noir, ce n'est pas une couleur, c'est un *statut*" [It was colonisation that made us blacks. To be black is not a claim, it is an injustice! A curse! [...] To be black is not a colour, it is a status] (LCdR, 285).

Yet Sané, like Djiraël in the novels, refuses to define the identity of his Sarcellois characters exclusively based on their ethnicity. Thus, even if he attributes much of the exclusion they experience to institutional racism, he complements ethnic and family genealogies with predominantly transnational intragenerational ties. Young characters of Caribbean, North African and sub-Saharan African descent who replace their unknown or missing fathers with intragenerational friends and rivals develop a transnational identity. Borrowed from the rhetoric of rap lyrics, the symbolic entities of the *city*, the *street* and the *ghetto*, and their metonymical markers, the concrete and the asphalt, play a key role in establishing a global, imagined community which is acknowledged by most youths as their shared community independently from their race and origins:

> La rue [...] elle raconte l'injustice, l'espoir et la chute. Pour hurler à la face blanche du monde qu'elle n'est pas Tobi mais Kunta Kinte, elle s'invente des notes bleues ; seul le ciel peut lui venir en aide... tal vez... Inch'Allah... si Dieu le veut. La rue, elle a la couleur pourpre, récite des incantations vaudous en invoquant le Christ en son nom propre.
>
> [The street [...] it tells of injustice, hope and fall. To scream at the white face of the world that she is not Tobi but Kunta Kinte, she invents blue notes; only heaven can help him ... tal vez ... Insh'Allah ... God willing. The street, it is color purple, recites voodoo incantations invoking Christ in his own name.] (DEM, 45, 113)

Self-identifying as postcolonial underdogs, ghetto boys or "street kids scarred by the asphalt" (DEM, 114), the novels' young protagonists develop a shared vision of history in which violence on black and Arab people feature prominently. They complement their parents' memories of colonial history and transnational migration with contemporary urban history interpreted as an extension of colonial domination. In their vision, ghetto youths are descendants of enslaved and colonised Africans who are today faced with police violence, political scapegoating or deportation as undocumented immigrants. Djiraël's younger brother

Alassane, who joins the rioters in November 2005, recognises himself in this interpretation of history:

> *Merde*, se disait-il, *j'suis pas africain, j'suis français!* Que devait-il attendre pour être considéré comme tel ? Et pourtant, il l'aimait, ce pays. Il l'aimait malgré l'Histoire. Il l'aimait malgré le Code Nègre, malgré *le bruit et les odeurs*, malgré Malik Oussékine, malgré l'Église Saint-Bernard. Il l'aimait envers et contre tout. Mais son amour restait sans écho, nourrissant sa rage. Cette indifférence, il la ferait payer.
>
> [Shit, he said to himself, I'm not African, I'm French! What did he have to wait for to be considered as such? And yet he loved this country. He loved it despite history. He loved it despite the Negro Code, despite the noise and the smells, despite Malik Oussékine, despite the Church of St. Bernard. He loved it against all odds. But his love remained echoed, fuelling his rage. This indifference, he would make it pay.] (PdC, 31f.)

While *Du plomb dans le crâne*'s deterritorialised banlieue experience shows that Sarcelles is just one of the many towns in France in which youths suffer from similar conditions, through its focus on Obama's election and subsequent assassination,[23] *Gueule de bois* argues that these conditions exist on a global scale. Through their identification with Obama, peripheral French youths who engage in rioting after his assassination demonstrate their awareness of the continuity between past colonial exploitation and present-day oppression of people of colour. By acknowledging the global salience of both the election and the assassination of Obama not only for black people but all marginalised populations in different national contexts,[24] Sané inscribes French banlieues into the global patterns of domination:

> Ce sont les chants d'esclaves marqués au fer rouge, fouettés, mutilés et piétinés dans les champs de coton du Mississippi ou les plantations de cannes à sucre de Guadeloupe ; c'est la lettre d'une épouse lue par une chair à canon sous les obus d'un champ de bataille, à Verdun ou aux Dardanelles, c'est le soleil que, chaque jour, rien ne peut empêcher de briller au-dessus du camp d'Auschwitz ; ce sont les têtes hautes d'hommes et de femmes qui enterrent un enfant à Gaza, à Baghdad, à Kabul, partout.
>
> [These are the songs of slaves branded, whipped, mutilated and trampled in the cotton fields of Mississippi or the sugar cane plantations of Guadeloupe; it is the letter of a wife read by cannon fodder under the shells of a battlefield, in Verdun or in the Dardanelles, it is the sun that, every day, nothing can prevent from shin-

ing above from the Auschwitz camp; these are the high heads of men and women who bury a child in Gaza, Baghdad, Kabul, everywhere.] (GdB, 127)

While banlieue life is depicted as a global experience, banlieue youths are also shown to develop solid local attachment to their neighbourhood. This neighbourhood belonging is strong enough to overwrite kinship relations. Thus Youba, Djiraël's cousin, becomes unwelcome in Sarcelles after Daddy's death sparks a war between the two neighbourhoods, which temporarily unites rival gangs in and around Sarcelles. Youths from the banlieue tend to resent their Parisian counterparts even if they belong to similar demographic groups and even if the working-class housing estates in the 19th arrondissement where Daddy's burnt body is found are just as stigmatised as the ones in Sarcelles. After the commemoration organised for Daddy, 6,000 youths from the surrounding areas disembark at Gare du Nord to carry out an organised attack against the capital:

> On venait de tous les quartiers de Sarcelles: Roisers, Merisier, Chantepie, Chardonneret, Cité Rose, Secte, Coop, Les sablons, Mozart… […] On avait sciemment oublié qui appartenait à quelle bande, qui venait de quelle cité […] On avait enterré désir de vengeance et haches de guerre. On avait fondé une patrie de misérables […] Envers et contre Paris l'orgueilleuse.
>
> [They came from all the districts of Sarcelles: Roisers, Merisier, Chantepie, Chardonneret, Cité Rose, Secte, Coop, Les sablons, Mozart… […] They had knowingly forgotten who belonged to which band, who came from which city […] They had buried desire for revenge and battle axes. They had founded a homeland of miserable people […] Towards and against the arrogant Paris.] (DEM 184–185)

After Sarcellois gangs ransack shops and attack local residents in the 19th arrondissement, Parisian youths retaliate, causing similar damage and taking hostages in Sarcelles. This outburst of violence, based on real events which occurred in 1995, is interpreted by Sané as a precursor to the 2005 uprising, which will become the most important outlet of the rage sparked by inequalities and institutional racism. This violent incident also allows Sané to question the assumed clear-cut difference between banlieues and central Paris neighbourhoods, demonstrating that banlieue-like high-rise inner-city neighbourhoods also exist in certain areas of Paris.

Sarcelles as a Translocal Contact Zone Where a Vernacular Cosmopolitanism Is Elaborated

The previous section has reviewed some key factors contributing to the emergence of new transnational identities in the French banlieues. These combine fragmented memories transmitted between generations in postcolonial immigrant families with local and global belongings to imagined communities such as the transnational neighbourhood and the delocalised *global ghetto*. This final section will focus on Sané's depiction of Sarcelles as a contact zone in which residents belonging to different clans, diasporas, racial and religious groups are in continuous contact, incessantly renegotiating their differences and affiliations. Through the incessant interaction with each other, they develop a high degree of cultural openness and sensitivity despite their initial reluctance to accept some forms of otherness. Unlike the elite cosmopolitans characterised by "an openness to, desire for and appreciation of social and cultural difference",[25] vernacular cosmopolitans do not necessarily engage with the Other out of choice. Nonetheless they show "an orientation, a willingness to engage with the Other".[26] Cosmopolitanism is generally associated with "transnational elites able to navigate between and within different cultures thanks to their education, confidence, cultural capital and money".[27] In recent years, however, the assumption that cosmopolitans are members of the elite has been increasingly challenged by scholars like James Clifford, Homi Bhabha, Kwame Anthony Appiah or Pnina Werbner.[28] Bhabha, to whom the oxymoron "vernacular cosmopolitanism" is attributed, defined it as a "cosmopolitan community envisaged in marginality".[29] The concept has been proven particularly useful to describe non-elite forms of travel and activities transcending national borders, such as the networks of global trade established by the Senegalese Mouridiyya brotherhood, a syncretic Sufi organisation whose members are predominantly working-class artisans and salesmen. The case of transnational banlieues is both similar to and different from globally mobile but self-centred diasporas like the Mourides.

According to Steven Vertovec and Robin Cohen,[30] vernacular cosmopolitanism has emerged in a global context which allowed transnational migrants to maintain stronger links with their home countries and develop new networks, living their lives "simultaneously across different nation-states, being both 'here' and 'there', crossing geographical and political boundaries".[31] This attitude is exemplified in the *Comédie urbaine* by Djiraël's father, who, like the Mouride migrants studied by Mamadou Diouf and Steven Rendall, Bruno Riccio or Giulia Sinatti,[32] returns to Senegal at frequent intervals and appears to be more invested in charitable activities there than in his life in the receiving society. Yet the similarities stop here. As Diouf and Rendall explain, Mouride religious leaders have succeeded to establish a distinctive community of mostly illiterate, rural traders and labourers that has been phenomenally successful at seeking fortune outside Senegal while maintaining and strengthening their spiritual and economic centres, Touba and Sandaga, in Senegal.[33] Mourides tend to occupy specific neighbourhoods in the receiving country, where they marginalise themselves, cloistering in crowded apartments, creating simultaneously ideological and territorial enclosures, to maintain their ritual community by drawing "on family relationships, appurtenance to the same village [...] and allegiance to the same marabout".[34] Although he maintains links with his co-nationals and invests his savings in Senegal rather than in France, Djiraël's father is an intellectual rather than a manual worker and he lives with his family in a multicultural French banlieue rather than in a shared apartment in a diasporic quartier. He saves to invest in the home country but instead of an ostentatious demonstration of wealth, he dedicates his resources to charitable donation. Despite his solidarity towards his co-villagers, he wants his children to grow up in France, study, achieve successful careers and found families with French partners to become fully French and have a better life than his.

In recent years, much scholarly attention has been dedicated to new forms of reterritorialised belonging developed by transnational migrants. Steven Vertovec, who has undertaken to disentangle the notion of *transnationalism*, has highlighted the intensification of cross-border activities and the emergence of a "'diaspora consciousness' marked by dual or multiple identifications" which can be "held together or re-created through migration or simply through cultural artefacts and a shared imagination":

> The awareness of multi-locality stimulates the desire to connect oneself with others, both 'here' and 'there' who share the same 'routes' and 'roots' [...] the condition of diaspora or transnationalism is comprised of ever-changing representations that provide an 'imaginary coherence' for a set of malleable identities.[35]

As Diouf and Rendall have shown, the imaginary coherence of the Mouride organisation relies on intense feelings of solidarity, affection, cooperation and mutual support and the image of Touba as an absolute reference to establish themselves in the world. The vernacular cosmopolitanism they create does not refer to the acquisition of an identity through assimilation, but rather to the display of a unique identity added to global temporality and not simply informed by the Western trajectory of modernity alone.[36] Thus, despite their openness to business opportunities in the world and adoption of capitalist business models, Mourides practise a cultural, religious and ideological enclosure in their receiving country which can be compared to the ill-defined notion of separatism penalised by the

French law championed by Macron. Yet, for Sinatti, even the urban settlements in Italy in which the Mourides congregate are highly dependent on the local contexts which provide the framework within which transnational relations develop. They become translocalities, defined by Appadurai as loci through which transnational relations anchor themselves to the ground to become regularised or institutionalised, through which collective modes of reference are created and new narratives of identification and belonging are developed.[37] In addition, Riccio, who has studied the internal tensions and the plurality of trajectories within the Mouride transnational space, has shown that even this relatively closed, highly cohesive, self-sufficient and group-centric community is far more complex and heterogeneous than has been previously thought:

> There exist different stages, different sending contexts (villages, post-colonial towns, the holy city, the capital), different backgrounds of class, urban or rural culture. Second, since a transnational circulatory model of migration is seen to be successful, it tends to be imitated. Finally, having an ambivalent audience to respond to, and a multi-polarised sending context to leave from, a Senegalese 'transnational community' can manifest itself in many different ways. I will, therefore, write against a construct of a monolithic ethnic group in the next section by considering the different experiences of Senegalese migrants in Italy.[38]

Riccio concludes that transnationalism is not a system of reified transnational networks but rather a dynamic process of constant networking within transnational spaces. In the light of this definition, we can argue that in Sané's *Comédie urbaine*, Sarcelles is represented as a translocal space in which the networking and negotiation of different belongings and allegiances is continually in progress. This is demonstrated through the plot centred on the members of a Senegalese household who maintain diasporic links with the extended family both in France and in Senegal, as well as with members of a transnational Senegalese intelligentsia who regularly visit the father: "vêtus de prestige, architectes, profs, médecins, encravatés" [dressed in prestige, architects, teachers, doctors, wearing ties] (LCdR, 171). Yet, at the same time, they also engage in new and constantly evolving relationships within and beyond their neighbourhood. The novels' transnational microcosmos in which residents of various national and ethnic origins live together, mirrors the banlieues' spatial and architectural heterogeneity rather than a diasporic homogeneity:

> Mon histoire est née en ville, dans une cité dortoir, un HLM, ou dans un pavillon avec vue imprenable sur les tours. Le cul entre la vie et la mort, mon histoire

s'exprime [...] dans un français qui baise avec le Maghreb, l'Afrique, l'Asie et les *States*, du coup ses mioches sont métis.

[My story was born in a city, in a sleepy suburb, a housing estate, or a detached house with a breath-taking view of the towers. The ass between life and death, my story speaks [...] a French that mates with the Maghreb, Africa, Asia and the States, thus her kids are mixed race.] (GdB, 11)

As opposed to the imagined harmony which characterises the republican ideal of *mixité sociale*, Sarcelles is depicted as a contact zone where tensions and frictions exist and require constant mitigation. Defined by Mary Louise Pratt as "social spaces where cultures meet, clash, and grapple with each other, often in contexts of highly asymmetrical relations of power, such as colonialism, slavery, or their aftermaths as they are lived out in many parts of the world today",[39] contact zones are territories in which the coexistence of different languages, religions, culinary traditions can be occasionally chaotic or conflictual. Raised in such a contact zone, Sarcellois youths learn to co-habit with the Other from an early age and acquire thereby a vernacular cosmopolitan orientation. This is exemplified by the ecumenic family rituals which precede each journey in Djiraël's family:

Quand j'ai regagné le séjour, tout le monde tenaient les mains dressées en l'air, qui à la façon des chrétiens, qui à la manière des musulmans. Tonton Hadj et Tonton Jean-Paul ont dirigé la prière. [...] Il restait encore une tradition à respecter – une tradition animiste, cette fois. La religion de ma mère. Elle a rempli une casserole d'eau devant le daron, qui se tenait immobile sur le seuil de la maison. Elle a versé le liquide au sol, puis elle a dit :
– Je t'attendrai, alors pars. Je t'attends, alors reviens.
Sans gêne, ils se sont embrassés sur la bouche. Ensuite, il a sauté par-dessus la flaque.

[When I returned home, everyone had their hands raised in the air, some Christian style, some Muslim style. Uncle Hadj and Uncle Jean-Paul led the prayer. [...] There was still a tradition to be respected – an animist tradition, this time. My mother's religion. She filled a pot of water in front of my old man, who stood motionless on the threshold of the house. She poured the liquid on the floor, then she said:
– I'll wait for you, so go. I'm waiting for you, so come back.
Without embarrassment, they kissed on the mouth. Then he jumped over the puddle.] (LCdR, 178f.)

Performed together in apparent harmony by Muslim, Christian and animist members of the same extended family, the departure ritual is one of the most successful examples of religious tolerance. The cultural capital acquired by the everyday exposure to otherness does not mean, however, that differences are always appreciated and actively sought after. Nonetheless the occasional clashes are never initiated by Sarcellois youths but rather the white, middle-class French residents of more affluent areas and State institutions. Djiraël's brother Tierno learns to fight as a child when he is attacked by a group of xenophobes in a middle-class neighbourhood. Djiraël's white friend, Armand, is not allowed to have dinner with the Senegalese family since his mother "hates Saracens" (SD, 163) and suspects the "Negroes" to be "cannibals" (SD, 275). Tatiana and her Parisian middle-class friends take Djiraël for a drug dealer and expect him to be a good dancer because he is black. Tatiana herself explains that she is attracted to him because of his sexualised black body (LCdR, 284). Such instances of rejection and racist stereotyping are regularly experienced by the novels' characters, in particular through their conflictual encounters with the French police:

> Maman a insisté que j'aille porter plainte au commissariat. […] Jamais je n'irai chez les poulets cafter. A chaque fois que j'avais eu affaire à la police, ç'avait été la même rengaine : « *Les mains contre le mur!* », « *Écarte les jambes* », « *Vides tes poches* »! Les agents de la paix ne s'adressaient à moi que par l'exclamative, à la deuxième personne singulier, et avec des injures. À chaque fois, je pouvais voir qu'ils étaient déçus de ne trouver ni drogue ni arme sur moi. Alors ils me disaient : « *Profite bien, p'tit pédé! Un jour tu vas dérailler et on sera là pour te cueillir!* »

> [Mum insisted that I go to the police station. […] I will never go to the cops to snitch. Every time I had dealt with the police it had been the same song: 'Hands against the wall!', 'Spread your legs', 'Empty your pockets'! Law enforcement officers only addressed me with exclamation, in second person singular, and name-calling. Each time, I could tell they were disappointed that they couldn't find drugs or guns on me. So, they told me, 'Enjoy, little fagot!' One day you will derail, and we will be there to get you!'] (LCdR, 267)

Such encounters with the police reinforce the young characters' impression that they are excluded from the national community both for their skin colour and their geographic marginality. They resist by cloistering in their transnational neighbourhood where transnational relationships are the rule rather than the exception. In the novels, groups of friends and couples are strictly multi-ethnic. At high school, Djiraël forms a solidary group with Armand and Sacha, who are white, Rania, who is Arab, and Jazz and Doumam, who are black. In *Gueule de bois*, another multi-ethnic trio is introduced which includes the Caribbean Freddy and the Maghrebi Samir and Farrel. In *Sarcelles-Dakar*, Djiraël starts a relationship with Farah, an Algerian girl from Kabylia. The mixed – black and Arab – couple is initially disapproved of by some members of the Maghrebi community: "Je sais que j'suis noir, ça fait longtemps que je le sais et je sais qu'on va avoir des problèmes par rapport à ça. Mais je sais aussi que je me bats les couilles des autres rageux. Tu vois, je m'en fous qu'on me montre de doigt ou qu'on m'insulte" [I know I'm black, I've known that for a long time and I know we're going to have problems with this. But I also know that I fight the balls of other haters. See, I don't care if anyone points a finger at me or insults me] (SD, 155).

Other mixed couples in the novels include the Moroccan Sonia who is in love with the black Freddy, or Alassane and his blonde French girlfriend, Babeth. Yet Djiraël's and his brothers' tolerance is challenged when their mother Abi announces that she is expecting a child from her partner, a white Frenchman, and when their younger sister Saly introduces her Cambodian boyfriend Phan. Farah, who confronts Djiraël with this injustice, highlights the fact that in practice the co-habitation of people of different ethnicities, religions and origins is more complex and difficult than the abstract political ideal of *mixité sociale* seems to suggest:

> Pourquoi tu n'acceptes pas que Saly sorte avec Phan ? Parce que ce mec a les yeux bridés? S'il était couleur café, voire avec un soupçon de lait en plus, la donne n'aurait pas été la même ? […] Si ça ne te pose aucun souci pour Alassane et Babeth, c'est parce que tu peux tolérer qu'un Noir couche avec une Blanche ou une Asiatique, alors que l'inverse, tu le condamnes. Ce qui fait de toi un raciste et un misogyne !
>
> [Why can't you accept that Saly is going out with Phan? Because this guy has slanted eyes? If he was coffee-coloured, even with a hint of extra milk, wouldn't the situation have been the same? […] If you don't mind Alassane and Babeth, it's because you can tolerate a black man sleeping with a white woman or an Asian, while the other way around, you condemn him. That makes you a racist and a misogynist!] (GdB, 200)

Sané, who in August 2021 announced the publication of the first episode of a new five-volume novel cycle, explained in an interview with TV5Monde that a more significant number of French people live in banlieues and experience diversity in their everyday life than politicians would admit. Polarising discourses accusing them of separatism are therefore not only inaccurate but, as Geisser suggests in his recent analysis of the anti-separatism law, also act as self-fulfilling prophecies which divide the nation by unfairly excluding large groups of peripheral citizens from official definitions of Frenchness.[40] As Sané argues:

> Quand nos élus parlent de séparatisme, ils font du tort à des gens comme moi qui ont grandi au milieu de chrétiens, au milieu de juifs, au milieu de musulmans, au milieu d'hindouistes, avec des blancs, avec des chaldéens, avec des noirs, avec des sémites; avec des communistes, des libéraux, des anarchistes ; qui ont essayé de se dire qu'on est frères. [...] [Ce sont] ces discours qui nous séparent, le séparatisme, ce n'est pas ces populations qui le créent, le séparatisme, c'est un séparatisme d'État.
>
> [When our elected officials talk about separatism, they are hurting people like me who grew up among Christians, among Jews, among Muslims, among Hindus, with whites, with Chaldeans, with blacks, with Semites, with communists, liberals, anarchists, who tried to say that we are brothers [...] These speeches [are the ones] that separate us, separatism is not created by these populations, this separatism, it a State separatism.][41]

For Sané, the most efficient way of responding to these divisive and stigmatising discourses is to include banlieue residents in fictional representations, thereby restoring their rightful place in the national imagination.

Conclusion: A Transnational Project Mirrored by Generic Diversity

This chapter has argued that Insa Sané's multi-volume cycle creates a vernacular cosmopolitan microcosmos to counter dominant political narratives depicting banlieues as sites where residents develop anti-republican, separatist tendencies. The *Comédie urbaine* counters this dystopian vision by showing that the constrained co-habitation of mostly working-class immigrant families from different regions of the world that results in banlieues like Sarcelles in a genuine version of the much desired French ideal of *mixité sociale*. Instead of erasing immigrant family ties, postcolonial memories, and ethnic, religious and racial identities, neighbourhood belonging can peacefully coexist with these ties. Sarcelles as a contact zone may not be perfectly harmonious at all times, but most differences are successfully negotiated by the residents, who practise open-mindedness by developing multi-religious practices and transnational friendships and relationships. The emergence of a vernacular cosmopolitanism demonstrates that identities developed in French banlieues are multiple and combinatory rather than binary: young residents like Djiraël are not either French or Senegalese, Parisian or Sarcellois, good students or lazy dunces; rather, they alternate and cumulate several of these identities.

The novels' hybrid form, which mixes various Western and exogenous genres and alternates different narrative viewpoints and attitudes, is a particularly effective support for Sané's ambitious project that aims to counter highly polarised, binary depictions of French banlieues in dominant media-political discourses. The *Urban Comedy* label, which reinforces the novels' intertextual links with Balzac, highlights that today's banlieues, like Sarcelles, are just as inalienable parts of the contemporary Paris as the urban margins depicted by realist novelists like Balzac or Zola were part of the 19th-century French capital. Thus, Sané invites his readers to recognise in Éléonore, the beautiful Congolese prostitute, the 21st-century reincarnation of Zola's Nana, who was attracted, celebrated and finally rejected by the City of Light, crushed by the ever-active dynamics of social determinism.

> Tu vois, copain, au 19e siècle, les quartiers à l'est de la capitale ressemblaient à ce qu'on appelle aujourd'hui *la banlieue*. Cette partie de Paris n'offrait que le sombre panorama d'édifices décrépits et de rues insalubres. Insécurité et violence rimant avec pauvreté et indigence […] Là s'entassaient les petits artisans et commerçants, mais surtout les ouvriers et les laissés-pour-compte d'une société qui rêvait désespérément de progrès… industriel. Hé, mon soce, t'as pigé : à l'époque déjà, Paris pouvait très bien accueillir toute la misère du monde.

> [You see, mate, in the 19th century, the neighbourhoods east of the capital looked like what we now call the suburbs. This part of Paris offered only the gloomy panorama of decrepit buildings and unsanitary streets. Insecurity and violence rhyming with poverty and indigence […] There were piled up small artisans and traders, but above all the workers and those left behind in a society that desperately dreamed of … industrial progress. Hey, mate, you got it: back then, Paris could very well accommodate all the misery in the world.] (DeM, 76f.)

The extraordinary narrative and stylistic diversity of the five volumes allows Sané to revisit various traditions and merge them in the same way banlieues integrate transnational populations and their disparate cultural baggage. *Sarcelles-Dakar* merges European genres and African oral traditions, including the proverb, the funeral praise poetry performed by griots and the fable. Divided into three acts, *Du plomb dans le crâne* resembles a Greek tragedy which progresses inevitably towards the death of Sonny/Prince, a Rabelaisian, carnivalesque character, while also recounting the defeat suffered by a generation of young men, exemplified by Alassane and his friends, who participated in the 2005 uprisings without being able to challenge the banlieues' political oppression. *Gueule de bois* is a dystopian novel anticipating Obama's assassination, *Daddy est mort* is a work of crime fiction divided into episodes reminiscent of a TV series. In addition, the novels are saturated with uncountable intertextual and intermedial references, some of which have been deconstructed by scholars such as Katelyn Knox, who studies musical intermediality in *Du plomb dans le crâne* and *Daddy est mort*, or Rym ben Tanfous in an ambitious thesis on intermediality in three banlieue novels.[42]

While the richness of the generic, stylistic and linguistic strategies elaborated by Sané requires further investigation, we can conclude that the extraordinary multiplicity of intertextual elements he combines in his novels is representative of the diversity of banlieues, which are simultaneously heterogeneous and quintessentially French. Sané's banlieue narratives are republican in their promotion of place-based rather than origin-based identities. However, the Frenchness he conceptualises in the *Comédie urbaine* is less based on a nationalist sentiment than on a combination of local, transnational and global belongings. By representing banlieues like Sarcelles as hubs where a vernacular cosmopolitanism is developed by multifarious social groups that mutually mistrust each other yet manage to overcome their differences, he counters accusations of separatism and returns the accusation of divisiveness towards the French State:

> Une nation c'est un groupe d'individus qui partagent les mêmes rêves et qui décident de vivre selon les mêmes règles [...]. Et justement, nos élus font en sorte de casser notre nation, de casser l'État lequel on a envie de défendre.
>
> [A nation is a group of individuals who share the same dreams and who decide to live according to the same rules [...]. Our elected officials are the ones who break our nation, who break the State which we want to defend.][43]

Notes

1. Macron, Emmanuel (2020): Speech Pronounced in Les Muraux on 2 October 2020, https://www.elysee.fr/en/emmanuel-macron/2020/10/02/fight-against-separatism-the-republic-in-action-speech-by-emmanuel-macron-president-of-the-republic-on-the-fight-against-separatism. Accessed 2 August 2021.
2. Dikeç, Mustafa (2007): *Badlands of the Republic: Space, Politics and Urban Policy*. Oxford: Blackwell, 22.
3. Collectif (2018): L'Appel des 100 intellectuels contre le 'séparatisme islamiste'. *Le Figaro* (19 March).

4. In his 2004 book Maurin has demonstrated that despite the 1990 Besson law and the 1991 Loi de l'Orientation pour la Ville obliging cities to build social housing, the most affluent French towns prefer to pay a fine rather than accepting social housing areas to be built on their territories. Maurin, Éric (2004): *Le Ghetto Français: Enquête sur le séparatisme social*. Paris: Seuil.
5. Hargreaves, Alec (1995): *Immigration, 'Race' and Ethnicity in Contemporary France*. London: Routledge, 66.
6. Avenel explains that by introducing the Aide personnalisée au Logement, the 1977 Barre law has significantly increased both the mobility of middle-class families and the access to social housing of those low-income families who remained excluded from homeownership. Avenel, Cyprien (2005): La mixité dans la ville et dans les grands ensembles: Entre mythe social et instrument politique. *Informations sociales* 125, 62–71; cf. also Tissot, Sylvie (2007): *L'État et les quartiers: Genèse d'une catégorie de l'action publique*. Paris: Seuil.
7. Avenel (2005).
8. These novels will henceforth be cited within the text using the acronyms SD, GdB, DEM, PdC and LCdR respectively.
9. Cited in Aubry, Bernard, and Michèle Tribalat (2009): Les Jeunes d'origine étrangère. *Commentaire* 126, 436.
10. INSEE (2021): *Revenues et pauvreté des ménages en 2018,* https://www.insee.fr/fr/statistiques/5011970?geo=UU2020-2A104. Accessed 2 August 2021.
11. Mulvey, Michael (2016): The Problem that Had a Name: French High-Rise Developments and the Fantasy of a Suburban Homemaker Pathology, 1954–73. *Gender & History* 28(1), 177–198.
12. Ibid., 178.
13. This type of personifying representation of the city, depicted as a monstrous being, is particularly prevalent is the crime novel *Daddy est mort*, where the omniscient narrator echoes the 19th-century preoccupation with a destructive urbanity, based on observations of aggressive and rapid industrialisation leading to the dissolution of close-knit communities: "Hum, Éléonore ! Tu te souviens, Éléonore ? Te souviens-tu de ta banlieue natale ? Te rappelles-tu comme l'adolescente sarcelloise que tu étais alors rêvait de voir les lumières de la ville, *la vraie* ? Tu les as vues, hein ? Paris, quelle aventure ! Mais la ville aime la chair, que reste-t-il de toi?" [Hmm, Eleanor! Do you remember, Eleanor? Do you remember your native banlieue? Do you remember how the teenager you were then in Sarcelles dreamed of seeing the lights of the city, the real one? You've seen them, huh? Paris, what an adventure! But the city loves the flesh, what is left of you?] (DEM, 17) While the character of Éléonore can be interpreted here as a transposition of Zola's Nana into a contemporary transnational urban context, it is also important to remember that this type of mythological representation of the city is common in the

noir genre, as Jean-Noël Blanc suggests. Blanc, Jean-Noël (1991): *Polarville: Images de la ville dans le roman policier*. Lyon: Presses Universitaires de Lyon.
14. Moretti, Franco (2005): *Graphs, Maps, Trees: Abstract Models for Literary History*. London: Verso, 57.
15. Sarkozy, Nicolas (2007): Speech Pronounced at the University of Dakar on 26 July 2007, https://www.lemonde.fr/afrique/article/2007/11/09/le-discours-de-dakar_976786_3212.html. Accessed 2 August 2021.
16. Anderson, Benedict (1984): *Imagined Communities: Reflections on the Origins and Spread of Nationalism*. London: Verso.
17. Appadurai, Arjun (1996): Sovereignty without Territoriality: Notes for a Postnational Geography. *The Geography of Identity*, edited by Patricia Yaeger. Ann Arbor: University of Michigan Press, 40-58; Sinatti, Giulia (2006): Diasporic Cosmopolitanism and Conservative Translocalism: Narratives of Nation Among Senegalese Migrants in Italy. *Studies in Ethnicity and Nationalism* 6(3), 30–50.
18. Appadurai, Arjun, and Carol Breckenridge (1989): On Moving Targets. *Public Culture* 2, i.
19. Knox, Katelyn (2021): Masculinity, Recognition, and Genealogy through Musico-Literary Intermediality in Insa Sané's Du plomb dans le crâne et Daddy est mort. *Contemporary French Civilization* 46(1), 1–25, 4.
20. Mbembe, Achille, and Anne Bocandé (2014): L'Afrique est plus qu'un ensemble géographique: Elle est et doit demeurer une question. *Africultures* 3/4(99–100), 104–107.
21. Gilroy, Paul (1993): *The Black Atlantic: Modernity and Double Consciousness*. London: Verso.
22. Tchumkam, Hervé (2015): *State Power, Stigmatization, and Youth Resistance Culture in the French Banlieues: Uncanny Citizenship*. Lamham: Lexington Books; Puig, Stève (2019): *Littérature urbaine et mémoire postcoloniale*. Paris: L'Harmattan; Beaman, Jean (2017): *Citizen Outsider: Children of North African Immigrants in France*. Oakland: University of California Press.
23. In the novel, President Obama is assassinated shortly after his victory, by one of his own bodyguards. Since this is the only significant distortion to reality in the novel cycle, and we can assume that the aim of Sané was not to produce a dystopian novel but to express his anxiety about this possibility. The novel was published in 2009, just one year into Obama's first mandate, and it was probably written at the time of the US elections or very shortly after. It may also be a prediction that did not come true.
24. "Ce meurtre ne portait attente qu'aux Noirs, mais aux exclus de tous bords de toutes nations" [This murder affected not only blacks, but all sorts of marginalised people in every nations] (GdB, 173).
25. Binnie, Jon, Julian Holloway, Steve Millington, and Craig Young (2006): *Cosmopolitan Urbanism*. London: Routledge, 7.
26. Hannerz, Ulf (1996): *Transnational Connections*. London: Routledge, 128.

27. Horvath, Christina (2011): The Cosmopolitan City. *The Ashgate Research Companion to Cosmopolitanism*, edited by Maria Rovisco and Magdalena Nowicka. Farnham: Ashgate, 87–106, 89.
28. Clifford, James (1992): Travelling Cultures. *Cultural Studies*, edited by Lawrence Grossberg. London: Routledge, 96–116; Bhabha, Homi K. (1996): Unsatisfied: Notes on Vernacular Cosmopolitanism. *Text and Nation: Cross-Disciplinary Essays on Cultural and National Identities*, edited by Laura Garcia-Moreno and Peter C. Pfeiffer. Columbia, SC: Camden House, 191–207; Breckenridge, Carol A., Sheldon Pollock, Homi K. Bhabha, and Dipesh Chakrabarty (2002): *Cosmopolitanism*. Durham, NC: Duke University Press; Appiah, Kwame Anthony (1998): Cosmopolitan Patriots. *Cosmopolitics: Thinking and Feeling Beyond the Nation*, edited by Pheng Cheah and Bruce Robbins. Minneapolis: University of Minnesota Press, 91–116; Werbner, Pnina (2006): Vernacular Cosmopolitanism. *Theory, Culture & Society* 23(2–3), 496–498; Werbner, Pnina (2008): *Anthropology and the New Cosmopolitanism: Rotted, Feminist and Vernacular Perspectives*. Oxford: Berg.
29. Bhabha (1996), 195f.
30. Vertovec, Steven, and Robin Cohen, eds. (1999): Introduction. *Migration, Diasporas, Transnationalism*. London: Edward Elgar.
31. Riccio, Bruno (2001): From 'Ethnic Group' to 'Transnational Community'? Senegalese Migrants' Ambivalent Experiences and Multiple Trajectories. *Journal of Ethnic and Migration Studies* 27(4), 583–599, 583.
32. Diouf, Mamadou, and Steven Rendall (2000): The Senegalese Murid Trade Diaspora and the Making of a Vernacular Cosmopolitanism. *Public Culture* 12(3), 679–702; Riccio (2001); Sinatti (2006).
33. Diouf (2000).
34. Ibid., 694.
35. Vertovec, Steven (1999): *Migration, Diasporas, Transnationalism*, edited by Steven Vertovec and Robin Cohen. London: Edward Elgar, 447-462, 450.
36. Diouf (2000), 702.
37. Cf. Appadurai, Arjun (1995): The Production of Locality. *Counterworks: Managing the Diversity of Knowledge*, edited by Richard Fardon. London: Routledge; Appadurai (1996).
38. Riccio (2001), 589f.
39. Pratt, Mary Louise (1991): Arts of the Contact Zone. *Profession* 2, 33–40, 34.
40. Geisser, Vincent (2021): Un séparatisme 'venu d'en haut' : rhétorique identitaire pour élites en mal de légitimité populaire. *Migrations Société* 183, 3–15.
41. Sané, Insa (2021): Cité des Argonautes: Premier acte d'un saga littéraire. Interview. *Le Journal Afrique, Culture, TV5Monde* (3 August).
42. Knox (2021); Ben Tanfous, R. (2018): *Décentrement et intermédiarité dans trois romans de Banlieue*. PhD Thesis. University of Tunis.
43. Sané (2021).

Works Cited

Primary Literature

Sané, Insa (2006): *Sarcelles-Dakar*. Paris: Sarbacane.
Sané, Insa (2008): *Du plomb dans le crâne*. Paris: Sarbacane.
Sané, Insa (2009): *Gueule de bois*. Paris: Sarbacane.
Sané, Insa (2010): *Daddy est mort... Retour à Sarcelles*. Paris: Sarbacane.
Sané, Insa (2017): *Les cancres de Rousseau*. Paris: Sarbacane.

Secondary Literature

Anderson, Benedict (1984): *Imagined Communities: Reflections on the Origins and Spread of Nationalism*. London: Verso.
Appadurai, Arjun (1995): The Production of Locality. *Counterworks: Managing the Diversity of Knowledge*, edited by Richard Fardon. London: Routledge, 204-225.
Appadurai, Arjun (1996): Sovereignty without Territoriality: Notes for a Postnational Geography. *The Geography of Identity*, edited by Patricia Yaeger. Ann Arbor: University of Michigan Press, 40-58.
Appadurai, Arjun, and Carol Breckenridge (1989): On Moving Targets. *Public Culture* 2:1.
Appiah, Kwame Anthony (1998): Cosmopolitan Patriots. *Cosmopolitics: Thinking and Feeling Beyond the Nation*, edited by Pheng Cheah and Bruce Robbins. Minneapolis: University of Minnesota Press, 91–116.
Breckenridge, Carol A., Sheldon Pollock, Homi K. Bhabha, and Dipesh Chakrabarty (2002): *Cosmopolitanism*. Durham, NC: Duke University Press.
Aubry, Bernard, and Michèle Tribalat (2009): Les Jeunes d'origine étrangère. *Commentaire* 126.
Avenel, Cyprien (2005): La mixité dans la ville et dans les grands ensembles: Entre mythe social et instrument politique. *Informations sociales* 125, 62–71.
Beaman, Jean (2017): *Citizen Outsider: Children of North African Immigrants in France*. Oakland: University of California Press.
Ben Tanfous, R. (2018): *Décentrement et intermédiarité dans trois romans de Banlieue*. PhD Thesis. University of Tunis.
Bhabha, Homi K. (1996): Unsatisfied: Notes on Vernacular Cosmopolitanism. *Text and Nation: Cross-Disciplinary Essays on Cultural and National Identities*, edited by Laura Garcia-Moreno and Peter C. Pfeiffer. Columbia, SC: Camden House, 191–207.
Binnie, Jon, Julian Holloway, Steve Millington, and Craig Young (2006): *Cosmopolitan Urbanism*. London: Routledge.
Blanc, Jean-Noël (1991): *Polarville: Images de la ville dans le roman policier*. Lyon: Presses Universitaires de Lyon.

Breckenridge, Carol A., Sheldon Pollock, Homi K. Bhabha, and Dipesh Chakrabarty (2002): *Cosmopolitanism*. Durham, NC: Duke University Press.
City Populations (n.d.): https://www.citypopulation.de/en/france/valdoise/sarcelles/95585__sarcelles/. Accessed 2 August 2021.
Clifford, James (1992): Travelling Cultures. *Cultural Studies*, edited by Lawrence Grossberg. London: Routledge, 96–116.
Cohen, Robin (1997): *Global Diasporas: An Introduction*. London: UCL Press.
Collectif (2018): L'Appel des 100 intellectuels contre le 'séparatisme islamiste'. *Le Figaro* (19 March).
Collectif Qui fait la France? (2007): *Chroniques d'une société annoncée*. Paris: Stock.
Dikeç, Mustafa (2007): *Badlands of the Republic: Space, Politics and Urban Policy*. Oxford: Blackwell.
Diouf, Mamadou, and Steven Rendall (2000): The Senegalese Murid Trade Diaspora and the Making of a Vernacular Cosmopolitanism. *Public Culture* 12(3), 679–702.
Geisser, Vincent (2021): Un séparatisme 'venu d'en haut' : rhétorique identitaire pour élites en mal de légitimité populaire. *Migrations Société* 183, 3–15.
Gilroy, Paul (1993): *The Black Atlantic: Modernity and Double Consciousness*. London: Verso.
Hannerz, Ulf (1996): *Transnational Connections*. London: Routledge.
Hargreaves, Alec (1995): *Immigration, 'Race' and Ethnicity in Contemporary France*. London: Routledge.
Horvath, Christina (2011): The Cosmopolitan City. *The Ashgate Research Companion to Cosmopolitanism*, edited by Maria Rovisco and Magdalena Nowicka. Farnham: Ashgate, 87–106.
INSEE (2021): *Revenues et pauvreté des ménages en 2018*, https://www.insee.fr/fr/statistiques/5011970?geo=UU2020-2A104. Accessed 2 August 2021.
Knox, Katelyn (2021): Masculinity, Recognition, and Genealogy through Musico-Literary Intermediality in Insa Sané's Du plomb dans le crâne et Daddy est mort. *Contemporary French Civilization* 46(1), 1–25.
Macron, Emmanuel (2020): Speech Pronounced in Les Muraux on 2 October 2020, https://www.elysee.fr/en/emmanuel-macron/2020/10/02/fight-against-separatism-the-republic-in-action-speech-by-emmanuel-macron-president-of-the-republic-on-the-fight-against-separatism. Accessed 2 August 2021.
Maurin, Éric (2004): *Le Ghetto Français : Enquête sur le séparatisme social*. Paris: Seuil.
Mbembe, Achille, and Anne Bocandé (2014): L'Afrique est plus qu'un ensemble géographique: Elle est et doit demeurer une question. *Africultures* 3/4(99–100), 104–107.
Mignolo, Walter D. (2013): Border Thinking, Decolonial Cosmopolitanism and Dialogues Among Civilizations. *The Ashgate Research Companion to Cosmopolitanism*, edited by Maria Rovisco and Magdalena Nowicka. London: Routledge, 329–348.

Moretti, Franco (2005): *Graphs, Maps, Trees: Abstract Models for Literary History*. London: Verso.

Mulvey, Michael (2016): The Problem that Had a Name: French High-Rise Developments and the Fantasy of a Suburban Homemaker Pathology, 1954–73. *Gender & History* 28(1), 177–198.

Pratt, Mary Louise (1991): Arts of the Contact Zone. *Profession* 2, 33–40.

Pratt, Mary Louise (1992): *Imperial Eyes: Travel Writing and Transculturation*. London: Routledge.

Pratt, Mary Louise (1999): *From Ways of Reading*, edited David Bartholomae and Anthony Petroksky. New York: Bedford/St. Martin's.

Puig, Stève (2019): *Littérature urbaine et mémoire postcoloniale*. Paris: L'Harmattan.

Riccio, Bruno (2001): From 'Ethnic Group' to 'Transnational Community'? Senegalese Migrants' Ambivalent Experiences and Multiple Trajectories. *Journal of Ethnic and Migration Studies* 27(4), 583–599.

Sané, Insa (2021): Cité des Argonautes: Premier acte d'un saga littéraire. Interview. *Le Journal Afrique, Culture, TV5Monde* (3 August).

Sarkozy, Nicolas (2007): Speech Pronounced at the University of Dakar on 26 July 2007, https://www.lemonde.fr/afrique/article/2007/11/09/le-discours-de-dakar_976786_3212.html. Accessed 2 August 2021.

Sinatti, Giulia (2006): Diasporic Cosmopolitanism and Conservative Translocalism: Narratives of Nation Among Senegalese Migrants in Italy. *Studies in Ethnicity and Nationalism* 6(3), 30–50.

Tchumkam, Hervé (2015): *State Power, Stigmatization, and Youth Resistance Culture in the French Banlieues: Uncanny Citizenship*. Lamham: Lexington Books.

Tissot, Sylvie (2007): *L'État et les quartiers: Genèse d'une catégorie de l'action publique*. Paris: Seuil.

Vertovec, Steven, and Robin Cohen, eds. (1999): *Migration, Diasporas, Transnationalism*. London: Edward Elgar.

Werbner, Pnina (2006): Vernacular Cosmopolitanism. *Theory, Culture & Society* 23(2–3), 496–498.

Werbner, Pnina (2008): *Anthropology and the New Cosmopolitanism: Rotted, Feminist and Vernacular Perspectives*. Oxford: Berg.

Werbner, Pnina (2011): Paradoxes of Postcolonial Vernacular Cosmopolitanism in South Asia and the Diaspora. *The Ashgate Research Companion to Cosmopolitanism*, edited by Maria Rovisco and Magdalena Nowicka. Farnham: Ashgate, 107–123.

SECTION I

VIRTUAL NEIGHBOURHOODS

"We will be ephemeral"

Encounter, Community and Unsettled Cosmopolitanism in Senthuran Varatharajah's *Vor der Zunahme der Zeichen* (2016)

MARIA ROCA LIZARAZU

Abstract

This chapter explores Senthuran Varatharaja's 2016 novel *Vor der Zunahme der Zeichen* as a literary manifestation of the transnational neighbourhood. In the novel, the experience of forced migration and displacement gives rise to new modes of encountering and living with the other and an 'unsettled' form of cosmopolitanism, which questions the notion of self-identity by foregrounding and performing, in the medium of writing, suspension, ephemerality and estrangement. In a similar manner to the transnational neighbourhood, understood as a space of chance encounters and uncommon grounds, this cosmopolitanism is not based on a shared essence or universalising principles but on fleeting associations, similarities and overlaps. Varatharajah's novel thus encourages us to revaluate much-debated concepts such as transnationalism, cosmopolitanism, conviviality and community from the vantage point of the everyday, transient encounters that constitute the transnational neighbourhood. As such, *Vor der Zunahme der Zeichen* also raises the question of whether and how the fugitive and precarious communities established in the novel can be translated into more lasting forms of togetherness. This is arguably where the medium of literature has a crucial role to play, as the novel itself can be read as a type of neighbourhood that is capable of expressing and providing space for ephemerality and unsettlement.

Introduction

Senthuran Varatharajah's 2016 debut novel *Vor der Zunahme der Zeichen* [Before the Signs Increase] has been read by many critics in the context of larger trends in German-language writing,[1] which, in recent years, has seen a proliferation of literary texts and scholarship responding to the so-called 'migrant and refugee crisis'.[2] The novel, presented in the form of a Facebook Messenger conversation, centres on the exchange between Senthil Vasuthevan, whose Tamil family fled the Sri Lankan Civil War when he was a toddler, and Valmira Surroi, whose Albanian family escaped the war in Kosovo when she was a child. The two encounter each other randomly on the social media platform and begin a conversation which lasts for a week and touches on their family histories of flight and expulsion, their experiences of growing up in Germany, their encounters with various forms of othering and racism, as well as their everyday lives and relationships. Given its publication date and subject matter, it seems plausible to read the novel as a commentary on the most recent migratory movements to Germany. Yet this perspective overlooks the fact that *Vor der Zunahme der Zeichen* is in many ways not about these current topics. The novel engages with displacements that took place several decades ago, in parts questioning the perception of the recent so-called 'refugee crisis' as an unprecedented and exceptional event. More importantly though, the novel, strictly speaking, does not depict direct experiences of flight and migration, but rather centres on the question of their aftermath and on the perspectives of those who actually have no personal experience of the events. Both Senthil and Valmira were small children when they were forced to flee their countries of origin and stress repeatedly that they have little to no memory of the events.[3] Apart from thus exploring the temporalities of departure and arrival, the book focuses mainly on language, narrative and memory in the face of a traumatic history that is the inaccessible yet all-pervasive precondition of one's existence. *Vor der Zunahme der Zeichen* reflects on how histories of flight and expulsion affect the very possibility of witnessing, recounting and transmitting such histories, while also exploring what kinds of connection and community might arise in their aftermath. As noted by Jonas Teupert, Varatharajah's text "reflects the condition of possibility of telling a story in times of mass-displacement and homelessness".[4] Additionally, I would argue that it also reflects the conditions of possibility of creating community and cosmopolitan outlooks in the absence of stable belongings and common grounds. The novel's relevance for the contemporary moment thus results less from its engagement with current political topics, but rather from its exploration of forms and figurations that may accommodate key experiences in the age of mass displacement and widespread transnational mobilities.[5] Varatharajah's text raises fundamental questions about what 'transnational', 'migrant' or 'refugee' writing is – is it writing by migrating and mobile subjects, writing about migrating and mobile subjects or, rather, a writing of mobile and fugitive forms and figurations?

In the following, I will examine how these themes relate to the notion of the transnational neighbourhood, which this volume seeks to explore. I want to suggest that the concept of the transnational neighbourhood brings to the fore a tangle of issues having to do with coexistence and conviviality, on the one hand, and transnationalism and cosmopolitanism, on the other. It thus provides a prism through which we may approach some of the key concerns shaping our age of mass migration and transnational mobility, namely the question of how we relate to the – literal and figurative – proximity of the stranger in all their difference and opacity. This question, which is central to Varatharajah's novel, also shapes my thoughts around the transnational neighbourhood, understood as a stage for exploring transnational convivialities, relational entanglements and everyday cosmopolitanisms. As a "densely packed contact zone",[6] the transnational neighbourhood is a space of chance and fleeting encounters, but also of unwanted proximities. It thus foregrounds the issue of having to coexist with others with whom we might seemingly not have anything in common, to whom we are connected solely by the fact that we share the same space. In an age of mass migration and various other forms of transnational movement, the question of how to encounter difference and "make some sort of common life together",[7] as Stuart Hall put it, is a central one. Varatharajah's novel, too, explores processes of encounter and of what it means to have something in common (or not). In a similar manner to the transnational neighbourhood, the virtual space presented in the novel offers opportunities for random and unexpected crossings, while also asking questions about encountering and living with others. I will approach these issues through the lens of Jean-Luc Nancy's ideas about community without unity, sharing and touching.[8]

Despite bearing the transnational in its name, the transnational neighbourhood is not the setting of the large-scale and border-crossing mobilities of people and goods that we often associate with the concept.[9] Rather, it is an urban microcosm defined by everyday interactions and intermingling, inviting us to expand established notions of the transnational. I want to argue here that the concept of the transnational neighbourhood can usefully complement the prevailing focus in transnational studies on border crossings, "mobility and flows" with a consideration of the ethics of coexistence and conviviality, which are also implied in the concept.[10] In his seminal book *After Empire*, Paul Gilroy defines the challenges of fostering more convivial cultures as follows:

> We need to know what sorts of insights and reflection might actually help increasingly differentiated societies and anxious individuals to cope successfully with the challenges involved in dwelling comfortably in proximity to the unfamiliar without becoming fearful and hostile. We need to consider whether the scale upon which sameness and difference are calculated might be altered productively so that the strangeness of strangers goes out of focus and other dimensions of the basic sameness can be acknowledged and made significant.[11]

Gilroy famously makes the case for a "vulgar" or "demotic" cosmopolitanism to address these issues, which "finds civic and ethical value in the ordinary virtues and ironies – listening, looking, discretion, friendship – that can be cultivated when mundane encounters with difference become rewarding".[12] The transnational neighbourhood, as "a fluid space in which various temporal and spatial axes intersect",[13] is uniquely suited to stage and explore such "mundane encounters with difference", thus contributing towards fostering a "vulgar" transnationalism, in Gilroy's sense, or a "cosmopolitanism of connections", to use Craig Calhoun's term.[14] Calhoun makes the case for grounding cosmopolitanism in "our relationships to each other", in the ways in which "we are affected and affect each other".[15] Such a transnationalism or cosmopolitanism would no longer be large-scale and universal, normative and prescriptive, which are criticisms that repeatedly have been levelled against these concepts.[16] While no longer describing an ideal state or grounding principle, this manifestation of transnationalism or cosmopolitanism would be the inevitable result of our entangled existences, which become particularly apparent in the everyday settings of the transnational neighbourhood. Such an approach to transnationalism and cosmopolitanism resonates with recent "post-foundational" re-framings of such terms,[17] which seek to move away from normative and universalising assumptions. The result is a self-critical and constantly self-interrogating version of transnationalism and cosmopolitanism, founded on "a degree of estrangement from one's own culture and history" and promoting "a plurality of fleeting and contingent groundings" rather than the one stable ground.[18] *Vor der Zunahme der Zeichen* approaches questions of conviviality, transnationalism and cosmopolitanism through the lens of micro-level, everyday interactions. Through tracing the mundane Facebook Messenger conversation between its main characters, the novel develops a notion of unstable and uncommon grounds, which become the basis for an unsettled and unsettling transnationalism or cosmopolitanism, based on suspension, ephemerality and estrangement. Paradoxically, this perpetual unsettlement becomes the condition of possibility for "dwelling comfortably in proximity to the unfamiliar" and providing refuge to the strange(r) in an era of mass displacement.[19]

Uncommon Grounds and Shared Experiences

I want to begin by exploring the virtual neighbourhood in which Senthil's and Valmira's meeting takes place, with a view to how it conditions and influences their ability to encounter one another. As mentioned above, both the virtual neighbourhood of the novel and the transnational neighbourhood are spaces of random encounter. The novel is presented in the form of a Facebook Messenger conversation, and while many use the platform to stay connected with people they already know, Facebook's "people you may know" feature enables unexpected contact. This feature shows users a list of people they may have a connection with, based on mutual friends or participation in the same Facebook groups or other networks, according to Facebook.[20] This is indeed how Senthil comes across Valmira, who seems "vertraut" [familiar] (9) to him, even though it turns out that the two have never met. The conditions of their encounter establish absent or uncommon ground as/at the basis of their fleeting connection: the two of them share no lived experiences, embodied space or substantial relationship; there are no grounds, as in good reasons, for their paring, which is the result of Facebook's algorithm; and the virtual space in which they cross paths is literally groundless, without substance. These circumstances connect to a more fundamental question in the text, relating to what it means to have something in common. Drawing on the philosopher of community Jean-Luc Nancy, we can say that Varatharajah's text explores the relationship between "common being" and "being in common".[21] The fact that Senthil and Valmira are randomly thrown together by computerised calculations and that they remain in an anonymous and disembodied space for the duration of their encounter makes it hard for them to refer back to a "common being", understood as a "substance, [...] essence, or common identity".[22] This lack of common ground, however, allows them to explore their "being in common", understood as a set of relations emerging from "commonalities which do not reduce their differences".[23] Rather than presuming and building on a pre-given connection, conditioned by national, ethnic, linguistic, gendered or generational belonging and identities, their exchange explores the very conditions of making connections, of encountering, of relating. The novel's emphasis on commonality or similarity over "common being" seems particularly important when considering the text's critical engagement with various practices of othering and racism, alongside the reductionism inherent to the notion of (self-)identity. By complicating manifestations of "common being", the text also tackles the issue of writing (after) displacement and so-called "migrant" or "refugee" literatures, which I briefly outlined in the introduction. In interview, Varatharajah has opposed a reading of his novel – and of literature more generally – as explicit political commentary, while also rejecting the idea that he speaks on behalf of or represents a particular group.[24] He highlights that flight and displacement render impossible such direct commentary and representation, since they destroy notions of pure origins and stable belongings, of tradition understood as continuity and of language as direct representation. What remains is the singularity of each human's experience, for which singular forms of expression need to be found. Such singularities might have something "in common", to use Nancy's language, but they cannot be subsumed under a stable category, a "common being". *Vor Der Zunahme der Zeichen* is concerned with precisely this labour of reflecting on and finding language and commonality in the face of the extreme ruptures and absent grounds produced by mass displacement.

The temporality of digital communication is another crucial aspect of encounter in *Vor der Zunahme der Zeichen*. Unlike the face-to-face encounter, as it would for example take place in the transnational neighbourhood, Senthil's and Valmira's communication is spatially and temporally displaced. Communication via the Messenger app involves differing physical locations and asynchronous modes of engagement. This creates a situation in which the two characters never respond directly to each other, producing a failed or displaced mode of encounter, or rather: failing as the mode of encounter. This communicative mode of "aneinander vorbei sprechen" [talking past each other] (14) is central to the text and refers to the delayed nature of Senthil's and Valmira's responses. In the book, each message is preceded by a timestamp, which makes readers aware of the amount of time that has passed before a response appears. In some cases, this gap encompasses only a couple of minutes; in other instances, several hours go by. In this context, every message sent is "ins leere geschrieben" [addressed toward emptiness] (50), as it remains uncertain when and if a response will come. Yet the asynchronicity of digital communication appears as an illustration rather than the cause of a more fundamental displacement in Senthil's and Valmira's ways of relating. Their exchange in the book is not really a conversation in the strictest sense, for they often talk past each other, also repeatedly stating their inability to respond: "Ich weiß nicht, was ich zu deiner Geschichte sagen soll" [I do not know how to respond to your story] (38). As Varatharajah himself has noted, the quality of their conversation is "monologisch" [monological] rather than dialogic: "Ihre gemeinsame Sprache ist eine einsame Sprache" [Their shared language is a language of separation].[25] Their exchange is an act of ceaseless addressing and sending, of suspended communication, in which the other – literally and figuratively – does not get the message.

This failure of dialogue and understanding is significant and relates back to my previous point about encountering the other and the role of commonality or similarity in this process. Anil Bhatti suggests that similarity represents a counter-model (or mode) to dialogic relations, which, driven by a desire to understand the other, "Differenz letztendlich stabilisieren" [ultimately stabilise difference].[26] Rather than unsettling the binary self/other, the dialogic model perpetuates it, because it presumes "deutlich voneinander abgegrenzten Einheiten oder Positionen" [discrete entities or positions].[27] By contrast, similarity destabilises this binary by emphasising and ontologically prioritising "Beziehungsgeflechte und grenzübergreifende Zusammenhänge" [webs of relations and border-crossing connections].[28] It is highly relevant in this context that Senthil and Valmira cannot understand each other through dialogue, but can relate to one another based on their "being in common", their commonalities or similarities. *Vor der Zunahme der Zeichen* thus appears critical of the notions of dialogue and understanding, particularly in the realm of intercultural encounter, which is how one could describe Senthil's and Valmira's exchange.[29] This lack of understanding, however, enables a different mode of encounter; it allows Senthil and Valmira to gravitate towards each other and *share* their experiences: "Wir können nur aus dieser Entfernung zueinander sprechen" [We can only talk to one another from a distance] (120). This idea of only being able to speak to one another from a distance strongly resonates with Nancy's thinking, who sees separation or spacing as the necessary precondition for the interrelation amongst singulars, for their "being-in-common". In *Being Singular Plural*, Nancy writes:

> From one singular to another, there is contiguity but not continuity. There is proximity, but only to the extent that the extreme closeness emphasizes the distancing it opens up. All of being is in touch with all of being, but the law of touching is separation; moreover, it is the heterogeneity of surfaces that touch each other.[30]

One could indeed describe Senthil's and Valmira's communication as a touching of heterogeneous surfaces in Nancy's sense.[31] Tactile metaphors and haptic experiences feature prominently in the writing of both Senthil and Valmira and contrast curiously with the immateriality of their communicative setting.[32] While touching conventionally connotes immediacy, *Vor der Zunahme der Zeichen* stresses mediation and distance. Not only are the haptic experiences in the text mediated verbally, the touching between Senthil and Valmira also happens figuratively rather than in a literal, embodied fashion and virtually, across spatial and temporal distance. Their messages touch subtly in that they relay certain themes and images but also words and phrases in each other's writing. For example, the theme of water pervades Senthil's writing but gradually bleeds into Valmira's passages, while the imagery of trees and forests moves from Valmira's into Senthil's texts. In other cases, direct quotes migrate between paragraphs, for instance when Valmira recounts that her father thought learning a language entailed "die Worte der anderen […] für die eigenen halten" [making someone else's words into your own] (195). A couple of pages later, Senthil attributes the following statement to his mother: "so würden wir die sprache erlernen; wenn wir die worte der anderen, wenn wir fremde wörter für die eigenen halten" [this is how we would pick up the language: by making someone else's words, foreign words, into our own] (208).[33] While commenting on the novel's overarching theme of migrating (into) language, these quotes also offer a meta-commentary on the relation between Senthil's and Valmira's particular languages, which constantly make the words of the other into their own. This ceaseless exchange destabilises the very concepts of self/other, strange/familiar, inside/outside, pure/impure, etc. This, again, aligns with Nancy's wider thinking on touch, which aims to go beyond binaries and notions of purity, in an attempt to think intimate distances and distant proximities, alongside the familiarity of the strange and the strangeness of the familiar.

Senthil's and Valmira's stories also touch in that, having studied in the same city, they have been in the same places and spaces physically and have had contact with the same people, albeit at different times. Yet again, we are presented with a displaced mode of touching, which does not restore "common being": "ich habe ins leere geschrieben. und du schreibst zurück, an stellen, an denen ich blind und taub für dich bin" [I addressed myself towards nothingness. and you have responded, and your responses hit my blind spots] (50). Although they share many experiences – both in the sense of having things in common and of telling each other things – this quote points to the fact that Senthil's and Valmira's sharing does not result in closure or unity. While undergoing similar experiences, temporarily inhabiting the same spaces and talking to the same people, they did so at different times and in a set of unique circumstances. The things they share thus also highlight the things that set them apart, the spatial and temporal distance between their similar experiences. This aligns with Nancy's understanding of touch as "a sharing out without fusion, a community without community, a language without communication, a being-with without confusion", as described by Jacques Derrida.[34]

The quote also highlights that touch can be an intrusion or impingement – if someone or something touches me in my blind spots ("an stellen, an denen ich blind und taub […] bin"), this means that I did not see this coming, that I am unprepared, exposed. This connects with a range of concepts that are important for Nancy's conceptualisation of community and that have to do with exposure, exposition, opening and spacing.[35] The kind of selves that Nancy tries to imagine are always separated but, as "heterogeneous surfaces",[36] they are also always open and exposed to an outside, to the possibility of touch. In *Vor der Zunahme der Zeichen*, this exposition is probably best captured in the layout of the text: between every message sent there is a visible gap that separates not only Senthil's and Valmira's respective communications, but also their own writing when they post two messages in succession or when, within one and the same message, they start a new train of thought. Varatharajah himself has pointed to the significance of these gaps, which are in equal parts ruptures and connection points: "Ich glaube, die wirkliche Geschichte in diesem Roman, das wirkliche Sprechen ereignet sich in den Bruchstellen, wo der eine Text zu Ende ist und der andere eigentlich anfangen könnte" [I think the actual story of this novel, the actual exchange, happens in the gaps where one text ends and the other one could potentially start].[37] Significantly, these "Bruchstellen" introduce typographical separation not only between the two singulars of Senthil and Valmira but also between their own messages, thus questioning the idea of a unified self with an untouched, unexposed interior.

The Poetics of Unsettlement

While the previous section reflected on the media-specific conditions of Senthil's and Valmira's failed or displaced encounter, I now want to turn to questions of history and memory. These are also domains of unstable grounds and displacements in the text, albeit for different reasons. As mentioned previously, *Vor der Zunahme der Zeichen* has been largely read as a comment on the so-called refugee crisis. While refugee experiences feature prominently in the text, it is important to note that Senthil and Valmira do not have direct experiences of flight – rather, they relate to their families' displacement via the mode of postmemory.[38] Marianne Hirsch famously defined postmemory as "the experience of those who grow up dominated by narratives that preceded their birth, whose own belated stories are evacuated by the stories of the previous generation shaped by traumatic events that can be neither understood nor recreated".[39] She coined the term in the (autobiographical) context of transgenerational Holocaust memory, seeking to describe the ways in which later generations with no personal experience of the period of World War II relate to it. While there are important differences between the (post-)Holocaust context of Hirsch's concept and the genocides and mass atrocities in Sri Lanka and Kosovo, which are at the centre of Varatharajah's novel, postmemory still provides a useful angle for capturing some of the conditions of experience and writing in the novel.[40] Hirsch's term describes a memory that is constructed on the absent grounds of inaccessible trauma and irretrievable loss, while also signifying a condition of displacement. Not only do experiences of genocide often entail physical displacement and diaspora, as did the Holocaust, postmemory also implies a displacement of memories across generations, displaced modes of witnessing, as argued by Shoshana Felman and Dori Laub in their seminal book on *Testimony*,[41] and the "risk [of] having one's own life stories displaced, even evacuated" by the memories of previous generations.[42] I therefore suggest reading the novel not so much as a 'refugee narrative' but rather as a literary engagement with postmemories of mass atrocity and genocide and their effects on language, memory and community. This engagement includes reflections on flight and displacement, but the focus is on aftereffects – what does it mean to live and write in the shadow of displacement and what other modes of displacement does physical dislocation produce?

Both Senthil and Valmira generate a narrative of ungrounded – in the sense of unstable and irrecoverable – origins, and of ruptured relationships between original and trace. This condition is illustrated when young Valmira is asked to bring photos of her as a baby and toddler to school, so that the children can reconstruct their family trees. Valmira's family tree remains conspicuously empty, and her photos show her as a seven-year-old, after the migration to Germany, rather than as a baby (83f.). Both her familial and her personal origins have been erased in the process of persecution and forced migration, which is also the case for Senthil. The obliteration of origins experienced by Senthil's and Valmira's families contrasts with a German obsession with determinable and all-determining origins, epitomised by the school's genealogical exercise: "Unsere Namen stehen über allem, was wir sagen, sie gehen jedem Satz voraus" [Our names dominate everything, they precede everything we say] (192). The quote illustrates that the obsession with traceable origins corresponds with a taxonomical obsession with properly naming and labelling things and people. Both practices assume a secure relationship between signifier and signified: a certain name, a certain skin colour, a certain accent must necessarily and unambiguously mean a certain thing and point to a certain origin. The novel's prominent theme of the unstable or even ruptured relationship between original and trace, signifier and signified, thus reflects on history and memory in the aftermath of destruction, while also questioning certain – racist and xenophobic – practices of signification, which assume that certain signs indisputably represent or correlate with certain attributes.

The ungroundedness of Senthil's and Valmira's origin narratives is a direct result of the attempted annihilation that both of their immediate families escaped. As a Sri Lankan Tamil and a Kosovo Albanian, both Senthil and Valmira are members of ethnic minorities who suffered persecution in the Sri Lankan Civil War and the Kosovo War respectively and had to flee their home countries.[43] As Senthil notes at various points in the novel, their personal existences in Germany are thus preceded and preconditioned by death:

> ich glaube, erst jetzt beginne ich zu verstehen, dass von anfang an der tod unserer sprache vorausging [...]. wir wären nicht in dieses land und nicht in diese sprache und ich vielleicht auch nicht in diese schrift gekommen, wenn er uns nicht erwartet hätte, in jaffna, in prishtina.
>
> [I am only now beginning to understand that death has always preceded our language [...]. we would not have entered this country, this language and, in my case, this writing system if death had not been waiting for us, in Jaffna, in Pristina.] (151)

This fact ungrounds and displaces their entire existence, not only by virtue of their families' physical dislocation. Their very survival can be understood as a form of displacement, as is implied in the term *überleben*/surviving itself, derived from the Latin word *supervivere*. The prefixes *über-* or *super-* suggest an existence that is somehow in excess, that has pushed past the point of its intended ending, beyond death. It is also an existence that is displaced in that it has taken the place of an other who did not survive: "an unserer stelle ist immer ein anderer gestorben" [someone else has had to die in our place] (152).

This emergence from the groundless ground of death means that Senthil's and Valmira's existences in Germany are built around various absences, encompassing their disappeared or dead relatives as well as their countries and languages of origin. These absences go beyond the loss of home that is often a theme in diasporic writing, in that their homes literally, as in materially, no longer exist, "weil es die Häuser, die Städte und Länder, aus denen wir kommen, nicht mehr gibt" [because the houses, cities and countries in which we grew up no longer exist] (173). This creates a rupture in the relationship between signifier and signified, original and trace, as is exemplified by the key to the house in Jaffna that Senthil's parents used to own. As Senthil remarks, the house "steht nicht mehr am selben ort" [is no longer in the same place] (228), so the key has become a trace that leads to nothingness, as the lock that it is meant to open has vanished. This key without a lock, itself a surviving and thus excessive object, could also be read as an image for Senthil's and Valmira's entire existence. The fact that they are in Germany refers to something, an origin story, but this something is irretrievable.

Traditionally, personal and cultural memory would be a domain in which acts of preservation and regeneration can take place, even in the face of utter destruction. The protagonists' position or condition of postmemory, however, only contributes further to the experience of groundlessness. While Senthil has virtually no memory of the life that preceded displacement, Valmira only has "Bruchstücke" [fragments] (125). Both of them thus depend on scarce family stories, a few objects that have survived displacement, such as the key or family photographs, and media coverage. What further complicates their postmemorial quest and sets it apart from, for example, post-Holocaust narratives, is the underrepresented and unresolved nature of the conflicts from which their families escaped. The Sri Lankan Civil War and the war in Kosovo have thus far not produced a global memory culture in the same way that other 20th- and 21st-century atrocities have. While such forms of canonisation and institutionalisation can be a problem in themselves for the generation of postmemory, cultural memories also provide a repository from which this generation can construct narratives. The underrepresentation of the conflicts which are at the heart of *Vor der Zunahme der Zeichen* reflects a "trauma economy", in which different traumatic experiences are valued differently and receive different levels of symbolic and material recognition.[44] Additionally, these conflicts are in many ways unresolved, producing contested memories and ongoing struggles for justice,[45] which hinder the establishment of a narrative that can be canonised, institutionalised and universalised, as eventually happened in the case of the Holocaust. This unresolved nature also means that the work of "imaginative investment, projection and creation",[46] which is so crucial to Hirsch's conception of postmemory, is disturbed, making both actual and symbolic healing or recuperation impossible.

Senthil and Valmira thus not only lack memories of decisive moments in their lives, rupturing their connection to the past, they also have nothing to transmit to the future:

> ich erinnere mich nicht an das ereignis, aber an die erzählungen von diesem ereignis erinnere ich mich, und wenn ich es erzähle, wenn ich es dir wiedergebe, gebe ich dir die spuren, die ich verwische, die letzten spuren, ich gebe dir nichts.
>
> [I do not remember the event, but I remember stories about the event. and when I tell you about the event, when I give an account of it, I give you traces which I then erase, I give you nothing.] (246)

Paradoxically, memory, aimed at preserving or at least retrieving the past, here becomes an agent of erasure and ephemerality. This fleetingness also marks the very language Senthil and Valmira use, which in the novel is described as ephemeral and transitory, as "flüchtig" (12) rather than preserving: "meine sprache bewahrt nichts" [my language preserves nothing] (246). This notion of language as an agent of erasure and ungrounding is also exemplified by the Tower of Babel imagery, which comes up several times in the text (106; 239). In the Babel narrative, language is also something that separates rather than unites, something that disperses rather than gathers. This observation relates back to the previous section, in which communication between Senthil and Valmira also featured as a lack of understanding, a separation and dispersal in the form of sharing. Yet, as I have illustrated, some mode of relating, of "being-in-common", is still possible – or might, indeed, only be possible – because of this separation.

These various figurations of groundlessness and ungrounding result in a condition of perpetual unsettlement, which manifests in several ways. The novel ends with a series of alternating paragraphs beginning with the phrases "Wir kommen" [We are coming/arriving] by Valmira and "wir gehen" [we are going/leaving] by Senthil (241ff.). These last paragraphs, and the back-and-forth between them, illustrate a condition of unsettlement, in which both the process of expulsion and of arrival are endless or suspended, as is also suggested by the use of the present tense. The back-and-forth between and touching of Valmira's and Senthil's paragraphs furthermore raises the question of how to distinguish between leaving and arriving – going and coming bleed into one another in these final passages of the novel. This problem of demarcation also surfaces at an earlier point in the text, when Valmira tells Senthil about a speaker who has been invited to one of her seminars and is introduced as an *"ehemalige[r] Flüchtling"* [former refugee, italics original] (31). This is a paradoxical term, because the adjective "former" would imply that, at least in terms of legal status, the person is no longer a refugee but, ideally, a citizen. Yet their history of flight still seems to be a constituent part of their identity, at least for the organisers of the seminar. The "former refugee" is thus another suspended figure, suggesting that the process of displacement is potentially without end. This impossibility of arrival and of definite beginnings and endings produces a condition of dispersion and fragmentariness:

> wenn wir uns nicht mehr an die letzten, die allerletzten dinge und auch nicht an die ersten und allerersten namen halten können, dann gibt es vielleicht nur verstreut einzelheiten, und der zusammenhang wird zufälliger sein.
>
> [when we can neither adhere to/hold on to the last and final nor to the first and originary things, then there may well be only fragments and the connections will be more random.] (187)

This inability to halt the unsettlement of displacement and to establish fixed origins, a necessary chain of events or a coherent life narrative goes to the heart of the novel, which is in itself a collection of fragments that are held together by associative and often serendipitous connections. In response to this condition, the text develops what I want to call a poetics of unsettlement, which has at least two dimensions. Firstly, it encompasses the constant unsettlement of the self, the other and language, understood as a process of alienation, of never feeling quite at home with oneself or in one's social and linguistic surroundings. One expression of this is Senthil's and Valmira's approach to the German language, which they initially experience from the perspective of the newcomer. This perspective gives rise to frequent misunderstandings, while also enabling a productive alienation that does not take the meaning of words for granted, enabling the creation of new meaning. The poetics of unsettlement turns this estrangement into a core principle, perhaps in the sense of Gilles Deleuze's and Félix Guattari's "minor" use of language, which they describe as becoming "a nomad and an immigrant and a gypsy in relation to one's own language".[47] Secondly, the poetics of unsettlement furthermore implies constant movement and translation and thereby the questioning of any stable, common and uncontested grounds. If there are indeed no definite departures or arrivals, no ends or beginnings, then what remains are acts of departing and arriving, processes of constant exploration with no fixed end point, as illustrated by the book's (non-)ending: "bis zur äußersten bedeutung müssen wir gehen und es wird nicht weit genug gewesen sein. wir gehen" [we have to go to the edges of meaning and we still will not have gone far enough. we are going] (250).

Strangers at Home: Unsettled Transnationalism and Cosmopolitanism

I want to conclude by returning to Jean-Luc Nancy and by considering his short autobiographical essay entitled 'L'intrus' [the intruder].[48] In this piece of writing, Nancy reflects on a period of serious illness in his life, during which he received a heart transplant and then later fell ill with cancer. In the first instance, his body was intruded upon by a stranger's organ, before turning against itself and becoming estranged from itself. The essay reflects on the boundaries between self and other, inside and outside and how they become precarious – or, rather, are exposed as always already precarious – through illness. In her comment on 'L'intrus', Anne O'Byrne reads the text as a reflection on the question of identity and the impossibility of self-identity specifically.[49] Building on O'Byrne's instructive reading, I want to suggest, perhaps somewhat counterintuitively, that this text about illness and intrusion can be related back to the key issues of transnational conviviality and cosmopolitanism introduced at the beginning. As noted by Calhoun, and corroborated by Gilroy, "cosmopolitanism is centrally about how well or poorly we relate to strangers – those we do not know and those outside our political and communal solidarities".[50] Questions of strangeness and familiarity, of difference and similarity, of inside and outside are thus central to cosmopolitanism as well as to the transnational neighbourhood, as I have interpreted it earlier in this chapter. As suggested previously, the transnational neighbourhood provides a particularly fruitful stage, on which to explore how to coexist and "dwell[…] comfortably in proximity to the unfamiliar".[51] Nancy's essay can be usefully connected to these larger issues as they surface in *Vor der Zunahme der Zeichen*, which, in the touching of Senthil and Valmira, models ways of encountering the intrusion of the stranger and of encountering the strangeness of one's self.

Nancy begins 'L'intrus' with a reflection on the stranger and the paradox that welcoming the stranger entails: one must necessarily welcome something that one did not expect and that is, therefore, unwelcome and an intrusion. As soon as one tries to avoid this intrusion, "by effacing his strangeness at the threshold", one is no longer "receiving" the stranger but welcoming someone who is familiar.[52] These opening passages of 'L'intrus' resonate with Jacques Derrida's thinking on hospitality, which is underpinned by a similar paradox: while "absolute hospitality" would require us to receive the "absolute, unknown, anonymous other",[53] the laws of hospitality, which provide the very conditions for creating a home that can receive the foreigner, require this foreigner to already have made themselves known. The laws of hospitality thus make it impossible for the foreigner to be "received" in Nancy's sense, as these laws are premised on effacing the intrusion of his nameless otherness. While Derrida, in *On Hospitality*, reflects further on the law and the conditions for an ethics of hospitality, Nancy in his essay tackles the question of identity. While the paradox of the stranger cannot be resolved, for Nancy it becomes a starting point for reflecting on the impossibility of self-identity and on self-estrangement as a mode of being in, or rather being-with, the world. His illness forces him to experience physically the exposedness of his bodily self to various outsides and the instability of the boundary that separates self/other. Through the heart transplant, the categories of inside and outside, of strange and familiar become unsettled, but for Nancy this only reveals the fact that they were not stable in the first place. In a similar manner, his cancer speaks to a confusion of the body as to what does and does not belong, in that it results from the use of immuno-suppressants after the transplant. Immunity, put simply, involves the capacity of recognising what is self and what is non-self and of either tolerating or attacking based on that distinction. Immuno-suppressants interfere with this basic operation, getting the body to tolerate a foreign part. In cancer, finally, some of the body's cells grow uncontrollably and attack healthy organs – what was formerly one's own becomes a potentially deadly intruder. The intrusion of the stranger's heart, the suppressed immune system and the cancer diagnosis thus exemplify the ways in which the self's inside is always permeated by various outsides, exposing the precarious boundary separating self and non-self. The self can at any point become a stranger to itself, a stranger at home. According to Nancy, "man himself"[54] is defined by these various moments of intrusion, by this exposedness: "The intrus is no other than me, my self; none other than man himself. No other than the one, the same, always identical to itself and yet that is never done with altering itself".[55] This realisation has two consequences: on the one hand, it destabilises binaries around self/other, inside/outside, strange/familiar, producing a condition in which "we are never quite at home even within our domestic space, and we are never simply strange, even in the most alien public arena", as noted by O'Byrne.[56] The self can arguably be located in this moment of suspension between the domestic and the public, between being at home and being a stranger. On the other hand, the self is not a completed or fixed category, but an open field of exposures and possibilities, "never done with altering itself", as suggested by Nancy. O'Byrne concludes that "identity is only ever a moment",[57] a fleeting glimpse, before the next alteration unfolds.

These conditions of suspension and of constant "altering" are reminiscent of the poetics of unsettlement that I have developed through my reading of Varatharajah's novel. In *Vor der Zunahme der Zeichen*, the characters are also suspended between sending and receiving, departure and arrival, between being at home and being a stranger, between knowing one another and anonymity. Furthermore, they present their identities as constantly shifting, as made up of several versions and variations, and as evolving in exchange with and through intrusion of the stories, phrases and words of the other: "Ich weiß nicht, ob irgendetwas, an das ich mich erinnern kann und das ich Dir in den vergangenen sieben Tagen geschrieben haben, so war oder so gewesen sein koennte, wie ich es Dir geschrieben habe" [I am not sure whether anything that I have remembered and that I have told to you in the last seven days has actually happened – or could have happened – in the way that I have told you] (242).

I want to suggest here that these constantly shifting selves and grounds can become the basis for an unsettled transnationalism and cosmopolitanism, understood as a fundamental estrangement from stable foundations but also from fixed identities. The historian Thomas Bender, for example, presents a version of cosmopolitanism as fundamental discomfort, as a state of never being quite at ease, "even at home".[58] This estrangement becomes the condition for "being open" to "novel experience",[59] or, one might add, the intrusion of the other. This is reminiscent of Paul Gilroy's understanding of cosmopolitanism in *After Empire*, in which he not only calls for a "vulgar" cosmopolitanism that thrives on "mundane encounters", as previously mentioned, but also advocates for a "planetary mentality" that is characterised by "an active hostility toward national solidarity, national culture, and their privileging over other, more open affiliations".[60] Bender and Gilroy connect with a tradition of "negative" cosmopolitanism as detachment or estrangement, which can be traced back to the Cynics and the Stoics, as noted by Bruce Robbins and Paul Lemos Horta.[61]

The unsettled transnationalism or cosmopolitanism that I am suggesting here, however, draws on more recent "post-foundational" reformulations of cosmopolitanism,[62] as mentioned in the introduction. The term "post-foundational" implies a scepticism towards "metaphysical figures of foundation",[63] or what Nancy would describe as "common being". As Tamara Caraus notes, much cosmopolitanism theory is characterised by "temptations of foundationalism",[64] not least by virtue of its drive toward universality. Post-foundationalism, however, does not claim that we are to do away with such founding principles or moments, as this is ultimately impossible – rather, the "post-" implies that we need to acknowledge their momentary and fleeting nature, turning them into contingent and contestable grounds. The gesture and practice of constant (self-)interrogation is therefore key to the post-foundational approach, which is itself a process of continuous grounding and ungrounding. The philosopher Oliver Marchart usefully applies these principles of contingency, contestability and ungrounding to his discussion of cosmopolitanism, introducing a theory of cosmopolitan democracy as based on the "unconditional demand of *self-alienation*, i.e. of accepting the impossibility of ever attaining a state of full self-identity" [italics original].[65] While Marchart is concerned with the macro level of global democracy, the notion of self-alienation as a demand is productive for framing the micro-level encounters with difference that characterise the transnational neighbourhood and Varatharajah's novel. Unsettled transnationalism and cosmopolitanism, as I have developed it through my reading of Varatharajah's novel, also question the notion of self-identity by foregrounding and performing, in the medium of writing, suspension, ephemerality and estrangement. *Vor der Zunahme der Zeichen* introduces the many-layered notion of being "flüchtig" to capture not only the groundlessness of displaced existence, but also the momentariness of any notion of identity, aiming to express this unsettled condition in the form of the novel. Varatharajah's text suggests that the only way to accommodate the "flüchtig" condition is through "fugitive" forms, as suggested by Teupert,[66] and through practices of constant estrangement from oneself, the other, and language, which unsettle any stable grounds. This entails becoming "a nomad and an immigrant and a gypsy" in relation to what one considers one's own, as suggested by Deleuze and Guattari,[67] or realising "[t]he intrus is no other than me", as posited by Nancy. Paradoxically, this fleetingness and groundlessness, which lets go of the need for understanding, for common ground and "common being", for others to be like us or become like us, provides the condition of possibility of "receiving" and relating to, of "dwelling comfortably" and "being-in-common" with,[68] the stranger, whose plight is central to our age of mass displacement and transnational mobility.

Notes

1. Varatharajah, Senthuran (2016): *Vor der Zunahme der Zeichen*. Frankfurt: Fischer. All translations into English are mine.
2. Notable literary examples include: Bazyar, Shida (2016): *Nachts ist es leise in Teheran*. Cologne: Kiepenheuer & Witsch; Erpenbeck, Jenny (2015): *Gehen, Ging, Gegangen*. Munich: Albrecht Knaus; Grjasnowa, Olga (2017): *Gott Ist Nicht Schüchtern*. Berlin: Aufbau; Khider, Abbas (2016): *Ohrfeige*. Munich: Carl Hanser; Köhlmeier, Michael (2016): *Das Mädchen mit dem Fingerhut*. Munich: Carl Hanser; Kirchoff, Bodo (2016): *Widerfahrnis*. Frankfurt: Frankfurter Verlagsanstalt; Rabinowich, Julya (2016): *Dazwischen Ich*. Munich: Carl Hanser; Vertlib, Vladimir (2018): *Viktor hilft*. Leipzig: Deuticke; Vermes, Timur (2018): *Die Hunrigen und die Satten*. Frankfurt: Eichborn. For recent academic explorations of the topic see: Ansari, Christine, and Caroline Frank, eds. (forthcoming): *Narrative der Flucht: Literatur-/Medienwissenschaftliche und didaktische Perspektiven*. Bern: Peter Lang; Arslan, Gizem et al. (2017): Forum Migration Studies. *The German Quarterly* 90(2), 212–234; Baltes-Löhr, Christel, Beate Petra Kory, and Gabriela Sandor, eds. (2018): *Auswanderung und Identität: Erfahrungen von Exil, Flucht und Migration in der deutschsprachigen Literatur*. Bielefeld: Transcript; Eigler, Friederike (2014): *Heimat, Space, Narrative: Toward a Transnational*

Approach to Flight and Expulsion. Rochester, NY: Camden House; Hardtke, Thomas, Johannes Kleine, and Charlton Payne, eds. (2016): *Niemandsbuchten und Schutzbefohlene: Flucht-Räume und Flüchtlingsfiguren in der deutschsprachigen Gegenwartsliteratur*. Göttingen: V&R unipress; Shortt, Linda (2021): Borders, Bordering, and Irregular Migration in Novels by Dorothee Elmiger and Olga Grjasnowa. *Modern Language Review* 116(1), 134–152; Shortt, Linda (2021): Writing the European Refugee Crisis: Timur Vermes' *'Die Hungrigen und die Satten'. Politics and Culture in Germany and Austria Today*, edited by Frauke Matthes, Dora Osborne, Katya Krylova, and Myrto Aspioti (= *Edinburgh German Yearbook* 14). Rochester, NY: Camden House, 15–33.

3. Chloe Fagan reads this memory loss as a symptom of personal trauma, whereas I interpret it more as a symptom of the protagonists' postmemorial condition, which I will analyse in more detail in the third section ('The Poetics of Unsettlement'. See Fagan, Chloe (2020): Senthuran Varatharajah's *Vor der Zunahme der Zeichen*. Representing the Kosovo War and the Tamil Conflict as an Absence and the Trauma of Language. *Germanistik in Ireland* 15, 211–224.
4. Teupert, Jonas (2018): Sharing Fugitive Lives: Digital Encounters in Senthuran Varatharajah's *Vor der Zunahme der Zeichen*. *Transit* 11(2), https://transit.berkeley.edu/2018/teupert/. Accessed 30 October 2020.
5. The importance of form is also stressed by Teupert (2018), and Klueppel, Joscha (2020): Emotionale Landschaften der Migration: Von unsichtbaren Grenzen, Nicht-Ankommen und dem Tod in Stanišić's *Herkunft* und Varatharajahs *Vor der Zunahme der Zeichen*. *Transit* 12(2), https://transit.berkeley.edu/2020/klueppel/. Accessed 30 October 2020.
6. Ehrig, Stephan, Britta C. Jung, and Maria Roca Lizarazu (2020): Conference Report: Exploring the Transnational Neighbourhood. Integration, Community and Co-Habitation. *Journal of Romance Studies* 20(1), 179–181, 179.
7. Hall, Stuart (2007): Living With Difference: Stuart Hall in Conversation with Bill Schwarz. *Soundings* 37, 148–158, 151, https://www.lwbooks.co.uk/sites/default/files/s37_15hall_schwarz.pdf. Accessed 1 December 2020.
8. As Joseph Twist notes, Nancy himself is critical of the notion of cosmopolitanism, as it does not take us beyond "closed forms of identity" but rather "perpetuates them on a transnational scale". I will illustrate in my conclusion how I think Nancy might take us towards a more open notion of "unsettled" cosmopolitanism. See Twist, Joseph (2018): *Mystical Islam and Cosmopolitanism in Contemporary German Literature: Openness to Alterity*. Rochester, NY: Camden House, 19. Berthold Schoene also explores Nancy's relationship with cosmopolitanism in the context of the British novel, see Schoene, Berthold (2009): *The Cosmopolitan Novel*. Edinburgh: Edinburgh University Press.
9. Steven Vertovec, for example, defines transnationalism broadly as "economic, social and political linkages between people, places and institutions crossing nation-state borders and spanning the world", see Vertovec, Steven (2009): *Transnationalism*. London: Routledge, 1.

10. De Cesari, Chiara, and Ann Rigney (2014): Introduction. *Transnational Memory: Circulation, Articulation, Scales*, edited by Chiara de Cesari and Ann Rigney. Berlin: De Gruyter, 1–25, 4.
11. Gilroy, Paul (2004), *After Empire. Melancholia or Convivial Culture?* London: Routledge.
12. Ibid., 75.
13. Ehrig, Jung, and Roca Lizarazu (2020), 179.
14. Calhoun, Craig (2017): A Cosmopolitanism of Connections. *Cosmopolitanisms*, edited by Bruce Robbins and Paul Lemos Horta. New York: New York University Press, 189–200.
15. Ibid., 196, 198.
16. For a brief overview of major criticisms of cosmopolitanism and recent developments in the field of cosmopolitanism studies, see Robbins, Bruce, and Paul Lemos Horta (2017): Introduction. *Cosmopolitanisms*, edited by Bruce Robbins and Paul Lemos Horta. New York: New York University Press, 1–17.
17. Caraus, Tamara, and Elena Paris, eds. (2017): *Re-grounding Cosmopolitanism: Towards a Post-foundational Cosmopolitanism*. London: Routledge.
18. Gilroy (2004), 75; Caraus, Tamara (2017): Introduction: Re-grounding Cosmopolitanism – Towards a Post-foundational Cosmopolitanism. *Re-grounding Cosmopolitanism: Towards a Post-foundational Cosmopolitanism*. London: Routledge, 1–26, 13.
19. Gilroy (2004), 75.
20. See https://www.facebook.com/help/336320879782850. Accessed 9 November 2020.
21. Nancy, Jean-Luc (1991): Of Being-In-Common. *Community at Loose Ends*, edited by Miami Theory Collective. Minneapolis: University of Minnesota Press, 1–12, 4.
22. Ibid., 8.
23. Teupert (2018).
24. Hampe, Lara, and Sibylla Vričić Hausmann (n.d.): Gespräch mit Senthuran Varatharajah. *Politischschreiben.net*, https://www.politischschreiben.net/ps-3/ps-im-gesprch-mit-senthuran-varatharajah. Accessed 9 November 2020.
25. Ibid.
26. Bhatti, Anil (2014): Ähnlichkeit. *Das neue Deutschland: Von Migration und Vielfalt*, edited by Oezkan Ezli and Gisela Staupe. Konstanz: Konstanz University Press, 161–163, 162.
27. Ibid.
28. Ibid.
29. Twist notes a similar complication of the idea of intercultural understanding in the work of Zafer Şenocak; interestingly, Twist also introduces touch and touching as an alternative mode of encountering the other in Şenocak. I will illustrate the importance of touch in Varatharajah's novel shortly, see Twist (2018), 27–55.

30. Nancy, Jean-Luc (2000): *Being Singular-Plural*. Palo Alto, CA: Stanford University Press, 5.
31. The theme and mode of touching is central to Nancy's thinking and has been explored in detail by Jacques Derrida in *On Touching – Jean-Luc Nancy*, translated by Christine Irizarry. Palo Alto, CA: Stanford University Press, 2005. While touch permeates many of Nancy's texts, it is probably most central to his exploration of bodies in *Corpus*, see Nancy, Jean-Luc (2008): *Corpus*, translated by Richard A. Rand. New York: Fordham University Press.
32. For example, on the first few pages, Senthil describes a haptic experience: "ich legte meinen zeigefinger auf die klingel, die grau war von berührungen" [i put my index finger on the door bell, which had gone grey from being touched so often] (22), which is followed by Valmira recounting a visit to the library in which her parents used to study: "und mit meinen Fingern fuhr ich die Maserungen auf dem dunklen Holz nach" [and with my fingers I traced the texture of the dark wood] (23).
33. Senthil's messages appear in lower case throughout the text, while Valmira sticks to the established typographic conventions of the German language. Jonas Teupert's reads Senthil's use of typography as an attempt to "democratize his use of words" by not singling out nouns and proper as somehow more substantial, see Teupert (2018), 4.
34. Derrida (2005), 195.
35. These themes are central to Nancy (2008) for example.
36. Nancy (2000), 5.
37. See Burgmann, Holm-Uwe, and Konstantin Schönfelder (n.d.): Vor/Zeichen #1 Senthuran Varatharajah. *Praeposition.com*, https://www.praeposition.com/text/vorzeichen/senthuran-varatharajah. Accessed 1 December 2020.
38. My interpretation thus differs slightly from Fagan's, who reads the novel through the lens of direct experiences of trauma and how they are addressed (or not) in the novel, whereas I see the postmemorial indirectness of traumatic experiences as central to Varatharajah's text, see Fagan (2020).
39. Hirsch, Marianne (1997): *Family Frames*. Cambridge, MA: Harvard University Press, 22.
40. While emerging from the post-Holocaust context, the notion of postmemory increasingly has been applied to a wide range of post-traumatic contexts. Hirsch herself also makes the case for a "'multidirectional' or 'connective' approach" to the concept, which not only sees the Holocaust in connection with other histories, but also posits postmemory as a set of wider "paradigms and strategies" for confronting traumatic pasts other than that of the Holocaust, see Hirsch, Marianne (2012): *The Generation of Postmemory: Writing and Visual Culture After the Holocaust*. New York: Columbia University Press, 21.
41. Felman and Laub famously construct testimony as an intersubjective and performative process, which functions through displacement. Echoing post-structuralist ap-

proaches to trauma, which were hugely popular when *Testimony* was written, Felman and Laub believe that the traumatised subject has no access to the traumatising event and can only come to witness it in a displaced fashion, through the act of testimony, which requires a listening other. Hirsch is strongly influenced by Felman and Laub, but in some ways de-spatialises and temporalises the testimonial framework, by applying it to inter- and transgenerational rather than the interpersonal, synchronous, face-to-face settings envisaged by Felman and Laub. See Felman, Shoshana, and Dori Laub (1992): *Testimony: Crises of Witnessing in Literature, Psychoanalysis, and History.* London: Routledge. For a critical engagement with post-structuralist trauma theory and its problematic implications, see Leys, Ruth (2000): *Trauma: A Genealogy.* Chicago: University of Chicago Press.
42. Hirsch (2012), 5.
43. For more details on this see Fagan (2020).
44. Tomsky, Terri (2011): From Sarajevo to 9/11: Travelling Memory and the Trauma Economy. *Parallax* 7(4), 49–60.
45. While Sri Lanka established a Lessons Learnt and Reconciliation Commission (LLRC) in 2010, Fagan notes that "the trauma of the Kosovo conflict and its war crimes have not yet been fully processed or recognized", see Fagan (2020), 215.
46. Hirsch (2012), 5.
47. Deleuze, Gilles, and Félix Guattari (1986): *Kafka: Toward a Minor Literature*, translated by Dana Polan. Minneapolis: University of Minnesota Press, 19.
48. Nancy, Jean-Luc (2002): L'intrus. *CR: The New Centennial Review* 2(3), 1–14.
49. O'Byrne, Anne E. (2002): The Politics of Intrusion. *CR: The New Centennial Review* 2(3), 169–187.
50. Calhoun (2017), 195.
51. Gilroy (2004), 75.
52. Nancy (2002), 12.
53. Derrida, Jacques (2000): *On Hospitality,* translated by Rachel Bowlby. Palo Alto, CA: Stanford University Press, 25.
54. Nancy (2002), 13.
55. Ibid.
56. O'Byrne (2002), 184.
57. Ibid., 185.
58. Bender, Thomas (2017): The Cosmopolitan Experience and Its Uses. *Cosmopolitanisms*, edited by Bruce Robbins and Paul Lemos Horta. New York: New York University Press, 116–126, 119.
59. Ibid., 117.
60. Gilroy (2004), 75f.
61. Robbins and Horta (2017), 5.
62. See Caraus and Paris (2017).

63. Caraus (2017), 2.
64. Ibid.
65. Marchart, Oliver (2017): The Political, the Ethical, the Global: Towards a Post-foundational Theory of Cosmopolitan Democracy. *Re-grounding Cosmopolitanism: Towards a Post-foundational Cosmopolitanism.* London: Routledge, 181–202, 195.
66. Teupert (2018).
67. Deleuze and Guattari (1986), 19.
68. Gilroy (2004), 75.

Works Cited

Primary Literature

Bazyar, Shida (2016): *Nachts ist es leise in Teheran.* Cologne: Kiepenheuer & Witsch.
Erpenbeck, Jenny (2015): *Gehen, Ging, Gegangen.* Munich: Albrecht Knaus.
Grjasnowa, Olga (2017): *Gott Ist Nicht Schüchtern.* Berlin: Aufbau.
Khider, Abbas (2016): *Ohrfeige.* Munich: Carl Hanser.
Kirchoff, Bodo (2016): *Widerfahrnis.* Frankfurt: Frankfurter Verlagsanstalt.
Köhlmeier, Michael (2016): *Das Mädchen mit dem Fingerhut.* Munich: Carl Hanser.
Rabinowich, Julya (2016): *Dazwischen Ich.* Munich: Carl Hanser.
Varatharajah, Senthuran (2016): *Vor der Zunahme der Zeichen.* Frankfurt: Fischer.
Vermes, Timur (2018): *Die Hunrigen und die Satten.* Frankfurt: Eichborn.
Vertlib, Vladimir (2018): *Viktor hilft.* Leipzig: Deuticke.

Secondary Literature

Ansari, Christine, and Caroline Frank, eds. (forthcoming): *Narrative der Flucht: Literatur-/Medienwissenschaftliche und didaktische Perspektiven.* Bern: Peter Lang.
Arslan, Gizem et al. (2017): Forum Migration Studies. *The German Quarterly* 90(2), 212–234.
Baltes-Löhr, Christel, Beate Petra Kory, and Gabriela Sandor, eds. (2018): *Auswanderung und Identität: Erfahrungen von Exil, Flucht und Migration in der deutschsprachigen Literatur.* Bielefeld: Transcript.
Bender, Thomas (2017): The Cosmopolitan Experience and Its Uses. *Cosmopolitanisms*, edited by Bruce Robbins and Paul Lemos Horta. New York: New York University Press, 116–126.
Bhatti, Anil (2014): Ähnlichkeit. *Das neue Deutschland: Von Migration und Vielfalt*, edited by Oezkan Ezli and Gisela Staupe. Konstanz: Konstanz University Press, 161–163.

Burgmann, Holm-Uwe, and Konstantin Schönfelder (n.d.): Vor/Zeichen #1 Senthuran Varatharajah. *Praeposition.com*, https://www.praeposition.com/text/vorzeichen/senthuran-varatharajah. Accessed 1 December 2020.

Calhoun, Craig (2017): A Cosmopolitanism of Connections. *Cosmopolitanisms*, edited by Bruce Robbins and Paul Lemos Horta. New York: New York University Press, 189–200.

Caraus, Tamara (2017): Introduction: Re-grounding Cosmopolitanism – Towards a Postfoundational Cosmopolitanism. *Re-grounding Cosmopolitanism: Towards a Post-foundational Cosmopolitanism*, edited by Tamara Caraus and Elena Paris. London: Routledge, 1–26.

Caraus, Tamara, and Elena Paris, eds. (2017): *Re-grounding Cosmopolitanism: Towards a Post-foundational Cosmopolitanism*. London: Routledge.

De Cesari, Chiara, and Ann Rigney (2014): Introduction. *Transnational Memory: Circulation, Articulation, Scales*, edited by Chiara de Cesari and Ann Rigney. Berlin: De Gruyter, 1–25.

Deleuze, Gilles, and Félix Guattari (1986): *Kafka: Toward a Minor Literature*, translated by Dana Polan. Minneapolis: University of Minnesota Press.

Derrida, Jacques (2000): *On Hospitality*, translated by Rachel Bowlby. Palo Alto, CA: Stanford University Press.

Derrida, Jacques (2005): *On Touching: Jean-Luc Nancy*, translated by Christine Irizarry. Palo Alto, CA: Stanford University Press.

Ehrig, Stephan, Britta C. Jung, and Maria Roca Lizarazu (2020): Conference Report: Exploring the Transnational Neighbourhood. Integration, Community and Co-Habitation. *Journal of Romance Studies* 20(1), 179–181.

Eigler, Friederike (2014): *Heimat, Space, Narrative: Toward a Transnational Approach to Flight and Expulsion*. Rochester, NY: Camden House.

Fagan, Chloe (2020): Senthuran Varatharajah's *Vor der Zunahme der Zeichen*. Representing the Kosovo War and the Tamil Conflict as an Absence and the Trauma of Language. *Germanistik in Ireland* 15, 211–224.

Felman, Shoshana, and Dori Laub (1992): *Testimony: Crises of Witnessing in Literature, Psychoanalysis, and History*. London: Routledge.

Gilroy, Paul (2004): *After Empire: Melancholia or Convivial Culture?* London: Routledge.

Hall, Stuart (2007): Living With Difference: Stuart Hall in Conversation with Bill Schwarz. *Soundings* 37, 148–158, 151, https://journals.lwbooks.co.uk/soundings/vol-2007-issue-37/article-7152. Accessed 1 December 2020.

Hampe, Lara, and Sibylla Vričić Hausmann (n.d.): Gespräch mit Senthuran Varatharajah. *Politischschreiben.net*, https://www.politischschreiben.net/ps-3/ps-im-gesprch-mit-senthuran-varatharajah/. Accessed 9 November 2020.

Hardtke, Thomas, Johannes Kleine, and Charlton Payne, eds. (2016): *Niemandsbuchten und Schutzbefohlene: Flucht-Räume und Flüchtlingsfiguren in der deutschsprachigen Gegenwartsliteratur*. Göttingen: V&R unipress.

Hirsch, Marianne (1997): *Family Frames*. Cambridge, MA: Harvard University Press.

Hirsch, Marianne (2012): *The Generation of Postmemory: Writing and Visual Culture After the Holocaust*. New York: Columbia University Press.

Klueppel, Joscha (2020): Emotionale Landschaften der Migration: Von unsichtbaren Grenzen, Nicht-Ankommen und dem Tod in Stanišićs *Herkunft* und Varatharajahs *Vor der Zunahme der Zeichen*. *Transit* 12(2), https://transit.berkeley.edu/2020/klueppel/. Accessed 30 October 2020.

Leys, Ruth (2000): *Trauma: A Genealogy*. Chicago: University of Chicago Press.

Marchart, Oliver (2017): The Political, the Ethical, the Global: Towards a Post-foundational Theory of Cosmopolitan Democracy. *Re-grounding Cosmopolitanism: Towards a Post-foundational Cosmopolitanism*, edited by Tamara Caraus and Elena Paris. London: Routledge, 181–202.

Nancy, Jean-Luc (1991): Of Being-In-Common. *Community at Loose Ends*, edited by Miami Theory Collective. Minneapolis: University of Minnesota Press, 1–12.

Nancy, Jean-Luc (2000): *Being Singular-Plural*. Palo Alto, CA: Stanford University Press.

Nancy, Jean-Luc (2002): L'intrus. *CR: The New Centennial Review* 2(3), 1–14.

Nancy, Jean-Luc (2008): *Corpus*, translated by Richard A. Rand. New York: Fordham University Press.

O'Byrne, Anne E. (2002): The Politics of Intrusion. *CR: The New Centennial Review* 2(3), 169–187.

Robbins, Bruce, and Paul Lemos Horta (2017): Introduction. *Cosmopolitanisms*, edited by Bruce Robbins and Paul Lemos Horta. New York: New York University Press, 1–17.

Schoene, Berthold (2009): *The Cosmopolitan Novel*. Edinburgh: Edinburgh University Press.

Shortt, Linda (2021a): Borders, Bordering, and Irregular Migration in Novels by Dorothee Elmiger and Olga Grjasnowa. *Modern Language Review* 116(1), 134–152.

Shortt, Linda (2021b): Writing the European Refugee Crisis: Timur Vermes' 'Die Hungrigen und die Satten'. *Politics and Culture in Germany and Austria Today*, edited by Frauke Matthes, Dora Osborne, Katya Krylova, and Myrto Aspioti (= *Edinburgh German Yearbook* 14). Rochester, NY: Camden House, 15–33.

Teupert, Jonas (2018): Sharing Fugitive Lives: Digital Encounters in Senthuran Varatharajah's *Vor der Zunahme der Zeichen*. *Transit* 11(2), https://transit.berkeley.edu/2018/teupert/. Accessed 30 October 2020.

Tomsky, Terri (2011): From Sarajevo to 9/11: Travelling Memory and the Trauma Economy. *Parallax* 7(4), 49–60.

Twist, Joseph (2018): *Mystical Islam and Cosmopolitanism in Contemporary German Literature: Openness to Alterity*. Rochester, NY: Camden House.

Vertovec, Steven (2009): *Transnationalism*. London: Routledge.

All Saints Catholic Church in Williamsburg, Brooklyn, NYC

From Religious Space to Transnational Territory of Multiterritorial Mexican Immigrants

EMILIO MACEDA RODRÍGUEZ

Abstract

The chapter investigates the All-Saints Catholic Church in Williamsburg, Brooklyn, NYC, as an example of a multiterritorial space for Mexican immigrants. The methodology in this research combines fieldwork, observation and semi-structured interviews which were carried out in Mexico and in New York City. While All-Saints Catholic Church is a multiterritorial space, it is equally a deterritorialised space, as individual immigrant groups within the church community maintain strong transnational ties to Mexico through continuous virtual interaction. In the church, the immigrant community of Piaxtla is territorialised, deterritorialised and reterritorialised, while simultaneously remaining in a territory established by those who come to this religious space but do not belong to the community. The fact that different groups coexist in the same space, each contributing their own characteristics, transforms the Church of All Saints into a multiterritorial and transnational space, since the links that immigrants have built with their places of origin influence the activities that take place in the church.

Introduction

In the Williamsburg neighbourhood in Brooklyn, the Church of All Saints is the central location for local Catholics to gather and participate in religious celebrations. The festivities have the characteristics and a style that often takes up the traditions of the places of origin of the different members, many of whom have migrated to the US themselves or are the descendants of immigrants. Depending on the time of year, the different coexisting denominational communities carry out their respective activities and celebrations within the church. Yet, at the same time, they share that space with the other communities, thus creating/performing a superposition of territories, not only as a physical space, but also conceived under a symbolic-cultural idea.

One of these immigrant communities that gathers in the church comes from Piaxtla, a small municipality located in the *Mixteca Puebla*, Mexico, and which has an important migratory tradition towards New York City. This community has been established in different parts of the city's five boroughs, but it has a strong presence in the Church of All Saints because there is a replica of the image of the Virgen de la Asunción, patron saint of the town of Piaxtla, which the same immigrants brought from their place origin.

In order to explain the way in which this church has been territorialised by this and other immigrant and non-immigrant communities, and the process that it has followed until defining itself as a transnational space, for this chapter I will use the theory established by human geographer Rogério Haesbaert,[1] who challenges us to rethink the concepts of territory and territoriality. Haesbaert proposes the concept of multiterritoriality, to explain the way in which spaces are conceived by each of the social groups and the people who pass through them. On the other hand, it also builds on Marcos Aurelio Saquet's explanation of the processes of territorialisation, deterritorialisation and reterritorialisation.[2]

The research underpinning this chapter is part of a larger project regarding the immigrant community from Piaxtla, in which I have identified the different characteristics of the migrants from this community, and the way they maintain a strong bond across borders.[3] Its aim was to better understand the way in which migrants have developed multiterritoriality and built their transnational ties, especially with *Piaxteco* immigrants living in New York City, and with immigrant and non-immigrant families in Piaxtla, Mexico. Furthermore, another aim was to try to examine the way the *Piaxteco* immigrants lead their daily life around the All-Saints Church in Williamsburg, with activities that take place across borders, and in virtual/digital spaces.

Theory

Space is not only understood in the material plane, but also thought of as something symbolic that gives way to the construction of the territory, as Haesbaert posits.[4] The territory changes its configuration over time and is not static or immobile. Following Henri Lefebvre, I propose to conceive it as a social construction, where the political, economic, cultural and natural dimensions interrelate.[5]

The relationship between space and territory is understood from the social processes that take place there. The territories arise from the power relations established between groups considered hegemonic and subaltern, who – within the conditions of power, inequality and precariousness – interact differently in space. Saquet affirms that space intervenes in the formation of society, being the support of life and the activities carried out by its inhabitants and relating to the territory because this is a socio-historical relational construction, which is defined by the appropriation and domination exercised by the inhabitants.[6]

Territorialities therefore refer to the practices that individuals develop due to the activities they carry out in the space they own; thus, territorialisation must be understood as the social appropriation of that space or a part of it. As social constructions in the historical evolution of spaces, multiple processes of territorialisation, deterritorialisation and reterritorialisation can be found, as well as heterogeneous and overlapping territories.[7]

Haesbaert has criticised how the concept of deterritorialisation has been understood as the destruction or abandonment of a territory, suggesting instead that it should be thought of as a process whereby the territory is rethought, reterritorialised, and whereby multiple territorialities emerge at the same time. Thus, it analyses the construction of territories but emphasises the current context, where mobility has intensified precarious processes and subordinate groups have the least control over their territories since control is out of their reach or is exercised by others, especially in the case of hegemonic groups.

In this sense, deterritorialisation is not only seen as negative, but also has a positive meaning where not only the idea of destruction is present, but also the reconstruction and construction of new territories. These subaltern groups are territorialised in spaces where, in general, they do not have the concrete and definitive ownership of the territory, but where they can have a more symbolic and experiential appropriation of the space.[8]

Migrants are one of the groups that experience the appropriation of space from multiple territorialities since, when travelling through different territories, they accumulate experiences and feelings along the way.[9] With this, migrants manage to develop multiterritoriality, whereby they have the possibility of having simultaneous experiences in different territories. In this context of migration, some migrants manage to establish strong ties with other members of their community, even in different countries. Other migrants develop the possibility of transiting through foreign territories, especially those who live in precarious conditions and are forced to enter or transit through foreign territories.[10]

To understand the transnational dynamics that takes place in the Church of All Saints, fieldwork was carried out in New York City, through the application of the participant observation technique, where the different activities carried out by those attending this space could be identified. The ethnographic work with this community began in 2015 and continued until 2020 as a long-term investigation, which allowed us to monitor the development of these processes over time, with their different changes, and not just as isolated fragments in time and space. During this observation process, many immigrants from different places and with different migratory statuses were registered. Moreover, semi-structured interviews were conducted during this period.

In this chapter, I propose that the Church of All Saints is the place where the original immigrants from Piaxtla have carried out their religious practices with greater force, linked to social and economic activities, and even political ones. This space has the characteristics of multiterritoriality, because members of different social groups, different immigrant communities, meet there, appropriating that space-territory, which functions in different ways, but does not symbolically change its meaning.

In the church, the immigrant community of Piaxtla is territorialised, deterritorialised and reterritorialised, while simultaneously remaining a territory established by those who come to this religious space and do not belong to the Piaxtla community. The fact that different groups coexist in the same space, and that each one contributes its own characteristics at the time of territorialisation, makes this church a multiterritorial and transnational space. The links that immigrants have built with their places of origin influence the activities that take place in the Church of All Saints.

The Transnational Space of the All-Saints Church

The All Saints Church, located in the Williamsburg neighbourhood of Brooklyn, New York City, was built in the second half of the 19th century, in approximately 1866, in an area of factories, warehouses and apartment buildings, where local workers resided (Figure 1). In the second half of the 20th century, Latino immigrants, coming mainly from Puerto Rico and Mexico, began to settle in this neighbourhood due to affordable housing and job opportunities for low-skilled workers in the nearby factories and warehouses.

Since the majority of residents were undocumented immigrants and the income was generally low, Williamsburg displayed the typical precariousness associated with many immigrant communities. Many lived crowded together with other compatriots, friends and relatives. Indeed, the accounts of some migrants report that in some of these apartments more than 20 people lived together. Additionally, some experienced racism and discrimination from the hegemonic groups in Williamsburg because of either their skin colour, their origin or their immigration status. Some of the migrants interviewed originating from Piaxtla reported that they had even suffered rejection and discrimination from other migrants who had arrived before them. Grouped by their place of origin, these different migrant demographics each continued to perform their identity-marker traditions, expressed in their daily life and diet, as well as the language they used to communicate. Some

Figure 1: Façade of All Saints Church, Williamsburg, Brooklyn, New York City © Emilio Maceda Rodríguez.

even managed to establish businesses where they sold products from their country of origin or took up some commercial activity that they had carried out in their place of origin before migrating. However, these same migrants also began to bond with other immigrant groups, from whom they copied some or many of their behaviours or attitudes, marking the process of cultural overlapping of territories.

Among the practices resumed by the members of this immigrant community in New York City were also religious ones. In their place of origin, these immigrants were mostly of the Catholic faith, so they sought to replicate the activities linked to the Catholic Church in the space they now occupied, a place within the Williamsburg neighbourhood where they could profess and maintain their faith. The Church of All Saints then transformed into a space where Catholic immigrants met. As an institution, the church started to operate transnationally, taking up a symbolic presence from the various migrational spaces of origin. As a territory, it therefore operates on the simultaneity of different traditions depending on the place where they were established, while it continues to have a similar symbolic meaning for all those who belong to the Catholic Church, itself a transnational institution.

As part of this process, the immigrants began to transfer replicas of religious images to the church, especially of the Saints and Virgins who were patrons of their places of origin, in order to carry out the religious activities to which they were accustomed before their emigration. However, they adapted them to the new space. In other words, while we can observe a process of deterritorialisation of the emigrants, the meaning of their practices remains intact. They only reterritorialised to another space, where they established a new territory in which they could live their religion, which in return overlapped with the territories that were already established before. Thus, the multiterritoriality of the Church of All Saints was established. At the same time, it developed as a transnational space, since some of the immigrants who territorialised this space had strong transnational ties that connected them across borders with their places of origin, as in the case of the immigrant community of Piaxtla.

One of the processes that influenced the development of these transnational ties was the political integration of undocumented Mexican immigrants to the United States, when immigrants obtained residency or citizenship, especially after the Immigration Reform and Control Act of 1986, which in turn allowed these immigrants to travel to their places of origin. In this context, some immigrants were able to travel more frequently, because in addition to residency or citizenship, they had a job that allowed them to have sufficient income, or they owned their own business. Some travelled to Mexico up to three times a year. Immigrants with these characteristics developed a strong transnational bond, became involved in activities and projects in the Williamsburg church and their place of origin, and had influence among the community that attended religious celebrations.

Seeing the strength of the transnational bond of these immigrants, the priest who oversaw the Church of All Saints accepted the invitation of the immigrants from Piaxtla (the biggest of the church's communities) to visit their place of origin. This visit is but one example of the level of transnationalism that has developed in this church among and between the different social groups: they identify as Catholics, yet as immigrants they also take their place of origin into account, i.e. the territorialised space they have left, and from which they have managed to transfer some of the practices from Piaxtla to the United States, albeit in an adapted form, thereby territorialising the spaces that they now occupy. In the case of Mexican immigrants, they identify themselves first as Latinos, then as Mexicans, third by the state where they were born, and finally by their community, reaching the point that in some communities, as in the case of the *Piaxtecos*, they even define themselves by the neighbourhood they come from.

Multiterritorial Immigrants: From Piaxtla to New York City

Piaxtla is a municipality that is located in the southwest of the state of Puebla, Mexico, within the region known as the *Mixteca Poblana* (Figure 2). The population is 4,585,[11] of whom 77% (3,232 inhabitants) experience a high degree of marginalisation, although the municipality has a medium degree of marginalisation. According to the data presented by CONEVAL, of the total population, 1,848 people live in moderate poverty and 1,014 in extreme poverty.[12]

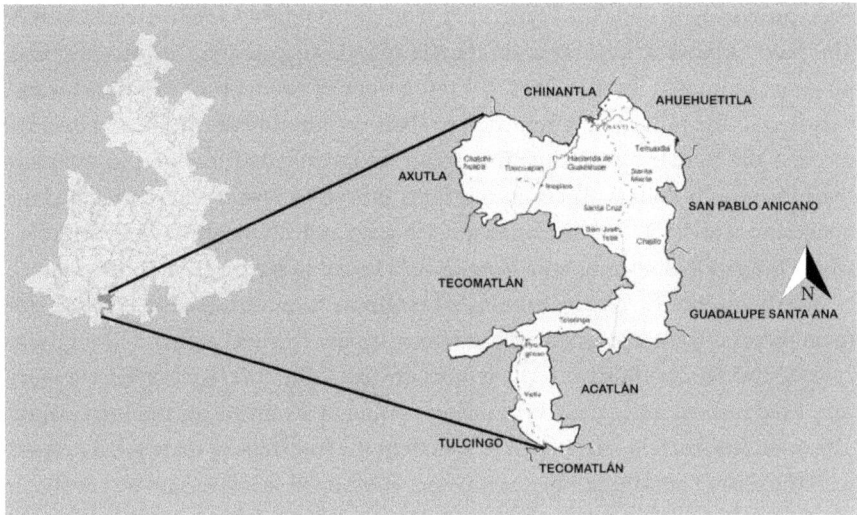

Figure 2: Map of Piaxtla Municipality in the Free and Sovereign State of Puebla, Mexico. Topographical information 1:250 000 © Own elaboration with data from INEGI (2005). *Marco Geoestadístico Municipal, version 3.1.*

The main economic activities that take place in the municipality are commerce and services. The characteristics of the local soil limit agricultural production, and according to data from INEGI only 11% of the land is suitable for agriculture, with corn being the main crop.[13] There is also a salt mine that is exploited in a rudimentary way, and a craft workshop that produces candles with beeswax. Based on these conditions, the level of marginalisation in this local population is not surprising. This has caused most of Piaxtla's inhabitants to be dependent on remittances of money made by migrants, which is why migrating, in this community, has become so important, and has made it possible to establish strong transnational links.

The international migration of the inhabitants of Piaxtla is not recent and has remained constant over time, destined for the United States, mainly the Tri-state Area of New York City, New Jersey and Connecticut. There are records that the first emigrants from Piaxtla arrived in New York City in 1940; however, at that time there was no real link between the community of origin and the space they occupied in the destination, because the migrants did not maintain constant communication with their family and transferring money back home was difficult.

During the United States' participation in World War II (1939–1945), the Bracero Program was established between this country and Mexico, which lasted from 1942 to 1964 and promoted the temporary entry of Mexican workers in a documented way. This programme "managed to mobilise, between 1954 and

1960, an average of 350,000 workers per year, and in total 4.5 million were hired."[14] The exact number of *braceros* from Piaxtla who participated during this period is, however, unknown. In the 1960s, the last groups of residents of Piaxtla who participated in the programme returned to their community of origin, and decided to cross the border again, this time in an undocumented manner, to maintain their income in dollars. These immigrants moved to places where they had acquaintances, so they went to California, Chicago and, above all, to New York City, where the group of immigrants from Piaxtla began to have a greater presence.

Starting in the 1970s, the number of migrants began to steadily increase due to an increase in undocumented border crossings. The undocumented migrants crossed the border hidden in the trunks of cars, with borrowed or false papers; they used tunnels and crossed the desert on foot or swam across the Rio Grande. The migrants from Piaxtla began to follow in the footsteps of their predecessors, with the idea of obtaining a better income, working in whatever job was available and in any unfamiliar space.

Most of these migrants made their way to New York City using the ties they had with friends, family and countrymen who already resided there. Although they knew neither the language nor the lifestyle, and their new jobs were not related to their previous economic activity, the advantage of being able to connect with immigrant networks that were already established made it easier for them to foray into this new space. While adapting to life in New York City, some immigrants began to reproduce the activities they carried out in Piaxtla, as a response to satisfy the needs generated by nostalgia, such as preparing food in the Mexican style or meeting in the apartment of a fellow migrant to celebrate their patron saint.

With the 1986 amnesty, many of the original immigrants from Piaxtla had the opportunity to regularise their immigration status, through which they obtained residency and later citizenship. These documents allowed them to leave and to return to the United States without legal problems, enabling them not only to visit their community of origin without problems but also, in some cases, to request residency for their relatives.

The ability to obtain permanent residence and citizenship allowed the ties between the immigrant communities of origin and destination to strengthen, giving rise to an incipient transnationalism with a constant flow of people, information, objects and resources. Now that their immigration status was regularised, immigrants who had started their own businesses in New York City also had to register their activities officially. On the one hand, this allowed them to fully integrate into the destination space and receive social protection and benefits; on the other hand, they now had to pay taxes as merchants and/or entrepreneurs. At the same time, some immigrants were able to bond more with their community of origin since not only did they have permission to enter and leave the country in a documented way, but they were also able to earn a better income that allowed them to save money and think about not only supporting their family, but also donating money for different projects in their home community.

These types of actions were not new among migrant communities established in places of destination: even without having documented migratory status, immigrants crossed the border to participate in their communities of origin and sent money to be used in projects there. The novelty was that the new immigration status and increased economic resources allowed them to become more independent, and thereby economic and cultural agents. They linked and influenced both spaces by transferring not only money, but also ideas, customs and projects. This in turn caused the governments of the places of origin to begin to see the migrants also as potential drivers of the development of their own communities. Therefore, immigrants with these characteristics can be called transmigrants, a concept that I will return to later.

This period marks the true beginning of the transnational community because the links between the places of origin and destination start to become institutionalised and formalised. Starting in the late 1990s, the municipal presidents and politicians of Piaxtla began to seek a rapprochement with transmigrants, and one of the activities they began to use was the celebration of *El Día del Migrante* [The Day of the Migrant], which takes place in the context of the patronal feast and consists of offering a meal and a dance to welcome the migrants. Those who have a greater influence among the community, or who possess significant economic resources, are invited to meet with the municipal president or with non-migrant groups, for proposals and projects to be presented to them, in order to seek the support of the transmigrants and link them with the rest of the community abroad. It is at this time that, as described by Alejandro Portes and Renato Pintor Sandoval, the transnational community is formed, within the process of immigrant transnationalism.[15]

The Transnational Patronal Religious Holiday in Williamsburg, NY

The patronal religious festival of the Virgen de la Asunción is one of the most important annual events for the inhabitants of Piaxtla, since it means the return of those who emigrated to other municipalities and states in Mexico, or indeed the United States, and who return for the season to their place of origin. This translates into the reunion of families and friends, the reaffirmation and construction of identities of migrants and their American children, the transformation of traditions and customs due to migration, and the emergence of projects derived from the reunion between migrants, visited by the community and representatives of the municipal and state government.

However, not all emigrants can return to celebrate the patronal feast of their town, either because they do not have their residence permit and they prefer not to risk crossing the border in an undocumented way, or, in the case of those who are already citizens or residents, because they cannot afford the trip or must work during the period of the celebration. Yet the inability to return to Piaxtla to celebrate the patronal feast was not necessarily an impediment to them reaffirming their faith and sense of belonging to the community of origin. As an alternative, they embarked on bringing a replica of the patronal image to New York City, which would allow them to celebrate the Virgen de la Asunción in their local church. This marks the beginning of the celebration of this patron saint in New York City.

Out of New York City's five boroughs, the *Piaxteco* community has had its greatest presence in Brooklyn, and developed its religious life particularly where the Williamsburg, Bedford-Stuyvesant and Bushwick neighbourhoods meet. The community found the support of a Dominican Catholic priest, who allowed them to celebrate the Virgen de la Asunción and helped them promote the project of moving a replica of their patron saint from its place of origin in Piaxtla. The fact of an icon migrating together with its people is by no means new, as Liliana Rivera Sánchez has illustrated.[16] In some cases, Rivera Sánchez explains, the icons would make a tour of the areas of the American Union where immigrants from the populations from which they originated were settled, to then later return to their communities of origin. However, as the example of Piaxtla shows, in some instances the migrants decided to carry the replica of the icon with them in order to continue the tradition in the new space they came to occupy and thereby maintain a link with their place of origin, i.e. with their faith and culture, but also with the distribution of positions, status and even power.

When interviewing the *Piaxteco* immigrants who arrived in New York City in the 20th century, they state that most of the community members maintained their faith and identity linked to the celebration of the Virgen de la Asunción. At the same time, some mention that they became Protestant Christians, especially because of the strong influence that this type of church has in the United States. Those who remained within the Catholic denomination, and especially linked to the patron saint of Piaxtla, sent money to support the arrangements of the church when necessary, gave alms, masses and tithes to ask favours of the Virgin, and, when they could, returned to the celebration of the patronal feast, even crossing the border in an undocumented way. Even so, those who could not go to this reaffirmation of their identity as *Piaxtecos* held a more modest celebration, in front of a small painting that represented the Virgin of their devotion, either in the house of one of the *Piaxtecos* who lived in New York City, or in a church where the icon was kept.

It was not until the second decade of the 21st century that a group of immigrants began to raise the idea of having their own image of the Virgin Patron of Piaxtla, in a church located in Brooklyn, so that in this way they could celebrate it as they did in their place of origin. This was also to do with wanting to feel more protected by having a place closer to them where they could go in time of need and comfort or simply when they wanted to demonstrate their faith. Therefore, the group organised and, after a series of formalities and religious celebrations, decided to collect money among the immigrant community to acquire a replica of the Virgen de la Asunción in Mexico.

This attempt to establish a territory linked to the profession of their religion, and the intention to resume the practices of their country of origin, is an example of that process of reterritorialisation. Instead of deterritorialising themselves, they began to build a territory in a space that was already territorialised by other communities. It is in this process that these multiterritorial spaces emerge, built by migrants with strong transnational ties, who in turn become multiterritorial migrants, as they move in different territories, appropriating them temporarily. Thus, deterritorialisation is not a final state, but just a transition between one moment and another.

The fundraising activities were carried out in the basement of the Church of All Saints, and consisted of kermesses, food sales at the end of Sunday mass, and visiting the homes and businesses of the immigrants from Piaxtla asking for their support. However, the activities were also met with hesitancy at times. During one of these home visits, for example, one of the families expressed uncertainty about what might happen to the icon once the members of this group pass away, fearing that perhaps their children did not feel the same devotion, that it could be relegated to a corner of the church or to the basement, without the festival taking place, and what was worse, without someone taking care of maintaining it. To them, the transfer of the replica from Piaxtla meant a great and lasting responsibility.

This fact underlines the importance of the cult of the Virgen de la Asunción among the *Piaxtecos*. Yet it also allows us to get a glimpse of the uncertainty immigrants face in their lives in terms of continuity. After all, the fear they experience concerning the future of the icon is the same one they experience in relation to the objects they have left behind, i.e. the land and houses in Piaxtla. They do not know what will happen to them once they leave and/or die and to what extent they and their offspring will still be connected to them: will they be buried in Piaxtla, where maybe their children and grandchildren cannot as easily visit them? Or will they be buried in New York City, far from the land where they were born?

Despite this hesitancy on the part of some members of the immigrant community, the group managed to collect the necessary funds, and – in August 2011 – a replica of the icon was taken to Piaxtla, where it was placed on the altar next to the original for its blessing. The mass was attended by non-emigrants and the representatives of the congregation in Piaxtla, as well as some emigrants who accompanied the icon on its trip from Williamsburg to Piaxtla and back again.

The *Piaxtecos* celebration of the Virgen de la Asunción in the US takes place on the weekend before the main festival in Piaxtla (15 August). The date was moved so that those who had emigrated to New York City and the Tri-state Area or indeed even further afield to cities such as Chicago have the possibility to attend both celebrations. It begins with a procession of the icon on the Friday, which is decorated with candles and flowers, through the streets (Figure 3). Those who have a request for the Virgin offer music or a strand of hair to serve as a makeshift wig for the icon. A dress, jewels and the crown are also offerings made by those seeking favour with the Virgin. However, should nobody present the Virgin with a dress and/or crown; these are donated by the festival's steward. Additionally, he oversees the adornment of the church, the candles and the mass, in which he fulfils similar functions to those performed by the steward in Piaxtla. The procession begins at the house of the steward for that year. If the house is located in walking distance to the church, those who accompany the Virgin walk the streets on foot. If it is further away, the procession travels in vans to a nearby street, where they organise and then begin the journey to the church, where the priest welcomes them and enters the church together with them to celebrate the main mass.

Like in Piaxtla, the stewardship of the Williamsburg procession is a great honour and it can significantly advance a person's standing within the *Piaxteco* community. Waiting lists can be long and those interested may have to wait several years for their turn. However, there are also years without contenders as the stewardship is predicated on the ability to dedicate sufficient (financial and human) resources to the event. While those who seek stewardship do so to honour the Virgin and to ask for her favour, the opportunity to advance one's own communal standing plays an important role and creates a certain competitiveness. Each steward seeks to trump the ones of the previous years, and failure may lead to a severe communal reprimand.

The procession itself is organised as follows: in front of the icon is a group of dancers interpreting the Dance of the *Tecuanis*, for which the *Mixteca* region is famous. It is therefore hardly a surprise that it has been adopted by the migrants from different populations of the *Mixteca Poblana* in the United States. Indeed, the communities invite the *Tecuanis* of the other communities for the celebration of the patron saint in their towns. The dancers are followed by a group of people carrying banners with images of other Saints and Virgins, or groups of migrants

Figure 3: Procession of the icon at the celebration of the *Virgen de la Asunción* (Friday) © Emilio Maceda Rodríguez.

who also celebrate the Virgen de la Asunción, and who gather to accompany the image of the *Piaxtecos* during the procession tour, along with the other faithful, who may or may not be from Piaxtla. At the centre of the procession walks the steward together with the banner of the Virgen de la Asunción and the people who are going to deliver offerings, such as the hair or the crown, accompanied by banners of the Virgen de Guadalupe and a group that plays wind band music. At the end of the procession comes a group of dancers from Piaxtla called *Los Tecuanis de Piaxtla*, who have maintained this tradition in New York City and have popularised it over the past 30 years.

The procession passes through several streets in Williamsburg, supported by the New York Police Department, who divert traffic and block off the streets. When the group accompanying the Virgin arrives in front of the church, the priest receives them in the street and blesses the banners, the offerings of the steward and the young women who accompany him. Then they enter the church, always accompanied by music, which only ceases when the mass begins.

In the street, the dancers continue dancing. At the end of the mass, the organisers provide the musicians and dancers who participated in the procession with food and drink, while people pass to take photos with the Virgin as a souvenir and to show that they attended the celebration. It is also common for participants to share it through social media. In doing so, they are not merely showing their family and friends that they attended the celebrations, but they are also demonstrating that – despite being outside their place of origin – they maintain a link with the traditions of their community, and that they continue to identify them-

Figure 4: Singing of the *mañanitas* and morning mass at All Saints Church during the celebration of the *Virgen de la Asunción* (Saturday) © Emilio Maceda Rodríguez.

selves as *Piaxtecos* and Catholics. Thus, photography and photo sharing on social media becomes another way of demonstrating the territorialisation of spaces.

At six in the morning on Saturday, when the dawn is breaking, a large part of the migrant community gathers to sing the *mañanitas* to their patron saint (Figure 4). After the *mañanitas* and morning mass, the main mass is celebrated at noon, where the devotees of the Virgin meet again, so that at the end they can go out in procession with the icon of their patron saint on their shoulders, accompanied by those from Piaxtla and migrants of various origins who live in the Tri-state Area. Some migrants from Piaxtla come from as far away as Chicago. This pilgrimage from other US states to Williamsburg is an important way to reconnect and reintegrate with the *Piaxteco* community, as well as to see family and friends.

The festivities last until late at night, with musical groups performing traditional songs from Mexico. On the one hand, and as mentioned before, participation in these festivities allows the migrants to reaffirm their identity as *Piaxtecos* and Mexicans; on the other hand, it also facilitates a continuous extension of their social and supportive networks with other migrant groups.

These practices are but one example of the way in which *Piaxteco* migrants have territorialised the Church of All Saints through sharing the space with other communities and religious groups, who in turn have also made this place a territory where they develop their activities. This superposition of territories is an example of the symbolic appropriation of spaces discussed in the theoretical section. Indeed, the transnational link is so strong in this territory that the priest of the Church of All Saints visited Piaxtla in 2015 (Figure 5). During

Figure 5: The priest of All Saints Church meets his counterpart in Piaxtla in 2015 © Emilio Maceda Rodríguez.

his visit, the immigrants from Piaxtla who had managed to obtain documented immigration status, had the economic resources that allowed them to travel back and forth between Mexico and the United States, and sought to get involved in activities and projects in their community had a strong influence. These immigrants are defined in this research as transmigrants, i.e. migrants who have a transnational link and who influence both their country of origin and the country of destination. In other words, they develop and maintain multiple relationships across borders – be they familial, economic, social, organisational, religious and/or political. These transmigrants, therefore, have multiple, overlapping commitments, both in their societies of origin and in the host societies, both of which they consider their home. They assume the role of active builders of transnational social fields.

In this context, a transmigrant is a person from Piaxtla who has moved to New York City, has obtained a residence permit and/or citizenship, and has sufficient financial resources through their economic activity to frequently return to their place of origin. The defining characteristic that differentiates a transmigrant from other migrants is their involvement with projects or activities in Piaxtla, which influences migrants and non-migrants alike. They organise meetings and groups of the *Piaxteco* community in the United States, which are linked with other immigrant groups, Mexican and non-Mexican, and they establish ties of reciprocal collaboration that have put them in contact with some political groups in New York City, as these other organisations have more institutionalised structures and links to politicians on both sides of the border.

As previously mentioned, the transmigrant moves constantly between their places of origin and destination. In the case of the *Piaxteco* community in Williamsburg, there is a group of migrants who visit Piaxtla every three to four months and actively participate in the two spaces they occupy. Therefore, they are the ones who practise multiterritoriality in its most advanced form. They are very conscious that they belong to multiple spaces, and that they have appropriated those spaces, not only symbolically, but also physically. Haesbaert defines this as successive multiterritoriality, while Ulrich Beck describes this as topopolygamy, i.e. being married to several places at the same time.[17]

The idea of transferring the icon to the Church of All Saints exemplifies the process of deterritorialisation experienced by the migrants from Piaxtla, who, faced with the need to leave their place of origin, sought a space where they could maintain the religious traditions of their birthplace. It is then reterritorialised in the Church of All Saints, which has already been territorialised by other groups. At the same time, the migrants from Piaxtla maintain a transnational link with their place of origin, with which they develop a multiterritorial relationship.

The Transnational Connection in Virtual Space

The activities that take place around the celebration carried out by migrants from Piaxtla of the Virgin of the Assumption were also influenced by tools that allow the use of social networks on the internet. In this virtual space, the *Piaxtecos* have established territories through the groups and profiles they have opened on Facebook, where it is possible to identify some iconographic elements of their place of origin, which allow them to show an identity linked to Piaxtla, despite its absence.

In these profiles and groups there are migrants who actively participate in activities and projects that have a simultaneous impact in Piaxtla and New York. The reterritorialisation, through the use of these virtual spaces, can be seen from the photographs and videos, which allow them to once again have a presence in their place of origin or destination, without having to physically move between the two spaces. The use of technological tools to link the place of origin with the spaces that migrants occupy in New York City is not something new. Before the arrival of the internet in Piaxtla, communication was carried out by sending letters, postcards, video cassettes and telephone calls that were made sporadically to the community's public telephone or to the homes of those who could pay for the service.

In the first decade of the 2000s, the internet was installed in Piaxtla and computer rental businesses began to appear, where photographs and emails were exchanged and the first video calls were made. These places, also called internet cafés, allowed a greater exchange of information between Piaxtla and New York. The first internet café that opened in Piaxtla had 12 computers and using the internet for an hour cost 10 pesos. When the community members realised that the business was a success, they opened two more internet cafés, with fewer computers, but with the same success.

The use of cell phones became popular between 2007 and 2008, when the first telephone masts were installed, although calls and messages were very expensive. The last change in communication between Piaxtla and New York City came with the advent of the smartphone, which was connected to the internet and allowed the use of online social networks such as Facebook, WhatsApp and Instagram, which are the platforms most used by migrants and non-migrants to communicate and disseminate information, photos and videos.

The use of these online social networks has facilitated the material and immaterial exchange between the places of origin and destination of the migrants from Piaxtla. Ideas, thoughts and data are transferred from one place to another in this virtual space, and it has even allowed material objects to be promoted and sold as well. Bracelets, T-shirts and hats adorned with Piaxtla's name have been offered and sold through these online social networks, manufactured in the place of origin and delivered in New York City.

But at the same time, the use of this virtual space has made it possible, under the protection of anonymity, for multiple accounts to be created without a defined personality. Some of these have been used to spread false information that accuses and incriminates those who participate in the municipal government, in any of the migrant or non-migrant organisations, and members of the *Piaxteco* community. Some of these anonymous profiles have a name that shows the purpose for which they were created, as in the case of the Facebook profile called *Veneno Piaxteco* [Piaxtec Poison], which has attacked people who worked in the municipal presidency, the police of the town and neighbours of the community. The topics in this profile were related to aspects of people's private lives, topics related to politics and the management of economic resources. The people who commented on these posts lived in Piaxtla, but migrants from this community living in New York City also posted.

At the same time, verified profiles of people and groups from Piaxtla who live in the place of origin or in the United States have been created, who use online social networks to communicate with their family and friends, with the municipal government of the place of origin, and even with the organisations that are also in charge of promoting projects in the church of Piaxtla and in the community. These groups, made up of locals and migrants living in New York City, have taken advantage of this non-physical space created on the internet to disseminate the plans and activities they propose to obtain resources and support community programmes and projects.

However, the presence of migrant groups in the virtual space has not been easy, mainly because there are barriers that limit the participation of the members, a disadvantage for some groups and an advantage for others. These limitations are due to the use of technology. In the United States, migrants have easy access to more and better technological devices, such as computers and cell phones, in addition to the fact that it is possible to connect to the internet via a smartphone from almost anywhere and with better quality. However, the research indicates that not all migrant groups use these tools. Most only use their cell phones to make calls and send text messages, and those who use virtual social networks use them for personal matters.

In the case of one of the groups linked to the construction of chapels in Piaxtla, the use of online social networks is common. The leader of the group took advantage of the reach of these types of tools, which facilitate constant communication between those who live in Piaxtla and migrants in the United States without having to travel. In the Facebook posts, this group presented recordings to convince people, showed lists of those who supported the project, and shared videos and photographs that show the progress of the construction. In doing so, the leader of the group sought to solve one of the problems that organisations face when requesting economic resources from the migrant community: how can you demonstrate that the money they were raising was actually used in the projects? The use of social networks and cell phones with cameras facilitated communication between the organisations and the *Piaxtecos* living in New York City and Piaxtla.

In contrast, a committee of migrants from Piaxtla that was formed to support the remodelling of the church in their place of origin did not have as much impact in the virtual space. The members of this committee had a cell phone that allowed them to have access to social networks on the internet, but they did not use it to share information, photos and videos of their activities. This meant that they did not have constant communication with the *Piaxteco* community on both sides of the border, and that the exchange of news and invitations to their events were only made to their friends or family. The number of attendees at their events depended on this information being shared orally, because the use of posters and other advertisements was often beyond the budget and was only possible when someone donated them.

With these two examples of the use of new technological tools by two migrant organisations, it is possible to appreciate the importance of the use of online networks for the development of projects. The most important means of communication for migrants today is the internet, as it allows them to share information instantaneously, has a greater scope and is not limited to a few contacts; instead, information can be shared among all those who are linked to the virtual network and is easily accessible to anyone with an internet connection.

However, it is not only written information that is disseminated through these media; photographs, videos, audio recordings and live broadcasts are also shared. Now migrants and non-migrants can witness what happens in the other space that the *Piaxteco* community occupies, without having to be physically present. These types of changes in the means of communication between Piaxtla and New York City have had positive and negative results for migrant organisations when developing programmes that seek to improve the community of origin: it is an opportunity to have a greater impact and obtain better support for projects, but, at the same time, those who do not have access to or do not know how to use these technological resources may have low participation and their activities may be ignored by the majority of the members of the community.

Conclusion

In a context where migrants constitute a significant presence, such as New York City, spaces such as the Church of All Saints arise. The state of precariousness in which many members of the community migrants find themselves pushes them to move into territories that have already been pre-established in New York City, in order to protect themselves, go unnoticed and earn an income. Yet they also try to appropriate a space that allows them to maintain their traditions and customs in an environment that is hostile to them. The Church of All Saints is but one example of the relationship between a religious space and the different migrant communities that utilise it. The religious practices developed in the church allow each community to interact with the space, appropriate it and turn it into their own territory – even if they do not dominate it. The different ways in which each community appropriates the space – the practices and activities they carry out – create an overlap of territories, which in the end turns the space into a place that allows the development of multiterritoriality. However, as the example of the immigrants from Piaxtla illustrates, the distinctive characteristics and abilities of certain migrant groups allow them to be multiterritorial agents that constantly move between different territories, affecting both their community of origin and destination. The recent technological advances have added yet another layer of transnational engagement.

The fieldwork also revealed that there are many other spaces where *Piaxtecos* and Mexican immigrants have established their territories, such as parks and public squares, streets, businesses, and even some schools. This has turned these places into transnational spaces, where the relationship with the places of origin is very close, with some moving constantly between them. The challenge is then to begin to analyse the transnational relationships that develop in these spaces, the relationship they maintain with the construction of territories, and the influence of multiterritorial migrants in the shaping of transnational places.

Notes

1. Haesbaert, Rogério (2011): *El Mito de la Desterritorialización: Del Fin de los Territorios a la Multiterritorialidad*, translated by Marcelo Canossa. Mexico City: Siglo XXI; Haesbaert, Rogério (2013): Del Mito de la Desterritorialización a la Multiterritorialidad. *Cultura y Representaciones Sociales* 8(15), 9–42.
2. Saquet, Marcos Aurelio (2015): *Por una Geografía de las Territorialidades y las Temporalidades: Una Concepción Multidimensional Orientada a la Cooperación y el Desarrollo Territorial*. La Plata: Universidad Nacional de La Plata, Facultad de Humanidades y Ciencias de la Educación.
3. Cf. Maceda Rodríguez, Emilio (2019): Migración, Territorio, Sociedad y Cultura en Piaxtla, Puebla: Una Comunidad en el Contexto del Transnacionalismo. *Migraciones Contemporáneas desde Puebla y Gestión Migratoria Extraterritorial*, edited by Cristina Cruz Carvajal, Adriana Sletza Ortega Ramírez, and José Luis Sánchez Gavi. Puebla: Benemérita Universidad Autónoma de Puebla, 34–52.
4. Haesbaert (2013), 27.
5. Haesbaert (2013), 19f. Cf. also Lefebvre, Henri (1984): *Everyday Life in the Modern World*, translated by Sacha Rabinovitch. London: Routledge.
6. Saquet (2015).
7. Ibid.
8. Haesbaert (2013).
9. Ibid.
10. Ibid.
11. INEGI (2009): *Prontuario de información geográfica municipal de los Estados Unidos Mexicanos*. Piaxtla, www.inegi.org.mx. Accessed 4 August 2021.
12. CONEVAL (2010): *Medición de la Pobreza en México 2010, a Escala Municipal*, http://www.coneval.gob.mx/Medicion/Paginas/Medici%C3%B3n/Informacion-por-Municipio.aspx. Accessed 4 August 2021.
13. INEGI (2009).
14. Durand, Jorge (2005): De Traidores a Héroes: Políticas Emigratorias en un Contexto de Asimetría de Poder. *Contribuciones al Análisis de la Migración Internacional y el Desarrollo Regional en México*, edited by Raúl Delgado Wise and Beatrice Knerr. Zacatecas: Autonomous University of Zacatecas, 15–39, 20.
15. Portes, Alejandro (2007): *Migration and Development: A Conceptual Review of the Evidence*. Working Paper, Center for Migration and Development, Princeton University, http://meme.phpwebhosting.com/~migracion/rimd/bellagio/2.pdf. Accessed 4 August 2021; Pintor Sandoval, Renato (2011): El Habitus y los Campos Transnacionales en el Proceso del Transnacionalismo Migrante. *Migraciones Internacionales* 6(2), 159–192.

16. Rivera Sánchez, Liliana (2006): Cuando los Santos También Migran: Conflictos Transnacionales por el Espacio y la Pertenencia. *Migraciones Internacionales* 3(4), 35–59.
17. Haesbaert (2013); Beck, Ulrich (2001): *¿Qué es la Globalización? Falacias del Globalismo, Respuestas a la Globalización*, translated by Bernardo Moreno and Ma. Rosa Borrás. Barcelona: Paidós.

Works Cited

Basch, Linda, Nina Glick-Schiller, and Cristina Szanton (1994): *Nations Unbound, Transnational Projects, Postcolonial Predicaments, and Deterritorialized Nation-States*. London: Routledge.

Beck, Ulrich (2001): *¿Qué es la Globalización? Falacias del Globalismo, Respuestas a la Globalización*, translated by Bernardo Moreno and Ma. Rosa Borrás. Barcelona: Paidós.

CONAPO (2016): *Índice de Marginación por Entidad Federativa y municipio 2015*. Mexico City: Consejo Nacional de Población, https://www.gob.mx/conapo/documentos/indice-de-marginacion-2015-284579. Accessed 4 August 2021.

CONEVAL (2010): *Medición de la Pobreza en México 2010, a Escala Municipal*, https://www.coneval.org.mx/Medicion/Paginas/Pobreza-municipal.aspx. Accessed 4 August 2021.

Durand, Jorge (2005): De Traidores a Héroes: Políticas Emigratorias en un Contexto de Asimetría de Poder. *Contribuciones al Análisis de la Migración Internacional y el Desarrollo Regional en México*, edited by Raúl Delgado Wise and Beatrice Knerr. Zacatecas: Universidad Autónoma de Zacatecas, 15–39.

Haesbaert, Rogério (2011): *El Mito de la Desterritorialización: Del Fin de los Territorios a la Multiterritorialidad*, translated by Marcelo Canossa. Mexico City: Siglo XXI.

Haesbaert, Rogério (2013): Del Mito de la Desterritorialización a la Multiterritorialidad. *Cultura y Representaciones Sociales* 8(15), 9–42.

INEGI (2009): *Prontuario de información geográfica municipal de los Estados Unidos Mexicanos*. Piaxtla, www.inegi.org.mx. Accessed 4 August 2021.

Lefebvre, Henri (1984): *Everyday Life in the Modern World*, translated by Sacha Rabinovitch. London: Routledge.

Maceda Rodríguez, Emilio (2019): Migración, Territorio, Sociedad y Cultura en Piaxtla, Puebla: Una Comunidad en el Contexto del Transnacionalismo. *Migraciones Contemporáneas desde Puebla y Gestión Migratoria Extraterritorial*, edited by Cristina Cruz Carvajal, Adriana Sletza Ortega Ramírez, and José Luis Sánchez Gavi. Puebla: Benemérita Universidad Autónoma de Puebla, 34–52.

Pintor Sandoval, Renato (2011): El Habitus y los Campos Transnacionales en el Proceso del Transnacionalismo Migrante. *Migraciones Internacionales* 6(2), 159–192.

Portes, Alejandro (2007): *Migration and Development: A Conceptual Review of the Evidence*. Working Paper, Center for Migration and Development, Princeton University, http://meme.phpwebhosting.com/~migracion/rimd/bellagio/2.pdf. Accessed 4 August 2021.

Rivera Sánchez, Liliana (2006): Cuando los Santos También Migran: Conflictos Transnacionales por el Espacio y la Pertenencia. *Migraciones Internacionales* 3(4), 35–59.

Saquet, Marcos (2015): *Por una Geografía de las Territorialidades y las Temporalidades: Una Concepción Multidimensional Orientada a la Cooperación y el Desarrollo Territorial*. La Plata: Universidad Nacional de La Plata, Facultad de Humanidades y Ciencias de la Educación.

Networking and Representing the Transnational Neighbourhood Online

The Linguistic Landscapes of Latin Americans in London's Seven Sisters

NAOMI WELLS

Abstract

Latin Americans in London have in recent decades established a more visible presence in neighbourhoods across the city, particularly in the market and commercial spaces in Seven Sisters and Elephant and Castle. While often studied and conceptualised as physical offline spaces, as Blommaert and Maly establish, much of what we observe offline is conditioned or made possible by the ways these spaces are networked and represented online. Focusing on the public web presence of the Latin American market in Seven Sisters, this chapter illustrates how the 'Latin American' identity of this space, and the associated community has been at least partly constructed and sustained as such through online representations. The chapter combines the study of contemporary and archived web content to provide diachronic insight into the changing linguistic and visual representations of the market online. It further illustrates how community members have made use of the rapidly evolving affordances of digital media and technologies to articulate the forms of transnational cultural heritage associated with these physical neighbourhood spaces.

Introduction

Since the 1990s, Latin American communities in London have established an increasingly visible presence in a number of areas across the city, most notably in the market and commercial spaces in the two neighbourhoods of Seven Sisters in North London and Elephant and Castle in South London. This growing visibility is reflected in a number of studies, initially from a more demographic perspective but more recent research has focused on the linguistic and cultural dynamics of these physical neighbourhood sites. However, given the consolidation of these physical sites as Latin American spaces alongside the rapid expansion in uses of digital media and technologies, the ways in which these sites operate at the intersection of online and offline worlds remain underexplored.

As Blommaert and Maly note, even when we focus our attention on concrete physical or 'offline' neighbourhoods, and the transnational communities who physically inhabit them, it is impossible to ignore the ways much of what we observe is increasingly conditioned or made possible online.[1] This includes more in-group and private communications through which gatherings and people's movements through the neighbourhood may be facilitated and coordinated. The focus of study in this chapter is, however, on more public and outward-facing online spaces, particularly websites, where physical spaces and the transnational communities associated with them are publicly represented. In the cases of the Seven Sisters and Elephant and Castle market and commercial spaces, a wealth of such representations has appeared online as they have come under increasing threat from local 'regeneration' initiatives.

As Márquez Reiter and Patiño-Santos note, this threat has constituted a critical moment in which London's Latin American community has needed to (re)position itself and (re)negotiate its place in the neighbourhood and wider city.[2] For example, what became known as the 'Latin American market' in Seven Sisters began when a small number of Colombian traders gradually from the early 2000s bought up several units in the existing indoor market space of the Wards Corner building. While as individual businesses some of these traders may have had an earlier online presence to promote their commercial interests, it was the threat of closure announced in 2007 that led to the emergence of a less commercially driven web presence from the late 2000s. From then until the present day, a number of webpages have been created by groups of traders and associated community members and campaigners that focus on representing the market as a specifically Latin American community space in order to communicate its cultural and social significance, and in the process asserting an identifiably Latin American presence within the neighbourhood and wider city.

This chapter results from a much larger project, *Cross-Language Dynamics: Reshaping Community*,[3] that explores the relationship between language and community from a range of disciplinary perspectives, with my own research exploring the role of digital media and technologies in relation to how language communities are formed, sustained and represented. Through the analysis of recent and archived webpages produced by Latin American community members, it is possible to trace how processes of community formation and (re)positioning have developed and been articulated online. Focusing primarily on the Latin American market in the Seven Sisters neighbourhood, the chapter will address the role of language and translation in relation to this positioning, as well as the ways these websites make use of the rapidly evolving multimedia affordances of the web to represent the cultural and social significance of these spaces.

London's Latin American 'Community'

London is renowned as a historic and contemporary centre of transnational flows of people, languages and cultures, and while the arrival of a significant number of Latin Americans is a relatively recent development, by 2011 they had become the eighth-largest and one of the fastest-growing non-EU-born communities in the city.[4] Latin Americans have, though, struggled to achieve visibility in London and in the wider national context, which has had major consequences for their ability to access similar levels of recognition and support as other communities in the city.[5] This is partly connected to their relatively recent establishment as a community in the UK, although some have also questioned how appropriate the label 'community' is to encompass individuals who may originate from the same broad geographic region but who have a "multiplicity of national, ethnic and linguistic identities".[6]

Such differences may previously have hampered efforts to mobilise a sense of collective identity, although recent years have seen important forms of cross-community solidarity emerge, most notably with the consolidation of a number of civic society groups. A coalition of these also successfully campaigned to have Latin Americans recognised as an ethnic group in a number of London boroughs since 2012.[7] As is common in contexts of migration, this sense of community identity is rooted in forms of political and economic marginalisation,[8] and in this specific case the desire to ensure the collective interests of Latin Americans are acknowledged by local institutions and services in London. This identity is also at least partly connected to language and, although the Latin American community also includes Portuguese-speaking Brazilians, the Spanish language is more dominant in the ways the community is represented.

While not then in any sense a uniform or homogenous community, particularly in more recent years there is evidence of a much stronger sense of collective identity and relationships of solidarity.[9] A number of spaces closely identified with Latin Americans have been consolidated across the city, the most important of which are the market and commercial spaces in the London neighbourhoods of Seven Sisters and Elephant and Castle. Although not used by all Latin American groups, or not necessarily identified with by all, these explicitly Latin American spaces play both symbolic and social roles in the construction of a sense of community identity. For as Cock notes, "[t]hese spaces are key to the formation of a sense of ethnicity because they are publicly and collectively accessible and they generate representations of those that are part of them."[10] These include digitally mediated representations, and with these spaces and the associated Latin American community having consolidated themselves in conjunction with the rapid growth of digital media and technologies, the web is an ideal space in which to trace this process by which a collective community identity has been forged and articulated at least partly online.

Researching the Web Presence of Latin Americans in London

Focusing specifically on the case of Latin Americans in London, this research combines the study of contemporary web materials that continue to circulate online, as well as archived web content in the UK Web Archive and the global Internet Archive from websites that have either disappeared or undergone significant changes over time. Web archives, in particular, allow for a more diachronic analysis through which we can simultaneously trace the ways the web has evolved as well as how Latin American individuals and groups in London have exploited the new affordances of the web to represent themselves and their collective interests. While the vast scale of web archives can present major methodological challenges for identifying or delimiting relevant research materials,[11] search terms to locate particularly significant community webpages were informed by 'offline' reading and research in relation to the physical presence of Latin Americans in London that allowed for the identification of both relevant keywords and important issues facing the community, such as the threatened closure of these market spaces.

The analysis of these online research materials draws partly on traditional approaches to the study of linguistic and cultural materials, such as textual and discourse analysis. At the same time, drawing on more recent approaches to the study of digital culture and digital language practices, it is important to recognise the specificity of these new media and to recognise the different capabilities or affordances of the web.[12] This includes in particular the greater multimodality of digital texts, which often feature "rich combinations of semiotic modes like writing, visuals and sound."[13] In relation to affordances, the diachronic approach requires attention to the rapidly changing circumstances of production of these online texts, and how the emergence of new platforms and technologies influences what people are able to do or produce online. This is not to suggest technologies alone determine our actions and interactions, with individuals and groups able to adapt and appropriate different technologies to serve their own specific goals,[14] as will be illustrated in the case of the Latin American traders and campaigners at the Seven Sisters market in London.

Language, Translation and Latin American Identities

Language choice and translation strategies on these public-facing websites offer insight into the communicative and symbolic role of language, with web archives further allowing us to trace how this has shifted over time. To a degree, public-facing websites can be treated as a form of digital linguistic landscape, and, like multilingual public signs in the physical landscape, they can offer at least partial insight into the linguistic and cultural dynamics at play within the associated communities and spaces.[15] Like the 'offline' world, the 'online' world is also made up of a multiplicity of texts with a range of discursive and generic norms in relation to language use. There are, for example, similar distinctions between speech and writing, although the development of the more participatory Web 2.0 era since the early 2000s, and in particular its intensification in the 2010s, has meant the rapid growth in more informal writing practices that blur traditional divisions between oral and written language norms.[16] In the cases of the websites under consideration here, and particularly their earlier archived versions, these do however replicate many of the traditional language norms of offline written texts, most notably with the clear separation of Spanish and English texts on the pages of the earliest website created for the Seven Sisters market.[17]

While, given that web archives do have gaps and absences, it is not possible to say with certainty that this is the first website created for the market, keyword searches in the UK Web Archive and Internet Archive point to this site as being one of the earliest websites that attempts to publicly represent the space as a specifically Latin American market. The earliest archived version of this site dates back to 2009, and from the description of its purpose, it is clear it was created in response to the threat of possible closure due to a redevelopment plan first announced by the local Haringey Council in 2007. This illustrates how, as Márquez Reiter and Patiño-Santos highlight, the proposed closure of these commercial spaces acted as a form of crisis point at which time it became necessary to articulate the significance of the space and the associated community formed around it. In particular, this threat created the need to create more public and visible representations of the site, with the web having by this time established itself as an increasingly accessible space in which to create and circulate such representations, and in particular offering opportunities to forge new "networks of solidarity" within and beyond the Latin American community.[18]

As a primarily Spanish-speaking space but operating within a primarily English-speaking country, one of the most important choices in creating such representations is in relation to language and an immediately noticeable feature of this website is its Spanish and English bilingualism. Languages here function both as communicative tools used to describe the community and the space, but simultaneously can in themselves be considered as representative of the community and space. In this sense, it is important to note that this Spanish and English bilingualism is not entirely equal and, in common with physical linguistic landscape studies, it is important to consider the relationships between languages on the page,[19] and in particular evidence of what Scollon and Scollon refer to as "code preference", whereby one language may be revealed to be the preferred or dominant code.[20]

Across the website, the Spanish-language name 'El Pueblito Paisa' is used as the sole heading and label applied to the market, without any attempt to provide an English translation. We will return to a later change in the labelling of the space, but to provide some background to this name, it reveals the strong connections of the site to a specific Latin American national and more specifically regional community. 'Paisa' is used to refer to those who come from the north-western Antioquia region of Colombia, while 'Pueblito' can be translated as 'little town' or 'village'.[21] The website describes the gradual and seemingly spontaneous initial adoption of the name among customers, with a group of the market's traders then formally adopting this name and forming El Pueblito Paisa Limited in 2005.

This label thus originated from within the community, and points clearly to the primarily Spanish-speaking clientele and business owners. It further highlights the regionally specific diasporic connections of the site with traders and customers primarily from the Colombian Paisa region.[22] Paying attention to the visual and graphic elements of the website's text,[23] the Colombian connections of the site are further reinforced by the fact that the name appears across the website in the three colours of the Colombian flag: 'El' in yellow, 'Pueblito' in red and 'Paisa' in blue. By 2013, the 'Misión & Valores/Values & Mission' page[24] also included a GIF of a fluttering Colombian flag, further illustrating the strong emphasis on the Colombian nationality of many of those who inhabit the market space.

Returning to language choice, despite this monolingual name for the market and the fact that those who run and visit it are primarily Spanish speakers, the website's menu uses bilingual labels for the different pages on the site, with Spanish appearing first, followed by English. Spanish is still however the clearly preferred code of the site, and on clicking through to both the 'Quienes Somos/Who we are'[25] and the 'Misión & Valores/Values & Mission'[26] pages, they both have Spanish appearing first, with English either appearing to the right of or below the Spanish text. The most self-evident explanation for the dominance of Spanish is that it is the first language of those who created the site, further reinforced by the ways the English syntax of the translations closely follows that of the Spanish versions. Given that the market has been noted as a primarily Spanish-speaking space, the language choice is also connected to the current visitors and users of the physical space. This demonstrates a partial connection to the daily language practices within the site, although there is likely to be a greater mixing of languages in everyday spoken language practices, while written text norms reinforce the more prescriptive division of languages that we see on this website.[27]

The dominance of Spanish may further function as a form of language display with a more symbolic purpose, with the monolingual heading in particular representing a resistance to translation for English-speaking audiences, for whom the name El Pueblito Paisa is likely to communicate little other than its 'non-Englishness'. This may thus be considered an attempt to overtly, as Clifford writes, "live inside, with difference",[28] by proudly displaying the market's identity as a Spanish-speaking space, even within a wider national context that promotes English-speaking monolingualism. At the same time, the location of the site in London is significant in terms of different attitudes towards linguistic and cultural diversity, as made explicit in the site's description of its mission and values, which refers to its potential as a tourist destination for those who would like to "experimentar la diversidad cultural de la ciudad/experience the diversity of the city".[29]

An exception to the dominance of Spanish is, however, on the page labelled 'Planeación Deficiente/Deficient Planning' where, in spite of this bilingual label, the text on the page appears in English alone.[30] This page describes the ongoing dispute with the local council in greater depth, and the more bureaucratic and legalistic tone suggests it was initially prepared for other purposes and later added to the website. This does, though, point to the intended audiences for this website, and in particular the need to go beyond the Spanish speakers who regularly visit and use the physical site. This is further reinforced by the 'Visitas Importantes/Important Visitors' page, illustrated on the menu with a picture of future Prime Minister Boris Johnson, who at this time was London Mayor and who visited the site and made a statement in support of it. His support again points to the different political dynamics of London, where support for cultural and linguistic diversity stands in marked contrast to national political discourse, particularly that of his own political party. The website's menu also includes a link to a video of a BBC news story on the market, uploaded to YouTube by a member of the group. These examples point to the major shift triggered by the planned closure of the market: the need to reach beyond the market's more immediate Spanish-speaking visitors in order to gain visibility and broader support for the market's continuation from English-speaking audiences.

In reaching such audiences, who may know little about the site and more importantly the community who use it, it is here that it becomes vital to create powerful representations of the space and community for those unable or unlikely to visit in person. In particular, and as later online representations illustrate, it becomes increasingly necessary to make the space and associated community more easily 'legible' for an English-speaking audience with potentially little understanding of the regional specificities and differences within the Latin American community. Seemingly in response to this, another label has emerged and, at least on the web, has become the more dominant label used to describe the market space: the 'Latin Village'. While Pueblito Paisa Ltd continued its activities and legal campaign under that name, it no longer had a public web presence from around 2015. Instead, a new group emerged, initially under the name Latin Corner[31] from 2015, and eventually becoming the Latin Village,[32] with a Save

Latin Village & Wards Corner Community Interest Company formally established in 2018. While Pueblito Paisa Ltd was originally founded to bring together the business interests of a group of traders connected to the market, this new group took the lead in the more public-facing campaigning activities the traders have been increasingly required to engage in. Importantly, this new group had strong connections to the original group, being led in particular by some of the daughters of the traders who formed Pueblito Paisa Ltd, but has a stronger focus on campaigning and fundraising activities, particularly through its website and associated social media activities.[33]

This has meant a greater emphasis on speaking to much broader English-speaking audiences, as is most evident in the use of the name Latin Village. While Pueblito Paisa continues to be used alongside this later label, it is Latin Village which has become the increasingly dominant name in public-facing communications. As well as the use of an English-language label, it is equally significant how in the translation process the regional specificity of the 'Paisa' label is subsumed into a more general 'Latin' identity. In efforts to reach wider audiences there is then a degree of simplification, with 'Paisa' likely to have little meaning for those external to the community associated with the market, while 'Latin' or 'Latin American' is a much more legible identity label that can more easily summon up pre-existing perceptions, including inevitably stereotypes, for the English-speaking reader unfamiliar with the site. The name Latin Village may also summon up associations with related 'ethnic' spaces, most notably Chinatowns in London and elsewhere across the globe, again pointing to efforts to draw on readers' pre-existing ideas and notions of 'ethnic' space.

In relation to the label 'Latin', which is also used by the campaigning group for the traders at Elephant and Castle, who go by the name Latin Elephant, it is important to highlight connections with the wider cross-London campaign to recognise Latin Americans as an ethnic group. The label is thus associated with efforts to increase the visibility of Latin American communities in the city, with public recognition necessitating efforts to consolidate a multiplicity of national, regional, cultural and linguistic identities under a single label. Such 'ethnic' labels, as has been widely noted, carry with them the risk of essentialising and fixing identities, and the increasing use of the 'Latin' label to designate these market spaces could be interpreted as a form of what Spivak termed "strategic essentialism". For as Brah notes, "[i]n their need to create new political identities, dominated groups will often appeal to bonds of common cultural experience in order to mobilise their constituency."[34]

While inevitably carrying risks of imposing a homogenising label that erases internal differences, such labels can be important for creating networks of solidarity between community members, something that earlier research noted as lacking among Latin Americans in the city.[35] In fact, while 'Latin American' or 'Latin' may now seem to be well-established terms for referring to the community, their recentness is highlighted by the fact that, while these labels are also used on the original Pueblito Paisa website, both the 'Quienes Somos/Who we are'[36] and the 'Misión & Valores/Values & Mission'[37] pages begin by referring to "la cultura Ibero Americana/Ibero-American culture" and the "Ibero Americanos/Ibero-Americans." This broader label, which also includes those from Spain, illustrates some uncertainty about which label should be used to refer to the *community* and who should be included within it. While 'Ibero-American' still continues to be used by some Latin American and Spanish groups, 'Latin' or 'Latin American' has in most recent years firmly established itself as the dominant label under which the community has mobilised itself.

The use of 'Latin' or 'Latin American' is likely also connected to the success or pre-circulation of these labels within the London and British context, unlike the rarely used term 'Ibero-American'. The name Latin Village thus speaks to this new group's aim to construct a more easily legible, and inevitably to a degree simplified, representation of the market space that derives its value from its association with a clearly identifiable Latin American community. The aim to speak outwards to wider audiences is further supported by the dominant use of English on the group's website, even if Spanish translations have been provided over time for some texts on the website. The success of such a strategy is evident from their fundraising campaigns that have allowed them to pursue major legal battles, as well as the ways their campaign has been picked up by local and national media, such as Channel 4 News and the Guardian. While the Pueblito Paisa group did have some success in leveraging media and political support, it is through the campaigning activities of this new group that the market has most significantly secured the intervention of the United Nations, which raised human rights concerns in relation to the market's closure.[38]

Returning, however, to the subject of transnational neighbourhoods, in addition to papering over differences within the Latin American community, the use of a single ethnic label to describe and at least partially lay claim to the space does risk obscuring the complexity of these transnational spaces. As we will return to later, while Latin Americans do represent the primary constituency of traders within both the Seven Sisters and Elephant and Castle sites, a number of businesses are run by individuals from other regions and continents, such as Africa, the Caribbean and the Middle East. Both markets do in fact sit within extremely diverse neighbourhoods, crosscut by a multiplicity of earlier and more recent migration trajectories. Despite the impossibility of either site acting as an isolated island within such neighbourhoods, the 'Latin' label does risk giving the impression of the creation of 'ethnic enclaves', or the often-critiqued 'parallel societies'. Something similar is at play in the display of languages on these websites, where parallel Spanish and English translations may function as representations of languages and their associated communities as clearly bounded and separable, which belies the ways both languages intersect in community members' repertoires, and may further obscure the multiplicity of other languages potentially present in the physical space.

Evidently it is important not to understand or see the authors' aims with these websites as being to create a mimetic representation of the physical space. Rather, the aim is to engage as wide an audience as possible and to reach those who may be able to lend their financial, campaigning, media and political support to their efforts to save the market. In this respect, while media and UN accounts also mention the wider diversity within these spaces, it is the site's recognisable 'Latinness' that appears to offer a more legible and compelling narrative for its continued existence than the ever-evolving and potential indeterminacy of transnational spaces. Due to their associations with trajectories of mobility, transnational neighbourhoods may risk being perceived as inherently transitory and temporary spaces, and while in practice it may be true that all spaces are, as Massey explains, always in a process of "becoming",[39] such a fleeting spatial identity can pose a real risk to those who inhabit these spaces and leave them without the means by which to sustain their continued existence within them. This points to the contradictions of political discourses that both seek to demonise 'ethnic enclaves' and 'parallel lives',[40] while simultaneously fostering a system whereby it becomes necessary to adopt a single and unified 'ethnic' identity to gain visibility and recognition. These websites thus operate within the realms of a political order, and a wider social and cultural order, that continues to demand the reduction of complex identities and communities into recognisable categories, also often identified with a single language, and in which clearly labelled 'ethnic' spaces may represent a more compelling and externally legible conceptualisation of space than the ever-embryonic transnational neighbourhood. Nevertheless, while the more textual content of both earlier and recent websites speaks to a certain 'taming' of the spatial order,[41] the increasingly multimedia affordances of the web point to new opportunities to represent the multiplicity and complexity of these sites.

Multimodal and Multivocal Representations of the Transnational Neighbourhood

As we move more squarely into the Web 2.0 era, and particularly in more recent years, we see an increasing dominance of multimedia content that to a degree replaces the earlier textual representations of the site. Mobile technologies, free social media platforms and easy-to-use web content management systems such as WordPress have made a far greater range of multimedia affordances available to a much wider range of actors than in the earlier days of the web.[42] This is not to ignore critical questions concerning the motivations of social media companies, in particular, in making their platforms freely available. Nevertheless, it remains undeniable that these platforms have taken on an increasingly important role as channels through which marginalised and minority groups are able to publish and share their stories, taking advantage of the distinct but complementary representational affordances of different platforms and media.

The original Pueblito Paisa website did already make some use of the earlier multimodal and multimedia affordances of the web, using photos and images for menu items, and as previously mentioned linking out to a YouTube video of a BBC news story about the market. What is noticeable, however, is the limited integration of the visual and textual, with the textual content remaining the primary mode for communicating and representing the market space. The Latin Village website, in contrast, makes use of a much wider range of multimodal and multimedia representations, beginning first with the homepage dominated by a large hand-drawn image of the external façade of the market.[43] A brief heading overlays the image with the words "Save Latin Village", with a smaller subheading and a button to "Donate" that links through to the organisation's crowdfunding page. This points to the primary function of this website in supporting the campaign's fundraising efforts, but what is important to note here is how the image is doing much of the representational work in terms of communicating the value of the market space. This is further reinforced by the gallery of images immediately below, which in the earlier versions of the webpage was made up of a series of children's hand-drawn representations of the market.

The organisation's homepage thus demonstrates how the organisation makes effective use of the multimodal affordances of the web to represent the market space in ways that more immediately communicate its value to an external audience. At the same time, the emphasis on hand-drawn images – both in the case of the main image and the gallery of children's drawings – may be a strategy to overcome the potentially distancing effects of 'purely' digital representations that may lack the affective resonances connected to the materiality of children's drawings in particular. The role of children in mediating these representations of the market serves to immediately communicate how it functions as a family and community space that goes beyond its commercial functions, with images of children playing also appearing across the many representations of the market. For example, in the more recent iteration of the website,[44] this internal website gallery has been replaced by an embedded gallery from the group's Instagram account, although images of children and families remain a primary feature.

Other subpages on the website are more dominated by text, and in particular with more legalistic and bureaucratic information about the continued campaign to save the market. But in terms of representing the market space, it is visual and audio-visual modes of communication that dominate. On the 'About Us' page, for example, the key page in which to explain the role and function of the market, the earliest versions included just a couple of lines on the market in English, while relying primarily on embedded YouTube videos to represent the space.[45] Different videos have been embedded on this page over time, with the text also changing, but what they have in common is an attempt to capture through audio-visual media the range of social and cultural practices associated with the space. The earliest videos used were trailers from a fly-on-the-wall documentary created about the market that captured some of the daily activities and interactions that take place within it. While later videos are created by the organisation itself and have a more explanatory function, with voiceovers and interviews narrating the background to the campaign, these are interspersed with Latin American music and seemingly unstaged scenes of food consumption and more informal interactions within the market. This is echoed across the organisation's YouTube channel, where recordings of council meetings, interviews and protests are interspersed with less explicitly campaigning videos of everyday activities and celebrations, with a particular emphasis on music, dance and food.

The interspersal of such content with more explicitly campaigning content illustrates how the threat to the market space created this new need to articulate and represent the cultural significance of the site. While these representations do not stand in for or substitute physical co-presence within the market building, audio-visual media are used to convey a sense of the daily embodied and emplaced cultural activities that occur within to a wider audience. Such activities could be categorised under the label of intangible cultural heritage, and here it is important to note that while the financial implications of the market closure for its traders are not to be overlooked, it is on the basis of the market's cultural significance that they have been able to secure media interest and most significantly the interventions of the United Nations. While intangible cultural heritage has historically often been associated with rural communities and notions of indigeneity, the United Nations' intervention points to a growing recognition of the cultural value of superdiverse or transnational urban neighbourhoods like Seven Sisters, and of forms of cultural heritage associated simultaneously with histories of mobility while also having become, albeit relatively recently, deeply rooted in a specific local context.

While discussions of forms of superdiverse or transnational urban heritage are not entirely new, what is significant here is the role that the web and social media play in terms of both capturing and communicating these forms of heritage. As Taylor notes, in contrast to the more historically stable written archive, embodied cultural practices associated with orality and performance historically relied on physical co-presence in the 'now', and as a result were associated with ephemerality and eventual erasure from the historical record.[46] While Taylor's work refers primarily to indigenous cultures within Latin America, embodied knowledge and practices are, I propose, central to understanding the value and cultural significance of the everyday cultural activities that take place within superdiverse or transnational neighbourhood sites such as the Latin American markets, particularly as migrant communities often face similar forms of exclusion from the 'official' written archive in its nationally bounded forms. Digital technologies, however, provide new ways of documenting and sharing these more ephemeral everyday practices, with video in particular able to capture "a sense of the kinetic and aural dimensions of the event/work, the physical and facial expressions of participants, the choreographies of meaning."[47] This is not to suggest they act as a substitute for a community's physical co-presence, but rather that they can allow for the practices and activities that take place in those physical spaces to be effectively mediated to wider audiences. This is illustrated by the many videos created and shared by the Save Latin Village campaign that are dominated by both dance and music performances, as well as more everyday activities like food preparation and consumption.

Video is evidently not a new technology specific to social media, but what is a distinct feature of most recent years is the massive increase in non-professional access to the means of production and dissemination through mobile devices and social media platforms. As mentioned, the earlier Pueblito Paisa did include a link to a YouTube video of a BBC story about the market, and the earlier versions of the Latin Village site, then known as Latin Corner, included embedded videos from an earlier documentary about the market. However, illustrative of the effects of the massive increase in mobile technologies is how the campaign's webpage and fundraising pages are now dominated by videos produced by the campaign itself. This is not to deny the continued prestige and power of more mainstream media, and leveraging the engagement of major UK media organisations has been a major success of the campaign, as highlighted on the website. Nevertheless, the multimedia affordances of social media and mobile technologies give those who work in and inhabit the market space far greater opportunities to shape and construct the representations of the market and associated community that circulate online.

This goes beyond the small group of campaigners who officially lead the Save Latin Village group, with a key feature of social media being its multivocal nature.[48] Thus, rather than the construction of a single authoritative narrative about the significance and value of the market space, what is noticeable is the way a multiplicity of representations and, in particular individual stories, are dispersed across different pages and platforms. This may partly compensate for some of the issues raised earlier in terms of the risk of representations that simplify the complexity and multiplicity of transnational neighbourhoods in order to construct a more easily legible and unified narrative. For example, across the group's pages and social media profiles, while Latin American groups and individuals are most visible, the stories and experiences of individuals and groups from a much wider range of backgrounds are also present. The website has from its early days included a simple floor plan of the space that uses national flags to indicate the different businesses and the countries of origin of the traders, which reveals the presence of a number of traders from outside of Latin America, including from Iran, Senegal, Ghana and Jamaica. While flags may also risk oversimplification of complex transnational identities, they do immediately communicate the greater porosity of the space, rather than it being a bounded or exclusively Latin American space. The earlier website[49] also linked to a version of this map that had an interactive function, created on the lesser-known platform ThingLink, where icons could be clicked on to reveal an image and written quote from some of these traders. However, while demonstrating the group's efforts to experiment with different platforms in order to fully exploit the affordances of the web to represent the market, it is the much greater use and integration of social media content that begins to give a sense of the multiplicity of stories of those who occupy and visit it.

Images and associated text are used, for example, on Instagram to recount the experiences of individual traders from both Latin America and elsewhere. YouTube and Instagram videos include the voices of campaigners from outside of the Latin American community who appear equally invested in its continuation. And while the majority of the group's textual content is in English, a number of Spanish-language hashtags are used, seemingly with the aim that these are taken up not just by Spanish-speaking community members, but the much wider network of local residents and campaigners who are supporting their efforts. In particular, the slogan and hashtag #SiSePuede is spoken and written repeatedly in textual and video content following English-language content, but without any English-language translation of the phrase. This points to the potential of social media to allow for more fluid flows between languages than the more rigid parallel translations of earlier web content. The presence of this phrase as a hashtag further points to a desire for it to be used more widely among their network of campaigners, functioning as what Blommaert describes as a "translingual framing device" that can be taken up across language and community boundaries.[50] In fact, this phrase has a longer intertextual history of crossing language and community boundaries, originating as a campaigning slogan in

César Chávez's labour movement in the 1970s in the US, and appearing to have inspired Obama's 'Yes, We Can' 2008 campaign slogan.[51] This specific use of the original Spanish-language version as a hashtag to be picked up and reused by others, however, may point to a desire for the market and its associated cultural and linguistic practices to function as a form of "multivocal" heritage[52] that can be claimed by the wider local community and including those who do not identify as Latin American.

These examples thus begin to point to the reality of transnational neighbourhoods not as made up of a collection of isolated national enclaves, but as spaces of a multiplicity of linguistic and cultural flows and encounters. While still evidently partial, and in particular representations shaped to further the campaigning and fundraising aims of the group, online and social media representations do appear to provide new ways of mediating this complexity and multiplicity of voices through the rich combinations of semiotic modes that these platforms afford. A particular feature of social media pages is further that they tend to be much less static than traditional webpages, which typically remained more stable over time. For example, the content of the original Pueblito Paisa site remained largely unchanged over several years, and consequently came to function as a fairly fixed representation of the market not entirely dissimilar to a printed text. In contrast, embedding the Instagram gallery on the homepage of the current Latin Village website conveys a sense of constant change and flux, giving a sense of both the website and the associated market space it represents as being "always under construction".[53] I use Massey's words here to illustrate the potential for online and social media representations to contribute to conceptualisations of transnational spaces as "processes" rather than "pregiven discrete entities".[54]

As discussed earlier, there is a risk here in terms of creating more complex, multivocal representations, also now dispersed over a number of pages and platforms, that may be less compelling or authoritative to an external audience than a singular and more stable narrative. While arguably contemporary audiences are increasingly familiar with transmedial representations and narratives that are dispersed across a range of pages and platforms, the content produced on social media platforms in particular is still often associated with more ephemeral and fleeting representations that lack the authority and stability of the traditional archive. Relatedly, the campaign associated with the other Latin American commercial space in Elephant and Castle recently created a new website, which functions more as a virtual exhibition gathering together and more explicitly curating a collection of social media content alongside a series of stories, poetry and artwork created during the organisation's many years of campaigning.[55] This site maintains a multiplicity of stories from traders and visitors, including many who identify with different communities, as well as incorporating a range of media and untranslated content in English and Spanish, thus retaining many of the features and affordances of the earlier-discussed social media content. However, the site displays a more explicit desire to guard against the potential ephemerality of this content, and to add greater value and authority to it through a more active process of curation. While as a web resource its longer-term archival stability is still not guaranteed, it points to the central role web and social media content are likely to play in the future as we look to document and more importantly sustain the complex and rapidly evolving cultural heritage associated with contemporary transnational urban neighbourhoods.

Conclusion

Despite the successes of the campaigns to protect both of these sites, illustrated in particular by the interventions of major media and international organisations, both were recently partially closed in their current forms. Nevertheless, both groups continue to campaign for the relocation of the traders, and more specifically for the provision of alternative community spaces that will allow for some form of continuity of the practices and activities associated with these original sites. In sustaining these and similar future campaigns, there is now a rich multimedia record from which community members can draw, and much stronger networks of solidarity within and beyond the community that have been at least partly forged by making use of the communicative and representational affordances of rapidly evolving digital media and technologies. This is not to support a simplistic techno-utopian view of these digital spaces as providing in any sense a substitute for these vital physical spaces. Indeed, it is precisely because they provide opportunities for physical co-presence, and associated embodied and emplaced practices and performances, that these markets have become such an important cultural centre for Latin Americans in the city. However, even if the main aim of these online and social media campaigns of maintaining these spaces has proven partly unsuccessful, they have allowed the community to articulate and represent the rich cultural heritage associated with these sites, with the potential also for this heritage to be more easily taken up and 'claimed' by current and future generations.[56]

Admittedly, this process has necessitated certain accommodations in reaching and becoming networked among wider audiences, most notably with the increasing use of English. This has also been accompanied by the adoption of a more general Latin American label in order to make the space and associated community more immediately legible to wider audiences. Given the campaign's focus on building solidarity and furthering the collective interests of the community, inevitably there will also be intracommunity tensions or differences documented in other studies, but which are papered over in these representations. Such strategic choices and compromises are understandable in light of the need to construct a narrative in relation to both the space and the associated community that is more meaningful and compelling to the wider audiences these campaigns aim to reach. At the same time, although the fragmented and ephemeral nature of web and social media content may pose a risk to the stability and authority of these representations, the new affordances of digital media and technologies appear to offer opportunities to create more complex, multivocal and rapidly evolving narratives that may more effectively reflect the "simultaneity of stories-so-far" that define the transnational neighbourhood.[57]

Notes

1. Blommaert, Jan, and Ico Maly (2019): Invisible Lines in the Online-Offline Linguistic Landscape. *Tilburg Papers in Culture Studies* 223.
2. Márquez Reiter, Rosina, and Adriana Patiño-Santos (2017): The Discursive Construction of Moral Agents among Spanish-Speaking Latin American Retailers in Elephant & Castle. *Tilburg Papers in Culture Studies* 194, 6f.
3. This project (AH/N004647/1) was funded by the UK Arts and Humanities Research Council, as part of the Open World Research Initiative.
4. McIlwaine, Cathy, and Diego Bunge (2016): *Towards Visibility: The Latin American Community in London.* Queen Mary University of London, Latin American Women's Rights Service and Trust for London, 14, https://www.trustforlondon.org.uk/publications/towards-visibility-latin-american-community-london/. Accessed 15 July 2021.
5. McIlwaine, Cathy, Juan Camilo Cock, and Brian Linneker (2011): *No Longer Invisible: The Latin American Community in London.* Queen Mary University of London and Trust for London, https://www.trustforlondon.org.uk/publications/no-longer-invisible-latin-american-community-london/. Accessed 15 July 2021.
6. Márquez Reiter and Patiño-Santos (2017), 4.
7. Montañez, María Soledad (2020): *Lemme Hablar: Community Engagement and the Latin American Community in Southwark.* Institute of Modern Languages Research, School of Advanced Study, University of London, 16, https://mariasoledadmontanez.files.wordpress.com/2020/12/southwark-report-october-2020.pdf. Accessed 15 July 2021.
8. Brah, Avtar (1996): *Cartographies of Diaspora: Contesting Identities.* London: Routledge, 238.
9. Montañez (2020); Román-Velázquez, Patria, and Jessica Retis (2021): *Narratives of Migration, Relocation and Belonging: Latin Americans in London.* London: Palgrave.

10. Cock, Juan Camilo (2011): Latin American Commercial Spaces and the Formation of Ethnic Publics in London: The Case of the Elephant and Castle. *Cross-Border Migration among Latin Americans: European Perspectives and Beyond*, edited by Cathy McIlwaine. London: Palgrave Macmillan, 175–195, 178.
11. Winters, Jane (2017): Coda: Web Archives for Humanities Research – Some Reflections. *The Web as History: Using Web Archives to Understand the Past and Present*, edited by Niels Brügger and Ralph Schroeder. London: University College Press, 238–247.
12. Hayles, N. Katherine (2007): Electronic Literature: What is it? *Doing Digital Humanities: Practice, Training, Research*, edited by Constance Crompton, Richard J. Lane, and Ray Siemens. London: Routledge, 197–226, 208.
13. Jones, Rodney H., Alice Chik, and Christoph A. Hafner (2015): Introduction: Discourse Analysis and Digital Practices. *Discourse and Digital Practices: Doing Discourse Analysis in the Digital Age*, edited by Rodney H. Jones, Alice Chik, and Christoph A. Hafner. London: Routledge, 1–17, 7.
14. Ibid., 11.
15. Paffey, Darren (2020): Hispanic London: Language Ideologies, Policies and Practices. *Researching Language in Superdiverse Urban Contexts*, edited by Clare Mar-Molinero. Bristol: Multilingual Matters, 79–105.
16. Lee, Carmen (2017): *Multilingualism Online*. London: Routledge, 5.
17. Pueblito Paisa, 31 May 2009.
18. Román-Velazquez and Retis (2021), 2.
19. Sebba, Mark (2013): Multilingualism in Written Discourse: An Approach to the Analysis of Multilingual Texts. *International Journal of Bilingualism* 17(1), 97–118.
20. Scollon, Ronald, and Suzanne B.K. Scollon (2003): *Discourses in Place: Language in the Material World*. London: Routledge.
21. There is also a model village in Colombia that uses the name Pueblito Paisa, and which is the place that appears in UK Web Archive searches prior to 2007, primarily as a tourist destination. It is unclear whether there was an intentional aim to borrow this name for the market given that 'Pueblito' has a more general use, and 'Paisa' is the widely used name for the region.
22. Cock (2011), 176.
23. Sebba (2013), 102.
24. Pueblito Paisa, 15 May 2013.
25. Pueblito Paisa, 7 April 2010.
26. Pueblito Paisa, 15 May 2013.
27. Weth, Constanze, and Kasper Juffermans (2018): The Tyranny of Writing in Language and Society. *The Tyranny of Writing: Ideologies of the Written Word*, edited by Constanze Weth and Kasper Juffermans. London: Bloomsbury, 1–18, 8.
28. Clifford, James (1997): *Routes: Travel and Translation in the Late Twentieth Century*. Cambridge, MA: Harvard University Press, 308.

29. Pueblito Paisa, 15 May 2013.
30. Pueblito Paisa, 7 April 2010.
31. Latin Corner UK, 20 March 2016.
32. Save Latin Village, 1 July 2019.
33. Taylor, Myfanwy (2019): The Haringey Council Housing & Regeneration Scrutiny Panel's scrutiny review of matters relating to Seven Sisters Market and Wards Corner. Written evidence from Dr Myfanwy Taylor, 4 June 2019, 14, https://trmcommunity-value.leeds.ac.uk/wp-content/uploads/sites/36/2019/09/19060-Scrutiny-Evidence-Submitted.pdf. Accessed 15 July 2021.
34. Brah (1996), 127.
35. Patiño-Santos, Adriana, and Rosina Márquez Reiter (2019): Banal Interculturalism: Latin Americans in Elephant and Castle, London. *Language and Intercultural Communication* 19(3), 227–241.
36. Pueblito Paisa, 7 April 2010.
37. Pueblito Paisa, 7 April 2010.
38. Office of the United Nations High Commissioner for Human Rights (2019): Plans to redevelop UK's Seven Sisters market pose human rights threat, say UN experts (26 March), https://www.ohchr.org/EN/NewsEvents/Pages/DisplayNews.aspx?NewsID=24409. Accessed 15 July 2021.
39. Massey, Doreen (2012): *For Space*. New York: Sage, 21.
40. Amin, Ash (2002): Ethnicity and the Multicultural City: Living with Diversity. *Environment and Planning A: Economy and Space* 34(6), 959–980.
41. Massey (2012), 20.
42. Giaccardi, Elisa (2012): Introduction: Reframing Heritage in a Participatory Culture. *Heritage and Social Media: Understanding Heritage in a Participatory Culture*, edited by Elisa Giaccardi. London: Routledge, 1–10.
43. Save Latin Village, 1 July 2019.
44. Save Latin Village, 10 May 2021.
45. Latin Corner UK, 8 July 2018.
46. Taylor, Diana (2010): Save As... Knowledge and Transmission in the Age of Digital Technologies. *Imagining America* 7, 6, https://surface.syr.edu/ia/7. Accessed 15 July 2021.
47. Ibid.
48. Deumert, Ana (2018): The Multivocality of Heritage: Moments, Encounters and Mobilities. *The Routledge Handbook of Language and Superdiversity*, edited by Angela Creese and Adrian Blackledge. London: Routledge, 149–164; Giaccardi (2012).
49. Latin Corner UK, 7 July 2018.
50. Blommaert and Maly (2019).

51. Hodges, Adam (2014): 'Yes, We Can': The Social Life of a Political Slogan. *Contemporary Critical Discourse Studies*, edited by Christopher Hart and Piotr Cap. London: Bloomsbury, 349–366.
52. Deumert (2018), 161.
53. Massey (2012), 9.
54. Ibid., 20f.
55. Latin Elephant, 10 May 2021.
56. Deumert (2018), 151.
57. Massey (2012), 9.

Works Cited

Amin, Ash (2002): Ethnicity and the Multicultural City: Living with Diversity. *Environment and Planning A: Economy and Space* 34(6), 959–980.

Blommaert, Jan, and Ico Maly (2019): Invisible Lines in the Online-Offline Linguistic Landscape. *Tilburg Papers in Culture Studies* 223.

Brah, Avtar (1996): *Cartographies of Diaspora: Contesting Identities*. London: Routledge.

Clifford, James (1997): *Routes: Travel and Translation in the Late Twentieth Century*. Cambridge, MA: Harvard University Press.

Cock, Juan Camilo (2011): Latin American Commercial Spaces and the Formation of Ethnic Publics in London: The Case of the Elephant and Castle. *Cross-Border Migration among Latin Americans: European Perspectives and Beyond*, edited by Cathy McIlwaine. London: Palgrave Macmillan, 175–195.

Deumert, Ana (2018): The Multivocality of Heritage: Moments, Encounters and Mobilities. *The Routledge Handbook of Language and Superdiversity*, edited by Angela Creese and Adrian Blackledge. London: Routledge, 149–164.

Giaccardi, Elisa (2012): Introduction: Reframing Heritage in a Participatory Culture. *Heritage and Social Media: Understanding Heritage in a Participatory Culture*, edited by Elisa Giaccardi. London: Routledge, 1–10.

Hayles, N. Katherine (2007): Electronic Literature: What is it?. *Doing Digital Humanities: Practice, Training, Research*, edited by Constance Crompton, Richard J. Lane, and Ray Siemens. London: Routledge, 197–226.

Hodges, Adam (2014): 'Yes, We Can': The Social Life of a Political Slogan. *Contemporary Critical Discourse Studies*, edited by Christopher Hart and Piotr Cap. London: Bloomsbury, 349–366.

Jones, Rodney H., Alice Chik, and Christoph A. Hafner (2015): Introduction: Discourse Analysis and Digital Practices. *Discourse and Digital Practices: Doing Discourse Analysis in the Digital Age*, edited by Rodney H. Jones, Alice Chik, and Christoph A. Hafner. London: Routledge, 1–17.

Latin Corner UK (captured 8 July 2018): "About Us", https://web.archive.org/web/20180708144930/http://www.latincorner.org.uk/mission-statement. Accessed 15 July 2021.

Latin Corner UK (captured 20 March 2016): "Homepage", https://web.archive.org/web/20160320132949/http://www.latincorner.org.uk/. Accessed 15 July 2021.

Latin Corner UK (captured 7 July 2018): "Homepage", https://web.archive.org/web/20180707112848/http://www.latincorner.org.uk/. Accessed 15 July 2021.

Latin Elephant (n.d.): *My Elephant Story*, https://myelephantstory.latinelephant.org/. Accessed 10 May 2021.

Lee, Carmen (2017): *Multilingualism Online*. London: Routledge.

Márquez Reiter, Rosina, and Adriana Patiño-Santos (2017): The Discursive Construction of Moral Agents among Spanish-Speaking Latin American Retailers in Elephant & Castle. *Tilburg Papers in Culture Studies* 194.

Massey, Doreen (2012): *For Space*. New York: Sage.

McIlwaine, Cathy, and Diego Bunge (2016): *Towards Visibility: The Latin American Community in London*. Queen Mary University of London, Latin American Women's Rights Service and Trust for London, https://www.trustforlondon.org.uk/publications/towards-visibility-latin-american-community-london/. Accessed 15 July 2021.

McIlwaine, Cathy, Juan Camilo Cock, and Brian Linneker (2011): *No Longer Invisible: The Latin American Community in London*. Queen Mary University of London and Trust for London, https://www.trustforlondon.org.uk/publications/no-longer-invisible-latin-american-community-london/. Accessed 15 July 2021.

Montañez, María Soledad (2020): *Lemme Hablar: Community Engagement and the Latin American Community in Southwark*. Institute of Modern Languages Research, School of Advanced Study, University of London, https://mariasoledadmontanez.files.wordpress.com/2020/12/southwark-report-october-2020.pdf. Accessed 15 July 2021.

Office of the United Nations High Commissioner for Human Rights (2019): Plans to redevelop UK's Seven Sisters market pose human rights threat, say UN experts (26 March), https://www.ohchr.org/EN/NewsEvents/Pages/DisplayNews.aspx?NewsID=24409. Accessed 15 July 2021.

Paffey, Darren (2020): Hispanic London: Language Ideologies, Policies and Practices. *Researching Language in Superdiverse Urban Contexts*, edited by Clare Mar-Molinero. Bristol: Multilingual Matters, 79–105.

Patiño-Santos, Adriana, and Rosina Márquez Reiter (2019): Banal Interculturalism: Latin Americans in Elephant and Castle, London. *Language and Intercultural Communication* 19(3), 227–241.

Pueblito Paisa (captured 31 May 2009): "Homepage", https://web.archive.org/web/20090531002909/http://www.pueblitopaisa.com. Accessed 15 July 2021.

Pueblito Paisa (captured 7 April 2010): "Misión & Valores/Values & Mission", https://web.archive.org/web/20100407181916/http://www.pueblitopaisa.com/vision/vision.htm. Accessed 15 July 2021.

Pueblito Paisa (captured 15 May 2013): "Misión & Valores/Values & Mission", https://web.archive.org/web/20130515115607/http://www.pueblitopaisa.com/vision/vision.htm. Accessed 15 July 2021.

Pueblito Paisa (captured 7 April 2010): "Planeacion Deficiente/Deficient Planning", https://web.archive.org/web/20100212035606/http://www.pueblitopaisa.com/haringey/haringey.htm. Accessed 15 July 2021.

Pueblito Paisa (captured 7 April 2010): "Quienes Somos/Who we are", https://web.archive.org/web/20100407181844/http://www.pueblitopaisa.com/who/who.htm. Accessed 15 July 2021.

Román-Velázquez, Patria, and Jessica Retis (2021): *Narratives of Migration, Relocation and Belonging: Latin Americans in London*. London: Palgrave.

Save Latin Village (captured 1 July 2019): "Homepage", https://www.webarchive.org.uk/wayback/archive/20190701070608/http://savelatinvillage.org.uk/. Accessed 15 July 2021.

Save Latin Village (2021): https://savelatinvillage.org.uk/. Accessed 10 May 2021.

Scollon, Ronald, and Suzanne B.K. Scollon (2003): *Discourses in Place: Language in the Material World*. London: Routledge.

Sebba, Mark (2013): Multilingualism in Written Discourse: An Approach to the Analysis of Multilingual Texts. *International Journal of Bilingualism* 17(1), 97–118.

Taylor, Diana (2010): Save As… Knowledge and Transmission in the Age of Digital Technologies. *Imagining America* 7, https://surface.syr.edu/ia/7. Accessed 15 July 2021.

Taylor, Myfanwy (2019): The Haringey Council Housing & Regeneration Scrutiny Panel's scrutiny review of matters relating to Seven Sisters Market and Wards Corner. Written evidence from Dr Myfanwy Taylor, 4 June 2019, https://trmcommunityvalue.leeds.ac.uk/wp-content/uploads/sites/36/2019/09/19060-Scrutiny-Evidence-Submitted.pdf. Accessed 15 July 2021.

Weth, Constanze, and Kasper Juffermans (2018): The Tyranny of Writing in Language and Society. *The Tyranny of Writing: Ideologies of the Written Word*, edited by Constanze Weth and Kasper Juffermans. London: Bloomsbury, 1–18.

Winters, Jane (2017): Coda: Web Archives for Humanities Research – Some Reflections. *The Web as History: Using Web Archives to Understand the Past and Present*, edited by Niels Brügger and Ralph Schroeder. London: University College Press, 238–247.

SECTION II

OVERLAPPING NEIGHBOURHOODS

The Translocalisation of Place

Sectarian Neighbourhoods, Boundaries and Transgressive Practices in Anna Burns' Belfast

ANNE FUCHS

Abstract
Drawing on Doreen Massey's notion of space as dynamically constituted through social interaction, the following chapter analyses the topography of segregation and the performance of subjectivity through boundary crossing in Anna Burns' novel *Milkman* (2018). Set in the early 1970s in a city modelled on Belfast, the novel predates the transnational urban reality of the globalised 21st century. I argue that *Milkman* can be classified a transnational neighbourhood novel because of the following features: the function of visible and invisible religious and social boundaries in the urban landscape; the 'ethnic' codes that define insiders and outsiders in the neighbourhood; the difficulty of inter-ethnic/inter-religious relationship building; language/idiom as an identity marker; and boundary crossing as a central aesthetic and political dimension of transnational writing. By focusing on the experiences of a young female protagonist, the narrative also foregrounds the gendered performance of subjectivity. I will also explore how in the context of sectarian surveillance the protagonist's practice of reading-while-walking is an act of resistance which recovers an interior space of subjectivity.

Introduction

Anna Burns' Booker Prize-winning novel *Milkman* (2018) must surely appear as an odd choice for a volume on the transnational neighbourhood. Set in Belfast during the 1970s at a time when the Northern Ireland Conflict, known as 'the Troubles', escalated and violence peaked, the novel deals with everyday sectarian life in a working-class Catholic neighbourhood. In this chapter I will argue that *Milkman* can be read as a transnational neighbourhood novel precisely because it explores boundary crossing as a transnational practice of resistance to ethnonationalism and sectarianism. In so doing, it exposes the 'ethnic' codes that define insiders and outsiders in the neighbourhood. The story is told as a first-person narrative by a nameless female narrator who, decades after the events, records her troubling encounter with the eponymous character as an 18-year-old young woman. Adopting the perspective of her younger alter ego, the narrator's style is marked throughout by a Northern Irish idiom and a wry and at times comical tone.

The story begins when the milkman – a 41-year-old married man and a powerful member of a paramilitary organisation who has the reputation of stalking young women – drives up in a van, offering the protagonist a lift as she is walking home from work while reading Walter Scott's *Ivanhoe*, a historical novel that allows her to escape into the world of medieval romance and chivalry. Her attraction to a genre which conveys the spirit and manners of a past period only accentuates her entrapment in a present which is characterised by deep sectarian divisions.[1] The title character is a creepy and dangerous man whose harmless name belies his violent character: "He wasn't our milkman. I don't think he was anybody's. He didn't take milk orders. There was no milk about him. He didn't even deliver milk. Also, he didn't drive a milk lorry."[2] A second intimidating encounter takes place in the local park, where he has preyed on her and starts jogging alongside her without her consent. The park episode gives rise to rumours in the gossipy world of her neighbourhood that she is having an affair with this man. A third encounter occurs when she is walking home after her French class. On this occasion, milkman threatens to kill her boyfriend if she does not break up with him. As the narrator retrospectively observes, "maybe-boyfriend was to be killed under the catch-all of the political problems even if, in reality, the milkman was going to kill him out of disguised jealousy over me" (115). Once again, she refuses to accept the stalker's offer of a lift because

> I knew I must not – as a crucial bottom line – ever get into his cars. It seemed everything had microscoped down to the last one threshold, as if to do so, to cross over, to get into one, would signal some 'end of' as well as 'commencement of'. (136)

A fourth encounter takes place after she has found out that her boyfriend is having an affair. Walking home feeling numb and confused, the milkman's van draws up, and this time she steps inside: "I was Milkman's *fait accompli* all along" (299).

The novel offers a forensic account of sectarian division by exploring the mechanisms hindering the building of mixed communities that could tolerate or even welcome diversity and difference. A particular focus is the gendered performance of power and violence: while sectarianism is a brutally enacted patriarchal project, it is, however, also contingent on the support of the powerful women in the community, a point to which I return later. By homing in on complex local mechanisms of social identity formation under extreme conditions, the novel lays bare everyday practices of inclusion and exclusion that pose obstacles to the formation of pluralistic neighbourhoods.

The following analysis focuses, firstly, on the various groups of characters that inhabit the sectarian world and negotiate its tribal rules in their everyday lives. The analysis of the topography of segregation then illuminates the sectarian encoding of place and space. In a third step, the chapter analyses transgressive practices that point to the possibility of a more diverse neighbourhood and transformative change. A brief sketch of the debates in anthropology, sociology, urban theory and geography attempts to provide conceptual clarity and a transnational lens for the ensuing narratological analysis.

Community, Neighbourhood and Space

Put simply, 'neighbourhood' is an everyday term, designating the daily experiences and practices of people who inhabit and share a defined local arena over a period of time. In contemporary urban studies, social geography and anthropology, the concept is widely used to debate competing notions of territorial belonging in the era of globalisation and hypermobility. For Talja Blokland a neighbourhood is "a geographically circumscribed, built environment that people use practically and symbolically".[3] Blokland's succinct definition points to three important features: firstly, a neighbourhood is a bounded place in a predominantly urban setting; secondly, neighbourhoods engender social relations through practices and rules; thirdly, neighbourhoods accrue symbolic meaning and capital which – depending on social and economic factors – can go up and down.

As a locality within an urban setting, neighbourhoods require other adjacent neighbourhoods for their self-definition. Even though the boundaries between neighbourhoods are often fluid, a shared sense of what constitutes a neighbourhood prevails. A neighbourhood appears, in the words of Arjun Appadurai, "to be simply a set of contexts, historically received, materially embedded, socially appropriate, naturally unproblematic."[4] From Appadurai's anthropological perspective, then, neighbourhoods have a particular function: they produce local subjects through "localized rituals, social categories, expert practitioners, and informed audiences, (who) are required in order for new members […] to be made temporary or permanent local subjects."[5] However, when local subjects engage in the reproduction of their own neighbourhood, they unwittingly create other contexts that potentially explode the material and symbolic boundaries of their locality. And so it is that the production of neighbourhoods always entails "a relational consciousness of other neighbourhoods."[6]

As Paul Watts and Peer Smets argue, in our own era of hypermobility neighbourhoods are "spatially fixed and determinate places"; they are, however, "also simultaneously being constantly made and remade via flows of people as they circulate in and out of, within and around these residential locales."⁷ Ulrike Hanna Meinhof aptly describes the contemporary city as a space of "negotiation and encounter between culturally diverse people", which is "in principle and practice disruptive of the often monocultural imaginary of the nation-state."⁸ Commonplace encounters with diversity and otherness in everyday life not only challenge the imaginary of the bounded nation-state,⁹ but they also corrode the notion of anchorage in local traditions. While the term 'neighbourhood' is sometimes used as a synonym for community, the latter is more narrowly associated with patriarchal norms of communal togetherness bounded by rootedness and heritage. 'Neighbourhood' designates a more porous, dynamic and diverse arena in which different forms of attachment can coexist. In response to migration and globalisation, urban studies and geography have re-theorised neighbourhood practices by deconstructing the conventional insider/outsider binary. For example, Michael Savage and his co-authors have coined the useful term "elective belonging" for forms of residential attachment that are no longer rooted in and authorised by historical ties to a particular locality. "Elective belonging", they write, embodies

> attachments that permit various kinds of global connections to be drawn. Fixed places thus play crucial roles within globalising processes. They become sites for new kinds of solidarities among people who chose to live in particular places, and whose deep concern about where they live is unlikely to be overlain with extraneous concerns arising from knowledge of others who have historically lived in the place. A new potential for collective action is made possible.¹⁰

In her seminal book *For Space,* the geographer Doreen Massey too tackled the "perniciousness of exclusivist localisms" on the one hand and "the grim inequalities of today's hegemonic form of globalisation" on the other.¹¹ Rejecting the idea of an organically grown place or neighbourhood as the source of a stable identity in a world in flux, she argues that such essentialising definitions turn local places into "the locus of denial, of attempted withdrawal from invasion/difference."¹² In order to overcome such defensive localism, Massey reclaims and redefines the notion of space. Liberating space from the shackles of structuralism, she understands space dynamically as the "product of interrelations; as constituted through interactions, from the immensity of the global to the intimately tiny."¹³ In so doing she promotes a pluralistic understanding of space "as the sphere of the possibility of the existence of multiplicity [...], as the sphere in which distinct trajectories coexist; as the sphere therefore of coexisting heterogeneity." Space is "always under construction";¹⁴ it is "a simultaneity of stories so far", that is, it is constituted by social practices and evolving narratives.¹⁵ For Massey, then, space is a political project which takes care of what she calls our *throwntogetherness*: space understood in this way is a chance which "may set us down next to the unexpected neighbour."[16] Faced with "the inevitable negotiations presented by our throwntogetherness", Massey makes the case for a new "relational politics of place", which would also give rise to a "politics of connectivity" in response to globalisation.[17]

People

The world so vividly evoked in *Milkman* is far removed from the challenges and opportunities of the transnational age of hypermobility. Burns' characters are moored in a society that is dominated by sectarian conflict, the militarisation of everyday life, and the absence of a horizon that extends beyond the parochial community. The main participants in the conflict – the IRA (Irish Republican Army), the INLA (Irish National Liberation Army), the UVF (Ulster Volunteer Force), the UDA (Ulster Defence Force) and the state actors (the British Army and RUC) – are never named in the novel. While the protagonist's own community is in the hands of the "renouncers-of-the-state", the enemy districts are controlled by the "defenders-of-the-state" and are as such absolute no-go areas (22). With the exception of the eponymous character whose family name turns out to be "Milkman",[18] none of the characters carry proper names. As in a medieval morality play, they are personified and either known through their roles and hierarchical positions in the community or through their tribal and family affiliations. The first-person protagonist is merely known as "middle sister" who lives with her "ma" and the "wee sisters". She is close to "third brother-in-law" but not to her "eldest sister" and "first-brother-in-law". Second sister is an outcast who

> brought disgrace upon the family as well as upon the community by marrying-out to some state-forces person then going to live in some country over the water, maybe even *that* country over *that* water, with the renouncers in our district warning her never to return. (48)

Middle sister is in a relationship with "maybe-boyfriend", a car mechanic who lives in another Catholic district. As the adverb indicates, their relationship is precarious because they are unsure about the right level of intimacy and closeness (43). A lover of classic cars, maybe-boyfriend gets into trouble over the motor components of an old Bentley which he won in a raffle and enjoys disassembling. Even though the broken engine is beyond repair and has no market value, the "supercharger" is quickly associated with the wrong kind of symbolic capital:

a neighbour suggests that the engine represents the "flag of the country from 'over the water'" which "was also that same flag from over the road" (26). The fact that the British flag is not engraved on any engine parts plays no role in the sectarian argument. Because the brand is viewed as a material manifestation of British domination, owning any bit of the car is emblematic of an act of treason: "to bring that flag in then, was divisive, indicative too, of a traitorous kowtowing and a betrayal most monstrous over which even informers and those who marry-out would be held in higher esteem" (26).

Even though the renouncers-of-the-state rule by means of a pervasive regime of intimidation, coercion and violence, they are considered "the good guys, the heroes, the men of honour, the dauntless, legendary warriors, outnumbered, risking their lives, standing up for rights, guerrilla-fashion, against all odds" (118). Members of the paramilitary faction range from the milkman to the narrator's second brother. Like middle sister's longest friend he is an active supporter of the cause. Both get killed in paramilitary action. "Somebody Mc Somebody" is a low-life type who falsely believes that he is "some top-drawer renouncer-of-the-state" (116) and attempts to rape the protagonist. The more high-ranking renouncers also keep trophy women: known as the "groupie women", their reputation in the community is extremely low because they are seen as parasitic hangers-on (121).

But it is the "pious women" and "gossip women" who pull the strings in the community and manage everyday life: they act as guardians of the status quo by circulating a cacophony of rumours that censor deviant behaviour. For example, the rumour about the protagonist's affair with the milkman is started by first brother-in-law, who instructs his wife to act as a conduit and tell the mother. However, the rumour is worthless without the collective endorsement by the "pious women of the neighbourhood" (47), who especially drop by to see "ma" in her house. Kai Wigendt points out that "rumour lies at the threshold of the individual and the crowd": while a rumour is often started by an individual who, like the first brother-in-law, tends to author the rumour with malicious intent, it is at the same time "an opinion attributed to no one specific but to 'everyone.'"[19] Rumours are kept alive by a chain of hearsay which involves the community as a whole. As pieces of news or stories that might be true or invented, rumours feed on contradictory claims. Rumours operate in the realm of imaginary storytelling and are subject to collective editing. As in the game of Chinese whispers, "every time a rumour is passed on there is a real possibility of deliberate or accidental distortion, and no corresponding possibility of correction."[20] And so it is that according to the pious women's rumour-mongering, middle sister's lover is the milkman but he is also a car mechanic; he is in his early forties but also "about his twenties"; he is connected and unconnected at the same time; he is an intelligence officer "who gathers the information on the target then hands it to the trigger men" (48). But at least he is, as the women sum up, a "renouncer-of-the-state and not a defender-of-the-state; something to be grateful for" (48). Their collective gossiping authenticates the rumour: the fact that their various pronouncements are incompatible does not matter at all because they demonstrate the pious women's central role as authorities in the community. While the men enact power through a regime of threats, coercion and violence within and outside the community, the women police the community discursively and performatively through everyday interactions. The implication is that patriarchal control of the district needs to enlist matriarchal backing.

The pious women thus occupy an ambivalent position: on the one hand, they are collaborators of the patriarchy by propping up a system that subjugates women; on the other, they have accrued a degree of power by mediating in inner-community conflicts and curbing the excesses of male violence. A central example is their handling of an escalating conflict between a small group of seven feminists from the district. Known as the "issues women", the feminists have dared to openly challenge the paramilitary control of the district by holding regular meetings in a garden shed: they have even invited a woman from "the other side's religion and also from the country 'over there'" to attend their gatherings (156). While the very idea of feminism is provocative in this male-dominated world, it is the presence of the woman from the other side that causes outrage. Local rumours quickly turn her into "an enemy to entrap into informership our seven naïve and dotty women" (157). When the renouncers threaten to kill the seven feminists because they refuse to disassociate themselves from the eighth woman, the traditional women throw themselves "into action" and make a deal with the paramilitaries (158). By tactically belittling the feminists and denying their transformative potential – "You can't kill them. They're simpletons. Intellectual simpletons. Academe! That's all they are fit for" (163) – they manage to appease the men. In return for not killing the defiant feminists, the eighth woman from downtown promises to stay out of the area (164). The women's mediation thus "spelled the end of any outside issue woman with expansive worldviews coming to visit our totalitarian enclave" (164). On the one hand, then, the normal women endorse and uphold the pernicious localism of a community that disciplines otherness. On the other, however, the community incorporates its own misfits, including "tablets girl", "nuclear boy", the "issues women", the protagonist, and the real milkman – a kind man who helps out "ma" but is generally known as "the man who didn't love anybody" (140).[21] Even though these characters are "deemed beyond the pale" (60), as long as they stay on the right side of the sectarian divide they are tolerated as the community's "own others". The notion that the community is bound by kinship, loyalty and a shared purpose is thus a convenient projection which covers over a much more fractured and diverse underlying reality. By inscribing otherness into sameness, Burns' ethnographic portrayal pulverises the very notion of homogenous community, while also tracking the first green shoots of a more pluralistic neighbourhood.

Places

At first sight, the sectarian topography of Burns' *Milkman* appears antithetical to Massey's pluralistic, interactive and performative understanding of a shared space. There are no uncontrolled flows of people circulating in and out of the segregated neighbourhoods to form elective bonds. Tribal roots and religious identities limit the geographical and social routes in and out of the neighbourhood. While the relational consciousness of other neighbourhoods (as identified by Appadurai) plays a pivotal role in local habitus formation, in the novel such relational knowledge is primarily used to bolster rather than explode existing boundaries. Evidently, there is little transformative scope in this sectarian setting. And yet, we will see that Burns' narrative subtly tracks the protagonist's pathways out of the community into areas that dislodge the accepted rules of community formation. The protagonist's choreography of movement in particular performs space as a "simultaneity of stories so far" in Massey's sense.

Burns' ethnographic perspective is simultaneously extremely local and universal: even though the setting is modelled on Belfast during the Troubles, it is abstracted from the actual geography of the city and from the real socio-political conflict to allow for an ethnographic analysis of the collective and bottom-up performance of sectarianism. The personification of characters is matched by the employment of abstract descriptors for all locations: real locales such as the Catholic Falls Road or the Protestant Shankill Road are replaced by nonpartisan terms such as "the area" (5), "the community" (12) and "the district" (45). The omission of the term "neighbourhood" is deliberate and signals the protagonist's emotional and cognitive distance from the parochial practices of social identity formation.

There are only two geographical reference points outside Belfast: mainland Britain is the country "over the water" (26). A mere extension of the inaccessible areas "over the road", it is enemy territory and as such a taboo: those who move there are stigmatised as outsiders for the rest of their lives and return at their own peril. On the other hand, the neighbouring Irish State is also obscurely referred to as the country "over the border". Even though the Irish tricolour provides a potent symbol for paramilitary funerals – the Irish flag is draped around the coffins of the 'martyrs' who have died fighting for the cause (130) – there is no sense that Burns' protagonists perceive the Irish Republic as a viable political alternative to the status quo. They inhabit an extremely parochial and partisan world without a transnational horizon.

And yet, even though this topography of segregation buttresses tribal belonging and a stagnant sense of rootedness in the locality, there is one district in which "elective belonging" (Michael Savage) and the green shoots of a new "politics of connectivity" (Doreen Massey) come into view. The so-called "red-light district" is a single street sandwiched between middle sister's and maybe-boyfriend's neighbourhoods:

> [I]t was called the red-light district not because red-light things went on in it but because it was where young couples went to live together who didn't want to get married or conventionally to settle down. It was not wanting to be wed at sixteen, babies from seventeen, to settle on the settee in front of the television to die like most parents by twenty. They wanted to try out – weren't sure but something else. (41)

As the locus of experimental co-habitation, the red-light district is a performative space in which translocal and inter-religious modes of living are tentatively explored. According to the narrator, the young people's lack of certainty of how to live a good life gives rise to a subculture of openness which, in the context of the para/militarised enforcement of segregation, appears as radically transgressive. The whispered rumour that "two men lived there, I mean together" (41) voices a titillating fear of otherness which is sutured by the subconscious recognition that the improper is the repressed flipside of the collective display of propriety. Media reports that the red-light district is "threatening to spill over into the next street" (41) amplify the perception that the strict boundaries between self and other, insider and outsider are already breaking down. Unsurprisingly, this small arena of practised co-habitation provokes a sectarian reaction from the "normal people, meaning married couples" (42), who move out of the area so as not to be contaminated by the "depravity, decadence, demoralisation, dissemination of pessimism, outrages to propriety and illicit moral affairs" (42). From the prevailing sectarian perspective, the immorality of sex outside wedlock is topped by inter-religious co-habitation. It is interesting to note that the protagonist's own knowledge of the red-light district is second-hand: she has never set a foot inside it because entering this zone of otherness would further stigmatise her as a social misfit in her own district. And so it is that she turns down her boyfriend's proposal to move together to the red-light district. In the life of the protagonist, the red-light district ultimately remains an imaginary island of outlandish otherness.

Burns' topography contains one further area that transgresses the sectarian schema of binary division. The so-called "ten-minute area" is a desolate and spooky no-man's land through which people hurry because it was "and always had been, some bleak, eerie, Mary Celeste little place" (81). Shaped in a round and dominated by three churches whose towers seem to converge to form a "witch's hat" (81), this area evokes extraterritorial otherness reaching back into mythical times (84).[22] Even though there are offices, residential buildings and even some shops, which display 'Open' signs on their doors, the ten-minute area appears to be completely devoid of human life. Nobody has been seen to ever enter or leave these shops nor do any people ever step on or off buses at the local bus stop. The ghostly symbolism of the ten-minute area accentuates its function in the collective unconscious. As a site of overdetermined uncanniness in Freud's sense, it uproots and defies the rigid norms of rooted and bounded belonging that organise and uphold social life on both sides of the sectarian divide.[23] The temporal signifier marks the ten-minute area as a dangerous zone of dislocation, upending the idea that identity can ever be (fully) anchored in place. This uncanny site is perhaps the only Foucauldian heterotopia in the novel "in which the real sites [...] that can be found within culture are simultaneously represented, contested and inverted."[24]

Practices

Immersed in a predominantly sectarian topography which curtails freedom of movement, middle sister engages in two practices of everyday life that aim to detach her from this entropied world: she enjoys running and reading novels while walking home. Far more than a typical fitness regime, her regular runs through the local parks performatively reclaim open space with different directions and trajectories. Even though the park is under the surveillance of state agents who hide behind shrubs with their cameras, the act of running transports her into a sphere of emancipatory mobility, agency and speed. In the history of emancipation, women runners had to fight hard for acceptance: until the mid-20th century, women were barred from long-distance running, which was associated with masculine endurance, muscular strength and virile speed.[25]

At the beginning of Burns' novel, we briefly encounter the protagonist running on her own before the milkman shows up out of nowhere, "falling into step beside me where he'd never been before: instantly we were running together and it looked as if always we were running together" (5). Enforcing an unwanted proximity, the milkman first controls the pace before slowing it down to a walk:

> He implied it was because of pacing, that he was slowing the run because of pacing, but I knew pacing and for me, walking during running was not that. I could not say so, however, for I could not be fitter than this man, could not be more

knowledgeable about my own regime than this man, because the conditioning of males and females here would never have allowed that. This was the 'I'm male and you're female' territory. (7f.)

Rather than indicating the milkman's defeat by the young woman's superior fitness, the reduction of speed down to a walking pace is a menacing act which asserts male dominance over women. By aborting the run, the milkman symbolically closes off the park as an open arena in which different routes and trajectories intersect. Burns' young protagonist understands very well that the milkman's demonstrative assertion of authority aims to harness her mobility by 'reterritorialising' this space. The episode finishes with the milkman censoring the protagonist's habits of running and walking: "Not sure [...] about this arunning, about all that awalking. Too much arunning and awalking" (9). For the milkman, then, middle sister's own fitness regime constitutes an intolerable violation of the very principle of sectarian control. Once more the tribal world has closed in on middle sister who, after this intimidating episode, stops her running, before resuming it in the company of third brother-in-law. Equipped with a "superb physicality and instinctive understanding of the combative male code of the district" (12f.), the latter figure is characterised by his "atypical high regard for all things female", and as such he is an obvious choice as running companion (12). Nevertheless, by seeking his protection middle sister inescapably assigns authority to her male chaperon. What was originally a liberating leisure activity now morphs into a quasi-military endurance test. And so it is that, in the course of their running, third-brother-in-law admonishes middle sister that her habit of reading-while-walking is "not safe, not natural, not dutiful to self, that by doing so you're switching yourself off, you're abandoning yourself, [...] that you're putting yourself at the mercy of hard and cunning and unruly forces" (58). Somebody could sneak up, he explains, as her defences are down, "no longer alert, no longer strenuously reconnoitring and surveying the environment" (58). In this sectarian society, both runners and pedestrians must act like paramilitary observers on the lookout for ambushes and traps. In the following I want to further explore the complexity of reading-while-walking in dialogue with Michel de Certeau's *The Practice of Everyday Life*.[26]

As many commentators have observed, de Certeau's book has become a major source for scholars of urban mobility, even though it is, on the whole, abstract and lacking "an empirical description of movement and walking in specific localities."[27] The success of de Certeau may have something to do with his anti-Foucauldian perspective: instead of illuminating the pervasive regime of power as constituted by discourse, he proposes a "science of singularity,"[28] which attributes emancipatory agency to urban dwellers in their everyday lives. Envisaging a theory of resistance to modernity, de Certeau famously distinguishes between strategies and tactics: while strategies service power by creating monolithic and static spaces, tactics are elusive, mobile and hard to pin down. Tactics are always "on the watch for opportunities that must be seized on the wing";[29] they are characterised by "microbe-like, singular and plural practices" and "surreptitious creativities" that pulverise centralising power.[30] Urban walking serves as a prime example: like the speech act, walking is an everyday act of expression and democratic emancipation,[31] which "affirms, suspects, tries out, transgresses, respects, etc., the trajectories it 'speaks'."[32] De Certeau describes the pedestrians' intersecting pathways in terms of illegible networks which "compose a manifold story that has neither author nor spectator, shaped out of fragments of trajectories and alterations of spaces" (93). In a move with significant consequences, de Certeau then characterises urban walking as a mode of illegible writing – a kind of collective automatic *écriture* unwittingly produced by the footfall of urban pedestrians.

To be sure, this celebration of walking as a mode of collective authorship accentuates the performative and transgressive effect of this quotidian practice, a point which is of immediate relevance for Burns' novel. And yet, the equation of urban walking with illegible writing results in a bizarre depreciation of reading: reading for de Certeau is neither a mode of creative immersion nor a form of critical engagement but merely an act of distancing from the fluid world of the everyday in the service of power and authority.[33] Evidently, de Certeau mistakes the reader for a mere scanner of surfaces: while the scanner's main operation is indeed optical, the reader's activity is not primarily surface-oriented. Reading requires active engagement of one's aesthetic and intellectual abilities as well as the imaginative capacity to engage with alternative worlds. Reading can be immersive or critical, pleasurable or blissful – to employ Roland Barthes' terminology.[34] Reading is a radical act of boundary crossing that activates the imaginary in the service of alternative world-making.[35]

Returning to Burns' novel, it is immediately evident that the conditions for walking as a collective practice of authorship in de Certeau's sense do not exist in her world. The sectarian practice of policing and blocking urban pathways inhibits the free movement of urban crowds, forestalling their intersecting choreography of emancipation. Middle sister's passage through the various districts is under constant surveillance by her own family, the wider community, the milkman, the renouncers-of-the-state, and even the state forces whose cameras she hears clicking whenever she goes running in the park. While tactical opportunities for transgressions exist, they are limited. The constant threat of violence also thwarts the mobility of the *flâneur*, who, as Benjamin famously observed, "goes botanizing on the asphalt".[36] As Anke Gleber comments, *flânerie* requires a leisurely pace which resists the functionalisation and objectification of modern life.[37] It feasts on visual thrills and electrifying diversions, offering "a survey of life in the metropolis that clings to the surface of things."[38] Reacting to the centralising forces of modernity, the *flâneur* thus cultivates a cinematic vision which scans urban life for interesting scenes and marginal details. Reacting to totalitarian sectarianism, middle sister's practice of reading-while-walking has the opposite effect: it deliberately shuts out any visual engagement with her environment: "I knew that by reading while I walked I was losing touch in a crucial sense with communal up-to-dateness and that, indeed, was risky" (65). Because sectarian vigilance excises the experience of the city as a pleasurable spectacle or scene, she retreats into the world of historical fiction while walking home: "Every weekday, rain or shine, gunplay or bombs, stand-off or riots, I preferred to walk home reading my latest book. This would be a nineteenth century book because I did not like twentieth-century books because I did not like the twentieth century" (5). By immersing herself in a world of make-belief, middle sister temporarily escapes the bleakness of a tribal reality which has impoverished the collective imagination by disavowing symbolic ambiguity. And so it is that middle sister's habit of reading-while-walking puts her "beyond the pale". Longest friend elaborates the sectarian dogmatism in the following way:

> 'It's the way you do it – reading books, whole books, taking notes, checking footnotes, underlining passages as if you're at some desk or something, in a little private study or something, the curtains closed, your lamp on, a cup of tea beside you, essay being penned – your discourses, your lubrications. It's disturbing. It's deviant. It's optical illusional. Not public-spirited' (200).

The implication here is that reading fiction in the privacy of the home would not cause such offence because, as a private act of purposeful study, it would not pose a challenge to the code of sectarian vigilance and conformist behaviour in the public domain. Reading-while-walking, by contrast, is a highly individualistic practice that visibly enacts middle sister's escape into her innermost self in defiance of the collective. In the sectarian setting, reading-while-walking is intolerably provocative precisely because it stages and asserts an impenetrable subjectivity under the public eye.

The subversive discovery of space "as the sphere of the possibility of the existence of multiplicity" (Massey) figures prominently in two central episodes which revolve around the perception of the colours of the sky. Maybe-boyfriend has invited middle sister for a drive to the seaside to look at the sunset, a romantic escapade which deviates from the sectarian cult of toughened masculinity. As she stands beside him, middle sister is at first unsure if "maybe-boyfriend should be going to sunsets" (75) at all before realising

> that something out there – or something in me – then changed. It fell into place because now, instead of blue, blue and more blue – the official blue everyone understood and thought was up there – the truth hit my senses. It became clear as I gazed that there was no blue out there at all. For the first time I saw colours, just as a week later in his French class also was I seeing colours. (77)

This epiphany of colours "blending and mixing, sliding and extending, new colours arriving, all colours combining, colours going on forever" (77) momentarily explodes the binary categories, stereotypes and clichés that regiment everyday language, down to the level of the sectarian inflection of words.[39] But this transitory sunset experience only gains a truly transformative dimension during one of the French classes when the teacher reads out a literary passage in which the sky is described in evocative terms. Because the students collectively assert that such "fancy footwork" is unnecessarily "complicating things" (69) – "'Yeah!' cried us and also we cried: 'A spade's a spade!', also the popular '*Le ciel est bleu!*' and '*What's the point? There is no point*'" (70) – the teacher confronts their obstinate righteousness and formulaic interpretation by marching them out of the classroom and making them look

> from a brand new perspective, where the sun – enormous and of the most gigantic orange-red colour – in a sky too, with no blue in it – was going down behind buildings in a section of windowpane.
>
> As for this sky, it was now a mix of pink and lemon with a glow of mauve behind it. It had changed colours during our short trip along the corridor and before our eyes was changing colours yet. An emerging gold above the mauve was moving towards a slip of silver, with a different mauve in a corner drifting in from the side. Then there was further pinking. Then more lilac. Then a turquoise that pressed clouds – not white – out of its ways. (73)

Both episodes employ the hackneyed image of the sunset to new effect: instead of framing a textbook romantic love story, here the sunset signifies liberation from the type of formulaic convention that blocks the recognition of otherness. Burns' evocative description of the changing colour palette reclaims the sky into an open space and cosmic horizon that transcends the pernicious localism of sectarianism.

Conclusion

For Appadurai, the long-term reproduction of a cohesive local neighbourhood "depends on the seamless interaction of localized spaces and times with local subjects possessed of the knowledge to reproduce locality."[40] We have seen that in Burns' *Milkman* such local knowledge revolves around tribal rules and identifiers which buttress a defensive notion of community and the sectarian division of society. Here the relational consciousness of other neighbourhoods is meant to suppress explorative cross-overs, mutual exchanges and elective belonging. The routes in and out of the neighbourhood are subject to rigid sectarian protocols which police and punish transgressive mobility.

Burns' novel especially highlights the gendered production of locality by means of the asymmetrical power of men over women. As the narrator observes, "in each of those totalitarian-run enclaves, it was the male paramilitaries who, more than anyone, ruled over the areas with final say" (120). A prime example of such totalitarian enforcement is the running episode: by forcing middle sister against her will to run alongside him and at his pace, the milkman symbolically harnesses the young woman's liberating mobility, while also 'reterritorialising' the park as a quasi-paramilitary zone. While the men's paramilitary practices operate on a scale of violence that ranges from intimidation and threats to murder, the women play their part by overseeing tribal affiliation and identity formation in everyday life: they sanction and promote marriage at a young age inside the community. Because unbridled male violence would lead to a collapse of the local community, the men need to recruit the women, who act as brokers in local conflicts. On the one hand, their rumour-mongering censors all signs of difference; on the other, it also provides a vernacular script for sectarian belonging. But Burns' novel also highlights the high effort and cost involved in the reproduction of the sectarian locality: the maintenance and reinforcement of boundaries against the threat of otherness necessitates constant vigilance and a regime of surveillance which is hard to maintain. And so it is that, in spite of the sectarian rule, the neighbourhood is exposed to corrosive effects that emanate from adjacent localities. The ten-minute area is the ghostly zone of non-belonging that uproots the very idea of safe anchorage in place: it is a site of projection for the collective unconscious which is latently haunted by the long-term effects of sectarian division and violence. By contrast, the red-light district signals the advent of experimental forms of elective belonging that give rise to new gender politics and inter-religious mixing. Burns' novel focuses on small-scale everyday practices which reveal the incremental nature of social change: the French class not only creates a rare contact zone for the sectarian communities, but it also prompts a deeper reflection on the symbolic function of language. Learning

French, looking at sunsets, running and reading-while-walking may be viewed as politically insignificant actions; and yet, in the sectarian and violent world of the novel, they are significant steps on the long road to the translocation and transnationalisation of place.

Notes

1. On the historical novel see Georg Lukács' classic: *The Historical Novel*, translated from the German by Hannah and Stanley Mitchel; introduction by Frederic Jameson. Lincoln: University of Nebraska Press, 1983.
2. Burns, Anna (2018): *Milkman*. London: Faber & Faber, 2. All page references are henceforth cited in the text.
3. Blokland, Talja (2003): *Urban Bonds*. Cambridge: Polity Press, 213.
4. Appadurai, Arjun (1996): The Production of Locality. *Modernity at Large: Cultural Dimensions of Globalization*. Minneapolis: University of Minnesota Press, 178–199, 185.
5. Ibid.
6. Ibid., 186.
7. Watts, Paul, and Peer Smets (2014): Introduction. *Mobilities and Neighbourhood Belonging in Cities and Suburbs*, edited by Paul Watts and Peer Smets. Basingstoke: Palgrave Macmillan, 1–23, 5.
8. Meinhof, Ulrike Hanna (2011): Introducing Borders, Networks, Neighbourhoods: Conceptual Frames and Social Practices. *Negotiating Multicultural Europe: Borders, Networks, Neighbourhoods*, edited by Heidi Armbruster and Ulrike Hanna Meinhof. Basingstoke: Palgrave Macmillan, 1–25, 7.
9. According to Benedict Anderson's famous definition the nation is "is an imagined political community – and imagined as both inherently limited and sovereign." Anderson, Benedict (1983): *Imagined Communities: Reflections on the Origin and Spread of Nationalism*. London: Verso, 5. Anderson's focus was on the role of print capitalism in the formation of the nation-state. Printed media enabled the standardisation of language across regions as well as the articulation of national consciousness. In the age of hypermobility and social media, such imagined cohesion is far more difficult to achieve.
10. Savage, Mike, Gaynor Bagnell, and Brian Longhurst (2005): The Limits of Local Attachment. *Globalization and Belonging*, edited by Mike Savage, Gaynor Bagnell, and Brian Longhurst. London: Sage, 29–55, 53.
11. Massey, Doreen (2005): *For Space*. Los Angeles and London: Sage, 6.
12. Ibid., 5f.
13. Ibid., 9.

14. Ibid. Similarly Tim Cresswell and Peter Merriman observe that "spaces are not simply contexts; they are also actively produced by the act of moving. [...] Practices of mobility animate and co-produce spaces, places and landscapes." See Cresswell, Tim, and Peter Merriman (2013): Introduction. *Geographies of Mobilities: Practices, Places, Subjects*, edited by Tim Cresswell and Peter Merriman. Farnham: Ashgate, 1–15, 7.
15. Massey (2005), 9.
16. Ibid., 151.
17. Ibid., 181.
18. However, the revelation that Milkman is his actual family name comes rather late in the novel. It is part of the narrator's ironising strategy that she keeps referring to this paramilitary man as 'the milkman': it accentuates the vast gap between the association of milk with whiteness, innocence and care on the one hand and paramilitary violence on the other.
19. Wiegandt, Kai (2008): Partial Truth: Rumour in Conrad's Heart of Darkness. *Poetica* 40(3/4), 397–424, 398.
20. Coady, David (2012): Rumors and Rumor-Mongers. *What We Believe Now: Applying Epistemology to Contemporary Issues*, edited by David Coady. Oxford: Wiley-Blackwell, 88. However, Coady sets out to show that rumours can be subjected to evaluation procedures involving estimates of plausibility, consistency and the channels of communication. He claims that "most of the people spreading the rumour are interested in whether it is true"; otherwise, "there would be little reason to warn people against believing them" (92). His focus on the truth value of rumours underestimates their illocutive and performative functions, which can range from stigmatising others to creating a discursive community.
21. The real milkman is deemed beyond the pale because he did not put up with a stockpile of arms which the renouncers were hiding in his back garden. Outraged, he dumped the stockpile in the middle of the street. In the eyes of the community, his unacceptable public confrontation with the paramilitaries is compounded by the fact that he started shouting at children who were playing close to the guns, which earns him the label of the man who did not love anybody (140).
22. The explosion of a bomb in the area destroys one of the three churches and gives rise to frenzied speculation about why anyone would want to plant a bomb "in a dead, creepy, grey place" (82), until it is established that it had been "a history bomb, an antiquity Greek and Roman bomb, a big, giant Nazi bomb" (83).
23. Freud, Sigmund (1999): Das Unheimliche. *Gesammelte Werke*, vol. 12, edited by Anna Freud et al. Frankfurt: Fischer, 292–368.
24. Foucault, Michel (1986): Of Other Spaces: Utopias and Heterotopias, translated by Jay Miskowiec. *Diacritics* 16(1), 22–27, 24.
25. Right up until World War I, the dress code made it very difficult for girls and women to run for any length of time. Running flouted the norms of feminine propriety and con-

duct, connoting danger and harm to the frail female body. Women were excluded from all Olympic track and field competitions until 1928, when the longest race was the 800 metres. After 1928 the 800 metres were banned once more and not reinstated until the Summer Olympics in 1960, where women were for the first time allowed to participate in five running events. However, it was only in 1984 that women were granted the right to compete in an Olympic marathon. As Jennifer Hargreaves shows, gender stereotyping has accompanied the history of the modern Olympics: arguments about the female ability, health and potential damage to their reproductive system show a deep-seated gender bias. See Hargreaves, Jennifer (1994): *Sporting Females: Critical Issues in the History and Sociology of Women's Sports*. London: Routledge, 209–235, 217.

26. De Certeau, Michel (1984): *The Practice of Everyday Life*, translated by Steven Rendall. Berkeley, Los Angeles and London: University of California Press.
27. Vergunst, Joe (2017): Key Figure of Mobility: The Pedestrian. *Social Anthropology/Anthropologie Sociale* 25, Issue 1, 13–27, 19. In the words of Jon Mitchell, it is best described as "a theology of the human spirit as redemptive counterpoint to the moral bankruptcy of modernity." Mitchell, Jon P. (2007): A fourth critic of the Enlightenment: Michel de Certeau and the Ethnography of Subjectivity. *Social Anthropology/Anthropologie Sociale* 15(1), 89–106, 103.
28. De Certeau (1984), ix.
29. Ibid., xix.
30. Ibid., 96. De Certeau's distinction not only reinforces the problematic space-time dichotomy but it also conceives of power as a monolithic and totalising instrument that is divorced from any agency. As Massey observes, "[n]ot only does this both overestimate the coherence of 'the powerful' and the seamlessness with which order is produced, it also reduces (while trying to do the opposite) the potential power of 'the weak' and obscures the implication of 'the weak' in power." Massey (2005), 45.
31. Vergunst rightly observes that the book is, on the whole, abstract and lacking "an empirical description of movement and walking in specific localities." See Vergunst (2017), 19.
32. De Certeau (1984), 99.
33. In line with this, de Certeau describes looking from the top of the World Trade Centre across New York in terms of static voyeurism: "His elevation [to the top of the WTC] transforms him into a voyeur. It puts him at a distance. It transforms the bewitching world by which one was possessed into a text that lies before one's eyes. It allows one to read it, to be a solar Eye, looking down like a God. The exaltation of a scopic and gnostic drive: the fiction of knowledge is related to this lust" (92). And: "The 1370-foot-high tower [...] continues to construct the fiction that creates readers, makes the complexity of the city readable, and immobilizes its opaque mobility in a transparent text" (ibid.). The association of textuality with immobility and readability is highly problematic as it erases the interaction between text and readers in the act of

reading. See Iser, Wolfgang (1980): *The Act of Reading: A Theory of Aesthetic Response*. Baltimore: Johns Hopkins University Press.

34. Barthes, Roland (1975): *The Pleasure of the Text*, translated by Richard Miller. New York: Hill and Wang.

35. Wolfgang Iser replaced the standard binary of the real and the fictive with the triad of the fictive, imaginary and the real in order to account for the work of *Vorstellung* in the act of reception. Because acts of fictionalisation invite the reader to move constantly between the imaginary and the real, readers perpetually "stage" themselves. In this way, readers can fashion new identities aesthetically in the act of reading, while also imagining alternative worlds. See Iser, Wolfgang (1993): *The Fictive and the Imaginary: Charting Literary Anthropology*. Baltimore. Johns Hopkins; Iser, Wolfgang (1986): Fictionalizing Acts. *Amerikastudien/American Studies* 31, 5–15. See also Thomas, Brook (2008): 'The Fictive and the Imaginary: Charting Literary Anthropology,' or, what's literature have to do with it? *American Literary History* 20(3), 622–631.

36. Benjamin, Walter (1991): Der Flaneur. *W. Benjamin, Abhandlungen. Gesammelte Schriften*, vol. I.2., edited by Rolf Tiedemann and Hermann Schweppenhäuser. Frankfurt: Suhrkamp, 537–569, 538.

37. Gleber, Anke (1999): *The Art of Taking a Walk: Flanerie, Literature and Film in Weimar Culture*. Princeton, NJ: Princeton University Press, 25f.

38. McBride, Patrizia (2011): Learning to See in Irmgard Keun's Das kunstseidene Mädchen. *The German Quarterly* 84(2), 220-238, 226. See also Anke Gleber. who with reference to Weimar culture comments that the *flâneur* "refuses to participate in a modern sense of productivity and rational labor." Gleber, Anke (1999), 26.

39. Burns shows that sectarianism is discursively policed on both sides of the divide: there are right or wrong first names, right or wrong TV programmes, right or wrong newspapers, murals, passports and: "The right butter. The wrong butter. The tea of allegiance. The tea of betrayal. There were 'our shops' and 'their shops'. Placenames. What school you went to. What prayers you said. […] How you pronounced your 'haitch' and your 'aitch'" (25).

40. Appadurai, The Production of Locality, 181.

Works Cited

Primary Literature

Burns, Anna (2018): *Milkman*. London: Faber & Faber.

Secondary Literature

Anderson, Benedict (1983): *Imagined Communities: Reflections on the Origin and Spread of Nationalism*. London: Verso.

Appadurai, Arjun (1996): The Production of Locality. *Modernity at Large: Cultural Dimensions of Globalization*. Minneapolis: University of Minnesota Press, 178-199.

Barthes, Roland (1975): *The Pleasure of the Text*, translated by Richard Miller. New York: Hill and Wang.

Benjamin, Walter (1991): Der Flaneur. *W. Benjamin, Abhandlungen. Gesammelte Schriften*, vol. I.2., edited by Rolf Tiedemann and Hermann Schweppenhäuser. Frankfurt: Suhrkamp, 537-569.

Blokland, Tanja (2003): *Urban Bonds*. Cambridge: Polity Press.

Coady, David (2012): Rumors and Rumor-Mongers. *What We Believe Now: Applying Epistemology to Contemporary Issues*, edited by David Coady. Oxford: Wiley-Blackwell, 86-109.

Cresswell, Tim, and Peter Merriman (2013): Introduction. *Geographies of Mobilities: Practices, Places, Subjects*, edited by Tim Cresswell and Peter Merriman. Farnham: Ashgate, 1-15.

De Certeau, Michel (1984): *The Practice of Everyday Life*, translated by Steven Rendall. Berkeley, Los Angeles and London: University of California Press.

Foucault, Michel (1986): Of Other Spaces: Utopias and Heterotopias, translated by Jay Miskowiec. *Diacritics* 16(1), 22-27.

Freud, Sigmund (1999): Das Unheimliche. *Gesammelte Werke*, vol. 12, edited by Anna Freud et al. Frankfurt: Fischer, 292-368.

Gleber, Anke (1999): *The Art of Taking a Walk: Flanerie, Literature and Film in Weimar Culture*. Princeton, NJ: Princeton University Press.

Hargreaves, Jennifer (1994): *Sporting Females: Critical Issues in the History and Sociology of Women's Sports*. London: Routledge, 209-235.

Iser, Wolfgang (1986): Fictionalizing Acts. *Amerikastudien/American Studies* 31, 5-15.

Iser, Wolfgang (1993): *The Fictive and the Imaginary: Charting Literary Anthropology*. Baltimore: Johns Hopkins.

Lukác, Georg (1983): *The Historical Novel*, translated from the German by Hannah and Stanley Mitchel; introduction by Frederic Jameson. Lincoln: University of Nebraska Press.

Massey, Doreen (2005): *For Space*. Los Angeles and London: Sage.

McBride, Patrizia (2011): Learning to See in Irmgard Keun's Das kunstseidene Mädchen. *The German Quarterly* 84(2), 220–238.

Meinhof, Ulrike Hanna (2011): Introducing Borders, Networks, Neighbourhoods: Conceptual Frames and Social Practices. *Negotiating Multicultural Europe: Borders, Networks, Neighbourhoods*, edited by Heidi Armbruster and Ulrike Hanna Meinhof. Basingstoke: Palgrave Macmillan, 1–25.

Mitchell, Jon P. (2007): A fourth critic of the Enlightenment: Michel de Certeau and the Ethnography of Subjectivity. *Social Anthropology/Anthropologie Sociale* 15(1), 89–106.

Savage, Mike, Gaynor Bagnell, and Brian Longhurst (2005): The Limits of Local Attachment. *Globalization and Belonging*, edited by Mike Savage, Gaynor Bagnell, and Brian Longhurst. London: Sage, 29–55.

Thomas, Brook (2008): 'The Fictive and the Imaginary: Charting Literary Anthropology,' or, what's literature have to do with it? *American Literary History* 20(3), 622–631.

Vergunst, Joe (2017): Key Figure of Mobility: The Pedestrian. *Social Anthropology/Anthropologie Sociale* 25 (1), 13–27.

Watts, Paul, and Peer Smets (2014): Introduction. *Mobilities and Neighbourhood Belonging in Cities and Suburbs*, edited by Paul Watts and Peer Smets. Basingstoke: Palgrave Macmillan, 1–23.

Wiegandt, Kai (2008): Partial Truth: Rumour in Conrad's Heart of Darkness. *Poetica* 40(3/4), 397–424.

The Quiet Unification of a Divided City

Jerusalem's Train-Track Park[1]

GAD SCHAFFER

Abstract

This chapter examines the recent redevelopment project of the City of Jerusalem, which has turned a derelict railway site into a new urban park: the Train-Track Park (TTP). The three central questions of the chapter are: (a) Does the TTP's accessibility and park quality serve all eight neighbourhoods equally as elements of environmental justice? (b) Has the new TTP created a new process of gentrification in the adjacent neighbourhoods? (c) To what extent are there any physical and mental changes to the TTP's borders and space?
The chapter illustrates how the park's very modern, neutral and non-site-specific design has become a connecting thread between eight demographically highly diverse neighbourhoods, constituting a space of security and unity for their residents. As such, the TTP has succeeded in creating a quiet unification of the adjacent neighbourhoods. Moreover, the construction of the TTP has provided an extra urban green area to all neighbourhoods, which has come to be particularly meaningful for the two disadvantaged neighbourhoods of Gonenim-Katamonim and Katamon Het-Tet. However, although the park was built to serve all neighbourhoods equally, there are notable differences in terms of accessibility and park quality. Historic sources and the conducted fieldwork suggest that these differences are due to historical and present-day physical limitations. Additionally, this chapter also reveals that the TTP has significantly contributed to the continued gentrification process in most of the adjacent neighbourhoods. Taking all aspects together, it seems that the TTP has indeed become the new central core and an area of transnational movement and encounters in between the adjacent neighbourhoods.

Introduction

Located at the physical and spiritual centre of the three Abrahamic religions, Jerusalem looks back on an extensive and eventful history. Tracing its origins back to the 4th millennium BC, the city has since then been attacked 52 times, captured and recaptured 44 times, besieged 23 times, and destroyed twice.[2] Since the end of the 19th century, it has expanded significantly from the 0.9 square kilometres of what has become known as the Old City to the 125,000 square kilometres of the present-day city.[3] The population has grown accordingly over the years, and reached 936,000 in 2019.[4] While borders between individual neighbourhoods are often fluid in many cities around the world, this is not the case in Jerusalem. On the contrary, Jerusalem's neighbourhoods are well defined physically and mentally. On a physical level, they include the barriers that separate some of the eastern Arab neighbourhoods from the rest of the city, as well as the barriers that are placed on the roads entering Jewish Orthodox neighbourhoods on Saturdays, i.e. the Jewish sacred day, to prevent vehicles from entering and passing through them. On a mental level, the barriers manifest themselves in the self-imposed seclusion and avoidance of passing through or staying too long in 'other' neighbourhoods. Indeed, the differences between the residential compositions of the individual neighbourhoods are self-evident, as they are segregated not only along ethno-religious lines in general, but also within the Arab and Jewish communities themselves.[5] While Jewish neighbourhoods are divided into secular, religious and orthodox groups, Arab neighbourhoods are divided into predominantly Christian or Muslim ones. This is further complicated by the fact that some Arabs living in Jerusalem have Israeli citizenship, while others only hold a residency permit.[6] In addition to these two dominant ethno-religious groups, some neighbourhoods contain a particularly high concentration of foreign residents. Likewise, as in every city, Jerusalem's neighbourhoods are diverse in socio-economic terms.

Urban green areas play an important role in modern city life and they provide many social benefits that can ultimately improve social equality. By providing pleasant, stress-free spaces for physical activity and relaxation, they facilitate health and wellbeing.[7] Indeed, urban green areas have been shown to decrease mortality rates.[8] Additionally, by their very nature they protect local ecosystems.[9] While these benefits are well known, it needs to be acknowledged that not all residents of these areas receive equal opportunities to use them.[10] *Environmental justice*, therefore, encourages the involvement of all people, regardless of gender, race, religion or class, in the planning, decision-making and implementation of different environmental policies and regulations for the purpose of reallocating resources more equitably throughout society.[11] In terms of urban green areas, environmental justice usually focuses on distributional justice, which includes quantity, accessibility, and park quality.[12] The consensus maintains that residents are in a more advantageous position the more urban green spaces they have. However, the mere existence of green urban areas does not guarantee frequent usage, so their accessibility and quality also have to be taken into consideration. Studies have shown that unjust spatial distribution of green urban spaces exists in cities in developed and developing countries alike, where more affluent residents have access to larger green areas than their less well-off counterparts.[13] While there are different methods of measuring accessibility to green urban areas,[14] none are comprehensive.[15] For example, the existing methods do not consider the psychological factors that can determine park accessibility.[16] Similarly, park quality comprises many factors, such as park conditions, the quantity of facilities and amenities, aesthetic features, cleanliness, and safety.[17] Yet none of the tools and methods to measure quality of a park are comprehensive either, each having its own advantages and disadvantages.[18] Furthermore, Glass and other scholars have argued that new urban green areas often encourage and accelerate the process of gentrification.[19]

Over the past decade, the Municipality of Jerusalem has grappled with a serious lack of available open spaces, especially in areas designated for new development. The root causes of this lacuna are first and foremost geopolitical factors. Since the end of the 19th century, both the Jewish and Arab populations set out to take control of as much land as possible around the Old City by building new residential neighbourhoods in a low-rise and low-densitymanner.[20] As a result, most open spaces have disappeared.[21] Indeed, since 1931 Jerusalem has expanded its borders six times, with the 1998 Safdie Plan proposing to expand the borders further westward – into an area dominated by open spaces with naturally high and valuable landscapes.[22] However, this plan was ultimately rejected in 2007, due to the successful opposition of environmental groups and local residents.[23] Following its rejection, the Municipality of Jerusalem decided to build upwards and redevelop areas wherever possible. In addition to employing a vertical rather than horizontal building policy, redevelopment of brownfield sites and other neglected areas can further promote the renewal of urban areas.[24]

There are many reasons to prioritise redevelopment over the development of new areas, with the promotion of *sustainable development* being perhaps one of the most important ones. The term 'sustainable development' refers to the promotion of a form of development that simultaneously enhances social equality and protects the environment.[25] For instance, the redevelopment of a neglected area can lead to economic growth by increasing municipal taxes, improving the quality of urban life, creating communal cohesion and promoting nature conservation.[26] One of Jerusalem's most significant redevelopment projects in the last few years is the park central to this chapter: the Train-Track Park (TTP) or Park HaMesila (Figure 1).

The TTP site comprises the former Jaffa–Jerusalem railway track, which operated from 1892 until 1998 when it closed for repair. In 2005, a new train station, Malha Station, was built five kilometres southwest of the original Jerusalem railway station, known as the First Station. As a result, the area between the First Station and Malha Station was neglected and became littered with environmen-

Figure 1: The Train-Track Park, section 2, northward facing view. On the right side, the original railroad track that has been converted into a walking path. On the left side, a bicycle lane. (Photo by Gad Schaffer)

tal and health hazards. Over the years, various redevelopment plans were put forward, but it was only in 2008 that plans to redevelop the site into a new urban park were approved. Two years later, in 2010, the construction of the TTP began. It was opened to the public in 2012, with its last instalments being completed three years later in 2015. Employing the slogan 'From Backyard to Central Core', the TTP passes through eight residential neighbourhoods that are a good representation of the human mosaic of Jerusalem. Indeed, after years of noise, pollution, neglect and division, the area had become a backyard, and the new TTP project sought to reinvent this area and turn it into the heart of its surrounding neighbourhoods to connect and unify, rather than divide and separate. Some were sceptical of how an unattractive area that acts as a physical and mental border between neighbourhoods could become a source of appeal and unity. Yet since its opening the TTP has become an area of transnational movement and encounters in between the adjacent neighbourhoods.

Building on the ideas of environmental justice and sustainable development, the following chapter seeks to examine three central questions:
(a) Does the TTP's accessibility and park quality serve all eight neighbourhoods equally as elements of environmental justice?

(b) Has the TTP created a new process of gentrification in the adjacent neighbourhoods?
(c) To what extent are there any physical and mental changes to the TTP's borders and space?

In order to do so, the chapter will first provide the historical-geopolitical context of the TTP and its adjacent neighbourhoods. It will explain the research methodology and present the results. This is then followed by a discussion of the results and a brief conclusion.

Historical-Geopolitical Contexts

Jerusalem's 20th-century history is characterised by different ethno-religious, military and political strife for control, beginning with the disintegration of the Ottoman Empire and its replacement by the British Mandate in 1917. At the end of the British Mandate in 1948 and after the First Arab Israeli War in the same year, Jerusalem was divided into two separate cities, one under Jordanian control and the other under Israeli control. Following the Six-Day War in 1967, Israel took full control of the entire city of Jerusalem and the West Bank. Yet the ethno-religious and political strife has remained unchanged and is still evident in the ongoing conflict between the Israelis and the Palestinians over land and the desire of the Palestinians for an independent sovereign state with Jerusalem as its capital.[27] The strife and struggle for control also impacted the Jaffa–Jerusalem railway track, which is located entirely within the territory of the State of Israel. During the 1948 War, Jordan occupied several sections of the tracks adjacent to the West Bank territory close to Jerusalem. In the 1949 Armistice Agreements between Israel and Jordan, Jordan returned these sections to Israel and thus allowed the train to continue operating almost without interruption. Moving into Jerusalem, the railway track comprises the neighbourhoods of Abu Tur, German Colony, Baka, Makor Haim, Gonenim-Katamonim, Katamon Het-Tet, Pat, Beit Safafa, and Malha – each of which will be introduced in the following section with the historic events mentioned above acting as key turning points.

The neighbourhood of Abu Tur was founded at the end of the 19th century, and initially contained two smaller sub-neighbourhoods, one Arab and the other Jewish. However, the Jewish neighbourhood failed to attract residents and the houses were eventually sold to members of the Arab community.[28] During the Arab–Israeli War of 1948, Abu Tur was divided, with Israelis and Jordanians occupying the west side and the east side of the neighbourhood respectively. After the war, Israel settled new Jewish immigrants, mostly from North Africa and the

Middle East, into the abandoned houses on the west side.[29] Today, Abu Tur is unified and predominantly Arab. However, the socio-economic differences are noticeable. On the Jewish side, the average ranking of the socio-economic status of households in the neighbourhood is ranked 14 out of 20, while on the Arab side it is ranked much lower, i.e. 4 out of 20.[30]

The German Colony was established at the end of the 19th century by German Christian Templars. During World War II, when Jerusalem was under British mandate, the German Templars – perceived as enemies – were deported from Palestine, and their confiscated property was sold to mostly affluent Christian Arabs.[31] During the Arab–Israeli War of 1948, some of the Arab residents abandoned their houses, while others were forced to flee, and Jewish residents took their place. With the gentrification process of the neighbourhood at the start of the 1970s, and later with the urban renewal process at the beginning of the 1990s, the German Colony transformed from disadvantaged to affluent with many foreign-born residents.[32]

The neighbourhood of Baka was intentionally built on the Jaffa–Jerusalem train route, as the latter was a central place of passage for people and goods at the time.[33] Indeed, the creation of the railway train track from Jaffa to Jerusalem prompted some Arab Muslims living in the densely populated Old City to move to this available open area, which also acted as a crossroads between the city of Jerusalem, Beit-Lehem and Hebron.[34] The history of Baka is similar to that of the German Colony. In the 1948 War, the Arab residents abandoned their houses, which were subsequently allocated to new Jewish immigrants. In the 1970s – and later, with the gentrification and urban renewal process – Baka transformed from a disadvantaged to an affluent neighbourhood, with many foreign-born residents choosing to live there.[35]

At present, Baka forms one larger neighbourhood together with Makor Haim. However, their historical development differs markedly. Built in 1924, Makor Haim was planned by German-Jewish architect Richard Kauffmann, who designed it to have but one central street. The houses along this street were to have large plots of land behind them that would serve as farms and vegetable gardens. The neighbourhood was built to serve the Mizrachi, members of a religious Jewish Zionist organisation.[36]

One of the largest neighbourhoods along the TTP was built between the 1950s and 1970s. Its three stages of construction have resulted in three different sub-neighbourhoods. The first area was named Gonenim-Katamonim, followed by Katamon Het-Tet, and then Pat. These sub-neighbourhoods were constructed by the government, which retained ownership of these houses until the 1970s, when it began selling them. The first houses were constructed to provide affordable housing for the new Jewish immigrants who survived the Holocaust, and later for Jews who fled Arab countries due to the deterioration of relations between these countries and Israel.[37] These social housing constructions were small and cheap,[38] and over the years other people looking for affordable housing moved into these neighbourhoods. Despite the municipality's attempts to improve the socio-economic conditions of Gonenim-Katamonim, Katamon Het-Tet and Pat, they nevertheless still rank low.[39]

In 1964, the Municipality of Jerusalem designated the area east of Gonenim-Katamonim as the Talpiot Industrial Area. In the 1970s, many garages and workshops moved from the city centre into this area, which at that time constituted the outskirts of the city. From the end of the 1980s, many shopping malls were being built there, and in 2013 the municipality decided to develop it as a mixed-use area that included an employment-commercial zone, an industrial zone, and on its outskirts a residential zone.[40]

Beit Safafa is an Arab neighbourhood. A small village during the 19th century, it was ultimately subsumed by the expanding city and grew into a large neighbourhood over the years. During the Arab–Israeli War of 1948, the neighbourhood was divided into two parts, one under Jordanian control and the other under Israeli control. After the Six-Day War in 1967, the neighbourhood was united under Israeli control. To this day, half of the residents of Beit Safafa are Israeli citizens (who lived under Israeli control between 1948 and 1967), while the other half (who lived under Jordanian control between 1948 and 1967) only hold a residency permit.[41]

A small Arab village in the 19th century, Malha was occupied by Israeli forces during the 1948 War. Houses there remained empty until 1951, when new Jewish immigrants from Kurdistan, Tunisia and Morocco arrived and moved into the area. Malha remained poor until the 1990s, when the Municipality of Jerusalem built a new neighbourhood around the old one. The new development included the biggest shopping mall in Jerusalem, a new technological compound and the construction of the Jerusalem sports stadium.[42]

Methodology

The researched area is located in West Jerusalem and includes the TTP, its eight surrounding neighbourhoods and one industrial area (Figure 2). It is approximately six kilometres long and covers an area of about 80,000 square metres. For the purpose of the research that underpins this chapter, the TTP was divided into five sections. Each section was separated from its adjoining section by an existing road or bridge. It is, however, important to note that the existence of bridges allows two areas of the park route to continue without any barrier. This division

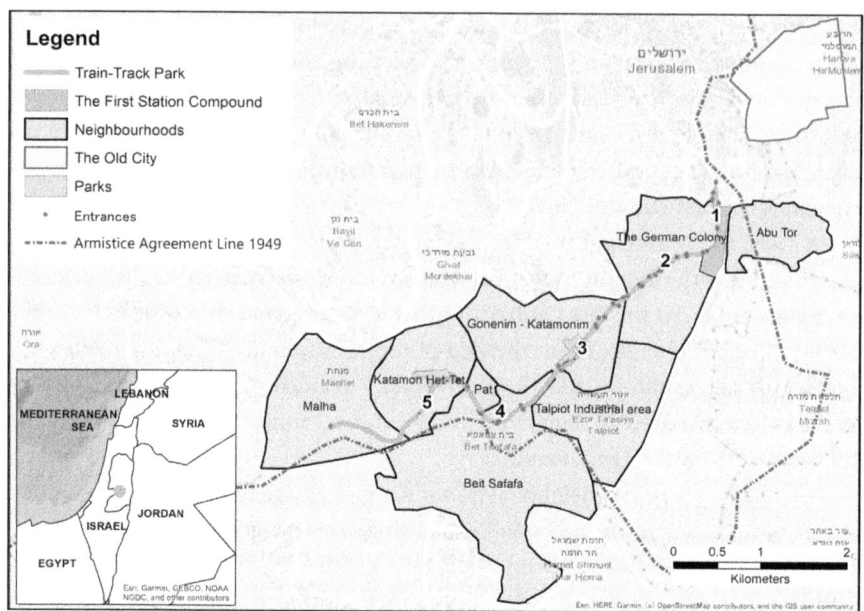

Figure 2: The Train-Track Park (TTP) (green line) starts at the First Station and ends near Malha Station. The white polygons are the surrounding neighbourhoods adjacent to the TTP. The TTP divides into five distinct Sections. Each Section of the park is separated from the adjoining Section by a main road or bridge.

of the TTP is not merely for the purpose of convenience, it also corresponds to the different neighbourhoods, which vary significantly from each other in their ethno-religious and socio-economic make-up. The longest sections of the TTP are 3 and 5, while section 1 is the shortest. Sections 2 and 4 are of similar medium length. Section 1 is a public open-space pedestrian centre consisting of cafés, restaurants and shops. There are also some restricted places around the area, both private and governmental. Section 1 is adjacent to Abu Tor and the German Colony, although a restricted area (an electric company) prevents direct access from the latter. Section 2 is situated between two neighbourhoods, the German Colony (which includes the Greek Colony) and Baka (which includes Makor Haim). As one of the longest sections, section 3 is situated mostly between Gonenim-Katamonim and the Talpiot Industrial Area. Section 4 is divided between Pat and Beit Safafa. Section 5 is shared by both Katamon Het-Tet and Malha.

One of the main features of sustainable development is the social aspect, and thus it was examined whether the TTP offers residents in all eight neighbourhoods adjacent to the park the same accessibility, conditions and park quality. First of all, the TTP's accessibility was examined by combining two methods to compensate for their individual shortcomings. While the first method measured the aerial distance from the various entrances to the closest and furthest houses in the neighbourhood, the second one measured a 500-metre buffer service zone from the various entrances of the park outwards to the neighbourhoods. Additionally, the overall accessibility of the TTP to bikes, strollers and disabled persons was surveyed at each of the park's entrances, as was their accessibility by public transportation in the form of nearby bus stops.[43] In order to assess the park quality, four types of facilities (i.e. sport fields, playgrounds, open-air sports facilities and public street libraries) and six amenities (i.e. bicycle and walking lanes, bicycle parking racks, benches, water dispensers and food facilities) were selected and assessed in terms of their quantity and quality. Indeed, the types of facilities, their conditions, cleanliness, safety and the planted vegetation were the same all along the TTP, since this park was created as one entity. The facilities and amenities of each section were counted, using the Quality Index of Parks for Youth (QUINPY).[44]

Since new development projects often result in the gentrification of the neighbourhoods in which they were constructed, a vital aspect of the research concerned the question whether this has also been the case with the TTP. Two different markers served as an indicator of gentrification: firstly, visual representations, such as signboards indicating new construction and redevelopment sites and street graffiti; and secondly, the development of the average apartment price over the past 15 years based on the data provided by the Israeli government website Gov-Real Estate.[45] A final aspect of the research concerned the physical and mental changes that the TTP has initiated through breaking down borders and its shared space. This part of the analysis is based on a collation of the historical background of the neighbourhoods and the events that are currently being organised in the TTP. The information was gathered from the relevant websites of the Municipality of Jerusalem as well as the neighbourhoods' community centres. Additional information was provided by newspaper articles in Hebrew and English by the *Jerusalem Post*, *Times of Israel* and *Haaretz*.

Results

Table 1 summarises the discrepancies in park accessibility in terms of aerial distance. The total average aerial distance from park entrances to neighbourhood houses is 571.4 metres. Nonetheless, the average aerial distance is higher in Abu Tur (834 metres), followed by Gonenim-Katamonim, Beit Safafa and Malha, with an average aerial distance of around 700 metres. The shortest aerial distance from the TTP to the neighbouring houses is in the German Colony (four metres), followed by Beit Safafa. Nonetheless, since Beit Safafa is a very large neigh-

Neighbourhood name	Distance (in metres)		
	Shortest	Longest	Average
Abu Tor	233	1,512	834
German Colony	4	1,433	563
Baka-Makor Haim	16	1,369	531
Gonenim-Katamonim	14	1,718	757
Pat	20	390	205
Beit Safafa	8	2,181	722
Katamon Het-Tet	16	779	391
Malha	354	1,103	729

Table 1. Table shows aerial distance in metres from the park's entrances to neighbourhood houses. The table shows the shortest, longest, and average distances.

Neighbourhood name	Total area (in sq. km)	Area of buffer (in sq. km)	% of cover
Abu Tor	0.739	0.251	33.9
German Colony	0.828	0.689	83.2
Baka-Makor Haim	1.125	0.920	81.7
Gonenim-Katamonim	1.307	0.749	57.3
Pat	0.136	0.136	100
Beit Safafa	3.147	0.829	26.3
Katamon Het-Tet	1.118	0.445	39.8
Malha	1.726	0.740	42.8

Table 2. Table shows the total area of each neighbourhood (in square kilometres). The table also shows the area (in square kilometres) covered by a buffer zone service area of 500 metres from the TTP's closest entrances outwards to the closest neighbourhoods.

bourhood, it also had the longest aerial distance from the park to the houses (2,181 metres), followed by Gonenim-Katamonim (1,718 metres).

Table 2 summarises the discrepancies in park accessibility in terms of the buffer zone service area. The TTP service area (defined by a 500-metre distance) covers 60.7% of the neighbourhood areas adjacent to the TTP. The service area covers 100% of Pat, followed by the German Colony and Baka–Makor Haim (~80%). The neighbourhoods that are least covered are Beit Safafa (26.3%), followed by Abu Tor and Katamon Het-Tet. Another finding showed that section 2 has the highest number of entrances, with an equal number of entrances for pedestrians, bicyclists, strollers and wheelchairs. The section with the least number of entrances is section 5, which is also the longest. The highest TTP accessibility by bus is in section 2, followed by section 1. Sections 4 and 5 are barely accessible, with each having only one bus stop.

THE QUIET UNIFICATION OF A DIVIDED CITY

Section of the TTP	Neighbourhood names adjacent to the TTP	Total no. of residents[46]	Neighbourhood area (in sq. km)	Ethnicity[47]	Socio-economic ranking[48]	% of foreign-born residents[46]	Section length (in metres)	Average aerial distance from the TTP to the neighbourhood (in metres)	% of cover by 500m buffer zone	Total no. of facilities	Facility score according to QUINPY[49]	Total no. of amenities	Amenities score according to QUINPY[49]
1	Abu Tor	12,870	0.7394	Arab-Jewish	4 / 14	3		834	33.9	2	2	27	2
2	German Colony	3,005	0.8280	Jewish	16	48	630	531	83.2	1	1	24	2
2	Baka-Makor Haim	12,856	1.1247	Jewish	14	45	1,040	563	81.7	1	1	24	2
3	Gonenim-Katamonim	17,264	1.3071	Jewish	9	27	1,040	757	57.3	4	2	32	2
4	Beit Safafa	13,731	3.1468	Arab	4	6	1,658	722	26.3	1	1	9	2
4	Pat	2,623	0.1356	Jewish	9	27	1,010	205	100	1	1	9	2
5	Katamon Het-Tet	6,502	1.1184	Jewish	4	35	1,010	391	39.8	2	2	11	2
5	Malha	4,205	1.7264	Jewish	13	21	1,970	729	42.8	2	2	11	2

Table 3. Table shows the differences found between the neighbourhoods adjacent to the TTP. The table also summarises the differences in accessibility and park quality – the services and amenities in each section of the TTP.

Table 3 summarises the discrepancies detected in park quality and accessibility (for more detailed results, see Appendix Table 1). Using the QUINPY index, it was found that there are two or more facilities in sections 1, 3, and 5. In examining the overall number of facilities, sections 1 and 3 possess, again, the greatest number of facilities, i.e. four facilities, while other sections only have one facility. Public street library facilities can be found in sections 2, 3 and 4. However, section 2 contains two public street library facilities, while sections 3 and 4 have just one. Two free-of-charge children's playgrounds are located in section 3, while section 1 has one that requires an entrance fee. Three open-air sports facilities exist, a small one in section 1 and two larger ones in sections 3 and 5.

Furthermore, the research has found that all TTP sections have two or more amenities. Examining the absolute number of amenities, the highest number can, again, be found in section 3 with 32 amenities, followed by section 1 with 27 amenities, and section 2 with 24 amenities. The section with the fewest amenities is section 4. Except for section 1, where there are no water dispensers, two to four water dispensers can be found in each section. There are many benches in sections 1, 2 and 3, but sections 4 and 5 have very few. Bicycle parking facilities can be found in sections 1, 2 and 3, but there are none in sections 4 and 5. Restaurants, shops and kiosks can be found mainly in section 1, and there is an additional local kiosk in section 4. Apart from two areas, bicycle and pedestrian paths run parallel to each other throughout the full length of the TTP. In some parts of section 4, the bicycle and pedestrian paths are shared, and section 5 only has a bicycle lane, although people do walk on it.

Discussion

One of the central questions of this chapter is to analyse whether the TTP's accessibility and park quality serve all eight neighbourhoods equally and can be considered environmentally just. In light of Jerusalem's historic division and its heterogeneity, this issue is particularly important, as previous research on two mixed Arab–Jewish cities in Israel, i.e. Ramle and Lod, has revealed that resources were unequally allocated within the cities.[50] In Jerusalem, the diversity found in the eight TTP neighbourhoods reflects the diversity of the city. For instance, while 97% of residents in Abu Tor are native born, only 52% of the residents in the German Colony are. Out of the eight neighbourhoods, two neighbourhoods are predominantly Arab – Abu Tor and Beit Safafa – while the others are predominantly Jewish. Moreover, there is a great disparity in terms of the socioeconomic ranking of the neighbourhoods: the German Colony ranks highest (16 out of 20), while Beit Safafa and Pat rank lowest (4 out of 20).

In terms of accessibility, scholarship suggests that the furthest people are willing to walk to a park is around 400–800 metres, or a 5–15-minute walk.[51] The research conducted for the chapter at hand has found that both the average aerial distance and the service area cover make the TTP accessible to most residents of the neighbourhoods adjacent to the park. Since accessibility is a strong indicator of whether a park serves all neighbourhood residents equally, it is difficult to prove any inequality regarding park accessibility when it comes to the TTP. Instead, most differences seemed to stem from physical planning obstacles. Moreover, three neighbourhoods, i.e. Beit Safafa, Abu Tor and Malha, have a slightly higher average aerial distance and a lower percentage of coverage, due to their greater size, the area of exposure to the park and the general topography.

Beit Safafa is the largest neighbourhood in size and expands southeast, away from the TTP, allowing only close-by residents to enjoy the park (Figure 2). Abu Tor, on the other hand, has two physical obstacles: first, the existence of Hebron Road, a busy four-lane thoroughfare that must be crossed to access the park; and second, the fact that most of the area is restricted and consists of private offices and other buildings. Moreover, its topography limits some residents' accessibility to the park: there is an elevation change of 94 metres from the bottom of the neighbourhood to TTP level. Indeed, topography is an important issue in terms of park accessibility, especially in a hilly city like Jerusalem. Jerusalem is built on several mountains, which range in height from 500 to 900 metres.[52] Although most of the neighbourhoods around the TTP are on the same level as the railway, Malha and Abu Tor are not. This can negatively affect the willingness of residents to utilise the park. In Malha, there are two factors limiting accessibility to the TTP. Like in Abu Tor, residents must cross a busy four-lane thoroughfare to access the park, as well as a working railway crossing. The topography further limits the access to the park for residents of Malha, as the elevation difference between the highest point in Malha and the TTP is 255 metres (Figure 3). Unlike Beit Safafa, Abu Tor and Malha, Pat has the shortest average aerial distance and has a full coverage to the TTP. This is not surprising, since Pat is the smallest neighbourhood in terms of size. The German Colony and Baka–Makor Haim follow closely behind Pat in terms of their aerial distances to the park. This is not surprising considering that Baka–Makor Haim was intentionally built along the railroad route itself at the end of the 19th century, as it was a central place of passage for people and goods.[53]

As mentioned above, Beit Safafa, Abu Tor (predominantly Arab and socio-economically disadvantaged) and Malha (predominantly Jewish and socio-economically advantaged) have less access to the TTP. Pat is the most accessible but ranks lowest on the socio-economic scale.

Another important factor is the number of TTP entrances and whether they include ramps for wheelchair and stroller access. Rigolon and Németh argue that

Figure 3: Section 5 near Malha neighborhood. The topography in Jerusalem can also play a role in limiting accessibility to the park, as seen in this case. (Photo by Gad Schaffer)

parks should support multiple age groups[5454]. Building a ramp at the entrances to the TTP would, therefore, attract more people who would otherwise find it hard to access. The fieldwork found that section 2 has the highest number of entrances – all of them with a ramp. Section 2 is adjacent to the German Colony and Baka, both predominantly affluent Jewish neighbourhoods. The large number of entrances in this section was possible thanks to a small road that runs along both sides of the TTP, enabling the construction of many entrances without restrictions. In contrast, other sections of the TTP are limited because they are blocked by backyard walls or buildings (Figure 4).

In accordance with its perception as a local park and/or a city park, it was found that park accessibility by public (bus) transportation was most convenient (less than a 100-metre walk) in sections 1 and 2 of the TTP. Accessibility is particularly important for section 1, since it consists of an open area with cafés and shops. Section 2 also has many bus stops close to the park, again because it runs parallel to Emek Refaim Street, which is a very busy commercial area that attracts many people. In conclusion, the fieldwork could not confirm any deliberate inequality regarding the accessibility of the TTP.

This chapter further attempts to discern whether park facilities and amenities are distributed evenly to the residents of all eight neighbourhoods. It is important to consider that, although the width of the park hardly varies, the length of each section greatly fluctuates. Obviously, larger sections allow for more facilities and amenities. An examination of the fieldwork results shows that, in most cases, facilities and amenities were divided equally between the sections. Where differences were found, there were valid planning explanations. Walking paths and bicycle lanes are considered important to sustainable development for three

Figure 4: Buildings and backyards adjected to the TTP limit accessibility to the TTP, section 3. (Photo by Gad Schaffer)

main reasons: they do not generate greenhouse gas emissions, they encourage physical activity – thereby promoting good health – and they take up minimal space.[55] The construction of walking paths and bicycle lanes in the TTP was planned in the aim of connecting the neighbourhoods. Moreover, the bicycle lane was intended to connect to the new Jerusalem Metropolitan Park, which begins near Malha Station and extends for 25 kilometres around Jerusalem. The fieldwork shows that there are bicycle and pedestrian paths along nearly the entire TTP. Exceptions were found in section 4, where a short section is a shared walking path and bicycle lane due to a small access road to private houses that runs parallel to the TTP, and in section 5, which has a shared path due to its declaration as an urban natural site.

An example of an explainable uneven distribution of facilities and amenities is the lack of restaurants and shops in all but section 1. The obvious explanation is the fact that the TTP passes through residential areas, between houses and backyards, and therefore space is limited. Additionally, section 1 was formerly the main central train station and was always a large, noisy space that was relatively far from residential areas. Thus, it was reasonable to transform it into an open mall, where people could come and enjoy themselves without disturbing nearby residents. Another example regarding facilities and amenities can be seen when comparing section 2 to section 3 of the TTP. Section 2 is adjacent to the German Colony and Baka, two predominantly Jewish and very affluent neighbourhoods. Section 3 is adjacent to Gonenim-Katamonim, a predominantly poor Jewish neighbourhood. Nonetheless, section 2 has only one facility (a public street library) and 26 amenities, in contrast to the four facilities (public street library, open-air sports facilities and two children's playgrounds) and 32 amenities in section 3.

Lastly, by looking at the present land cover of the area, we can see that the TTP is one of the only available long green areas around. One major issue of environmental justice focuses on the distribution of green urban areas.[56] The amount of green urban areas (parks) within the research area is very small. Some small parks can be found in Abu Tor, the German Colony and Baka, but the rest of the neighbourhoods were lacking in parks. Although the TTP is very narrow, its length provides another green area for residents and creates the impression of a big park. Moreover, with the development of the TTP, two additional large parks in Gonenim-Katamonim (section 3) and Katamon Het-Tet (section 5) were created (Figure 2). This was possible due to the fact that these areas were previously empty and had no important natural or historical features. The addition of two large parks that supply these less privileged neighbourhoods with more green urban spaces can be seen as a path towards a more just distribution.

Reportedly, improving the environment does not often bring about social equality, but rather inequalities.[57] The rationale behind this claim is that the improvement of a neglected place often creates a process of gentrification in which the socio-economically disadvantaged population is pushed out of the neighbourhood and more advantaged populations move in, thus negating the primary purpose of reaching environmental justice. Yet Gould and Lewis also argue that this might be avoided if the disadvantaged residents mobilise early in the stages of the process.[58]

It is important to note two important factors. First, in general terms, average real estate prices in Jerusalem have increased by 35.3% between 2010 and 2020.[59] This has driven many disadvantaged people and families to search for cheaper housing in other peripheral areas and cities.[60] Second, the process of gentrification started in several Jerusalem neighbourhoods beginning in the 1970s.[61] In the context of this chapter, since the 1970s the German Colony and Baka have witnessed a slow process of gentrification.[62]

Since the TTP only opened in 2012, it is too early to claim with certainty that its construction has triggered a process of gentrification. Nonetheless, in some areas there are signs that the TTP has strengthened an already ongoing gentrification process, while other areas show the first signs of gentrification. The area where this process can be most prominently discerned is section 2 of the TTP, adjacent to the German Colony and Baka. For instance, the German Colony has a new construction site next to the TTP. The new development is

Figure 5: A new residential construction site, *HaMesila* (The Train-Track), built adjected to section 2 of the TTP in the German Colony. (Photo by Gad Schaffer)

Figure 6: Graffiti on the signboard of new construction project, HaMesila (The Train-Track). The writing says: "We want our public pool back!! Swimming is <u>not only</u> for the rich!! And our public fitness room too!! Residents of Baka, Katamon, Katamonim, Greek Colony, German Colony, Makor Chayim". (Photo by Gad Schaffer)

called HaMesila (The Train Track). The construction site is surrounded by a wall with an advertisement that reads "Luxury Residence" alongside the photo of a future private swimming pool (Figure 5). Until a few years ago, this site was a public swimming pool called Brehat Yerushalaim (Jerusalem Swimming Pool), which operated from 1958 to 2018. Feelings of alienation and resistance on part of some of the residents, who feel this development is taking away what belongs

Figure 7: A new Israeli National Outline Plan 38A project adjacent to the TTP in section 2 – Baka neighborhood. The signboard reads, "Luxury project for the whole family" and "14 high-end cottages and penthouses". (Photo by Gad Schaffer)

to them and changing the neighbourhood, can be found in different graffiti written on some of the signboards surrounding the construction site (Figure 6). Interestingly, after a few months the signboard with the graffiti was replaced with a more simplistic, discreet, photo-free signboard. It is significant to note that the signboard for this new development is all in English, which indicates that this development is intended to attract foreign buyers and internationally oriented parts of the population.

On the other side of the TTP, i.e. in Baka, there are various redevelopment projects adjacent to the park. The largest project is under the Israeli National Outline Plan 38A (TAMA 38A), which aims to reinforce buildings against earthquakes and increase housing stock in highly sought-after areas. The developers improved the buildings for the sake of the residents living there. At the same time, they added

Figure 8: "Ghost apartments" adjected to the TTP in section 2 – Baka. Many of the apartments in the German Colony and Baka are owned by foreign residents who come to live in these apartments for a short period every year. On most days of the year, these apartments are sealed off, which is noticeable from the closed shutters. (Photo by Gad Schaffer)

floors to these buildings and can thus sell these additional units at market prices. The new redevelopment project applies to social housing buildings. The advertisement for this project reads "Luxury project for the whole family" (Figure 7). If we examine the real estate prices in this section of the TTP we can see that between 2010 and 2020 house prices increased by 154%.[63] Specifically in the German Colony and Baka, new residents are mostly American and British Jews who buy second homes in Israel for the holidays.[64] Many of these houses and apartments are nicknamed "ghost houses", since they remain empty for most of the year (Figure 8).

The other neighbourhood that shows early signs of a gentrification process is Makor Haim. Over the past few years, new projects have been constructed in Makor Haim, some of them adjacent to the TTP. Since 2012, the neighbourhood has seen an increase of 40–60% in real estate prices.[65] New construction developments there have attracted new residents, many of whom are French Jewish immigrants. Originally only one synagogue operated in Makor Haim, but the relocation of many French residents to the area who wanted a synagogue that suited their prayer style led to the construction of the new synagogue, Beit Yosef, funded by the donations of these new residents. Moreover, many new housing projects/developments have sprung up near the TTP, with the many advertisements emphasising their proximity to the park.

In the other neighbourhoods, no direct link could be found between other signs of gentrification and the opening of the TTP. The creation of the TTP has made the area much more attractive, with real estate companies also becoming more involved. Calls for the redevelopment of the old train track area into an urban park came from residents of all adjacent neighbourhoods, who were full partners in the planning and implementation stages.[66] Nonetheless, in this case, it seems that the effort did not successfully avoid the gentrification process, as argued by Gould and Lewis (2016).[67] There are other examples of such a process. One such case is High Line Park in New York City (USA). The High Line was an abandoned train track on Manhattan's west side, which was redeveloped into an urban park and opened in 2009. The redevelopment project has reinforced the gentrification process in this instance as well – a process that had originated back in the 1980s. Today, the neighbourhoods adjacent to High Line Park are mostly upper-class neighbourhoods.[68] Another similar redevelopment project is the Atlanta Belt project, an abandoned train track that was transformed into a park. Here, the value of the houses closest to the park have also risen and consequently become much less affordable.[69] It seems that in the case of the TTP, as in other similar cases, the market has been a stronger force than the community.

A "Quiet Unification"

Jerusalem is a city of many contradictions. Such contradictions can be found between the east side and the west side, between modernity and tradition, between Jewish and Arab residents, and within each of these groups. Many of these contradictions can also be found in the neighbourhoods surrounding the TTP. The TTP passes through affluent and disadvantaged neighbourhoods, between predominantly Jewish and predominantly Arab neighbourhoods, between neighbourhoods with a higher percentage of foreign residents and others with mostly local-born residents. Since the opening of the TTP in 2013, it has become a major attraction for residents of nearby neighbourhoods and Jerusalem in general.

The park attracts different visitors at different times of the day and during different seasons. Some come to work out, run or use the open-air sports facilities; others borrow a book from the public street library (Figure 9). Some come to meet friends and family, or just walk alone, while others use the park as a more attractive route from one place to another. For instance, in the mornings, mostly during spring and summer, one can find older people and parents with babies strolling around, or the occasional person who comes there to exercise. In the afternoons, most park visitors are there to work out or pass through the park on their way back home from work. In the evenings, one will most likely encounter more people exercising and younger people hanging out. The TTP is also used for neighbourhood and city events. The neighbourhoods bordering the park are ascribed to five

Figure 9: On the left, a public street library (in section 2 of the TTP) and on the right, an open-air sport facility (in section 3 of the TTP). Similar facilities can be found in different locations along the TTP. (Photos by Gad Schaffer)

different community centres. These community centres organise various activities in the park throughout the year, such as music performances, plays and story hours for children, marches for various purposes, and activities that promote the environment and the local community. Moreover, the Jerusalem Municipality also organises events that take place in the TTP. Some of the major sporting events that take place there are the Jerusalem Marathon, with over 10,000 participants passing through sections 1 and 2, and the Cycling in the Capital City event, with over 7,000 cyclists passing through all sections of the TTP. Furthermore, in the last few years, the Hebrew Book Week event has taken place in section 1 of the TTP.

The TTP has created "a quiet unification" in a city rife with contrast and strife.[70] While this "quiet unification" is mostly a physical one, there are also first small signs of a mental change. There are different factors that could explain how the creation of the TTP has successfully produced a special and attractive transcultural space that allows everyone to feel part of it. One obvious factor is the fact that it is new, clean, well lit at night, and only steps away from people's homes. Another obvious factor is that the park offers different facilities for different people. There are open-air sports facilities, cycling and walking lanes, benches, water dispensers, public street library facilities, and others. Furthermore, the park has different entrances for pedestrians, people with disabilities, strollers and cyclists, which ensures easy access for everyone. The TTP has also created a place of connection, belonging and security. One of the reasons for this could be found in relation to the design of the space itself – the creation of a globalised modern green urban space.

The TTP has two parallel historical narratives. One narrative tells the story of how the area of the railway itself changed from a small stream to a major busy railway and, finally, a modern urban park. The second narrative covers the unique urbanisation process of the neighbourhoods adjacent to the TTP and how it resulted from a combination of historical-political events. With regard to its natural environment, the TTP is located in the Mediterranean phytogeographic region. When looking at the general landscape of the park, we can see that it could have been at home anywhere else in the world. Its design is very modern, neutral and non-site-specific. The park's facilities and amenities and plants do not have unique features or local stylistic touches. While during the reconstruction of the new TTP some old trees were preserved, most of the area was replanted, and although the planners included some native plants, it is the foreign vegetation which stands out. The only place where some connection to the past can be seen in sections 1, 2 and 3, where some signs in Hebrew, English and Arabic describe and illustrate the history of the old railway line. It could very well be that because the design of the TTP is, in a way, neutral, all visitors experience a sense of belonging and safety there. The TTP resulted in the exposure of visitors to different areas and residents. The transnational neighbourhoods "can be both urban and rural, and are often multiterritorial, re-/deterritorialized places/spaces for transmigrants, in an artificial and partially even forced setting".[71] Indeed, one can look at the TTP as a forced, artificial space. Nonetheless, this artificial space, simultaneously of no one and everyone, has created a place of encounters between strangers but where all share this common space. In recent years, shared activities organised between Jewish and Arab residents have taken place, with the aim to try and change the mental gap which still exists.[72] Undoubtedly, the TTP has created a route that physically connects the neighbourhoods, and only time will tell if this connection also succeeds in creating new deep connections between the residents themselves.

Conclusion

This chapter examined a redevelopment project in Jerusalem by investigating historical-geographical changes in land cover and surroundings, and whether the TTP was redeveloped in a socially equal way. The fieldwork found that the area in and around the TTP has undergone dramatic land cover changes in the past 140 years. From the end of the 19th century until today, modernisation and regional political competition have contributed to change it from an open green space to a dense urban area. The fieldwork has shown that differences in accessibility to the TTP were mostly caused by one or a combination of the following reasons: neighbourhood size and the area of exposure to the park, physical obstacles, and topography. With regard to park quality, differences found in the number of facilities and amenities across the various sections of the TTP were due to disparities in each park section's physical attributes and limitations. It can be said that this park has become a central core for the residents of the adjacent, culturally diverse neighbourhoods that now overlap. Despite the short time period between the construction of the park and this examination, there is evidence that the park might be the cause of a gentrification process in one neighbourhood and that it has reinforced this process in two other affluent neighbourhoods where it was already underway.

Unlike new development, which is often done in vacant areas, the redevelopment of neglected sites is much more challenging due to the existing limitations of the surrounding area. Ideally, the goal is to develop such sites in a sustainable manner that takes social issues into account. To achieve this goal, the redevelopment of neglected sites requires meticulous planning and often calls for out-of-the-box solutions. Jerusalem is still a very heterogeneous and divided city. Yet, sometimes, having to coexist with others with whom we might not have anything in common, to whom we are connected solely by the fact that we share the same space, can transform a place into a unifying one. The TTP has become the new central core of its surroundings, and, in being a no man's land, has transformed the area into a connecting thread between the neighbourhoods and the residents. There are the first small signs that the TTP has unintentionally fostered a more integrated community, and created a quiet unification in this divided city.

Appendix

		1	2	3	4	5
No. of amenities	Bicycle lanes	yes	yes	yes	yes	yes
	Walking paths	yes	yes	yes	mostly yes	shared with bicycle lane
	Shops, cafés, kiosks	15	0	0	1	0
	Bicycle parkings	2	1	5	0	0
	Benches	10	21	23	6	8
	Water dispensers	0	2	4	2	3
No. of facilities	Sports fields	0	0	0	0	1
	Open-air sports facilities	1	0	1	0	1
	Children's playgrounds	1	0	2	0	0
	Public street libraries	0	1	1	1	0
Bus stops – easy access		3	5	3	1	1
Number of entrances to the park	by bicycle, stroller and wheel-chair	4	11	8	5	2
	on foot	6	11	10	6	2
Section length (in metres)		630	1,040	1,658	1,010	1,970
Section of the TTP		1	2	3	4	5

Table A.1.: Summarisation of the quantity of facilities and amenities in each section of the TTP.

Notes

1. I would like to thank Mr. Refael Gabay for his help collecting portions of the data from the present-day Train-Track Park in Jerusalem.
2. Cline, Eric, H. (2010): *Jerusalem Besieged: From Ancient Canaan to Modern Israel*. Ann Arbor: The University of Michigan Press.
3. Amirav, Moshe (2017): Jerusalem: A City without Borders [Hebrew]. *Stop No Border in Front of You! About Borders and the Lack of Them in Israel*, edited by Raanan Zubida and Hani Lipschitz. Jerusalem: Yediot Acharonot.
4. Assaf-Shapira, Yair (2020): *Population of Jerusalem*. Jerusalem: Jerusalem Institute for Policy Research.
5. Rokem, Jonathan, and Laura Vaughan (2018): Segregation, Mobility and Encounters in Jerusalem: The Role of Public Transport Infrastructure in Connecting the 'Divided City'. *Urban Studies* 55(15), 3454–3473; Hasson, Shlomo (2001): Territories and Identities in Jerusalem. *GeoJournal* 53, 311–322.
6. Romann, Michael, and Alex Weingrod (1991): *Living Together Separately: Arabs and Jews in Contemporary Jerusalem*. Princeton, NJ: Princeton University Press.
7. Brown, Greg, Morgan Faith Schebella, and Delene Weber (2014): Using Participatory GIS to Measure Physical Activity and Urban Park Benefits. *Landscape and Urban Planning* 121, 34–44.
8. Wolch, Jennifer R., Jason Byrne, and Joshua P. Newell (2014): Urban Green Space, Public Health, and Environmental Justice: The Challenge of Making Cities 'Just Green Enough'. *Landscape and Urban Planning* 125, 234–244.
9. Bolund, Per, and Sven Hunhammar (1999): Ecosystem Services in Urban Areas. *Ecological Economics* 29(2), 293–301; Tratalos, Jamie et al. (2007): Urban Form, Biodiversity Potential and Ecosystem Services. *Landscape and Urban Planning* 83(4), 308–317.
10. Germann-Chiari, Christina, and Klaus Seeland (2004): Are Urban Green Spaces Optimally Distributed to Act as Places for Social Integration? Results of a Geographical Information System (GIS) Approach for Urban Forestry Research. *Forest Policy and Economics* 6(1), 3–13; Heynen, Nik, Harold A. Perkins, and Parama Roy (2006): The Political Ecology of Uneven Urban Green Space. *Urban Affairs Review* 42(1), 3–25.
11. Schlosberg, David (2007): *Defining Environmental Justice*. Oxford: Oxford University Press; Walker, Gordon P. (2012): *Environmental Justice*. London: Routledge.
12. Rigolon, Alessandro (2018): Access to Urban Green Space in Cities of the Global South: A Systematic Literature Review. *Urban Science* 2(3), 67, doi.org/10.3390/urbansci2030067.
13. Rigolon, Alessandro (2016): A Complex Landscape of Inequity in Access to Urban Parks: A Literature Review. *Landscape and Urban Planning* 153, 160–169; Schüle, Steffen Andreas et al. (2019): Social Inequalities in Environmental Resources of Green and Blue Spaces: A Review of Evidence in the WHO European Region. *International*

Journal of Environmental Research and Public Health 16(7), 1216, doi.org/10.3390/ijerph16071216.
14. Talen, Emily (2003): Neighborhoods as Service Providers: A Methodology for Evaluating Pedestrian Access. *Environment and Planning B: Planning and Design* 30(2), 181–200.
15. Nicholls, Sarah (2001): Measuring the Accessibility and Equity of Public Parks: A Case Study Using GIS. *Managing Leisure* 6(4), 201–219; Talen (2003).
16. Gimblett, Randy, and Hans Skov-Petersen, eds. (2008): *Monitoring, Simulation, and Management of Visitor Landscapes*. Tucson: University of Arizona Press.
17. Cavner, Mario M. et al. (2004): Evaluating the Quality of Recreation Facilities: Development of an Assessment Tool. *Journal of Park and Recreation Administration* 22(1), 96–114; Rigolon et al. (2018); Chen, Yiyong et al. (2018): Emerging Social Media Data on Measuring Urban Park Use. *Urban Forestry & Urban Greening* 31, 130–141.
18. Rigolon, Alessandro, and Jeremy Németh (2018): A QUality INdex of Parks for Youth (QUINPY): Evaluating Urban Parks through Geographic Information Systems. *Environment and Planning B: Urban Analytics and City Science* 45(2), 275–294; Broomhall, Melissa H. (2004): *Quality of Public Open Spaces Tool (POST)*. Perth: The University of Western Australia Publishing, 1-9; Bird, Madeleine E. et al. (2015): A Reliability Assessment of a Direct-Observation Park Evaluation Tool: The Parks, Activity and Recreation among Kids (PARK) Tool. *BMC Public Health* 15, 906, doi.org/10.1186/s12889-015-2209-0.
19. Glass, R. (1964): Introduction: Aspects of Change. *London: Aspects of Change*, edited by Centre for Urban Studies. London: MacKibbon and Kee, 1–12. Moskowitz, Peter E. (2017): *How to Kill a City: Gentrification, Inequality, and the Fight for the Neighborhood*. New York: Bold Type Books; Lees, Loretta, Tom Slater, and Elvin Wyly (2007): *Gentrification*. London: Routledge.
20. Kliotand, Nurit, and Yoel Mansfeld (1999): Case Studies of Conflict and Territorial Organization in Divided Cities. *Progress in Planning* 52(3), 167–225; Amirav (2017); Yiftachel, Oren (2006): *Ethnocracy: Land and Identity Politics in Israel/Palestine*. Philadelphia: University of Pennsylvania Press.
21. Schaffer, Gad, and Noam Levin (2014): Mapping Human Induced Landscape Changes in Israel between the End of the 19th Century and the Beginning of the 21st Century. *Journal of Landscape Ecology* 7(1), 110–145.
22. Ramon, Uri, Tal Schwartz, and Iris Bernstein (2001): *West Jerusalem: Landscape Survey and Planning Principles* [Hebrew]. Jerusalem: Open Landscape Institute.
23. Rokem, Jonathan (2012): Politics and Conflict in a Contested City. *Bulletin du Centre de recherche français à Jéruslem* 23.
24. Alker, Sandra et al. (2000): The Definition of Brownfield. *Journal of Environmental Planning and Management* 43(1), 49–69; Yount, Kristen R. (2003): What Are Brownfields? Finding a Conceptual Definition. *Environmental Practice* 5(1), 25–33.

25. Campbell, Scott (1996): Green Cities, Growing Cities, Just Cities? Urban Planning and the Contradictions of Sustainable Development. *Journal of the American Planning Association* 2(3), 296–312.
26. Greenberg, Michael et al. (2001): Brownfield Redevelopment as a Smart Growth Option in the United States. *Environmentalist* 21(2), 129–143; De Sousa, Christopher A. (2008): *Brownfields Redevelopment and the Quest for Sustainability*. Oxford: Elsevier.
27. Oren, Michael B. (2002): *Six Days of War: June 1967 and the making of the modern Middle East*. Oxford: Oxford University Press.
28. Oren-Nordheim, Michal, and Ruth Kark (1995): *Jerusalem and its Environments: Quarters, Neighborhoods, Villages 1800–1948*. Jerusalem: Academon.
29. Israeli, Raphael (2002): *Jerusalem Divided: The Armistice Regime 1947–1967*. New York: Routledge.
30. The Central Bureau of Statistics (2018): *Localities and Population, by District, Sub-District, Religion and Population Group*. Jerusalem. Available online at https://www.cbs.gov.il/he/publications/DocLib/2018/2.%20ShnatonPopulation/st02_16x.pdf.
31. Rutland, Suzanne D. (2005): 'Buying out the Matter': Australia's Role in the Restitution for Templar Property in Israel. *Journal of Israeli History* 24(1), 135–154.
32. Kroyanker, David (2008): *The German colony and Emek Rephaim Street*. Jerusalem: Keter Books.
33. Kroyanker, David (1996): *A Guide to Neighborhoods and Buildings: An Architectural View*. Jerusalem: Keter Books.
34. Ibid.
35. Ibid.
36. Rosenblatt, Samuel (1951): *The History of the Mizrachi Movement*. New York: Mizrachi Organization of America.
37. Lissak, Moshe (2003): The Demographic-Social Revolution in Israel in the 1950s: The Absorption of the Great Aliyah. *Journal of Israeli History* 22(2), 1–31.
38. Hananal, Ravit (2017): From Central to Marginal: The Trajectory of Israel's Public Housing Policy. *Urban Studies* 54(11), 2432–2447.
39. The Central Bureau of Statistics (2008): *Census Data 2008*. Jerusalem. Available online at http://www.cbs.gov.il.
40. Jerusalem Municipality (2017): *Jerusalem Neighbourhoods*. Available online at https://www.jerusalem.muni.il/City/Neighborhood/Pages/default.aspx.
41. Romann and Weingrod (1991).
42. Jerusalem Municipality (2017).
43. Examining nearby bus stops up to 100 metres walking distance from the TTP.
44. Rigolon and Németh (2018). The overall score for each section of the TTP was calculated as follows: 0 – no facility or amenity; 1 – one facility/amenity; 2 – two or more facilities/amenities.

45. Survey of Israel (2020): Israeli Government Real Estate Website. Available at https://www.nadlan.gov.il/.
46. Jerusalem Municipality (2017).
47. Jerusalem Institute for Policy Research (2016): Table III/5 – Population of Jerusalem by Population Group, Quarter and Sub-Quarter. Jerusalem.
48. Data from the Israel Centre of Bureau of Statistics. The socio-economic status index ranges from 1 to 20, with 1 the lowest and 20 the highest·
49. The score was calculated using the Quality Index of Parks for Youth (QUINPY).
50. Omer, Itzhak, and Udi Or (2005): Distributive Environmental Justice in the City: Differential Access in Two Mixed Israeli Cities. *Tijdschrift voor Economische en Sociale Geografie* 96(4), 433–443.
51. Boone, Christopher G. et al. (2009): Parks and People: An Environmental Justice Inquiry in Baltimore, Maryland. *Annals of the Association of American Geographers* 99(4), 767–787; Nicholls (2001); Forsyth, Anne (2000): Analysing Public Space at a Metropolitan Scale: Notes on the Potential for Using GIS. *Urban Geography* 21(2), 121–147; Miyake, Keith K. et al. (2010): Not Just a Walk in the Park: Methodological Improvements for Determining Environmental Justice Implications of Park Access in New York City for the Promotion of Physical Activity. *Cities and the Environment* 3(1), 1–17; Su, Jason G. et al. (2019): Associations of Green Space Metrics with Health and Behavior Outcomes at Different Buffer Sizes and Remote Sensing Sensor Resolutions. *Environment International* 126, 162–170.
52. Efrat, Elisheva (1999): *The Land of Israel: Physical, Local and Regional Geography* [Hebrew]. Tel Aviv: Achiasaf.
53. Kroyanker (1996).
54. Rigolon, Alessandro, and Jeremy Németh (2018): A QUality INdex of Parks for Youth (QUINPY): Evaluating Urban Parks through Geographic Information Systems. *Environment and Planning B: Urban Analytics and City Science* 45(2), 275–294.
55. Pucher, John, and Ralph Buehler (2017): Cycling towards a More Sustainable Transport Future. *Transport Reviews* 37(6), 689–694.
56. Rigolon (2018); Schüle et al. (2019).
57. Gould, Kenneth A., and Tammy L. Lewis (2016): *Green Gentrification: Urban Sustainability and the Struggle for Environmental Justice*. New York and London: Routledge.
58. García-Lamarca, Melissa (2017): Green Gentrification: Urban Sustainability and the Struggle for Environmental Justice. *Local Environment* 22(12), 1563–1565; Gould and Lewis (2016)
59. Madlan (2020): *Apartment Prices in Jerusalem*. Available at https://www.madlan.co.il/.
60. Choshen, Maya, and Michal Korach (2014): *Leaving Jerusalem 2011–2013: The Characteristics of the Migrants and Their Reasons for Migrants*. Jerusalem: Jerusalem Institute for Policy Research.

61. Gonen, Amiram (2002): Widespread and Diverse Neighborhood Gentrification in Jerusalem. *Political Geography* 21(5), 727–737.
62. Zaban, Hila (2019a): 'Once There Were Moroccans Here – Today Americans': Gentrifications and the Housing Market in the Baka Neighborhood of Jerusalem. *City* 20(3), 412–427; Zaban, Hila (2019b): The Real Estate Foothold in the Holy Land: Transnational Gentrification in Jerusalem. *Urban Studies* 57(15), 3116–3134.
63. Survey of Israel (2020).
64. Zaban (2019a); Zaban (2019b).
65. Survey of Israel (2020).
66. Rotman, Diego, and Eytan Shouker (2019): Building and Developing HaMesika Park: From Resistance to Collaboration. *Understanding Campus-Community Partnerships in Conflict Zones: Engaging Students for Transformative Change*, edited by Dalya Yafa Markovich, Daphna Golan, and Nadera Shalboub-Kevorkian. London: Palgrave, 117–156.
67. Gould and Lewis (2016).
68. Alvarez, Ariel B. et al. (2012): *New York City's High Line: Participatory Planning or Gentrification?* Working Paper, Pennsylvania State University; Loughran, Kevin (2014): Parks for Profit: The High Line, Growth Machines, and the Uneven Development of Urban Public Spaces. *City & Community* 13(1), 49–68.
69. Immergluck, Dan, and Tharunya Balan (2018): Sustainable for Whom? Green Urban Development, Environmental Gentrification, and the Atlanta Beltline. *Urban Geography* 39(4), 546–562.
70. Friedman, Matti (2013): Trains, Bikes and Shoppers: The Quiet Unification of Jerusalem. *The Times of Israel* (3 March).
71. Ehrig, Stephan, Britta C. Jung, and Maria Roca Lizarazu (2020): Conference Report: Exploring the Transnational Neighbourhood. Integration, Community, and Co-Habitation. *Journal of Romance Studies* 20(1), 179–181.
72. Saidov, Yossi (2016): Join the Bottom-Up Movement for Change. *Palestine–Israel Journal of Politics, Economics, and Culture; East Jerusalem* 21(4): 78–80; Eglash, Ruth (2015): The Jewish-Arab running club that's uniting some of Jerusalem's teens. *The Washington Post* (16 June).

Works Cited

Alker, Sandra et al. (2000): The Definition of Brownfield. *Journal of Environmental Planning and Management* 43(1), 49–69.

Alvarez, Ariel B. et al. (2012): *New York City's High Line: Participatory Planning or Gentrification?* Working Paper, Pennsylvania State University.

Amirav, Moshe (2017): Jerusalem: A City without Borders [Hebrew]. *Stop No Border in Front of You! About Borders and the Lack of Them in Israel*, edited by R. Zubida and H. Lipschitz. Jerusalem: Yediot Acharonot.

Assaf-Shapira, Yair (2020): *Population of Jerusalem*. Jerusalem: Jerusalem Institute for Policy Research.

Bird, Madeleine E. et al. (2015): A Reliability Assessment of a Direct-Observation Park Evaluation Tool: The Parks, Activity and Recreation among Kids (PARK) Tool. *BMC Public Health* 15, 906, doi.org/10.1186/s12889-015-2209-0.

Bolund, Per, and Sven Hunhammar (1999): Ecosystem Services in Urban Areas. *Ecological Economics* 29(2), 293–301.

Boone, Christopher G. et al. (2009): Parks and People: An Environmental Justice Inquiry in Baltimore, Maryland. *Annals of the Association of American Geographers* 99(4), 767–787.

Broomhall, Melissa H. (2004): *Quality of Public Open Spaces Tool (POST)*. Perth: The University of Western Australia Publishing.

Brown, Greg, Morgan Faith Schebella, and Delene Weber (2014): Using Participatory GIS to Measure Physical Activity and Urban Park Benefits. *Landscape and Urban Planning* 121, 34–44.

Campbell, Scott (1996): Green Cities, Growing Cities, Just Cities? Urban Planning and the Contradictions of Sustainable Development. *Journal of the American Planning Association* 2(3), 296–312.

Cavner, Mario M. et al. (2004): Evaluating the Quality of Recreation Facilities: Development of an Assessment Tool. *Journal of Park and Recreation Administration* 22(1), 96–114.

Chen, Yiyong et al. (2018): Emerging Social Media Data on Measuring Urban Park Use. *Urban Forestry & Urban Greening* 31, 130–141.

Choshen, Maya, and Michal Korach (2014): *Leaving Jerusalem 2011–2013: The Characteristics of the Migrants and Their Reasons for Migrants*. Jerusalem: Jerusalem Institute for Policy Research.

Cline, Eric, H. (2010): *Jerusalem Besieged: From Ancient Canaan to Modern Israel*. Ann Arbor: The University of Michigan Press.

Conder, Claude Reignier, and Horatio Herbert Kitchener (1881): *Palestine Exploration Fund: Survey of Western Palestine 1:63,000 Map*. London: Palestine Exploration Fund.

De Sousa, Christopher A. (2008): *Brownfields Redevelopment and the Quest for Sustainability*. Oxford: Elsevier.

Efrat, Elisheva (1999): *The Land of Israel: Physical, Local and Regional Geography* [Hebrew]. Tel Aviv: Achiasaf.

Eglash, Ruth (2015): The Jewish-Arab running club that's uniting some of Jerusalem's teens. *The Washington Post* (16 June).

Ehrig, Stephan, Britta C. Jung, and Maria Roca Lizarazu (2020): Conference Report: Exploring the Transnational Neighbourhood. Integration, Community, and Co-Habitation. *Journal of Romance Studies* 20(1), 179–181.

Forsyth, Anne (2000): Analysing Public Space at a Metropolitan Scale: Notes on the Potential for Using GIS. *Urban Geography* 21(2), 121–147.

Friedman, Matti (2013): Trains, Bikes and Shoppers: The Quiet Unification of Jerusalem. *The Times of Israel* (3 March).

García-Lamarca, Melissa (2017): Green Gentrification: Urban Sustainability and the Struggle for Environmental Justice. *Local Environment* 22(12), 1563–1565.

Germann-Chiari, Christina, and Klaus Seeland (2004): Are Urban Green Spaces Optimally Distributed to Act as Places for Social Integration? Results of a Geographical Information System (GIS) Approach for Urban Forestry Research. *Forest Policy and Economics* 6(1), 3–13.

Gimblett, Randy, and Hans Skov-Petersen, eds. (2008): *Monitoring, Simulation, and Management of Visitor Landscapes*. Tucson: University of Arizona Press.

Glass, R. (1964): Introduction: Aspects of Change. *London: Aspects of Change*, edited by Centre for Urban Studies. London: MacKibbon and Kee, 1–12.

Gonen, Amiram (2002): Widespread and Diverse Neighborhood Gentrification in Jerusalem. *Political Geography* 21(5), 727–737.

Gould, Kenneth A., and Tammy L. Lewis (2016): *Green Gentrification: Urban Sustainability and the Struggle for Environmental Justice*. New York and London: Routledge.

Greenberg, Michael et al. (2001): Brownfield Redevelopment as a Smart Growth Option in the United States. *Environmentalist* 21(2), 129–143.

Hananal, Ravit (2017): From Central to Marginal: The Trajectory of Israel's Public Housing Policy. *Urban Studies* 54(11), 2432–2447.

Hasson, Shlomo (2001): Territories and Identities in Jerusalem. *GeoJournal* 53, 311–322.

Heynen, Nik, Harold A. Perkins, and Parama Roy (2006): The Political Ecology of Uneven Urban Green Space. *Urban Affairs Review* 42(1), 3–25.

Immergluck, Dan, and Tharunya Balan (2018): Sustainable for Whom? Green Urban Development, Environmental Gentrification, and the Atlanta Beltline. *Urban Geography* 39(4), 546–562.

Israeli, Raphael (2002): *Jerusalem Divided: The Armistice Regime 1947–1967*. New York: Routledge.

Jerusalem Institute for Policy Research (2016): *Table III/5 – Population of Jerusalem by Population Group, Quarter and Sub-Quarter*. Jerusalem.

Jerusalem Municipality (2017): Jerusalem Neighbourhoods, https://www.jerusalem.muni.il/City/Neighborhood/Pages/default.aspx. Accessed 5 July 2021.Kliotand, Nurit, and Yoel Mansfeld (1999): Case Studies of Conflict and Territorial Organization in Divided Cities. *Progress in Planning* 52(3), 167–225.

Kroyanker, David (1996): *A Guide to Neighborhoods and Buildings: An Architectural View.* Jerusalem: Keter Books.

Kroyanker, David (2008): *The German colony and Emek Rephaim Street.* Jerusalem: Keter Books.

Lees, Loretta, Tom Slater, and Elvin Wyly (2007): *Gentrification.* London: Routledge.

Lissak, Moshe (2003): The Demographic-Social Revolution in Israel in the 1950s: The Absorption of the Great Aliyah. *Journal of Israeli History* 22(2), 1–31.

Loughran, Kevin (2014): Parks for Profit: The High Line, Growth Machines, and the Uneven Development of Urban Public Spaces. *City & Community* 13(1), 49–68.

Madlan (2020): *Apartment Prices in Jerusalem.* Available at https://www.madlan.co.il/.

Miyake, Keith K. et al. (2010): Not Just a Walk in the Park: Methodological Improvements for Determining Environmental Justice Implications of Park Access in New York City for the Promotion of Physical Activity. *Cities and the Environment* 3(1), 1–17.

Moskowitz, Peter E. (2017): *How to Kill a City: Gentrification, Inequality, and the Fight for the Neighborhood.* New York: Bold Type Books.

Nicholls, Sarah (2001): Measuring the Accessibility and Equity of Public Parks: A Case Study Using GIS. *Managing Leisure* 6(4), 201–219.

Omer, Itzhak, and Udi Or (2005): Distributive Environmental Justice in the City: Differential Access in Two Mixed Israeli Cities. *Tijdschrift voor Economische en Sociale Geografie* 96(4), 433–443.

Oren, Michael B. (2002): *Six Days of War: June 1967 and the making of the modern Middle East.* Oxford: Oxford University Press.

Oren-Nordheim, Michal, and Ruth Kark (1995): *Jerusalem and its Environments: Quarters, Neighborhoods, Villages 1800–1948.* Jerusalem: Academon.

Paton, Lewis Bayles (1907): Jerusalem in Bible Times II: The Valleys of Ancient Jerusalem. *The Biblical World* 29(2), 86–96.

Pucher, John, and Ralph Buehler (2017): Cycling towards a More Sustainable Transport Future. *Transport Reviews* 37(6), 689–694.

Ramon, Uri, Tal Schwartz, and Iris Bernstein (2001): *West Jerusalem: Landscape Survey and Planning Principles* [Hebrew]. Jerusalem: Open Landscape Institute.

Rigolon, Alessandro (2016): A Complex Landscape of Inequity in Access to Urban Parks: A Literature Review. *Landscape and Urban Planning* 153, 160–169.

Rigolon, Alessandro (2018): Access to Urban Green Space in Cities of the Global South: A Systematic Literature Review. *Urban Science* 2(3), 67, doi.org/10.3390/urbansci2030067.

Rigolon, Alessandro, and Jeremy Németh (2018): A QUality INdex of Parks for Youth (QUINPY): Evaluating Urban Parks through Geographic Information Systems. *Environment and Planning B: Urban Analytics and City Science* 45(2), 275–294.

Rokem, Jonathan (2012): Politics and Conflict in a Contested City. *Bulletin du Centre de recherche français à Jéruslem* 23.

Rokem, Jonathan, and Laura Vaughan (2018): Segregation, Mobility and Encounters in Jerusalem: The Role of Public Transport Infrastructure in Connecting the 'Divided City'. *Urban Studies* 55(15), 3454–3473.

Romann, Michael, and Alex Weingrod (1991): *Living Together Separately: Arabs and Jews in Contemporary Jerusalem*. Princeton: Princeton University Press.

Rosenblatt, Samuel (1951): *The History of the Mizrachi Movement*. New York: Mizrachi Organization of America.

Rotman, Diego, and Eytan Shouker (2019): Building and Developing HaMesika Park: From Resistance to Collaboration. *Understanding Campus-Community Partnerships in Conflict Zones: Engaging Students for Transformative Change*, edited by Dalya Yafa Markovich, Daphna Golan, and Nadera Shalboub-Kevorkian. Jerusalem: Palgrave Macmillan, 117–156.

Rutland, Suzanne D. (2005): 'Buying out the Matter': Australia's Role in the Restitution for Templar Property in Israel. *Journal of Israeli History* 24(1), 135–154.

Saidov, Yossi (2016): Join the Bottom-Up Movement for Change. *Palestine–Israel Journal of Politics, Economics, and Culture; East Jerusalem* 21(4), 78–80.

Schaffer, Gad, and Noam Levin (2014): Mapping Human Induced Landscape Changes in Israel between the End of the 19th Century and the Beginning of the 21st Century. *Journal of Landscape Ecology* 7(1), 110–145.

Schlosberg, David (2007): *Defining Environmental Justice*. Oxford: Oxford University Press.

Schüle, Steffen Andreas et al. (2019): Social Inequalities in Environmental Resources of Green and Blue Spaces: A Review of Evidence in the WHO European Region. *International Journal of Environmental Research and Public Health* 16(7), 1216, https://doi.org/10.3390/ijerph16071216.

Su, Jason G. et al. (2019): Associations of Green Space Metrics with Health and Behavior Outcomes at Different Buffer Sizes and Remote Sensing Sensor Resolutions. *Environment International* 126, 162–170.

Survey of Israel (2020): Israeli Government Real Estate Website, https://www.nadlan.gov.il/. Accessed 5 July 2021.

Talen, Emily (2003): Neighborhoods as Service Providers: A Methodology for Evaluating Pedestrian Access. *Environment and Planning B: Planning and Design* 30(2), 181–200.

The Central Bureau of Statistics (2008): *Census Data 2008*. Jerusalem. Available online at http://www.cbs.gov.il.

The Central Bureau of Statistics (2018): *Localities and Population, by District, Sub-District, Religion and Population Group*. Jerusalem. Available online at https://www.cbs.gov.il/he/publications/DocLib/2018/2.%20ShnatonPopulation/st02_16x.pdf.

Tratalos, Jamie et al. (2007): Urban Form, Biodiversity Potential and Ecosystem Services. *Landscape and Urban Planning* 83(4), 308–317.

Travis, Anthony S. (2009): *On Chariots with Horses of Fire and Iron: The Excursionists and the Narrow Gauge Railroad from Jaffa to Jerusalem*. Tel Aviv: Manes Press.

Walker, Gordon P. (2012): *Environmental Justice*. London: Routledge.

Wolch, Jennifer R., Jason Byrne, and Joshua P. Newell (2014): Urban Green Space, Public Health, and Environmental Justice: The Challenge of Making Cities 'Just Green Enough'. *Landscape and Urban Planning* 125, 234–244.

Yiftachel, Oren (2006): *Ethnocracy: Land and Identity Politics in Israel/Palestine*. Philadelphia: University of Pennsylvania Press.

Yount, Kristen R. (2003): What Are Brownfields? Finding a Conceptual Definition. *Environmental Practice* 5(1), 25–33.

Zaban, Hila (2019a): 'Once There Were Moroccans Here – Today Americans': Gentrifications and the Housing Market in the Baka Neighborhood of Jerusalem. *City* 20(3), 412–427.

Zaban, Hila (2019b): The Real Estate Foothold in the Holy Land: Transnational Gentrification in Jerusalem. *Urban Studies* 57(15), 3116–3134.

Zevi, Shlomi and Avigdor Yair (2015): The 'Hamsila' leisure and recreation axis in Jerusalem – from a backyard to the center of things [Hebrew]. *Landscape Architecture* 55, 40–42.

Ruins and Representation

Remembering Flushing Meadows–Corona Park in Queens, New York City

DANIELA BOHÓRQUEZ SHEININ

Abstract

Through archival research and oral history, this chapter reveals how personal narratives of everyday life in Flushing Meadows–Corona Park and its neighbouring communities contributed to the construction of a new kind of transnational neighbourhood in Queens, New York. In the aftermath of the 1964–1965 New York World's Fair, formerly spectacular structures remained in an abandoned and decaying state; the ruins came to serve as markers of memory, closely intertwined with racial and ethnic community formation. Residents have narrated these transformations in their own lives, refracting their experiences with the park and its surrounding neighbourhoods through diverse personal and communal experiences. The idea of neighbourhood is one inextricably tied up in ideas about the past – in memory. Neighbourhoods thus become shifting entities, at once physical and imagined, shaped in part through individual and collective recollections of past significance. In their testimonies, residents demonstrate the ways in which the experience of the park and its environs is tied to deeper and broader histories encompassing subjects' country of origin, multi-national family history and ethnic and racial identification.

Introduction

Willy asked if I wanted to see inside the pavilion. It was no problem, he assured me; the stray kittens needed feeding anyway. I marvelled at my good fortune as Willy walked me through the doors of the old New York State Pavilion. The glass roof was entirely gone, the ground broken, weeds growing through the cracks. I could see the faded imprint of an old Texaco sign painted on the side wall. He led me through a door to one of the rooms along the edge. Mounds of trash covered the large space from floor to ceiling. It was indecipherable junk, too dangerous to sift through in that moment, Willy informed me. Still, I imagined the old pieces of the pavilion's many lives that might be submerged in the pile of rubble. A diligent scavenger, I thought, might find pieces of the old stage on which the Grateful Dead, Led Zeppelin and The Ramones had performed or shards of the pavilion's formerly majestic stained-glass roof. When the pavilion opened for the 1964–1965 New York World's Fair, a terrazzo highway map of New York state covered the structure's floor, inviting excited visitors to search for their hometown. Now, I wondered if one might dig long enough in that pile to find bits of the Empire State – maybe a shard of Watertown, of Albany or Rochester. As I attempted to locate memories that others had left behind in this dusty room, I could hear the animated yelps from a nearby soccer game, and the concrete roll of the skatepark merely steps away.

Willy, my guide on this expedition, noticed none of it. Born in Ecuador, he moved to Queens as a child in the 1970s. Before his resettlement, he had visited numerous times; his grandmother already lived there. He remembered visiting during the summer of 1964, just in time for the Fair. But he did not go. He urged his grandmother to instead take him to Coney Island, evidently the preferred destination for a young Ecuadorian boy's afternoon amusement. The Fair's projected prestige had not transcended international boundaries. All of this was a strange admission from a man whose work revolved, in large measure, around the Fair and its afterlives. The ongoing historical significance of the former fairgrounds was central to his work as the Director of the Queens Theatre, an institution that currently stands in Flushing Meadows–Corona Park, beside the former New York State Pavilion.

Notwithstanding his late preference for Coney Island, Willy had become an enthusiastic booster for the old fairgrounds and its structures by the time I met him in 2017. Flushing Meadows–Corona Park is something special, he explained, emphasising his attachment to the old pavilion:

> I take pride in that building, I love that building, you know... you probably heard that I was the one who painted the stripes. Like I was the one, picked them back in '91 and I left them there. Then the paint got chipped and all... I used to take care of that building. I used to like, pull the weeds out, when my kids were little, I used to go in there and like clean it up (Willy M.).[1]

Willy was part of a burgeoning multi-generational and multi-national Latin American immigrant population in Queens, a population whose own history had little to do with the Fair. All the same, he felt compelled to claim it as his own because "[he] grew up in this park, coming to this park when [he] was younger." He now occupies space within an institution materially tied to the history of the World's Fair, though integrates his own history and knowledge of cultural practices within the park. In Willy's hands, Flushing Meadows–Corona Park and its buildings were not the ruins of a past mega-event but rather a gathering space for new communities and a stage for ongoing memory-making (Willy M.).

The experience of Anni, however, was different. The granddaughter of Jewish Austrian and Hungarian immigrants, Anni was born and raised in Kew Gardens Hills, a neighbourhood adjacent to Flushing Meadows–Corona Park. Although a major expressway ran north–south along the park's eastern border separating her neighbourhood from the park grounds, she considered Flushing Meadows–Corona Park "practically [her] backyard", just down the hill and across the highway. While Anni conceived of the park as her backyard, it was also the neighbourhood park, *and* the site of something long departed. "The park when I grew up was ruins," she said. It was the "ghost of something" that had been there before. That "something" was the New York World's Fair – Anni was born during its opening season (Anni P.).

When she was 9 or 10 years old, she discovered a 1964 issue of *Life* magazine at her grandmother's house. Shockingly, her neighbourhood park was on the cover. It featured a photo of an illuminated Unisphere, the 140-foot steel globe in the centre of a fountain at the north end of the park. She learned this had been a symbol of the Fair's theme, 'Peace Through Understanding', a celebration of the United States' industry and technological prowess, their cultural offerings, and the promise of a bright and harmonious future. Anni could not believe it. Just 10 years prior millions of visitors had come to see the park, to marvel at space race technologies and the achievements of industry titans. This was the very same seemingly empty park she had visited many times and the contrast with the *Life* spread was jarring – and disappointing. It was "kind of like someone had Disneyland in their backyard, and it slipped away before you could see it" (Anni P.).

First conceived in the 1930s, Flushing Meadow (later Flushing Meadows–Corona) Park was built to house the 1939 New York World's Fair. Accessible by water, rail and road, Flushing Meadow sat roughly nine kilometres from midtown Manhattan and was promoted as the geographic and demographic centre of the city. Into this highly accessible space, city planners hoped to lure Fair visitors from across the city, state and country, but also from the neighbourhoods immediately adjacent to the park – Flushing, Kew Gardens, Forest Hills and Corona. Kew Gardens Hills was later developed as part of the Flushing Meadow Fair project along the park's south-eastern border.[2] In the aftermath of the 1939 World's Fair, the New York City Department of Parks drew on the original commercial appeal of the Fair to push the construction of a state-of-the-art recreational space to serve the adjoining neighbourhoods: "a public park second to none in the entire world".[3] The onset of World War II, however, prevented meaningful progress on this plan. After a second and final World's Fair in 1964–65, planners again moved to realise the conclusion of the park plan, part of a broader post-war current in urban development that saw the opening of Manhattan's Lincoln Center, the completion of the metropolitan arterial highway programme and the opening of Shea Stadium on the park grounds. Once again, however, the regimented, carefully planned world-class park that planners imagined failed to materialise.

As Willy's and Anni's testimonies show, however, Flushing Meadow did emerge as an important site for Queens residents, notwithstanding the failed (elite) aspirations for the site. On its 1,200 acres (4.8 square kilometres), city residents eventually found soccer fields and cricket pitches, festival grounds, playgrounds and afternoon amusements. In the coming decades, the park itself shaped the five neighbourhoods surrounding the park, transforming Queens into a new kind of urban community of rapidly changing politics, ethnicities, racial identities and immigrant spaces. In their own ways, Willy and Anni model the varying modes in which residents have narrated these transformations in their own lives, refracting their experiences with the park and its surrounding neighbourhoods through diverse personal and communal experiences. In their testimonies, each demonstrates the ways in which the experience of the park and its environs is tied to deeper and broader histories encompassing subjects' country of origin, multi-national family history and ethnic identification.

At the same time, their experiences are only two of the innumerable narratives that Queensites have crafted to help them make sense of themselves, their communities, their neighbourhoods and their relationship to the park. In this chapter I draw on a small sample of these stories – over 60 oral histories collected in Queens, NY in 2017. English- and Spanish-language interviews provided insight into the importance of language and personal experience in neighbourhood formation and the intersections of nationality, ethnicity and urban space. Participants varied by age, gender, ethnicity, race and citizenship status; their sole unifying trait was that they were, or had once been, a resident of Queens, New York. A diverse array of local knowledge brings a focus to those excluded from traditional, or even radical, archives. Oral histories reveal previously dismissed or obscured stories and experiences allowing affective responses from those whose perspectives are not as frequently recorded in traditional archives. They offer intensely personal histories of broad historical events.[4]

What these personal narratives tell us is that everyday life in Flushing Meadows–Corona Park and its neighbouring communities contributed to the construction of a new kind of transnational neighbourhood. The experience of having moved across borders (or not) exercised a profound influence on how residents understood themselves and their communities – subjects' status as recent immigrants, second-generation immigrants, native-born, undocumented or US citizens played a key role in shaping how they formulated narratives about the park and neighbourhood space. But while life in the transnational neighbourhood was profoundly shaped by the forces of global mobility, subjects' ethnic, national or citizenship status did not guarantee shared beliefs. More forces were at play, and the interviews collected here reveal often-obscured connections between green spaces and neighbourhood identity; between recreation, leisure and memory; and between the traumas of displacement, migration and neighbourhood change.

White Ethnic Memory and the Rhetoric of Ruin

The idea of neighbourhood is one inextricably tied up in ideas about the past – in memory. Neighbourhoods are neither geographic facts nor static locations, but are rather the culmination of a set of entangled and uneven historical processes through which constructions of belonging, home, ownership, insider, outsider, familiar and unfamiliar come into being. These constructions are determined by both material and ideological factors. They are malleable and mobile. Their borders are constantly in flux. Neighbourhoods operate as discursive sites in addition to physical spaces, originating in, constituted through and maintained by local recollections and emotional attachments to place. Neighbourhood, in this context, becomes a construct of the past. It both exists as a space neighbours occupy while also functioning as memory. Understandings of place form in both immediate perceptions of one's surroundings and remembered imaginings.[5]

For many descendants of European immigrants, or white ethnics, the ruins of the World's Fair have served as markers of memory – material safeguards of a past where a trip to the German-American butcher shop was an intimate social gathering or where a Jewish grandparent hollering across the street was the call to supper (P.S.). Conceptions of neighbourhood in this context are closely intertwined with World's Fair projections for the future, as well as the wave of proud enthusiasm that swept over surrounding neighbourhoods before and during the Fair. Residents absorbed Flushing Meadows–Corona Park into their concerns for the neighbourhood. They developed a sense of ownership over the park and the structures within. They had consumed the show from the side-lines, sometimes even *partaking* in the show on the side-lines. Neighbours urged each other to ensure their homes reflected the themes of progress and American ingenuity that were on display at the Fair. They delighted in the cachet they imagined the Fair brought to the area, certain that visitors from across the country would admire their beautiful neighbourhoods. Through this participation, the Fair neighbours cultivated a sense of familiarity in ways tourists or New Yorkers from other boroughs could not experience; they could never claim the Fair was their neighbour.

For white ethnic Queensites, however, the Fair's monuments also serve as trenchant reminders of loss. The end of the 1964–65 New York World's Fair brought to a close the park's and the surrounding neighbourhoods' moment in the global spotlight, a fact made all the more painful by the degradation of the park's structures in subsequent years. Due in part to the World's Fair's financial failure, the city never rehabilitated the space as the grandiose park once imagined, and promised.[6] Demolition remained half-finished for decades as permanent structures fell into disrepair. Letters poured in from residents of all ages pleading with city officials to restore Flushing Meadows to a park that evoked the grandeur of the World's Fair.[7] By the end of the 1960s, these letters had become more of a nuisance than a friendly communication with a troubled citizen, a reminder of lost promise. The place where "64 million fair visitors strolled, is virtually deserted, a half-fulfilled dream." The Unisphere stood alone in "the nearly deserted area where a park was supposed to be developed."[8]

Local publications bolstered the rhetoric of ruin that many residents adopted in their letters to municipal officials, and in the way they described their neighbourhood park years later. Newspapers focused extensively on the graffiti that marred old Fair structures through the 1970s and 1980s, conjuring images of the "once-majestic" park features rendered "inoperable" and "gutted by vandals".[9] Reporters often used language of violent destruction; "the wreckers ripped apart building after building and carted away the rubble." The imagery of the active disassembling leaving only "rubble" behind further emphasised the horrors of dismantling the previously pristine buildings.[10] New York City reporters compared the abandonment, interior looting and ultimate demolition of the Fair's United States Pavilion to the nation-wide federal neglect that had resulted in overwhelming amounts of building abandonment and urban destruction. The US Pavilion, "still impressive from a distance, seems headed on a slow trip to the junkyard, a journey which its ravaged interior suggests has already begun".[11]

The image of the "caved-in roof"[12] – in both text and reality – haunted nearby residents. Anni revealed that when she was a child, it was "a strange experience watching buildings deteriorate. For kids, things have more permanence." The decay was confusing, especially because she only observed such ruinous markings in the same places she went to play. Throughout her childhood and adolescence, every time she drove down the Van Wyck Expressway along the park's eastern border, she claimed she would see that more glass had fallen from the roof of the New York State Pavilion – the same pavilion that she would see her friend climb for fun just a few years later, and at which Willy would let his children play even later. The playgrounds vandalised and eventually dismantled, in the park and in her neighbourhood, were all part of urban decay – "for a child," she said, it was a "haunting thing to happen" (Anni P.).

Anni's understanding of this place as urban, and in striking contrast to her "old school suburban" neighbourhood, was moulded by what she knew of other US cities during the 1970s. By the late 1960s, news of the disastrous urban renewal projects in Manhattan, Brooklyn and the Bronx reached US Americans across the country. Queens inhabitants saw other boroughs' residential areas become sites for bulldozers, blasts and thousands of displaced residents. Many attributed the wave of white residents that moved to Long Island, the rising number of shuttered stores and the still vacant Flushing Meadows–Corona Park to the city-wide downward trend. In some cases, these concerns arose not entirely because residents feared for their own displacement or the destruction of the neighbourhood they had inhabited for decades, but just as much for the implication of labelling their neighbourhood as a place that might benefit from urban renewal. To propose a site for an urban renewal project in New York City and elsewhere, Queens neighbours believed, was degrading. It branded the neighbourhood as ugly, deprived and non-white. It was offensive to first- and second-generation European immigrants who considered themselves on the margins of white American society, but white Americans nonetheless.[13]

In this way, the World's Fair 'ruins' became touchstones for the Queens experience of what historians have called the urban crisis. Amidst the growth of the post-war United States emerged pockets of economic depression within urban centres, propelled by isolation from the labour force, public transportation, civic services and government subsidised or affordable housing.[14] Population shifts to the suburbs left cities underfunded, and federally subsidised housing loan programmes, like the Federal Housing Administration and Homeowners' Loan Corporation, exacerbated racial disparities, thus prompting an increasing racialised spatial conception of urban/suburban space.[15] By the late 1960s, Americans came to understand the spatiality of inequality, materialising through neighbourhood aesthetics, *and* in the way policymakers and the public talked about the neighbourhood. They attributed moral and individual fault to the material outcomes of economic inequalities and racial segregation. Well-kept homes and neighbourhoods became standard, "tangible evidence of hard work, savings and prudent investment, the sign of upward mobility and middle-class status".[16] By contrast, neighbourhoods labelled slums and targeted for redevelopment projects were often thought to be the product of moral failings. Vandalism, theft and ultimately uprisings in various US cities during the 1960s became racialised behaviours, relegated to only some neighbourhoods – the products of their own residents' shortcomings.[17] The ruins, in this context, represented a critical moment for European white ethnic residents, who through the 1960s, 1970s and 1980s would witness the large-scale demographic and aesthetic evolution of their neighbourhoods.

In recent years, scholars have traced the cultural history of the urban crisis, from the significance of cultural producers in utilising particular imagery and narrative to metaphorical framings of city elements associated with the crisis.

As the film and news media industries capitalised on urban decline, regions like the South Bronx in New York City became nationally branded as the "iconography of urban ruin in America".[18] Brian Tochterman argues that these narratives shaped policy and political ideology while the media pushed tropes of decay and disease in need of a solution.[19] Peter L'Official posits that terms for urban spaces, like "blight" and "inner city", might be considered "metaphorical constructions of place that continue, to this day, to characterize cities and, more pointedly, the people in them – as versions of urban legends as well".[20]

The former World's Fair structures at Flushing Meadows–Corona Park signified this crisis, and its legacy, to surrounding residents. Just two years after the World's Fair vacated Flushing Meadows, the *New York Times* reported: "At a number of points the area was, simultaneously, in process of destruction and creation. Where the Chrysler building once drew lines, there is now a broken skeleton of red steel beams".[21] While their rusty appearance prompted alarm from many who feared *their* neighbourhood might be thought of in the same urban categories as the South Bronx, the structures became critical monuments in the construction of neighbourhood memories. They still represented the Fair itself, but the decrepit structures no longer conjured images of an imagined modernity, nor progress, but the very symbols residents had grown accustomed to seeing in the news of deteriorating and abandoned structures across the United States. Still, the structures played a role in the fabrication of collective memory, albeit differently for different groups. There are many for whom the structures were simply just *there*. The ground on which they cast shadows held significance as sites of cultural display and ritual, while the ruins were relegated only to the background in photographs.[22] Queens neighbourhood oral histories reveal alternative understandings of the urban crisis and the post-war decay of urban structures.

Transnational Negotiations

Eventually, the Fair's ruins came to symbolise a loss of another kind to many white ethnic residents. The end of the Fair had coincided with profound changes in the park's surrounding communities, as Italian-, German-, Jewish- and Irish-dominated neighbourhoods transformed into (still-growing) Latin American and Asian enclaves. White ethnics no longer recognised the languages spoken in shops or restaurants, and familiar faces seemed to move away in droves. As businesses began catering to a new local clientele, European white ethnic residents lost their sense of comfort and familiarity. 'Their' neighbourhood now belonged to someone else, in their eyes, leaving only Flushing Meadows behind (George P., P.S.). Residents used the decaying Fair structures as a means to process their changing neighbourhoods. The Fair represented their 'perfect' former neighbourhood that they watched fall apart every time they visited the park. Through this sense of ownership of the spectacle of the first billion-dollar World's Fair in contrast to new immigrant cultures, the myth of Flushing Meadows–Corona Park materialised. One Forest Hills resident shared, "the world of *Leave it to Beaver* and those kinds of sitcoms was the world we grew up in. And after that it became a very different world." He referenced the World's Fair as a temporal marker, signifying a turning point from a perceived harmonious and homogenous domestic ideal to what "the neighbourhood [had] become." The new neighbourhood he referenced, by contrast, was one filled with new immigrants who, by his observation, remained in isolated sects, unwilling to interact with their neighbours (Ken U.).[23]

Organisations representing white ethnics attempted to make sense of these urban transformations through the 1960s and 1970s. Prime among these organisations' concerns was the perception that federal, state and municipal funding had been directed elsewhere in the city. Neighbours to Flushing Meadows–Corona Park wondered why impoverished neighbourhoods in other boroughs received funding for renewal projects, when decaying structures remained crumbled at the park, unaware of (or perhaps ignoring) the colossal displacement and segregation many renewal projects caused.[24] Debates in which the residents of Flushing Meadows neighbourhoods found themselves embroiled after the Fair were grounded in arguments that drew upon representations of the transnational neighbourhood. Many believed that in their claims as descendants of European immigrants, and thus the diffusers of particular urban cultures, they might make a stronger case for neighbourhood defence and appeals to municipal officials. In 1975, for example, the American Italian Historical Association hosted a conference at Queens College in Flushing themed 'The Urban Experience of Italian Americans'. Speakers revealed a different kind of experience of the urban crisis; they "were never included in the crisis equation [...] Italian-Americans were upwardly mobile some scholars assumed. They had made it. They were moving to the suburbs. Hence, urban living constituted no difficulty for them".[25] Political scientist and historian Patrick J. Gallo and others advised this was not the case; they found themselves economically and racially wedged between the inner city and the affluent suburbs.

Anni, for example, speculated that her parents relocated to Kew Gardens Hills from Astoria and the Bronx because of the neighbourhood's ethnic composition. She shared what she described as her Eastern European Jewish background with many in the neighbourhood, along with others of Greek and Italian descent. At the same time, she suggested, it might have been part of a broader trajectory for young parents – moving to Queens from elsewhere in the city, where something like a quadplex with a backyard was reasonably attainable (Anni P.). But the attainable suburban experience was short-lived.

The feeling of in-betweenness was common. As immigrants began moving to Queens in greater numbers, ethnic groups such as Italian and Jewish Americans found in Flushing Meadows' monuments an assertion of their whiteness. What had been a previously ambiguous status between African Americans and Anglo European Americans was solidified by contrast to new residents from Latin America and Asia. Still, as part of this transition, speakers at the 1975 conference and oral history subjects in 2017 reflected on (and resented) the loss of Italian identity through the process of being identified as white suburban dwellers, as well as the loss of Italian community during the influx of new immigrants.

Others saw African American and Latino residents as a threat to their own unstable social positions within the urban racial hierarchy; the Italian American neighbourhood needed protection. Speaker Joseph M. Conforti claimed that "[w]hen the new arrivals are members of groups generally ranked low in status in the American racial-ethnic hierarchy, they further pose the threat of status contamination." The Italian Americans had already fashioned their own "version of the suburban dream" between the city and the exclusively white suburbs and they were not about to share these spaces with supposedly untrustworthy neighbours. Like other white Americans, many Italian Americans fled these urban spaces.[26]

When I interviewed Italian American George P., he shared a fairly typical story about grandparents who had arrived to Ellis Island, then moved from Manhattan to Brooklyn to start a family. Their children made a final move to Queens when George was a child. His father-in-law still lived in a small house just three blocks from where the three of us sat in William F. Moore Park, a tiny triangle where 108th Street, 51st and 52nd Avenue converge. One could traverse the park in about a minute or so. To the north, just beyond the bocce courts, they would see Park Side Restaurant, an institution for Italian dining, and to the south, perhaps a line of people waiting for their Italian ice at the Lemon Ice King of Corona. Had I been to Flushing Meadows–Corona Park, he asked, making sure I knew that it was just a 10-minute walk.

Our conversation in English was an infrequent occurrence in the centre of the formerly Italian enclave. Now the population is predominantly Spanish-speaking, from South and Central America. "It was back in the sixties that a lot of whites were moving to Long Island," he shared. Though he opted to stay in Queens, much of his family and friends moved to Long Island because some parts of Queens became "very, very bad […] just like East New York", a predominantly Black and Latino Brooklyn neighbourhood. He was purposely vague when talking about neighbourhoods "getting bad", though did not attribute this change to anything more specific than "blockbusting", the deceitful real estate practice wherein agents convinced white homeowners that non-white residents would soon move into their neighbourhood, thus prompting them to sell their house quickly at a reduced price. Later in the conversation, however, it became clear he regrets the massive cultural shift that left him unable to understand the new owners of a store where he had shopped for decades. He has an especially difficult time with others who moved away and now reminisce about the old neighbourhood. "Well, the neighbourhood wouldn't be like that if people like you would have stayed, instead of panicking and moving because a minority family moved next door to you" (George P.).

At the same time, conversations with George often drifted toward his love of the World's Fair. Did I know, he asked, that young boys wore jackets and ties when they attended? A loss of a distinguished, respectable moment in time, he mused. He later proposed to his wife at the Fair's still standing centrepiece, the Unisphere, signalling the continued significance of the space as a grand background for important moments in his life. As he and I conversed, surrounded by some of the few remaining Italian neighbourhood institutions, it was clear that sharing memories of the World's Fair was comforting to George. His descriptions of the fun and awe he felt as a young child, and continued appreciation for Flushing Meadows and the Fair ruins contrasted with his defeated portrayals of the changing neighbourhood and his place within (George P.).

In the late 1960s, councilman Arthur J. Katzman, a representative for roughly 125,000 residents in a number of neighbourhoods in the Flushing Meadows area, criticised the John Lindsay administration publicly for their "neglect" of the predominantly Jewish "Forest Hills–Rego Park community". In all areas of civic service, from education and housing, to police protection and transit, he condemned the municipal government's "disregard for middle-class citizens' needs".[27] The city's failure to provide them with appropriate services threatened their stability, he claimed, increasing still "as more and more other neighbourhoods have slid over the brink of crisis." These shortcomings would lead to their own crisis, he and his supporters predicted. Katzman called for neighbours to insist on transit and infrastructure development. He demanded answers to why the Forest Hills–Rego Park area, whose high school had classrooms in the basement and only two guidance counsellors for 4,000 students, had not been considered when the New York City Board of Education had allocated resources for one hundred additional schools in the city. Implicit in this call to action was that they had also failed to protect them from urban incursions they had managed to resist for a century.[28]

Queens newspaper the *Long Island Post* also took a stance against the administration: "Neither the Councilman, nor we [the paper], feel any immediate peril that our fine residential communities face imminent disaster, or looming deterioration into blighted, undesirable neighbourhoods. That's not the point".[29] The point, however, was to use the rhetoric of ruin to spark fear-motivated action among residents and lawmakers. They believed Lindsay's administration set a precedent for the kind of municipal neglect that other cities and neighbourhoods around the country experienced; the final step was tax-paying middle-class residents, or the "voiceless ones", fleeing to the suburbs. Residents and their allies drew on their identities as the daughters and sons of immigrants to both explain their perceived oppression, as well as to assert their claims to the neighbourhood.

The World's Fair remnants thus became heritage sites for the material consequences of the urban crisis. Monuments, counter-monuments and architecture often serve as motors for urban collective memory, as well as the spatial organisation of racial and ethnic identities. They became pieces of the many "vernacular ruins" scattered throughout the United States, often remnants that signify neither aesthetic prestige nor a defining moment, but rather the passage of time itself.[30] And because the structures did not rely on historical knowledge nor cultural capital to understand their significance, they became accessible to all, moulded in the neighbour's image. Here, nostalgia features prominently as a contrast to the changing neighbourhood, determining *how* and *what* people remembered. In relying on old Fair structures as markers of their past, European white ethnic Queens residents relied on nostalgic constructions to mask realities – a neighbourhood that never was, and that becomes increasingly unattainable as it evolves in memory.[31]

From Ruins to Rebirth

In the coming decades, local newspapers continued to employ the rhetoric of ruin in their coverage of Flushing Meadows–Corona Park, despite the fact that weekend crowds had, by the mid-1970s, started to top 200,000. Part of Flushing Meadows' rehabilitation through the 1970s and 1980s had been the restoration of some former Fair structures, including the Hall of Science and the Queens Museum. It was also home to some massive entertainment venues with Shea Stadium and the National Tennis Center, as well as the smaller scale zoo and the Queens Playhouse. Tens of thousands travelled to watch the New York Mets take the field and tennis greats compete at the US Open.[32] These developments, however, fell well short of the expectations of many white ethnic residents, who tended to judge the park according to the spectacular criteria set by the Fair. Anything else was ignored.

If white Queensites felt underwhelmed by the Hall of Science and even Shea Stadium, they were sometimes wholly oblivious to the dynamic recreational culture that had begun to take shape in the park as New Yorkers – including a very large proportion of recent immigrants – appropriated the space for casual play, multi-ethnic and multi-national festivals, family gatherings, soccer games, kite flying and cycling. Reporter Caryn Eve Weiner commented at the time on the park's centrality to the lives of immigrant as well as non-immigrant New Yorkers, noting that many parkgoers "consider themselves the naturalized citizens of Flushing Meadows–Corona Park. They are the Hispanic soccer players from around Queens, the solitary cyclist from Forest Hills, and the young Brooklyn families on picnics." White ethnic citizens found symbols of a collective identity and a shared history in the park's ruins. But as Weiner pointed out, the park could serve to crystallise other identities, rooted less in an experience of collective loss than in a sense of new beginnings.[33] While not all foreign-born parkgoers' immigration status was "naturalized citizen", the display of community on park grounds solidified their belonging in the neighbourhood. While Anni and many others perceived in Flushing Meadows a story of "decline", others saw in the space opportunity.

For many immigrants the park represented the best, most dynamic aspects of the city itself, as well as an antidote to some of its inconveniences. Willy, for example, marvelled at the park's overwhelming diversity:

> If you come here on a Sunday for instance, springtime, summer day on a Sunday, it's beautiful 'cause you'll see families of Jewish people on bicycles, and then you'll see the Chinese people, you see the, mainly more Latinos, you know what I'm saying, but it's a mixture of everything. Everybody just enjoying the day in the park, it's very mixed. It's cool (Willy M.).

Silvia, a Queens resident born in Colombia, found in the park a respite from her overcrowded living conditions. She remembered: "I brought my son here, and you know, when he has kids, I hope he brings them here. We don't have to pay, we don't have to buy anything. And you know, when we moved here, we lived with my sister and her kids [...] they needed to *run*" (Silvia, her emphasis). Manhattanites Darren Leung and Timothy Wong travelled to Flushing Meadows in the 1980s rather than the closer Central Park because there were "too many muggers [...] Here, it's a family type of thing".[34] For Silvia, Darren and Timothy, Flushing Meadows–Corona Park functioned as an escape, operating as a family-friendly (sub)urban getaway. Particularly for residents like Silvia, the space played a critical role in her family's history in a new country. There her children played sports, celebrated holidays and birthdays, and learned to identify as citizens of a heterogeneous American Republic. Visiting and playing in Flushing Meadows is now a critical memory in the formation of herself and her sons as US Americans. They "think of themselves as Colombian-Americans," Silvia says, but she and the children were also aware of their place in a broader sweep of American diversity: "You know, you have the Ecuatorianos, the Mexicans. Bueno, they're all Americans" (Silvia).

Conversely, these accounts differ from a white, lifelong resident's relationship to Flushing Meadows. After delighting in his memories of the World's Fair, he revealed that he had returned very few times:

> A couple of visits to the Queens Museum. Maybe when the kids were small, maybe one visit to the zoo. I could walk over the highway to that part of Flushing Meadow Park where there's a Lake, I think I was there, twice. I tried to jog around there once, and it's a low-lying area, and the lake came up, and it was swampy, and I found nothing interesting about that park. Just flat, you know, I'd rather go to Central Park. So this is what I'm talking about, about my connection with this neighbourhood. I mean, here's a big park there, but I never go there […] If I was there in that park a half a dozen times in thirty-two years, that's probably the most. It's not, it doesn't grab me. Like I said, I can go to Central Park […] but Flushing Meadow, you know, there's guys playing soccer, and picnicking, you know, locals picnicking and things, but it's not a, I don't find anything there for, you know, that interests me (Ken U.).

For Willy and Silvia, there was plenty. It was a recreational space in which to see the beauty of the neighbourhood's diversity, and of children as they grow. Moreover, it was a much-needed escape from the cramped apartments in which many residents lived. The lifelong Queens resident, however, felt no attachment beyond the close of the World's Fair.

In their understandings of the park, recent immigrants also registered feelings of loss, though of a very different kind than that of their white ethnic neighbours. As recent arrivals to the United States, many had experienced a loss of place-based identity as they attempted to adjust to the foreign geography of New York. Many found themselves in a foreign place to which they felt little personal connection, an alienation compounded by the discrimination many experienced both from outside and from within their own 'communities'. As I sat with a young Bolivian woman on a park bench, she murmured,

> You know what, I can tell you. I'm undocumented… it's who I am, it's who I work for [referring to her activism on behalf of undocumented residents in Queens]. You know, you look around and you never know here. I feel supported here, but sometimes people are not how they seem. They could really have a problem with it. You know, if they came here *the right* [interviewee's emphasis] way. But I can't help how I came here. I'm here. I am their neighbour (Anonymous 1).

Some also revealed racial divisions within their community. "They are so ugly," an Afro-Dominican woman said of her neighbours who complained of the newcomers. She had been living in Corona for 20 years, after moving to join her brother there as an adult in the late 1990s. She was not speaking of her white neighbours of European descent, but her Latino neighbours who held disdain for new migrants; "I'd like to know what they think of me… but I know. You should see, when they see me speaking Spanish? What a fuss!" She proceeded to chuckle, mostly to herself, at her dramatisation of the neighbours realising that she, a black woman, also spoke Spanish. She equated her neighbours' contempt for new immigrants with their disdain for Afro-Latinas like her, no matter how long they had lived in the neighbourhood. "You'll see," she said, "they're not the Italians, but what's the difference?" (Anonymous 2).

Just as imported race relations had impacted New York's Puerto Rican population decades prior, the increasingly varied Latin American population across the city brought with them vague and diverse understandings of racial status and identity.[35] Walter, a Peruvian man who arrived in Queens in the 1970s, shared with me his struggles with not only US American conceptions of racial identification, but also those held by his neighbours from multiple Latin American nations. He was quiet and soft-spoken; he took a few seconds to consider every story he shared with me. Though Walter had been an anthropologist in Peru, on arriving in the United States he found work at a grocery store where, he claimed, he was mistreated by the Mexican "kids" with whom he worked. Nobody wanted to get to know him because of his dark skin and he felt as though no one in his adopted country had ever really understood him. They had strange ideas about Peru, and strange ideas about him. He quickly learned that it was too much effort to try to share anything of himself or his past with his new co-workers and neighbours. Although he had the support of his sister, with whom he lived, their neighbours were not particularly friendly, nor helpful. It was foolish, he said, to have hoped for something different. "How do I insert myself into the world of others?" he asked rhetorically. "Silence" (Walter S.).

These stories are at least partly a function of the rising diversity within New York's Latin American enclaves since 1970, as well as the city's peculiar human geography. Whereas 'Latino' had once been nearly synonymous in New York with Puerto Rican politics and identity, by the 1980s, the term signalled a far broader sweep of potential geographic origins, encompassing much of Central and South America.[36] Unlike other US cities with substantial Latino populations, New York's Latin American community is not dominated by a single nationality. Nor are New York's various Latin American national communities particularly segregated from one another. In many cases, a single block that might once have been home to a Puerto Rican, Dominican or Cuban majority now houses immigrants from multiple Central and South American nations. The Spanish language is an important unifier for these pan-national communities, as is the fact that many immigrants share similar motivations for coming to the United States.[37] Additionally, the close proximity in which these various national communities live to one another can, as Willy pointed out, serve as a source of dynamism. But Walter's experience is no less valid: diversity in this context can also contribute to misunderstandings and increased tensions.

Conclusion

Flushing Meadows–Corona Park and its environs stood at the intersection of local history and memory, post-war urban history, and the cultural histories of the urban landscape. The culmination of fairground destruction, the decay of buildings left behind, rising immigration numbers, and an increasing national emphasis on slum clearance and urban development had a profound impact on Queens' landscape in the two decades following the World's Fair. The residents of Flushing, Corona, Forest Hills, Kew Gardens and Kew Gardens Hills navigated at once a local and transnational space. While neighbourhood demographics shifted over time, the park remained, suffused each day with multi-national and multi-ethnic meanings by its diverse occupants who refashioned the space in their neighbourhood's image.

In general terms, Flushing Meadows has operated in different modes of identity formation for different populations. For ethnic whites, the park has come to operate as a material buttress for memory, a touchstone for the specific transnational constellation of communities the park and its neighbourhoods once housed decades ago. For many first- and second-generation Latin American immigrants, however, Flushing Meadows–Corona Park became a material and symbolic marker of the present and the future, with all of the opportunities, anxieties, harmonies and contestations implied thereby. Willy, for example, not only felt a personal connection to the park in which he worked, but his connection was reinforced by the ever-evolving new meanings parkgoers instilled in the park and structures within every day. As a musician whose music reflected the many nationalities, cultures and histories that surrounded him, he explained to me that he planned to shoot a music video at a particular place on the park grounds:

> [I]n the early 20th century, there was a Peruvian composer who wrote the song, 'El Cóndor Pasa', The Condor Passes. You know, condors, symbolically, that's the bird represents Bolivia, represents Ecuador, Columbia, like about five, like seven countries, in Latin America. You know how the eagle represents the United

States? Well, the condor, you know, is the symbolic bird for those. So, when this guy wrote this, he wrote it as an instrumental. Then, throughout the decades of the 20th century, people were recording the song with their own lyrics, like putting, writing lyrics. Everybody would write their own lyrics or they'll, their own take on the song […] I went and recorded it last year, with a, with a female singer, a singer from Ecuador. She's a good friend of mine. And, I did it in Spanglish and I wrote my own lyrics. This summer we're gonna shoot the video pretty much underneath the Unisphere. Underneath America (Willy M.).

As Willy recounted this particular song's permeation through US American music, it was clear that for him, the ideal visual representation of the song was the connected Americas on the Unisphere. He saw in the steel structure a background for the traditional instruments and garments he would have the band wear, a fascinating contrast illustrated every day by park goers. While he liked the contrast of traditional garb against the modern steel, he also liked that it was his to use. He could claim the Unisphere, just as his neighbours had, and just as the Fair planners and the millions of Americans who had descended upon the fairgrounds 50 years prior had. In his vision of integrating the old and the new, he established an ownership of, and familiarity with, the park.

While Flushing Meadows–Corona Park has often been portrayed by longtime residents, real estate firms and neighbourhood associations as an exclusive space inundated by "foreign aliens", this study reveals that there have *always* been unfamiliar "newcomers" in the park and surrounding neighbourhoods, but that immigrants from across the globe found in Flushing Meadows a site for negotiations over the meanings of 'neighbour', 'neighbourhood', and even 'American'. Rather than a disruption to the community, the park with its diverse throngs of newcomers has served as the very engine of a renewed sense of neighbourhood in Queens and beyond. How people enjoy a city park – and in so doing change it – is part of an urbanising process that transforms newcomers into residents, neighbours, community stakeholders and citizens in a transnational United States.

Notes

1. Interview participants will be referred to by first name, first name/last initial, first and last initials, or "Anonymous", per their request. Anonymous participants are numbered to indicate different speakers. For the purposes of this study, participants of Latin American origin and descent are overrepresented. This is representative of their population numbers in the region studied, and driven by the interviewer's ability to communicate in Spanish with non-English speakers. All interview references are cited in the text.

2. Bulletin (1936): *The Flushing Meadow Improvement* 1(3).
3. Clarke, Gilmore D. (1939): Landscape Architecture at the New York World's Fair: A Portfolio of Photographs of Modern Design. *Landscape Architecture* 29(4), 153–166, 166.
4. Mallon, Florencia E. (2005): *Courage Tastes of Blood: The Mapuche Community of Nicolás Ailío and the Chilean State, 1906–2001.* Durham, NC: Duke University Press; Rúa, Mérida M. (2012): *A Grounded Identidad: Making New Lives in Chicago's Puerto Rican Neighborhoods.* Oxford: Oxford University Press; Ruiz, Vicki L. (1998a): *From out of the Shadows: Mexican Women in Twentieth-Century America.* Oxford: Oxford University Press; Lipman, Jana K. (2009): *Guantánamo: A Working-Class History between Empire and Revolution.* Berkeley: University of California Press. See also Shopes, Linda (2015): Community Oral History: Where We Have Been, Where We Are Going. *Oral History* 43(1), 97–106; Kline, Carrie Nobel (1996): Giving It Back: Creating Conversations to Interpret Community Oral History. *The Oral History Review* 23(1), 19–40; Ruiz, Vicki L. (1998b): Situating Stories: The Surprising Consequences of Oral History. Theme Articles: Practice and Pedagogy. *The Oral History Review* 25(1), 71–80.
5. The theoretical framework here draws from Pierre Nora's "sites of memory".
6. New York World's Fair, New York, N.Y. (1960): *Preparation of the Site for World's Fair 1964–1965: Flushing Meadow Park, the City of New York.* New York, 10.
7. Rotner, Eileen (1964): Letter to Robert Moses (7 January). Box 248, Folder M3 Request for Information 1963–1964, Restoration of Park (L–Z), Maintenance. N.Y. World's Fair Corp. Maintenance. New York World's Fair 1964–1965 Corporation records, Manuscripts and Archives Division, The New York Public Library; Class 5–4 at PS 196 (1965): Letters to Robert Wagner (10 February). Box 250, Folder M3 Restoration of Park (1965) N.Y. World's Fair 1964–65 Corps. Maintenance A–L. New York World's Fair 1964–1965 Corporation records, Manuscripts and Archives Division, The New York Public Library; Yordan, Raymond M. (1965): Letter to Robert Moses (8 September). Box 250, Folder M3 Restoration of Park (1965) N.Y. World's Fair 1964–65 Corps. Maintenance A–L. New York World's Fair 1964–1965 Corporation records, Manuscripts and Archives Division, The New York Public Library; Carrano, Ralph (1964): Letter to Robert Moses (30 May). Box 248, Folder M3 Request for Information 1963–1964, Restoration of Park (A–K), Maintenance. New York World's Fair 1964–1965 Corporation records, Manuscripts and Archives Division, The New York Public Library; Beckley, Arlene (1964): Letter to Robert Moses (23 May). Box 248, Folder M3 Request for Information 1963–1964, Restoration of Park (A–K), Maintenance. New York World's Fair 1964–1965 Corporation records, Manuscripts and Archives Division, The New York Public Library.
8. Forlorn Place: Site of N.Y. World Fair. *Los Angeles Times* (12 December 1969).
9. Ames, Charlotte (1974): The World's Fair 10 Years After: Ruin and Hope. *Long Island Press* (14 April). Folder: Parks. Queens Co. Flushing Meadows Corona Park 1974. Archives at Queens Public Library.

10. Ibid.
11. Klein, H.L. (1975): A White Elephant Wastes Away. *Long Island Press* (17 August).
12. Ibid.
13. Iachetta, Michael (1971): City Clears the Rubble From 5 Blitzed Homes. *Daily News* (27 October); Iachetta, Michael (1978): New Corona Label – 'Worse Than Ever'. *Daily News* (15 November); Orin, Deborah (n.d.). Where we live – Part II. *Corona History*. The Archives at Queens Library.
14. Sugrue, Thomas J. (1996): *The Origins of the Urban Crisis: Race and Inequality in Postwar Detroit*. Princeton, NJ: Princeton University Press, 5ff.
15. Avila, Eric (2004): *Popular Culture in the Age of White Flight: Fear and Fantasy in Suburban Los Angeles*. Berkeley: University of California Press, 34ff.
16. Sugrue (1996), 213.
17. Weaver, Timothy (2017): Urban Crisis: The Genealogy of a Concept. *Urban Studies* 54(9), 2039–2055, 2045.
18. L'Official, Peter (2020): *Urban Legends: The South Bronx in Representation and Ruin*. Cambridge, MA: Harvard University Press, 2.
19. Tochterman, Brian (2017): *The Dying City: Postwar New York and the Ideology of Fear*. Chapel Hill: University of North Carolina Press, 6ff.
20. L'Official (2020), 7.
21. Schumach, Murray (1967): Moses Gives City Fair Site as Park: Flushing Meadows in Queens. *New York Times* (4 June).
22. Oats, David (1974): The Ruins of Flushing Meadows. *Flushing Tribune* (22 November). Folder: Parks. Queens Co. Flushing Meadows Corona Park 1974. Archives at Queens Public Library; Rabin, Bernard (1980): It's a Park for Vandals in the Dark. [publication unknown] (31 October). Folder: Parks. Queens Co. Flushing Meadows Corona Park 1980–81. Archives at Queens Public Library. See also: The Shame of Flushing Meadow. *Sunday News* (7 April 1974). Folder: Parks. Queens Co. Flushing Meadows Corona Park 1976. Archives at Queens Public Library; 'Ideal' Play Spot a Shambles. *Daily News* (11 April 1978). Folder: Parks. Queens Co. Flushing Meadows Corona Park 1978. Archives at Queens Public Library.
23. Gershowitz, Mike (1967): Poverty, War, Renewal Bogged Down. *Long Island Star-Journal* (20 January). Folder: Corona – East Elmhurst, The Archives at Queens Library. See also: Steve Letzer (1977): U.S. Pavilion is Coming Down. *Long Island Press* (6 February). Folder: Parks. Queens Co. Flushing Meadows Corona Park 1977, Archives at Queens Public Library; U.S. Hall Tumbles Down. *Daily News* (17 May 1977). Folder: Parks. Queens Co. Flushing Meadows Corona Park 1977, Archives at Queens Public Library; Oats, David (1977): The End of the U.S. Pavilion. *Flushing Tribune*, (12 April). Folder: Parks. Queens Co. Flushing Meadows Corona Park 1977, Archives at Queens Public Library.

24. See also: Corona – Unity Turns into a Schism. *Daily News* (4 July 1971). Housing. Corona. The Archives at Queens Public Library.
25. Gallo, Patrick J. (1977): The Urban Experience of Italian-Americans. *Proceedings of the Eighth Annual Conference of the American Italian Historical Association.* The American Italian Historical Association, 11.
26. Conforti, Joseph M. (1977): Italian-Americans and the Urban Crisis: A Sociological Perspective. *Proceedings of the Eighth Annual Conference of the American Italian Historical Association.* The American Italian Historical Association, 103.
27. Raps City Neglect of Forest Hills – Rego Park. *Long Island Post* (9 November 1967).
28. Ibid.
29. End Neglect! *Long Island Post* (16 November 1967).
30. Yablon, Nick (2009): *Untimely Ruins: An Archaeology of American Urban Modernity, 1819–1919.* Chicago: University of Chicago Press, 8ff.
31. Shackel, Paul A. (2001): *Myth, Memory, and the Making of the American Landscape.* Gainesville: University Press of Florida, 1ff. See also: Lowenthal, David (1996): *Possessed by the Past: The Heritage Crusade and the Spoils of History.* New York: Free Press.
32. Collins, Tom (1974): Thousands enjoy Flushing Meadows. *Sunday News* (7 July). Folder: Parks. Queens Co. Flushing Meadows Corona Park 1974. Archives at Queens Public Library; Ames (1974).
33. Weiner, Caryn Eve (1985): The Park; Borough's Backyard. *Newsday* (14 July).
34. Leung and Wong quoted in Weiner (1985).
35. Rodríguez, Clara E. (2010): Racial Themes in the Literature: Puerto Ricans and Other Latinos. *Hispanic New York: A Sourcebook*, edited by Iván Claudio Remeseira. New York: Columbia University Press, 183–186.
36. Sanjek, Roger (1998): *The Future of Us All: Race and Neighborhood Politics in New York City.* Ithaca, NY: Cornell University Press, 61ff.
37. Remeseira, Iván Claudio, ed. (2010): *Hispanic New York: A Sourcebook.* New York: Columbia University Press, 2f. and 5f.; Jones-Correa, Michael (1998): *Between Two Nations: The Political Predicament of Latinos in New York City.* Ithaca, NY: Cornell University Press, 109–123.

Works Cited

Personal Interviews

Anonymous 1. Interview. Conducted by Daniela B. Sheinin, 22 May 2017.
Anonymous 2. Interview. Conducted by Daniela B. Sheinin, 22 May 2017.
D., D. Interview. Conducted by Daniela B. Sheinin, 30 July 2017.
M., Willy. Interview. Conducted by Daniela B. Sheinin, 27 March 2017.

L., A. Interview. Conducted by Daniela B. Sheinin, 5 February 2017.
P., Anni. Interview. Conducted by Daniela B. Sheinin, 5 February 2017.
P., George. Interview. Conducted by Daniela B. Sheinin, 29 July 2017.
Silvia. Interview. Conducted by Daniela B. Sheinin, 22 May 2017.
S., P. Interview. Conducted by Daniela B. Sheinin, 29 January 2017.
U., Ken. Interview. Conducted by Daniela B. Sheinin, 23 March 2017.
S., Walter. Interview. Conducted by Daniela B. Sheinin, 22 April 2017.

Primary Literature

Ames, Charlotte (1974): The World's Fair 10 Years After: Ruin and Hope. *Long Island Press* (14 April). Folder: Parks. Queens Co. Flushing Meadows Corona Park 1974. Archives at Queens Public Library.
Anonymous (1967): End Neglect! *Long Island Post* (16 November).
Anonymous (1967): Raps City Neglect of Forest Hills – Rego Park. *Long Island Post* (9 November).
Anonymous (1969): Forlorn Place: Site of N.Y. World Fair. *Los Angeles Times* (12 December).
Anonymous (1971): Corona – Unity Turns into a Schism. *Daily News* (4 July 1971). Housing. Corona. The Archives at Queens Public Library.
Anonymous (1974): The Shame of Flushing Meadow. *Sunday News* (7 April). Folder: Parks. Queens Co. Flushing Meadows Corona Park 1976. Archives at Queens Public Library.
Anonymous (1977): U.S. Hall Tumbles Down. *Daily News* (17 May). Folder: Parks. Queens Co. Flushing Meadows Corona Park 1977. Archives at Queens Public Library.
Anonymous (1978): 'Ideal' Play Spot a Shambles. *Daily News* (11 April). Folder: Parks. Queens Co. Flushing Meadows Corona Park 1978. Archives at Queens Public Library.
Beckley, Arlene (1964): Letter to Robert Moses (23 May). Box 248, Folder M3 Request for Information 1963–1964, Restoration of Park (A–K), Maintenance. New York World's Fair 1964–1965 Corporation records, Manuscripts and Archives Division, The New York Public Library.
Bulletin (1936): *The Flushing Meadow Improvement* 1(3).
Carrano, Ralph (1964): Letter to Robert Moses (30 May). Box 248, Folder M3 Request for Information 1963–1964, Restoration of Park (A–K), Maintenance. New York World's Fair 1964–1965 Corporation records, Manuscripts and Archives Division, The New York Public Library.
Clarke, Gilmore D. (1939): Landscape Architecture at the New York World's Fair: A Portfolio of Photographs of Modern Design. *Landscape Architecture* 29(4), 153–166.
Class 5-4 at PS 196 (1965): Letters to Robert Wagner (10 February). Box 250, Folder M3 Restoration of Park (1965) N.Y. World's Fair 1964–65 Corps. Maintenance A–L. New

York World's Fair 1964–1965 Corporation records, Manuscripts and Archives Division, The New York Public Library.

Collins, Tom (1974): Thousands enjoy Flushing Meadows. *Sunday News* (7 July). Folder: Parks. Queens Co. Flushing Meadows Corona Park 1974. Archives at Queens Public Library.

Conforti, Joseph M. (1977): Italian-Americans and the Urban Crisis: A Sociological Perspective. *Proceedings of the Eighth Annual Conference of the American Italian Historical Association.* The American Italian Historical Association.

Gallo, Patrick J. (1977): The Urban Experience of Italian-Americans. *Proceedings of the Eighth Annual Conference of the American Italian Historical Association.* The American Italian Historical Association.

Gershowitz, Mike (1967): Poverty, War, Renewal Bogged Down. *Long Island Star-Journal* (20 January). Folder: Corona – East Elmhurst, The Archives at Queens Public Library.

Iachetta, Michael (1971): City Clears the Rubble From 5 Blitzed Homes. *Daily News* (27 October).

Iachetta, Michael (1978): New Corona Label – 'Worse Than Ever'. *Daily News* (15 November).

Klein, H.L. (1975): A White Elephant Wastes Away. *Long Island Press* (17 August).

Letzer, Steve (1977): U.S. Pavilion is Coming Down. *Long Island Press* (6 February). Folder: Parks. Queens Co. Flushing Meadows Corona Park 1977. Archives at Queens Public Library.

New York World's Fair, New York, N.Y. (1960): *Preparation of the Site for World's Fair 1964–1965: Flushing Meadow Park, the City of New York.* New York.

Oats, David (1974): The Ruins of Flushing Meadows. *Flushing Tribune* (22 November). Folder: Parks. Queens Co. Flushing Meadows Corona Park 1974. Archives at Queens Public Library.

Oats, David (1977): The End of the U.S. Pavilion. *Flushing Tribune* (12 April). Folder: Parks. Queens Co. Flushing Meadows Corona Park 1977. Archives at Queens Public Library.

Orin, Deborah (n.d.). Where we live – Part II. *Corona History.* The Archives at Queens Public Library.

Rabin, Bernard (1980): It's a Park for Vandals in the Dark. [publication unknown] (31 October). Folder: Parks. Queens Co. Flushing Meadows Corona Park 1980–81. Archives at Queens Public Library.

Rotner, Eileen (1964): Letter to Robert Moses (7 January). Box 248, Folder M3 Request for Information 1963–1964, Restoration of Park (L–Z), Maintenance. N.Y. World's Fair Corp. Maintenance. New York World's Fair 1964–1965 Corporation records, Manuscripts and Archives Division, The New York Public Library.

Schumach, Murray (1967): Moses Gives City Fair Site as Park: Flushing Meadows in Queens. *New York Times* (4 June).

Weiner, Caryn Eve (1985): The Park; Borough's Backyard. *Newsday* (14 July).
Yordan, Raymond M. (1965): Letter to Robert Moses (8 September). Box 250, Folder M3 Restoration of Park (1965) N.Y. World's Fair 1964–65 Corps. Maintenance A–L. New York World's Fair 1964–1965 Corporation records, Manuscripts and Archives Division, The New York Public Library.

Secondary Literature

Avila, Eric (2004): *Popular Culture in the Age of White Flight: Fear and Fantasy in Suburban Los Angeles*. Berkeley: University of California Press.
Jones-Correa, Michael (1998): *Between Two Nations: The Political Predicament of Latinos in New York City*. Ithaca, NY: Cornell University Press.
Kline, Carrie Nobel (1996): Giving It Back: Creating Conversations to Interpret Community Oral History. *The Oral History Review* 23(1), 19–40.
Lipman, Jana K. (2009): *Guantánamo: A Working-Class History between Empire and Revolution*. Berkeley: University of California Press.
L'Official, Peter (2020): *Urban Legends: The South Bronx in Representation and Ruin*. Cambridge, MA: Harvard University Press.
Lowenthal, David (1996): *Possessed by the Past: The Heritage Crusade and the Spoils of History*. New York: Free Press.
Mallon, Florencia E. (2005): *Courage Tastes of Blood: The Mapuche Community of Nicolás Ailío and the Chilean State, 1906–2001*. Durham, NC: Duke University Press.
Nora, Pierre (1989): Between Memory and History: Les Lieux de Mémoire. *Representations* 26, 7–24.
Remeseira, Iván Claudio, ed. (2010): *Hispanic New York: A Sourcebook*. New York: Columbia University Press.
Rodríguez, Clara E. (2010): Racial Themes in the Literature: Puerto Ricans and Other Latinos. *Hispanic New York: A Sourcebook*, edited by in Iván Claudio Remeseira. New York: Columbia University Press, 183–200.
Rúa, Mérida M. (2012): *A Grounded Identidad: Making New Lives in Chicago's Puerto Rican Neighborhoods*. Oxford: Oxford University Press.
Ruiz, Vicki L. (1998a): *From out of the Shadows: Mexican Women in Twentieth-Century America*. Oxford: Oxford University Press.
Ruiz, Vicki L. (1998b): Situating Stories: The Surprising Consequences of Oral History. Theme Articles: Practice and Pedagogy. *The Oral History Review* 25(1), 71–80.
Sanjek, Roger (1998): *The Future of Us All: Race and Neighborhood Politics in New York City*. Ithaca, NY: Cornell University Press.
Shackel, Paul A. (2001): *Myth, Memory, and the Making of the American Landscape*. Gainesville: University Press of Florida.

Shopes, Linda (2015): Community Oral History: Where We Have Been, Where We Are Going. *Oral History* 43(1), 97–106.

Simmons, LaKisha Michelle (2015): *Crescent City Girls the Lives of Young Black Women in Segregated New Orleans*. Chapel Hill: University of North Carolina Press.

Sugrue, Thomas J. (1996): *The Origins of the Urban Crisis: Race and Inequality in Postwar Detroit*. Princeton, NJ: Princeton University Press.

Tochterman, Brian (2017): *The Dying City: Postwar New York and the Ideology of Fear*. Chapel Hill: University of North Carolina Press.

Weaver, Timothy (2017): Urban Crisis: The Genealogy of a Concept. *Urban Studies* 54(9), 2039–2055.

Yablon, Nick (2009): *Untimely Ruins: An Archaeology of American Urban Modernity, 1819–1919*. Chicago: University of Chicago Press.

The Materiality of the Wall(s)

Mural Art and Counterspace Appropriation in El Paso's Chihuahuita and El Segundo Barrio

ANNA MARTA MARINI

Abstract

Binational metropolitan areas along the US–Mexico border are – historically and culturally – inherently transnational, as well as strictly related to the definition of space dictated by the materiality of the boundary. Since the emergence of Chicano art in the mid-1960s, mural art has become one of the visual articulations of the quest to frontier liminal identity, explored by claiming urban space and becoming visible. Wall art and Mexican mural traditions have thus supported the creation of an urban counterspace intrinsic to the appropriation of the neighbourhood. Hemmed by the now militarised border, the case of Central El Paso's south side – composed chiefly by Chihuahuita and El Segundo Barrio – is particularly interesting; marked by the historical demographic and cultural presence of Mexican Americans, in recent years the area has been also characterised by a conflictual relationship with the border itself and the presence of incoming migrants. Aside from crystallised paradigms, through the analysis of street art and local border discourse it is possible to trace the community's strong simultaneous connection with the boundary – characterised by overbearing presence and intrinsic controversial conflicts – and the 'other side', embodied in the hybrid reproduction of Mexican traditions and iconography.

Introduction

The binational metropolitan areas scattered along the US–Mexico border are – historically and culturally – inherently transnational, as well as strictly related to a definition of public and private space dictated by the materiality of the boundary. Immersed in a same composite and vast natural landscape, these urban spaces often share a diverse, hybrid cultural landscape and a common built environment cut across by the border infrastructure. Since the emergence of the Chicano Movement and the related visual art production in the mid-1960s, on the US side of the border street art has become one of the visual articulations of the quest for a hybrid, liminal identity distinctive of the frontier regions. Painting walls has represented a means of exploration of the borderland heritage, as well as a material claim to urban space.[1]

Mexican American communities compose a culturally silenced ethno-linguistic group, which became visible by opposing the imposed assimilation to the dominant national monoglossic culture, developing political and social justice activist movements, and exploiting the recovery of vernacular art traditions. In the early 1970s, the Chicanx mural movements developed and disseminated throughout the Southwest, directly linked to the political activism for civil rights fomented by the US ethnic minorities. Murals have often embodied a synthesis of a Chicanx rediscovery and wishful return to past imaginaries, reconstructed through Mexican iconography and the embrace of the ideological belonging to the *raza mestiza* [mixed race].[2] Wall art and Mexican mural traditions have supported the creation of an urban counterspace and its intrinsic reappropriation of and identification with the Mexican American neighbourhood.[3]

Hemmed by the now militarised border, the case of Central El Paso's south side – composed chiefly by Chihuahuita and El Segundo Barrio – is particularly interesting, due to the historical interconnectedness with the urban and social fabric of Ciudad Juárez on the Mexican side. Marked by the historical demographic and cultural presence of Mexican Americans, in recent years the area has been also characterised by a conflictual relationship with the border infrastructure itself, the presence of incoming migrants and the related immigration enforcement strategies. When the Chicano Movement arose and spread throughout the Southwest, the south side was an area where the social and ethnic struggle was strongly felt, in particular against the structural violence associated with housing matters and urban planning. Several murals realised in such a complex historical conjuncture expressed the possibility for the community to assert control on its barrios (neighbourhoods populated by a Latinx majority), populated by a Mexican American majority of farm and factory workers. Through the following decades, the original ideological nature of the first Chicanx murals – realised in the early 1970s – has evolved and transformed up to the present. The political message intrinsic to muralism has developed and adapted to the local barrios' everyday reality on a micro and macro scale, juxtaposing personal storytelling, Mexican mytho-historical tropes and the struggle to maintain the community's cohesive action.

Aside from crystallised paradigms, through the analysis of street art and local border discourse it is possible to trace the south side community's connection with the boundary itself – characterised by its overbearing presence and intrinsic controversial conflicts – and with the other side, embodied by the hybrid reproduction of Mexican heritage, its folklore, traditions and iconographies.

Chicanx Murals: Cultural Resistance and Spatial Justice

Chicanx street art surged in the 1960s, strictly related to the contemporary political ferment, and flourished during the 1970s, destabilising the analyses several sociologists had been making of the phenomenon of ethnic minority resistance expressed through visible artefacts. For example, Glazer and Moynihan foresaw a progressive overcoming of the melting pot notion through integration – a position Glazer would later on review and rearticulate.[4] Nonetheless, an increasing emphasis on a rediscovery of ethnic heritage and the subsequent quest for identification have allowed, as Simpson argues, a "revitalization of folk art and the emergence of new artistic expressions representing a synthesis of a specific group's cultural heritage and experiences."[5] When it comes to street art, clearly a consequent revitalisation of the ethnic minority neighbourhood's spaces can be observed. Simpson's work focused on the configuration of 49 Chicanx murals in East Los Angeles, realised in the 1970s on non-commercial buildings and often – at least partially – financed by public agencies. Her analysis revealed that in the majority of cases the representations revolved around themes and depictions connected with "ethno-racial identity and heritage of Mexican Americans", reflecting "the ethnic, religious and social background of their creators."[6]

Through the decades, the construction and transformation of the (American) Mexicanness have often been a blend of different, even opposite, processes.[7] Cultural resistance to assimilation and the necessity to define a Mexican American identity have led to a search for elements to identify with and, at the same time, strategies to dissociate from imposed cultural paradigms. The fundamental trope embodied by Aztlán and the reprisal of pre-Hispanic imaginaries, folklore and myths reveal a tension toward heritage roots[8] necessary to structure an articulated otherness, opposed to the US-dominant, monoglossic national culture. Aztlán represented the mytho-historical, fundamentally transnational locus of Chicanx resistance, a heterotopic space connected to an idealised place of origin and where colonial oppression and racialisation could be remapped. Retrieving the myth of origin embodied by a symbolic land the Mexican people would have come from, the Chicano Movement adapted it to its struggle and identified that place with the territories the Mexican government ceded to the US with the Treaty of Guadalupe Hidalgo (1848), indeed roughly corresponding to the Southwest region.

In the 1960s, Chicanx nationalist political groups stressed the importance of retaining heritage identification and, vice versa, the literary and artistic production was "informed by the new nationalist and separatist philosophy of Chicano activism" and openly embraced post- and decolonial stances.[9] 'Chicanx' is indeed a term usually identifying the politicised members of the Mexican American minority, who advocate the defence, preservation and flourishing of its peculiar ethnic heritage. When the political Chicano Movement began to develop, folklore became – and still is – an integral part of the ethnic activism for civil rights;[10] likewise, it was crucial for the embedding of pre-Hispanic, indigenist iconographies in the visual artistic expressions connected to the Movement.[11] Besides pre-Hispanic elements, religious icons are also fundamental in the expression of Mexican and Mexican American heritage. In particular, the Virgen de Guadalupe, which corresponds to the Marian apparition to a Mexican Indigenous boy in 1531, has a markedly syncretic background rooted in Aztec mythology and has become an identity symbol for Mexican Catholics. Mexican faith is, indeed, profoundly syncretic and imbued with pre-Hispanic myths and cosmogonies, aspects that were rediscovered and reinterpreted by the Chicanx artistic movements.

Despite being characterised by a vast diversity of expressions and configurations, Mexican American identity and the related cultural production have often been connected to a reinterpretation of themes and tropes distinctive of a perceived Mexican authenticity. It is relevant to mention that Mexico has seen a rather long history of mural painting,[12] from the very articulated examples of the pre-Hispanic murals up to the work of muralists such as Diego Rivera, David Alfaro Siqueiros, José Clemente Orozco and Aurora Reyes Flores. The popular mural tradition has blended with religious motifs, it has become recognised as fine art, and it is very much alive up to the present day in many configurations. Moreover, mural paintings are a visible common element in the architectural landscape of towns and *pueblos* [villages] both in Mexico and in the Southwest.[13] Therefore, the Chicanx street art movement has necessarily referred to Mexican heritage, focusing on its reinterpretation and adaptation to the American reality. As Herrera-Sobek underlined, folklore became "a significant self-empowering tool in [the Chicanx population's] journey of self discovery, identity formation, cultural and political resistance, and self affirmation."[14] Pre-Hispanic themes and motifs, as well as scenes related to the conquest and to historical moments fundamental to the formation of the post-revolutionary Mexican state, figure among the most common reproductions in Chicanx murals realised during the 1970s.[15] With time, the transformations intrinsic to the Chicanx movement(s) have also been reflected in the production of cultural artefacts, embracing a more diverse range of subjects. In the 1980s, the Movement saw the breakthrough of openly queer intellectuals and creators such as Cherríe Moraga, Gloria Anzaldúa and Francisco Alarcón, among many others.[16] Aztlán expanded and became more inclusive, centring more on the diverse needs of the Mexican American population. Increasingly less focused on nationalist themes and more on social and cultural justice, Chicanx street art drew inspiration from the Mexican muralist tradition of the 1930s and its well-known artists. The pre-Hispanic elements remained central to the mural representation, but they did so without "displacing contemporary concerns"[17] and blending a variety of thematic elements related to local communities. Quite often, the imagery and choice of subjects connected directly to issues and figures that were relevant within the barrio, visually producing arguments specific to each urban context and its uniqueness.

Very often, neighbourhoods historically inhabited mostly by ethnic minorities suffer from urban decline, derived from a systemic administrative neglect rooted in a history of segregation and repression. Their urban configuration has been marked by the visible manifestation of the structural violence intrinsic to differential developments of urban planning, leading to underdevelopment and a progressive deterioration of urban conditions. Institutional abandonment and the consequent local devaluation of real estate have been key pre-existing factors that in many cases have led to the advent of gentrification of the minority neighbourhood. The unfair distribution of resources has been known to facilitate the exploitation of space as a form of domination and segregation, as locational discrimination can be exerted by means of differential access to services.[18] In the case of borderland Mexican American neighbourhoods, urban segregation and social isolation were the fundamental features of a consolidated internal colonialism that had developed since the annexation of the Southwestern territories by the United States. Living conditions and the discrimination of segregation transformed as a consequence of the Civil Rights Movement and related minority activism. However, the Latinx barrios have continued to suffer from a pervasive relative isolation and structural abandonment, as well as from urban planning strategies that have – whether purposely or not – neglected the needs of the ethnic minority communities. Thus, the defence of the local community networks and their neighbourhood space has been crucial in Chicanx activism. Reasserting the community's control and – at the same time – its belonging to the urban space represents a "reaffirmation of culture, a defense of space, an ethnically bounded sanctuary, and the spiritual zone of Chicano/a and Mexicano/a identity."[19] The necessity to fight for spatial justice[20] evidences that space and its (re)arrangement are strictly related to the sociocultural milieu. The implementation of unequal urban policies evidently has a role in (re)producing a context of social injustice. The tentative counter-appropriation of the neighbourhood and the creation of spaces that represent the community allow the minority population to assume a position that is simultaneously marginalised by the dominant society and centred within the neighbourhood.[21]

Murals produce a visible form of activism against spatial injustice, fostering at the same time social development[22] and an enhancement of barrio aesthetics,[23] to an extent compensating for the institutional neglect and consequent urban deterioration. Murals can transform "abandoned space into community space, a space for rallying together as a community against the city bureaucracy",[24] providing an alternative vision that embodies the minority resistance "to entrenched systems of power, exclusion and negation."[25] Murals also characterise free spaces within the barrio, public spaces where community members can reassert their identity and belonging to a minority heritage group – as Evans and Boyte have defined them.[26] The epideictic practice of mural painting and, in general, of painting external walls according to the Mexican architectural traditions, allows the members of the ethnic minority community to visibly distinguish themselves, and their publicly shared spaces, from the mainstream Anglo-American culture.

It is necessary to briefly clarify the difference between graffiti and muralism, although both practices express appropriation of the public space and the process of visibly marking it with signs connected to identity. Graffiti and tagging represent an art form initiated by individuals who write their tag as a personal revindication of space and social justice, as "behind every tag is a story about survival and about striving to be seen",[27] reflecting through wall-writing the struggles implicit in segregated urban contexts and issues of oppression.[28] On the other hand, murals are strongly linked to the community living in the area and often they are the result of a collaborative effort. Even when a single artist or a group of artists develop the mural project and materially realise its painting, the local community is involved, and the chosen location has an intrinsic symbolic meaning. As will be analysed further on, the majority of murals that can be observed in El Paso's south side are located on walls of buildings that are either private property or local public spaces, dedicated to social sharing or activities related to education.

Besides these general yet fundamental reflections, it is worth stressing that the configuration of barrios and the community engagement with street art forms also depend on the local macro context. As will be noted, the peculiarity of the binational metropolitan area composed of Ciudad Juárez and El Paso marks the history and sociocultural development of El Paso's south side, located right on the border line and across two main international border bridges.

El Paso's Historical South Side and Its Murals

Even though the definition of El Paso's south side at times includes a larger urban area connected to the city's downtown neighbourhoods – in particular, the peripheral part of El Segundo Barrio in Central El Paso – it will be here circumscribed to the historical areas represented by El Segundo Barrio and Chihuahuita. The boundaries of this area are constituted by the Rio Grande river to the south – and therefore the border fence – the Santa Fe Railroad to the south-west, and Paisano Drive to the north. Nowadays, El Segundo Barrio is a densely populated area – with about 20,000 inhabitants per square mile, against El Paso's average of 2,750[29] – whose population of about 8,000 is, for the 97.2% who are of Latinx (mostly Mexican) heritage, marked by a low median income and a well-established presence of farm and factory worker residents. Chihuahuita comprises a smaller, similarly composed community of approximately 200 residents, and it is cut across by El Paso Street, connected to the Paso del Norte international bridge over the Rio Grande. The south side area is also directly connected to the neighbouring Ciudad Juárez by the Stanton Street bridge, which operates with limited access.

Like many other neighbourhoods, such as Boyle Heights in Los Angeles or the Barrio Logan in San Diego, El Paso's south side has been populated by a consolidated Mexican community marked by a distinct transnational character, and has been the object of a continuous afflux of migrants since its establishment. As a consequence of the Mexican–American War (1846–1848), the Mexican populations living in the US borderlands often chose to remain and seek to obtain American citizenship. During the second half of the 19th century and in particular during the dictatorship of Porfirio Díaz (1884–1911), Mexican workers from the northern regions crossed to find better labour and economic conditions. El Paso was a fundamental railroad hub connecting the border to mines and industry in the Southwest, as well as the core location for transnational commerce. Segregated in predominantly Mexican neighbourhoods adjacent to the border, immigrants reconstructed structured barrio communities comprising small businesses catering to the local population and community newspapers.[30] In 1910, the binational region of El Paso–Juárez turned into a strategic site for the revolutionary conflicts and especially for those involving Francisco 'Pancho' Villa and his *División del Norte* armed faction, with whom he occasionally raided border towns and sought support in the Mexican border communities. Chihuahuita became a place where revolutionary fighters would flee from the military; at the same time, poor families would try to recover from the devastating economic consequences of the conflicts, finding shelter in some tenements purposely built in the area in 1916.[31] Due to its proximity to the Santa Fe Railroad, the barrio also became a crucial spot where migrants could be recruited for indentured labour. Through the 1910s, 1920s and 1930s, the low income levels characterising its inhabitants and the institutional neglect led to several community health issues – mostly related to the poor conditions of the sewage system and narrow dirt roads, as well as to the inexistence of a functioning garbage collection service.[32]

Besides the dominant society's tendency to isolate them, the urban segregation of Mexican communities on the border was also due to self-isolating mechanisms. The ethnic-minority and migrant members tended to recreate a sociocultural network based on shared heritage; furthermore, their belonging to low-income strata also facilitated their concentration in specific urban areas.[33] Being located right on the border, the connection of El Paso's south side to Ciudad Juárez has been, to an extent, almost seamless and characterised by a highly porous boundary up to the present. Many Mexicans either work, go to school or live on the respective other side: some prefer to reside in the US but still do their daily business in Juárez, while others live on the Mexican side and work in El Paso, engaging in "mixed daily transnational practices".[34] The proximity and the relative ease for locals to cross daily have definitely shaped the configuration of the barrios, as both El Segundo Barrio and Chihuahuita share evident similarities with the specular barrios in Ciudad Juárez. Despite the institutional neglect and the original segregating character of the area, both El Segundo Barrio and Chihuahuita developed a lively, thriving cultural life, fostering the surge and flourishing of social justice activism and activities related to the Chicano Movement for civil rights. For the Chicanx communities, the preservation of everyday customs, intangible heritage elements, and shared sets of values and beliefs has been a crucial aspect of the resistance to assimilation, as well as a means to cope with urban decline, structural violence and institutional abandonment. As argued in the introduction, murals – executed on publicly accessible surfaces that constitute the built environment of the community[35] – have represented visible sources of heritage pride and identification, otherwise invisibilised within the dominant national culture. Furthermore, the murals have an intrinsic educational function directed to the community itself, as they depict fundamental themes embraced by Chicanx activism and present stories of well-known individuals who hailed from the barrio, historical figures who were based there, and people who contributed to the wellness and development of the community. The location and scale of the wall paintings are also crucial to conveying the messages they articulate: the chosen surfaces are usually connected to public spaces and specific milieux, and their dimensions make it impossible for them to go unseen. Characterised by vibrant colours, themes linked to history – of both Mexico and the Chicanx struggle – and Mexican traditional arts, each mural in the south side embodies the community's efforts to preserve and celebrate Chicanx culture throughout the decades, starting with the Chicanx mural movement in the late 1960s and 1970s.

The wall paintings scattered throughout El Paso's south side can be divided into three main typologies, according to the main contents and features of the visual representation: they can be either political, commercial or personally oriented murals, although these categories can also partially overlap.

Political murals are characterised by the intrinsic connection with Chicanx activism – linked to both the original Chicano Movement and its following configurations up to the present day. The ideological messages are not necessarily overt: most murals of this typology depict relevant community members or traditions, often accompanied by more traditional iconographies and references to heritage expression. In El Segundo Barrio, murals with an implicit political mes-

Figure 1: El Segundo Barrio, mural painted by Francisco Delgado in 2006 on the wall of the then gymnasium of the Sacred Heart Parish, 2017. © El Paso Times.

sage are scattered throughout the whole urban area, located in particular on the premises of educational centres and religious community spaces. The mural titled *Segundo Barrio* (1975) represents one of the emblems of the neighbourhood; it was realised in an area where working-class tenements were built – and then progressively demolished over the years – and it evidently reprises pre-Hispanic elements in a geometric composition dominated by vibrant yellow, green and brown. Painted in 2007, a well-known mural (Figure 1) spans across the façade of the *tortillería* and restaurant managed by the Sacred Heart Parish, the Catholic heart of the south side. Founded by Jesuits in 1892, the parish flourished in particular in the 1950s during the appointment of Harold Rahm as assistant pastor, as his outreach helped consolidate the social networks internal to the barrio. Rahm appears in the mural riding his bicycle and forming part of an articulated depiction of the shared history of the local religious community. Most figures represented are, in fact, other relevant members of the community who contributed in one way or another to its thriving through the years – such as the founder of the Sacred Heart parish Father Carlos Pinto – or iconic historical figures, such as Pancho Villa. Significantly, the mural is enriched by Mexican Catholic iconographies. In particular, the Virgen de Guadalupe, the crucified Christ and the flaming Sacred Heart are the main religious symbols connected to Mexican and Mexican American identity. A more implicitly political mural is definitely the painting on the main wall of Chihuahuita's community centre, depicting a train of the Santa Fe Railroad and thus the strong connection of the barrio with the railroad marking its boundaries.

Commercial murals are linked to the practice of painting exteriors of businesses and shops for commercial advertising purposes,[36] characterising neighbourhoods with a predominantly Latinx population throughout the Southwestern region. As mentioned earlier on, mural paintings constitute a rooted vernacular folk tradition in the architectural configuration of Mexican towns and, consequently, of predominantly Mexican American urban areas in the Southwest. Muralist Diego Rivera himself identified mural paintings on the walls of bars and eateries – such as *pulquerías* and *cantinas* – as a most relevant manifestation of Mexican painting.[37] The wall paintings are, in fact, mostly found on the premises of businesses related to food; nonetheless, painted *letreros* or signs accompanied by painted characters or depictions of the offered products and services can be found on the walls of any type of shop. This typology of murals serves "the pragmatic function of advertisement, but [it is] also [a] powerful expression of identity",[38] as the wall paintings are evidently infused with shared aesthetic values and cultural references.

In El Segundo Barrio, the mural found on the wall of Mata's grocery store (realised in 2007) in the neighbourhood's market area would be a good example of the *pulquería* type of murals, with its realistic depiction of the shop's offerings. Shop owners often accompany the actual sign composed of painted letters with elements of personal identification, such as caricatures and religious iconographies,[39] revealing an emotional connection informed by their social networks and realised to elicit the community members' interaction. A well-known example is *La Tiendita de Irma* in Park Street (Figure 2). The wall has been repainted several times through the years, but a few elements remain unchanged: the words written on the wall – signalling products offered by the small grocery shop – and the one-storey-high Virgen de Guadalupe painting. The verbal element reprises the aforementioned Mexican tradition, advertising the main products offered by the shop, while the shop's name has been repainted unchanged after each renovation. Once again, the religious motif is key to embodying the Mexican American identity: the Virgen is reproduced according to the canonic iconography and complemented with a *hoja de nopal* (the pad of the Opuntia cactus) – a symbol of the foundation of Mexico-Tenochtitlan, the heart of the Aztec empire.

The majority of the personal typology of murals can be found on the walls of private houses, scattered all over the south side and in particular in the narrow streets of Chihuahuita. One of the most well known is the memorial depiction of two historical residents of the barrio, on the wall of the house they used to live in on Bandera Way (Figure 3). The mural was dedicated to the memory of Joe and Carmen by their family members; their realistic portraits are accompanied by red roses, symbols reminiscent of the Virgen de Guadalupe and thus Mexican identity. The way in which the couple is represented is also remindful of stylisations

Figure 2: La Tiendita de Irma, mural by anonymous local artist. Photograph taken by Dave Matthews, 2014. © Dave Matthews.

typical of the *Época de Oro* of Mexican cinema (1936–1956), whose films marked the early Mexican– American borderland broadcast and media in general. The residential areas of El Paso's south side are also characterised by houses painted with vibrant, saturated colours – whether as a uniform colour block or with frames in contrast – a feature that becomes even more evident in the oldest parts of Chihuahuita, where the one-storey buildings are smaller and closely packed together. Here, the Mexican architectural heritage also emerges in the widespread use of wrought metal railings and window bars – traditionally painted white – and the presence of religious icons and ex-votos hanging on external walls.

Sometimes different typologies of murals are juxtaposed: this is the case of the building of the Barrios Grocery (sic) in Father Rahm Avenue at South Virginia Street. On the wall where the shop's entrance is located, painted descriptions of the services offered and a rose can be found. On the side wall, though, a definitely political mural was painted in 1991 by a group of artists led by Carlos Callejo (Figure 4). The scene is meant to represent Texas, its rural reality and the blend of cultures characterising it, playing as well on the suggestion that Mexican American farm workers are both deeply American and Mexican at the same time. The mural's title recalls the Pachuco subculture strongly rooted in the borderlands, as well as the phrase "Vamos al chuco" – peculiar to this specific binational area – indicating the border-crossing Mexican workers used to do daily to work in El Paso at a shoemaking company.

Figure 3: Silva Rodriguez and the mural dedicated to the memory of her parents Joe and Carmen, on the façade of her home, 2017. © El Paso Times.

Figure 4: El Chuco y qué? (1991) blends Mexican American Pachuco culture and more traditional borderland imagery, 2018. © Roberto José Andrade Franco.

The Border Wall and the Reshaping of Urban Perceptions

Despite its transnational nature and historical origins, in recent years the area has been characterised by an increasingly conflictual relationship with the border infrastructure itself. Before the current wire-mesh border fence was built in 2008, Chihuahuita in particular used to be a favoured crossing point, as migrants would only need to cross the riverbed, jump the existing chain-link fencing and go through private backyards, as private houses are located right along the border itself. On the one hand, some locals welcomed migrants and even nourished them if needed; on the other hand, though, the relative ease of crossing allowed the passage of criminals and gang members, who would break into the houses and put the inhabitants in danger. The construction of the wire-mesh fence partially hindered illegal crossing, but it also blocked the view of the canal area adjacent to Chihuahuita, the Rio Grande itself and the green riverbed natural landscape the residents could previously enjoy.

As a consequence of the increased restrictions and the immigration policies implemented from the mid-1980s on, a series of incidents happened in the border barrios due to questionable Border Patrol operations. A well-known exemplary case linked to a civil rights lawsuit was instituted in 1992 and won by Bowie High School, located in a peripheral area near the historical part of El Segundo Barrio and a few tens of metres away from the border barriers. Border Patrol agents were known for regularly "stopping, detaining, and questioning Hispanic individuals within the Bowie High School district",[40] harassing and abusing students and staff of apparent Mexican origin both verbally and physically, without any reasonable suspicion of criminal activity or illegal immigrant status. Nonetheless, in 1993 the Border Patrol in El Paso initiated Operation Blockade (also known as Hold-the-Line), changing the approach to border militarisation and enforcement by shifting from a low-intensity conflict to what was the foundation of the post-9/11 border strategies, based on "prevention through deterrence".[41] In the early 2000s, the presence of Border Patrol and Immigration and Customs Enforcement (ICE) agents became pervasive along the border and the sudden increase in the number of apprehensions pushed the migrants to choose crossing points farther away from urban areas, where the crossing itself is much more dangerous for orographic reasons. The deterrence mechanisms led to a dramatic rise in migrant deaths, as well as uncontrolled and unnecessarily harmful persecutions by the members of the border enforcement agencies. The militarisation of the border – often accompanied by extrajudicial practices – has inevitably influenced the locals' daily life, as enforcement agents have been an overbearing presence added to the – reduced but still persisting – phenomenon of migrants' attempts to cross.

During Trump's 2016 presidential campaign and subsequent administration, El Paso generally stood up against the necessity of building a different, even more militarised fence. Trump gained around 26% of the vote in El Paso County and several local politicians – including Republicans such as El Paso's mayor Dee Margo – publicly expressed their criticisms of the false claims the former president made about border security.[42] The realisation of the militarised fence in 2008 notwithstanding, from 2006 to 2014 the crime rate in El Paso rose by 17%, whereas it had decreased by 34% since the implementation of Operation Blockade.[43] In fact, El Paso has historically been one of the US cities with the lowest crime rates.[44] In the past two decades, thorough research and analysis of crime rates statistics have shown that in many cities in which the Latinx migrant presence is dense, immigration does not usually increase local crime rates and it often corresponds to decreasing violent crime rates.[45]

However, the El Paso locals' perception of border issues and the presence of the fence is not homogeneous nor simple to unravel. Since 2006, the federal response to immigration and border issues has focused on the construction of the militarised fence, an increased collaboration with local police and the reliance on ICE operations, reinforcing racial-related anxieties in the local populations.[46] Even though surveys such as the one funded by the National Institutes of Health (NIH) in 2012 revealed that the vast majority of El Paso residents interviewed – 919 scattered across the whole urban area – perceived their city as safe,[47] it would be relevant to focus on the south side's inhabitants in the current political climate. A transnational survey realised in May 2016 by Cronkite News with the support of Arizona State University – with the support of the Univision network and Dallas Morning News – revealed that out of 1,500 residents of 14 border towns on both sides of the border, an average of 80% declared that the implementation of a new infrastructure was unnecessary.[48] An average of 65% of the interviewees also evaluated Trump's wall discourse during the presidential campaign as harmful for the region, an area "that's one of the most culturally vibrant parts of both countries."[49] The transnational preoccupation has emerged through interviews realised in the last few years with residents of Chihuahuita in particular, where the backyards of private houses are delimited by the existing border fence and the pillars of the border freeway that is under construction. When talks about the new fence began to be concretised in 2017, the president of the Chihuahuita neighbourhood association, Manuela 'Mannys' Silva Rodriguez, expressed her concern about the fact that Chihuahuita residents cannot help migrants anymore "because the Border Patrol sees [them], and they think [they]'re helping [the migrants] cross" and thus take action against them,[50] highlighting the issue represented by the complex relationship between the Border Patrol agency and the residents. As used to happen in the 1990s when the Border

Patrol enforcement was upscaled and refocused, today the daily coexistence between the enforcement agencies and the local population remains problematic. Silva Rodriguez revealed another source of internal conflict, as she asserted that the neighbourhood community learned about the upcoming fence rebuilding through media reports, as no authority or federal official contacted the locals on the topic.

Some long-time residents have expressed their disapproval and worries concerning the substitution of the current fencing with a taller concrete wall, as they feel it would disrupt the neighbourhood's daily life and its intrinsically transnational feel.[51] When the work on rebuilding of the fence started at the beginning of 2019, local community members declared that they had not seen immigrants crossing their border neighbourhoods in years, so they thought the modification of the existing infrastructure and the "waste [of] taxpayers' money on a wall" it would entail were unnecessary.[52] Local historian and resident David Romo shared the stance stance by other neighbours against the construction of the wall, feeling "under threat from the extreme militarization" on a daily basis.[53] Conversely, others have supported the wall building plans and even some residents of Chihuahuita welcomed the reconstruction of the barrier as they felt that it would make the area even safer. Some El Pasoans might not openly approve of the wall construction in itself but claimed that the existing militarised fence has made a positive difference. As construction works seemed to start toward the end of the Trump administration, Silva Rodriguez still supported the reinforcement of the wire-mesh fence, as she stated that she could still see immigrants climbing it and crossing through the neighbourhood.[54] Aside from the possible position taken in favour of the new border infrastructure or against it, the community's shared feelings have seemed to centre on the uncertainty represented by the infrastructural plans and not knowing "what is going to happen" as a consequence of the rebuilding works.[55]

Conflicting stances and issues in defining the peculiar heritage of the area have, in fact, increased in parallel with the progressive strengthening of border and anti-immigration measures. Since 1972, the Institute of Oral History of the University of Texas at El Paso has collected hundreds of interviews with Mexican American locals, expressing themselves on a variety of subjects. Many interviews throughout the years have covered topics related to daily life in the south side barrios, as well as the interconnectedness of their community with the other side of the border, and the activism of the local factions of the Chicano Movement and MEChA (Movimento Estudiantil Chicano de Aztlán). Many interviewees were born or grew up in the barrios, experiencing first hand the transformations the area has gone through. Nonetheless, in recent years the presence of the militarised border fence has become overwhelming, as has the political and media attention given

Figure 5: Mural Sister Cities/ Ciudades Hermanas, realized in 2015. © LxsDos.

to immigration issues, reducing El Paso's identity to the image of port of entry for illegal immigrants. In reality, the south side is still a lively cultural locus of heritage preservation, thanks to social interconnectedness and projects fostered by groups such as the local faction of MEChA, struggling against discriminatory discourses and practices imposed on a national level. El Paso's Republican mayor Dee Margo has been outspokenly opposing the border wall discourse since he took office in 2017, clarifying in interviews and public appearances that a "bigger" fence cannot be the panacea to solve immigration issues and that – to intervene on the border – it is crucial to understand that El Paso is "the largest city on the Mexican border that's been intertwined with Mexico for almost 400 years."[56] The politician has also been clear on the transnational character of the city, stressing that it is home to "a highly binational, bilingual, bicultural workforce" and represents "a global metroplex seamlessly blending U.S. and Mexican traditions and cultures",[57] insisting on communicating how close-knit El Paso and Juárez are.[58]

It is crucial to highlight that the realisation of murals throughout the south side has remained a pivotal expression of resistance and preservation. Despite the federal imposition of increased militarised enforcement, El Paso's City Council launched a public art programme in 2002, and rebooted it in 2014, in order to "enhance the quality of life of residents, promote economic revitalization, and strengthen authentic images of El Paso as a unique place."[59] The Museums and Cultural Affairs Department purposely began to reach out to local artists, supporting the realisation of murals in strategic public spaces, recognising the relevance of the city's mural practices and their strong connection with the community.

In 2015, the art duo LxsDos – formed by Ramon and Christian Cardenas – realised a mural entitled *Sister Cities/Ciudades Hermanas* (Figure 5), dedicated to

Figure 6: A mural depicting a Chicana woman purposely oriented toward Mexico, featuring Mexican heritage symbolic iconographies, at the corner of Tays Street and Delta Drive, © El Paso Inc, 2019.

the binational metropolitan area to celebrate its transnational nature. Living and working between El Paso and Ciudad Juárez, the couple realised several murals in the south side through the 2010s; nonetheless, *Sister Cities/Ciudades Hermanas* conveys a most effective intrinsic meaning and its underlying purpose was to be a "straight-up political comment on the borderland".[60] The location of the wall painting is fundamental: it can be found on Father Rahm Avenue – the axis of the south side's community – at the junction with El Paso Street, and it is visible right after crossing the Paso del Norte border bridge from Mexico. The mural is part of a larger project called *Make Shift*, funded by El Paso's Museum and Cultural Affairs Department, for the realisation of several murals depicting everyday life and residents of the barrio, as well as representing a "homage to [local] artisans and farmworkers".[61]

Murals have also been a form of protest directed explicitly against the Trump administration and the border wall discourse. When then-president Trump visited El Paso in February 2019 for a campaign rally, a group led by Jesus 'Cimi' Alvarado – one of the most active muralists in the south side for the past couple of decades – realised a mural in El Segundo Barrio to stress the border's unity and safety (Figure 6). The piece features a Chicana woman purposely oriented toward Mexico and it reprises Mexican heritage symbolic iconographies such as the Virgen de Guadalupe and the Monarca butterfly. The latter in particular comes to signify the process, hope and struggle intrinsic to migration, as the species notoriously embarks on an annual migratory cycle across North America.

It is worth mentioning that street art collectives such as LxsDos or those led by Alvarado are working on both sides of the border, and that Ciudad Juárez – and particularly the central and historical neighbourhoods closest to the boundary – is also characterised by the pervasive presence of murals. Particularly interesting was the urban renovation and regeneration of the area around the space now known as Gran Plaza Juan Gabriel – dedicated to the much-celebrated Mexican pop icon – as the project was marked by the realisation of colourful murals dedicated to Mexican and borderland heritage.

Conclusion

Even from such a brief analysis, the existence of a shared perception emerges that an enhanced border infrastructure revolving around a concrete wall would serve as a symbolic sign of division. Local residents who support the rebuilding of the fence rarely express a firm stance on the topic, as the question for them is far more complex and concrete than it is often presented as being on national news or through the political discourse centred on the topic. The new infrastructure might provide an increased sense of safety, and yet it influences the lives of the barrios' inhabitants directly and inevitably; such a heavily militarised border barrier has been imposed by the federal government without consulting the local residents, nor has it been carried out in agreement with local institutions.

Conversely, on the local level there has been an evident, persistent collective interest in the preservation of the south side's historical and cultural heritage. In 1991, the city of El Paso designed Chihuahuita as a historic district and since 2016 the barrio figures on the list of the Most Endangered Historic Places compiled by the National Trust for Historic Preservation. As of the beginning of 2020, El Paso County was considering seeking the designation of El Segundo Barrio as a historic district as well. Promoted by the University of Texas in El Paso, in 2010 the Museo Urbano was created as a public history project actively promoting the history of El Segundo Barrio. The project is characterised by an openly transnational perspective, as it "reclaims, researches, preserves, exhibits, and interprets the history of the borderlands, especially El Paso-Ciudad Juárez",[62] collaborating with local grassroots groups, educational institutions and heritage-oriented cultural projects. The efforts to counter the border wall discourse have been overt and synergistic, and the realisation of murals has been a concrete part of such a process. Albeit less widely known than cases such as LA's Echo Park and its acclaimed murals, it is evident that the collective identity of El Paso's south side is inextricably intertwined with the practice of muralism. In Chihuahuita and El Segundo Barrio, the development and evolution of the Chicano Movement and Chicanx social justice activism have been connected to the realisation of meaningful wall paintings as a means of expression against spatial injustice. The rich history of Chicanx street art and Mexican mural traditions have supported the creation of an urban counterspace; the development of such a space is intrinsic to processes aimed at reasserting the presence and strong cultural bonds of the local transnational Mexican American community, making it visible both materially and metaphorically.

Notes

1. See among others, Simpson, Eve (1980): Chicano Street Murals: A Sociological Perspective. *Journal of Popular Culture* 13(3), 516–525; Arreola, Daniel D. (1984): Mexican American Exterior Murals. *Geographical Review* 74(4), 409–424; LaWare, Margaret R. (1998): Encountering Visions of Aztlan: Arguments for Ethnic Pride, Community Activism and Cultural Revitalization in Chicano Murals. *Argumentation and Advocacy* 34(3), 140–153; Diaz, David R. (2005): *Barrio Urbanism: Chicanos, Planning, and American Cities*. London: Routledge; Corrigan Correll, Timothy (2014): Productos Latinos: Latino Business Murals, Symbolism, and the Social Enactment of Identity in Greater Los Angeles. *The Journal of American Folklore* 127(505), 285–320.
2. See Goldman, Shifra M. (1977): Resistance and Identity: Street Murals of Occupied Aztlán. *Latin American Literary Review* 5(10), Special Issue of Chicano Literature, 124–128.
3. Corrigan Correll (2014).
4. Glazer, Nathan (1997): *We Are All Multiculturalist Now*. Cambridge, MA: Harvard University Press.
5. Simpson (1980), 516.
6. Ibid., 518.
7. Villoro, Juan (2011): Identidades Fronterizas. *Conflictos Interculturales*, edited by Nestor García Canclini. Barcelona: Editorial Gedisa, 29–30.
8. Among many, see Rodríguez, Mariángela (1998): *Mito, Identidad y Rito: Mexicanos y Chicanos en California*. Mexico City: CIESAS, 191–222.
9. Goldman (1977), 125.
10. Herrera-Sobek, María (2011): Folklore and Ethno-Nationalism in Mexican American Literary Production: Adaptation and Transformation of Indigenous Folk Icons in the Chicano Movement. *Traditiones* 40(3), 131–144, 132.
11. For a thorough study, see Latorre, Guisela (2008): *Walls of Empowerment: Chicana/o Indigenist Murals of California*. Austin: University of Texas Press.

12. Among many, see Rodríguez, Antonio (1970): *El Hombre en Llamas: Historia de la Pintura Mural en México*. London: Thames and Hudson.
13. LaWare (1998), 147.
14. Herrera-Sobek (2011), 133.
15. Simpson (1980), 519.
16. Aldama, Frederick Luis (2005): *Brown on Brown: Chicano/a Representation of Gender, Sexuality, and Ethnicity*. Austin: University of Texas Press, 21ff.
17. Goldman (1977), 126.
18. See Diaz, David R. (2005): *Barrio Urbanism: Chicanos, Planning, and American Cities*. London: Routledge; Soja, Edward W. (2010): *Seeking Spatial Justice*. Minneapolis: University of Minnesota Press.
19. Diaz (2005), 3.
20. Soja (2010).
21. See Soja, Edward W. (1996): *Thirdspace: Journeys to Los Angeles and Other Real and Imagined Places*. Hoboken, NJ: Wiley-Blackwell.
22. Castañeda, Ernesto, et al. (2015): Walking through Contemporary North American Barrios: Hispanic Neighborhoods in New York, San Diego, and El Paso. *Walking in Cities: Quotidian Mobility as Urban Theory, Method, and Practice*, edited by Evrick Brown and Timothy Shortell. Philadelphia: Temple University Press, 60–78, 75.
23. Arreola, Daniel D. (1984): Mexican American Exterior Murals. *Geographical Review* 74(4), 409–424, 409; Simpson (1980), 521; Ybarra Frausto, Tomás (1993): Arte Chicano: Images from a Community. *Signs from the Heart: California Chicano Murals*, edited by Eva Sperling Cockcroft and Holly Barnet-Sánchez. Albuquerque: University of New Mexico Press, 54–67.
24. LaWare (1998), 140.
25. Ybarra Frausto (1993), 67.
26. Evans, Sara M., and Boyte, Harry C. (1986): *Free Spaces: The Sources of Change in America*. New York: Harper and Row, 17.
27. Bloch, Stefano (2019): *Going All City: Struggle and Survival in LA's Graffiti Subculture*. Chicago: University of Chicago Press, 3.
28. Ferrell, Jeff (1995): Urban Graffiti: Crime, Control, and Resistance. *Youth & Society* 27, 73–92.
29. According to USCB and El Paso County's 2017 data.
30. For a thorough study, see García, Mario T. (1982): *Desert Immigrants: The Mexicans of El Paso, 1880–1920*. New Haven, CT: Yale University Press.
31. Romo, David Dorado (2005): *Ringside Seat to a Revolution: An Underground Cultural History of El Paso and Juarez: 1893–1923*. El Paso: Cinco Puntos Press.
32. See García (1982); Morales, Fred M. (2007): *La Chihuahuita*. El Paso/Juárez Historical Museum.

33. Jiménez Muñoz, Jorge H. (2006): Las Colonias del Imperio: Segregación Urbana en la Frontera México-Estados Unidos. *Bitácora Arquitectura UNAM* 15, 10–15, 10.
34. Castañeda et al. (2015), 73.
35. LaWare (1998), 143.
36. Arreola (1984), 410.
37. Rivera, Diego (1926): Mexican Painting: Pulquerías. *Mexican Folkways* 2(7), 6–15.
38. Corrigan Correll (2014), 286.
39. Ibid., 288.
40. *Murillo v. Musegades*. Case summary, 809 F.Supp. 487, W.D.Tex, 1992.
41. For a thorough study, see Dunn, Timothy J. (2010): *Blockading the Border and Human Rights: The El Paso Operation that Remade Immigration Enforcement*. Austin: University of Texas Press; Martin, John L. (1993): *Operation Blockade: Bullying Tactic or Border Control Model?* Report. Washington DC: Center for Immigration Studies (1 December).
42. Romero, Simon (2019): El Paso's Message for Trump Before Rally: Don't Speak for Us. *The New York Times*, (10 February).
43. FBI Crime Data Explorer, 1985–2014 statistics.
44. FBI Uniform Crime Reports, Crime Data Explorer, 1985–2019 statistics.
45. For an overview, see Castañeda, Ernesto, and Chiappetta, Casey (2020): Border Residents' Perceptions of Crime and Security in El Paso, Texas. *Social Sciences* 9(24), 1–15.
46. Provine, Doris Marie, and Roxanne Lynn Doty (2011): The Criminalization of Immigrants as a Racial Project. *Journal of Contemporary Criminal Justice* 27, 261–77, 261.
47. Castañeda and Chiappetta (2020).
48. Bilker, Molly (2016): New Poll by Cronkite News, Univision News and the Dallas Morning News Shows Strong Sense of Community on Both Sides of the U.S.-Mexico Border. *Cronkite News* (16 July).
49. Ibid.
50. In Sanchez, Sara (2017): Chihuahuita: A Border Community Rooted in History. *El Paso Times* (10 January).
51. Ibid.
52. Robert Vega Jr. in CBS4 (2019): Chihuahuita Residents React to President Trump's Replacement Wall. *Interviews by Adriana Candelaria*, aired on 11 January.
53. PBS (2019): How Residents from El Paso Feel About Border Barriers. Interviews by Angela Korchega. *PBS News Hour*, aired on 20 March.
54. Ibid.
55. Gutierrez, Rudy, and Sanchez, Sara (2017): Residents of El Paso's Oldest Neighborhood Have Lived with a Border Fence for Years. Video. *El Paso Times* (10 January).
56. PBS (2019): Dee Margo, Mayor of El Paso, TX, on Border Wall Politics. Interview with Christiane Amanpour. *Amanpour & Co*, aired on 12 February.

57. Margo, Dee (2019): El Paso's Safety Transcends President Trump's Claim about Border Fence. *El Paso Times*, (9 February).
58. Margo, Dee (2020): On the Border. *The Brookings Cafeteria* podcast, hosted by John Hudak. The Brookings Institution, aired on 22 September.
59. Bressi, Todd W., and McKinley, Meridith C. (2014): *Public Art Master Plan*. El Paso: MCAD, 5.
60. Christian Cardenas in Martinez, Freddy (2016): On the Streets of El Paso and Juarez, 'Sister Cities' Art Project Pays Tribute to Border Communities. Interview with Ramon and Christian Cardenas. *Remezcla* (7 July), https://remezcla.com/features/culture/interview-los-dos/. Accessed 29 June 2021.
61. Ramon Cardenas in Martinez (2016).
62. Museo Urbano at UTEP (n.d.): Official page, https://www.utep.edu/liberalarts/oral-history/public-history/museo-urbano.html. Accessed 12 July 2022.

Works Cited

Aldama, Frederick Luis (2005): *Brown on Brown: Chicano/a Representation of Gender, Sexuality, and Ethnicity*. Austin: University of Texas Press.

Anonymous (1992): *Murillo v. Musegades*. Case summary, 809 F.Supp. 487, W.D.Tex.

Arreola, Daniel D. (1984): Mexican American Exterior Murals. *Geographical Review* 74(4), 409–424.

Bilker, Molly (2016): New Poll by Cronkite News, Univision News and the Dallas Morning News Shows Strong Sense of Community on Both Sides of the U.S.-Mexico Border. *Cronkite News* (16 July).

Bloch, Stefano (2019): *Going All City: Struggle and Survival in LA's Graffiti Subculture*. Chicago: University of Chicago Press.

Bressi, Todd W., and McKinley, Meridith C. (2014): *Public Art Master Plan*. El Paso: MCAD.

Castañeda, Ernesto, et al. (2015): Walking through Contemporary North American Barrios: Hispanic Neighborhoods in New York, San Diego, and El Paso. *Walking in Cities: Quotidian Mobility as Urban Theory, Method, and Practice*, edited by Evrick Brown and Timothy Shortell. Philadelphia: Temple University Press, 60–78.

Castañeda, Ernesto, and Chiappetta, Casey (2020): Border Residents' Perceptions of Crime and Security in El Paso, Texas. *Social Sciences* 9(24), 1–15.

CBS4 (2019): Chihuahuita Residents React to President Trump's Replacement Wall. *Interviews by Adriana Candelaria*, aired on 11 January.

Corrigan Correll, Timothy (2014): Productos Latinos: Latino Business Murals, Symbolism, and the Social Enactment of Identity in Greater Los Angeles. *The Journal of American Folklore* 127(505), 285–320.

Diaz, David R. (2005): *Barrio Urbanism: Chicanos, Planning, and American Cities*. London: Routledge.

Dunn, Timothy J. (2010): *Blockading the Border and Human Rights: The El Paso Operation that Remade Immigration Enforcement*. Austin: University of Texas Press.

Evans, Sara M., and Boyte, Harry C. (1986): *Free Spaces: The Sources of Change in America*. New York: Harper and Row.

Ferrell, Jeff (1995): Urban Graffiti: Crime, Control, and Resistance. *Youth & Society* 27, 73–92.

García, Mario T. (1982): *Desert Immigrants: The Mexicans of El Paso, 1880–1920*. New Haven, CT: Yale University Press.

Glazer, Nathan (1997): *We Are All Multiculturalist Now*. Cambridge, MA: Harvard University Press.

Glazer, Nathan, and Daniel P. Moynihan (1963): *Beyond the Melting Pot*. Cambridge, MA: MIT Press.

Goldman, Shifra M. (1977): Resistance and Identity: Street Murals of Occupied Aztlán. *Latin American Literary Review* 5(10), Special Issue of Chicano Literature, 124–128.

Gutierrez, Rudy, and Sanchez, Sara (2017): Residents of El Paso's Oldest Neighborhood Have Lived with a Border Fence for Years. Video. *El Paso Times* (10 January).

Herrera-Sobek, María (2011): Folklore and Ethno-Nationalism in Mexican American Literary Production: Adaptation and Transformation of Indigenous Folk Icons in the Chicano Movement. *Traditiones* 40(3), 131–144.

Institute of Oral History (n.d.): *Institute of Oral History Collections*. Interviews, UTEP, 1972–present, https://scholarworks.utep.edu/oral_history/. Accessed 29 June 2021.

Jiménez Muñoz, Jorge H. (2006): Las Colonias del Imperio: Segregación Urbana en la Frontera México-Estados Unidos. *Bitácora Arquitectura UNAM* 15, 10–15.

Latorre, Guisela (2008): *Walls of Empowerment: Chicana/o Indigenist Murals of California*. Austin: University of Texas Press.

LaWare, Margaret R. (1998): Encountering Visions of Aztlan: Arguments for Ethnic Pride, Community Activism and Cultural Revitalization in Chicano Murals. *Argumentation and Advocacy* 34(3), 140–153.

Margo, Dee (2019): El Paso's Safety Transcends President Trump's Claim about Border Fence. *El Paso Times* (9 February).

Margo, Dee (2020): On the Border. *The Brookings Cafeteria* podcast, hosted by John Hudak. The Brookings Institution, aired on 22 September.

Martin, John L. (1993): *Operation Blockade: Bullying Tactic or Border Control Model?* Report. Washington DC: Center for Immigration Studies (1 December).

Martinez, Freddy (2016): On the Streets of El Paso and Juarez, 'Sister Cities' Art Project Pays Tribute to Border Communities. Interview with Ramon and Christian Cardenas. *Remezcla* (7 July), https://remezcla.com/features/culture/interview-los-dos/. Accessed 29 June 2021.

Morales, Fred M. (2007): *La Chihuahuita*. El Paso/Juárez Historical Museum.

Museo Urbano at UTEP (n.d.): Official page, https://www.utep.edu/liberalarts/oral-history/public-history/museo-urbano.html. Accessed 12 July 2022.

PBS (2019): Dee Margo, Mayor of El Paso, TX, on Border Wall Politics. *Amanpour & Co*, aired on 12 February.

PBS (2019): How Residents from El Paso Feel About Border Barriers. Interviews by Angela Korchega. *PBS News Hour*, aired on 20 March.

Provine, Doris Marie, and Roxanne Lynn Doty (2011): The Criminalization of Immigrants as a Racial Project. *Journal of Contemporary Criminal Justice* 27, 261–277.

Rivera, Diego (1926): Mexican Painting: Pulquerías. *Mexican Folkways* 2(7), 6–15.

Rodríguez, Antonio (1970): *El Hombre en Llamas: Historia de la Pintura Mural en México*. London: Thames and Hudson.

Rodríguez, Mariángela (1998): *Mito, Identidad y Rito: Mexicanos y Chicanos en California*. Mexico City: CIESAS.

Romero, Simon (2019): El Paso's Message for Trump Before Rally: Don't Speak for Us. *The New York Times*, (10 February).

Romo, David Dorado (2005): *Ringside Seat to a Revolution: An Underground Cultural History of El Paso and Juarez: 1893–1923*. El Paso: Cinco Puntos Press.

Sanchez, Sara (2017): Chihuahuita: A Border Community Rooted in History. *El Paso Times* (10 January).

Simpson, Eve (1980): Chicano Street Murals: A Sociological Perspective. *Journal of Popular Culture* 13(3), 516–525.

Soja, Edward W. (1996): *Thirdspace: Journeys to Los Angeles and Other Real and Imagined Places*. Hoboken, NJ: Wiley-Blackwell.

Soja, Edward W. (2010): *Seeking Spatial Justice*. Minneapolis: University of Minnesota Press.

Villoro, Juan (2011): Identidades Fronterizas. *Conflictos Interculturales*, edited by Nestor García Canclini. Barcelona: Editorial Gedisa, 29–30.

Ybarra Frausto, Tomás (1993): Arte Chicano: Images from a Community. *Signs from the Heart: California Chicano Murals*, edited by Eva Sperling Cockcroft and Holly Barnet-Sánchez. Albuquerque: University of New Mexico Press, 54–67.

SECTION III

NEGOTIATING STRANGENESS AND MOBILE NEIGHBOURHOODS

Transnational Neighbourhoods in Barbara Honigmann's *Das überirdische Licht* (2008) and *Chronik meiner Straße* (2016)

GODELA WEISS-SUSSEX

Abstract

This chapter sets out to analyse two recent texts by German-Jewish author Barbara Honigmann, *Das überirdische Licht* [The Supernatural Light] (2008) and *Chronik meiner Straße* [Chronicle of My Street] (2016), focusing on the literary depiction of her experience of living in New York and Strasbourg. Reading the texts in the context of Honigmann's aesthetics of minor literature, I aim to show how the author/narrator establishes a balance between distance and belonging and depicts transnational urban neighbourhoods, from a vantage point of *Vertrautheit* [familiarity], as places of encounters and interaction, constant mobility, and change.

Introduction

In accordance with the other contributions to this volume, I understand the concept of the urban neighbourhood as defined in spatial and relational terms – or, to be more precise, as based on space, but without fixed or even describable borders, constantly changing over time, and constituted by social practice and encounters between different, at times even antagonistic, city dwellers: "localized everyday life", to borrow Ulf Hannerz's phrase.[1] Heterogeneity and fluidity are characteristics of all neighbourhoods understood in this way, but the transnational neighbourhoods investigated here bring these constitutive elements to the fore.

My focus, in this chapter, is to investigate how literary writing can capture and support the idea of a successful, vibrant transnational neighbourhood. How can it reflect – and what possibilities does it have to reflect upon – the constantly shifting spatial and relational characteristics that make up these neighbourhoods? How can it provide a sense of the "productive social and cultural friction [of the] throwntogetherness"[2] that constitutes them, while resisting expectations of cohesion and notions of harmonisation?

I shall address these questions through case studies of two literary texts by Barbara Honigmann, an author who straddles various cultural identities, as a German writer of Jewish faith living in Strasbourg. The two texts are *Das überirdische Licht*, published in 2008, recording Honigmann's experience as a writer in residence in Manhattan in the winter of 2006; and *Chronik meiner Straße* (2016), a depiction of the multicultural world in the Strasbourg street and neighbourhood she has lived in for over 30 years.

Barbara Honigmann's writing is well positioned to grapple with the experience of the transnational neighbourhood: blurring the lines between author and narrator, her "autofiction"[3] provides personal reflection as well as literary transcendence. Both her texts under discussion here reflect the author-narrator's position as an observer, but also as taking part in the lives of these cities characterised by their diverse migrant communities. This liminal position is characteristic for Honigmann's writing and identity more generally: in her poetological text 'Eine "ganz kleine Literatur" des Anvertrauens' [A Truly Minor Literature of Confiding], she positions herself "am Rande und zugehörig zugleich" [on the margins and yet belonging at the same time].[4] With implicit reference to Gilles Deleuze's and Félix Guattari's concept of minor literature, she thus defines her writing as an expression of deterritorialisation and of not-quite-belonging. Following Deleuze and Guattari further, this kind of writing is well placed to creatively posit models or provide glimpses of potential future communal lives: "this situation allows the writer all the more the possibility to express another possible community and to forge the means for another consciousness and another sensibility."[5]

Reading Honigmann's texts in the context of theories of urban space production and conception by Michel de Certeau, Doreen Massey, Sara Ahmed and others will help to map and understand the realm of co-production that exists between social theory and literary world-making. I aim, firstly, to show how the author-narrator situates herself vis-à-vis the transnational neighbourhoods of Manhattan and Strasbourg featured in her texts, and more specifically, how she constitutes the relationship between space and self through spatial practice and through a negotiation of distance and belonging. Having established her liminal position and the understanding of her attachment as not only related to space but also as shifting with time, I will, secondly, analyse how Honigmann depicts these pluralist heterogeneous neighbourhoods, emphasising the importance of transnational encounters, the *Gestus* of motion and change, and the motif of new beginnings.

Situating the Self: Performing Belonging

Both *Das überirdische Licht* and *Chronik meiner Straße* highlight the performative aspect of city life. In *Licht*, Honigmann refers to "Szenerien" [stage settings] and the "vierte Wand des Theaters" [the theatre's fourth wall];[6] in *Chronik*, she configures her street as a stage: "Vor dem Abrauschen der Autos gibt es ein ganzes Konzert, dann stürze ich oft auf den Balkon, um auch die Choreographie zu sehen" [Before the cars zoom off there is an entire concert, I often rush onto my balcony then so I can see the choreography as well].[7]

In both cases, the author-narrator identifies herself as a spectator, watching from her window or, respectively, her balcony. The narrators' positions differ, however, quite markedly in the two texts, as they are characterised by different degrees of distance between the observing self and the scene observed. In *Das überirdische Licht*, the scene evokes Hitchcock's *Rear Window*, focusing on a set of windows seen from the viewer's own window, Honigmann conveys the strangeness of the not-fully-knowing, awareness of only façade: "Ich beobachte die fremden Menschen in ihren fremden Leben" [I observe the strange/unknown people in their strange/unknown lives] (*Licht* 9). A reference to Edward Hopper's paintings of urban alienation further underlines the distance between observer and the observed scene. This static description contrasts with the depiction of the street scene in *Chronik meiner Straße* as a choreography of sound and movement. What the narrator experiences here is clearly a repeat performance, one that is anticipated and enjoyed. Though not part of it, the observer is "at home" in her position "auf meinem Sonnenplätzchen auf dem Balkon" [in my little place in the sun on the balcony] (*Chronik* 151); she is a connoisseur rather than an outsider.

The comparison between these two passages, which use the same motif but show a different relationality, captures the subtle but clear difference between the gaze of the newly arrived transient visitor (in New York) and that of the settled migrant (in Strasbourg). However, this gaze – and the relationship it implies – changes and develops throughout both texts. The relationship between the observer/narrator and the urban neighbourhood in which she moves is constantly explored anew through shifts along the spectrum of distance and belonging.

Both texts evoke and celebrate the freedom of the stranger in a new city; the narrators' migration has occurred by choice and is framed as an act of leaving behind a bounded state of being, the deterritorialisation of the self is seen as a productive and energising force. In *Das überirdische Licht*, indeed, Honigmann constructs the city of New York as a congenial space for the loosening of bonds; a key word in the New York text is "ledig" [unmarried, but also "free of…" (for instance worries)], configured here as a "Wohlgefühl" [sense of wellbeing] and freedom (*Licht* 30). Once the narrator's husband joins her, the sense of liberation extends to him too: "[u]nsere provisorische Geborgenheit [...], die kurze, freie Bindung an die Stadt machen uns ganz glücklich, ja euphorisch" [our provisory feeling of being settled and safe [...], the brief, free/open bond with the city make us really happy, even euphoric], Honigmann writes (*Licht* 82). Yet this euphoric state of freedom/openness is predicated on the balance between being strange and belonging ("einem seltenen Zustand der Ausgeglichenheit" [a rare state of equilibrium] (*Licht* 83). To achieve this balance, complete, disorienting strangeness must be overcome but at the same time the necessity to commit that comes with complete belonging must be avoided, too. It is a state of being that needs to be kept in constant flux – a process of adjusting and re-adjusting – and which can only be defined, with a dose of vagueness, as a "gewisse Vertrautheit" [a certain intimacy/familiarity] (*Licht* 82).

Such a state is – by definition – transitory, and fittingly, all groups of belonging described in this text on New York are transitory, too; they are temporary, constituted with the awareness of their impermanence, and they are conscious of their heterogeneity: a group gathering for a talk and discussion at the "Remarque Center"[8] is addressed as "Leute in diesem Raum" [people in this room], the speaker deliberately avoiding the more binding "wir" [we/us] (*Licht* 106), and the members of a Jewish "shul" are referred to as "Leute von Brzezan" [people from Brzezan], a paradoxical use of a name that seemingly defines belonging to a particular *shtetl* but actually (as the result of a historical process of widening and transformation) refers to a most eclectic mix of Jewishness ("ein sehr breites Spektrum" [a very broad spectrum] (*Licht* 113)).

The fluidity of belonging that is implied here is inclusive to the stranger, and it places no demands on her. It is based on common intellectual interest or spiritual orientation, but eschews affective commitment. Movement, not stasis, and the opportunity for independent joining and leaving characterises this kind of belonging; and an active effort is required to maintain the balance between distance and closeness that it implies:

> Ich spüre die Versuchung, mich jetzt entweder ganz fallen zu lassen oder viel mehr / auf Distanz zu gehen. Beides ist aber nicht meine Art, ich möchte gern versuchen, das gefährdete Gleichgewicht zu halten und ein Beobachter zu bleiben, der trotz allem etwas sieht.
>
> [I feel the temptation to either drop my guard completely or to assume a stance of much greater distance. Neither is in my nature, I would like to try to maintain the precarious balance and to remain an observer who sees something in spite of it all.] (*Licht* 125f.)

Belonging is thus in the individual's own hands; traditional categorisations lose their meanings and are open to be transcended or deconstructed. A little vignette of a Yiddish-speaking Jew from the "Borschtsch-Belt", who learns Spanish and "[rettet] sich damit erfolgreich in eine andere Welt hinüber[…]" [successfully makes it across into a different world] (*Licht* 146), testifies to this. We may even see a hint of gender boundaries being overcome in the narrator's joy at being part of a group of four female writers whose last names all end on "-mann" (see *Licht* 145).

It is her sense of *Vertrautheit* [intimacy/familiarity], though, that keeps the narrator from "unravelling" in this boundless state,[9] while at the same time offering a safe platform from which to explore the plurality of city life. Honigmann's narrator finds this *Vertrautheit* in her magic triangle of spatial and cultural at-homeness:

Zwischen dem Deutschen Haus, der Maison Française und der koscheren Mensa finde ich mich also in einem Perimeter von weniger als zwanzig Metern in genau jenem magischen Dreieck wieder, in dem sich mein Leben nun schon seit so vielen Jahren abspielt.

[Between the Deutsche Haus, the Maison Française and the kosher refectory I find myself in a perimeter of less than twenty metres in precisely that magic triangle in which my life has been playing out for so many years now.] (*Licht* 20)

Her text, then, concentrates (mainly) on this section of Manhattan – a section that is not necessarily representative of the city as a whole but that is marked by personal experience and observation and into which the writer-narrator has "inscribed" herself. Describing her daily routine as a process of "mich mit den alltäglichen Handlungen in die Stadt ein[zu]schreibe[n]" [inscribing herself into the city with her everyday activities] (*Licht* 21), Honigmann conjures up the idea of the city walker as co-author of the text of the city that Michel de Certeau explored in his seminal text, 'Practices of Space'. Just like de Certeau, whose essay was equally inspired by an experience of Manhattan,[10] she alludes to a rhetoric of space that allows city inhabitants to appropriate the city sites through their everyday activities and, interpreting these activities as "utterances",[11] to contribute to writing the urban text in this way. This metaphor helpfully points to the balance between an already existing urban system that provides orientation and the fluidity of this system, which can be changed and shaped by the individual city walker.

Experiencing the Transnational Neighbourhood: Plurality, Fluidity, Motion and Change

Even beyond this – rather narrow – triangle, the experience of finding herself in a city in which being Jewish is an unremarkable fact[12] provides the narrator with a sense of *Vertrautheit* [intimacy/familiarity], too. References to Jewish tradition, from kosher delis and restaurants via seasonal wishes of "Happy Hannukah" to an African American sales assistant closing his deal in Yiddish (*Licht* 126, 79), are ubiquitous in New York; at the same time, however, the variety of the performances of Jewish practice the narrator encounters in New York opens the door to another crucial element in her city experience: the intense sense of plurality. The "Mischung der verschiedensten Juden aller Arten und Gattungen" [mixture of the most diverse Jews of all sorts and species] (*Licht* 114) at times produces irritation and disorientation (most acutely felt in an encounter with a circle of elderly Holocaust survivors living in an enclosed world of their own (see *Licht* 121ff.)), but, ultimately, the text embraces the plurality it presents.

Honigmann is here picking up a motif again that she foregrounded in her novel *Soharas Reise* [Sohara's Journey] (1996):[13] working against a homogenising view of what it means to be Jewish, she explores, both in the earlier novel and in *Das überirdische Licht*, the plurality of Jewish groups who have immigrated from various geographic regions and have fled different political systems, and who practise a whole range of cultural and religious rituals and customs, displaying and insisting on the richness and heterogeneity of Jewish religious and cultural practice.

New York thus emerges as a city that defies monolithic characterisation. How appropriate, then, that the narrator's favourite café bears the name 'Space Untitled': the city space is defined by its resistance to be named and thus tied down/bounded; it is a city in movement, and, most crucially, a city of encounters. Apart from different forms of Jewish experience, Honigmann's narrator herself encounters old friends and acquaintances from her GDR past (some expected, some by chance), as well as family members she hardly knows, and makes new acquaintances through her everyday engagement with life in New York. But it is the encounters that she observes among the city's inhabitants that stick most vividly in the readers' minds and that most forcefully emphasise the view of the city as a bustling, heterogeneous meeting place of cultures.

Two of these scenes stand out especially, as they both convey a sense of particular city spaces as microcosms: "eine improvisierte Rollerblade-Bahn" [a makeshift rollerblading rink] in Central Park (*Licht* 151) and "OUR Schul" on the Lower East Side (*Licht* 112ff.). Extended enumerations of the physical characteristics of the rollerbladers, their movements and their clothes reveal the significance of this image as a microcosm ("Latinos, Schwarze, Weiße, Chinesen, Inder und andere Asiaten, Juden mit Kippa und auch einer in voller orthodoxer Montur [...] eine beschwingte *brotherhood of men*" [Latinos, Blacks, Whites, Chinese, Indians and other Asians, Jews with kippah and also one in full Orthodox garb [...] a vivacious brotherhood of men] (*Licht* 152f.), and as a place of encounters, of "immer neue Verbindungen" [ever new interactions]: "die Leute holen sich ein, drehen sich umeinander, fassen einander, lösen sich wieder, überholen sich, auch der Hin-Her-Vor-Zurück-Opa wird von einem besonders virtuosen Paar kurz umschwärmt und mitgezogen" [people catch each other up, twirl/ pivot around one another, separate again, the here-there-back-forth-granddad, too, briefly finds himself buzzed around by a particularly virtuoso/artistic couple and pulled along with them] (*Licht* 152).

Honigmann emphasises the provisory, spontaneous nature of the encounters this space engenders (the "office" of the African American who sells his music at the centre of the improvised rink, consists of a revamped bicycle), and the inclusivity of the resulting interactions. These encounters, full of vitality and hope, point to new forms of community, in which heterogeneity is embraced wholeheartedly; they replace a sense of community built on commonality and go beyond an understanding of inclusiveness that still focuses on a norm that reaches out to include the "stranger". They are, in Sara Ahmed's terms, "ethical encounters": encounters which do not fetishise the other as "other" or "stranger"[14] and which, rather than juxtaposing two fully constituted entities, allow identities to meet and be changed through these meetings. These encounters "shift the boundaries of what is familiar",[15] and in so doing, create the basis for a new understanding of community, one that "moves beyond the opposition between common and uncommon, between friends and strangers, or between sameness and difference": "a 'we'" that "must be worked for".[16]

***

For *Chronik meiner Straße*, the same basic tenet applies: here too, Honigmann's narrator writes herself as an observer into a pluralist world. Having lived in Strasbourg for over 30 years, the author does not convey the same transitory experience here; living in the city does not require the same balancing act in an obvious sense. But here, too, the oscillation between the poles of distance and belonging needs to be negotiated.

Strasbourg, the narrator explains, has always been a place of refuge for her, a city "wo das Jüdischsein nicht dem Totsein gleich[kommt]" [where being Jewish does not equate with being dead], after the constraints of life as a Jew in East Berlin, "[die] Stadt, aus der ich mich [...] so sehr wegwünschte" [the city I was

[...] so desperate to leave] (*Chronik* 74 and 79). Yet the process of settling in has been a long one. In a text published in 1999, 15 years after her move, Honigmann had referred to herself as "nur ein Zuschauer, ein Gast, eine Fremde" [merely a spectator, a guest, a stranger] in Strasbourg ('Selbstporträt als Jüdin' 17). Now, in *Chronik meiner Straße*, 17 years on, she still describes herself as a spectator, an observer, but the vantage point is one of belonging: "Ich sitze auf meinem Sonnenplätzchen" [I sit in my little place in the sun] (*Chronik* 152). Still, hers is a place on the margins – literally, as she observes her street from her balcony, and metaphorically, as she positions herself as living in a continual state of "in-between-ness" between Berlin and Strasbourg: "so ist es ein Auseinandersein mit beiden Orten" [it is a state of being separate with both places] (*Chronik* 79).

However, she is also anchored now in the community of Orthodox Jews in Strasbourg, a minoritarian community, with history, rituals, resting in itself, yet lively, changing, being shaped by its members. Emily Jeremiah has shown, in her analysis of Honigmann's earlier work, that the author "understands Jewishness not as a fixed condition but as an exploratory, performative, collective journey involving both dispossession and nomadic potential."[17] This observation holds true here, too. There is an underlying sense of precariousness in her text, which is, however, countered (and thus contained) through instances of community spirit: the exchange of cooking recipes twice concludes conversations about the threat of anti-Semitism (*Chronik* 112 and 130), and the reminder of the precariousness of Jewish existence in the diaspora, symbolised by the Feast of Tabernacles (Succoth), is made bearable through the sense of togetherness and a communal "schallendes Gelächter" [resounding laughter] about the lack of cultural knowledge of their non-Jewish neighbours (*Chronik* 138).

As in *Das überirdische Licht*, though, the narrator's exploration of her own sense of belonging is complemented by her observation and presentation of the different characters that make up the transnational neighbourhood, and in particular the street, in which she lives. As in the New York text, the observed city is, first and foremost, a space of encounters and plurality.

We are not presented, here, with the same idea of microcosms in city locations themselves; instead what comes to the fore is an emphasis on the interconnectedness of the small community she focuses on with global events and political constellations. This idea is most clearly developed in the depiction of the market, where Arabs, Turks and Indian stallholders jostle for space with a *Front National*-voting Frenchman as well as their Jewish and non-Jewish customers. When Honigmann writes of the "Nachbeben" [aftershocks] of events in world politics "auf unserem Markt" [in our market] (*Chronik* 114), it is impossible not to see an echo of Fontane's *Der Stechlin*, the novel of interconnectedness and social evolution in the German literary canon, in which a remote lake in northern Germany echoes international upheavals by featuring a red cockerel rising from the water and raising its voice at times of natural catastrophe or political crisis.

Depictions of the plurality of the cities' inhabitants and their encounters are in both of Honigmann's city books deeply connected with a sense of openness and possibilities. In this sense, these texts gesture at future communities. "Eigentlich führe ich einen Feldzug, um die Territorien eines möglichen Lebens zu erobern" [in essence I lead a crusade to capture the territories of a potential life], Honigmann writes,[18] and through this, makes the same link as that suggested by Deleuze and Guattari, between the marginalised writer and their potential for imagining futurity. The "potential life" – or future communities – she explores are imagined as based on the heterogeneous bustle she perceives, they are heterogeneous, and – crucially – not always and necessarily harmonious, and they are constantly shifting and changing. Indeed, it is worth exploring in further detail how Honigmann's writing, her city descriptions, her use of text structure and of genre, reflect this emphasis on motion and change.

✳✳✳

In *Das überirdische Licht*, already the very first paragraph untethers all spatial anchoring. What was understood to be static moves ("Ein siebzehnstöckiges Hochhaus schiebt sich den Hudson runter" [a seventeen-storey skyscraper is moving down the Hudson] (*Licht* 5)). Spatial orientation is not based in the city itself, in the ground it stands on, but aligned to the sky and its directions, the "Himmelsrichtungen" [cardinal points]; all streets end in sky and clouds and sea, and a few lines on, we learn, through a quotation from a poem by Georg Heym, that the sky itself dissolves in wind and light: "die Gestade des Himmels dahinter / zergehen in Wind und Licht" [the shores of the sky beyond / dissolve in wind and light] (*Licht* 5).[19]

Later, in her description of the area around Washington Square, the narrator speaks of "die kleinen Streets, die um [die Gegend] herumquirlen" [the little streets swirling around [the area]] (*Licht* 8): the city is animated, resists all fixation, "die unwahrscheinlichsten Dinge wirbeln über Straßen und Gehsteige, heben ab und fangen an zu fliegen" [the most improbable items whirl across streets and sidewalks, take off and start to fly] (*Licht* 6).

This sense of motion with which the text is imbued is as much an indicator of energy as it is of a state of flux – and of constant change. This is most evident in Honigmann's contrasting of a museum (the Whitney) with the Greenwich Village neighbourhood: "der Kontrast könnte nicht größer sein: Hier bewegt sich nichts, alles bleibt an seinem Platz […] Keine Ausdehnung und keine Beschleunigung!" [the contrast could not be any starker: here nothing moves, everything stays in its place […] no expansion and no acceleration!] (*Licht* 150f.). This idea of expansion in acceleration is indirectly taken up and developed again in the image of the "improvisierte Rollerblade-Bahn" a few lines later (*Licht* 151): both accentuate the significance of movement as initiator of encounters and, thus, communal activity.

We find a similar dynamic in *Chronik meiner Straße*: here, too, the neighbourhood focused on, the narrator's street, is configured as a space of perpetual motion. In a phrase that clearly echoes the descriptions of New York in the earlier text, we read: "Weil sie so schmal ist, bildet unsere Straße einen Korridor für den Wind, für Autos und für Vögel, die hindurchjagen" [Because it is so narrow our street forms a corridor for the wind, for cars and for birds chasing through it] (*Chronik* 34). This notion of a corridor, a passageway, also applies to parents taking their children to the École Internationale, and of course to the various ethnic groups who settle briefly and leave again. Honigmann lists them extensively to emphasise their diversity, and she underlines both the idea of heterogeneity and of motion by dwelling on the different speeds of their passage through the street ("daherkommen", "eilen", "laufen gemächlicher", "entgegenschiebt" [come along, hurry, walk more leisurely, push against] (*Chronik* 10–11). As in *Das überirdische Licht*, poetic imagery supports the impression created; here it is particularly the references to the slightly surreal or fantastic realm – a bird that looks like a dog, and a "flying" tree to which she provides a home (*Chronik* 34 and 32) – that untether the supposedly factual "chronicle" from the constraints of the genre.

Change is initiated by encounters between the narrator and the other inhabitants in her street – relationships, acquaintances, at times even friendships develop. What Honigmann provides here is not a gushing celebration of multiculturalism, but an indication, too, of the frictions caused by the *throwntogetherness* of people being "set [...] down next to the unexpected neighbour".[20] Katja Garloff has observed that in *Chronik meiner Straße* Honigmann indicates not only the interactions but also the separations between people, and not just individual differences but, more problematically, also those delineated by ethnicity[21] – or, indeed, class: we may well ask whether evoking members of the working class, for instance, as "das 'andere Frankreich' [...], unförmig und dick, ohne *savoir vivre*" [the 'other France' [...], shapeless and fat, with no *savoir vivre*] (*Chronik* 11) is not in fact a dangerously de-individualising practice.

However, as Garloff goes on to say, "the focus on ethnic groups [...] gradually gives way to the stories of individual people and families".[22] And, going beyond this, I would contend that it is also possible to read this naming of difference in a context of heterogeneous world-making, and as a reminder that the chance to unsettle "the givenness" of our social world and to create new, more democratic, more inclusive configurations of communal life or neighbourhood relies, to no small extent, on productive negotiation of difference and even antagonism. As

Doreen Massey writes, it is this antagonism that allows us productive negotiation of "the terms of connectivity" in urban spaces that go beyond mere coexistence.[23] It is important, then, not to forget, that in her text, Honigmann does not leave it at the statement of difference, but leaves us with a deep impression of her Strasbourg neighbourhood as constituted despite these differences. The neighbourhood market gathers all economically, politically and/or ethnically antagonistic groups in the common purpose of selling and buying food. The relationships are "nicht spannungsfrei" [not free of tensions] (*Chronik* 114); but often it takes only a little initiative to reach beyond separation or hostility. Such is the case of the Arab neighbour who – after years of resistance – suddenly responds to a "Friedensinitiative" [peace initiative] of friendly small talk: "Und plötzlich fing auch der Sheriff an zu sprechen, seine Zunge löste sich, sein Gesicht entspannte sich, erzählte Peter später, 'es war als hätte ich einen neuen Kontinent entdeckt'" [And suddenly the sheriff too started to speak, his tongue loosened, his face relaxed, Peter later told us, "it was as if I had discovered a new continent"] (*Chronik* 55f.). The use of the adverb "plötzlich" [suddenly] here indicates the jolt or "choc" (to use Benjamin's term) of the new, which brings understanding through a new way seeing.

This idea of seeing differently, seeing anew, is linked to the idea of new beginnings, which figures largely in both texts. In *Das überirdische Licht*, it is briefly touched upon at the very end of the book, in the form of a thought experiment: "Aus dem Kontinent meines alten Lebens auswandern. Nach Amerika. […] Das möchte doch jeder! Alle Rollen des Lebens noch einmal umbesetzen können, Verwandlung, neuer Text, neues Dekor, eine andere Gestalt" [To emigrate from the continent of my old life. To America. […] Everyone wants this, surely! To be able to re-cast all parts of your life, transformation, new text, new décor, a new shape] (*Licht* 155). The potential new beginning here appears as seductive thought, the possibilities it implies are clearly appealing, but the commitment required for this new beginning is rejected. This unwillingness to commit may be the narrator's loss – the reason she gives is her lack of courage – but what she gains through it is the free, at times almost hallucinatory quality of her writing on New York.

In Honigmann's Strasbourg text, the idea of new beginnings is developed further into a leitmotif. Indeed, the first words of the book read: "Wenn wir sagen, daß wir in der Rue Edel wohnen, antwortet man uns meistens, ach ja, da haben wir am Anfang auch gewohnt. Unsere Straße scheint also eine Straße des Anfangs und des Ankommens zu sein" [Most of the time, when we say that we live in Rue Edel, we are told, oh yes, we used to live there too in the beginning. So our street seems to be a street of beginning and arrival]. And, a little later: "wir sind hier nie ausgezogen und wohnen noch heute in der Straße, in der man nur 'am Anfang' wohnt" [we have never moved out and still today we live in the street in which you only live "in the beginning"] (*Chronik* 5f.).

The *Gestus* of new beginning is here extended into a mode of living – a habitus – through the emphasis on duration, which is made even more explicit when the leitmotif is taken up again later in the book: "in der Straße des Anfangs und des Ankommens, das nun schon so lange dauert" [in the street of beginning and arrival, which has now been going on for so long] (*Chronik* 76).

Again, Honigmann recurs here on ideas explored in previous works: her configuration of life in the diaspora as a new beginning appears in the essay 'Von meinem Urgroßvater, meinem Großvater, meinem Vater und von mir' [About my Great-Grandfather, my Grandfather and Me] for instance, published in 1999. The new beginning is here further represented as a precondition for her writing:

> wurde Frankreich […] das Land der Freiheit für mich. Keiner meiner Vorväter hatte dort jemals gelebt, und es war also leichter, gerade dort noch einmal ganz von vorne anzufangen. Anfangen, eine 'richtige' Jüdin und anfangen eine 'richtige' Schriftstellerin zu sein, ich könnte auch sagen, wieder anfangen.
>
> [France […] became the land of freedom for me. None of my ancestors had ever lived there and so it was easier to start once more from the very beginning there. To start being a 'proper' Jewess and to start being a 'proper' writer, I might also say, to start again.][24]

It is important not to misunderstand the meaning of *Ankommen* [process of arriving], which is not used in the sense of a completion of a journey leading to unequivocal belonging, but in the sense of "new arrival" and new beginning. For, as Petra Renneke very rightly explains: "Das Niemals-Ankommen und der Atopos sind das wesentliche Sujet in Honigmanns Büchern" [The condition of never-arriving and the a-topos are the essential subject of Honigmann's books].[25]

In the same way as another Jewish writer, Hélène Cixous, thinks of herself as always "in *passance*", explaining "I have always rejoiced at having been spared all 'arrival' […] I want *arrivance*, movement, unfinishing in my life",[26] Honigmann stresses the procedural aspect of her extended *Ankommen* in Strasbourg, understanding it as open and ongoing.

***

The sense of unboundedness, untethering, movement and possibility that has emerged so far in the two city portraits is supported by the author's use of text, genre and structure. The texts themselves resist fixity and the closed form usually implied in a published text.

The narrator of *Das überirdische Licht* destroys all evidence of her time in New York at the end of her stay, she divests herself of "[a]lles, was ich habe aufheben wollen, um später […] meinem Gedächtnis Halt geben zu können" [everything I had intended to keep so as to be able […] to provide support to my memory later on] (*Licht* 156). The written text is thus the product of her memory without this "support" – a memory that is free, also free to change: at the time of writing, her memory of her stay in New York "treibt […] wie eine Insel ungebunden herum, ohne an eines der großen Erinnerungsterritorien anzudocken" [drifts […] like an island, untethered, without mooring on one of the big territories of memories] (*Licht* 157). This compositum, "territory of memory", interestingly combines time and space in that it refers to the special conceptualisation of a particular time recalled, a continent in the map of memories. The New York memories, floating, untethered, not (yet) bound to space and time, are still as mobile and malleable as the city itself. It is – the author leads us to this conclusion quite deliberately – a deterritorialised memory in the Deleuzian sense, one that preserves the freedom of affiliation.

Of course, there is a paradox here of the conceptualisation of memory as fluid but being fixed in a published text; and the paradox is reinforced as the narrator rejects the idea of writing down her New York experiences. At a party, when asked whether she will write about her stay in New York later on, she responds quite categorically: "Nein, nein, natürlich nicht, […] wie denn das?" [No, no, of course not, […] how would I?] (*Licht* 86). We are thus meant to read the book as a direct communication: Honigmann stresses the immediacy, but also the fleetingness, of this moment of remembering and communicating through the repeated use of "jetzt" [now] and "noch" [still] in the final two short paragraphs of the book. (*Licht* 156f.).

***

In *Chronik meiner Straße*, we see a similar aspect of resistance to boundedness and fixity. Contrary to what is to be expected from a 'Chronik', the narrative resists a linear structure and a finite ending. Honigmann has described this book as a record of her "observing the time passing",[27] and she provides the reader with a sense of ongoing change and of evolution taking place in a perpetual rhythm.

The passing of time is acknowledged in the somewhat paradoxical situation that social constructs such as the street market remain in place – the market stallholders convene in the same place at the same time, and indeed remain a focus of community life – over a long period of time, while the people involved in the buying, selling and gossiping at the market change. "Es ist derselbe Markt und doch nicht derselbe" [It is the same market and yet not the same], Honigmann succinctly concludes (*Chronik* 116), and she similarly refers to the people who make up her neighbourhood as "viele [...] Völker [...], die sich nach dem Rhythmus der Weltkonflikte erneuern" [many [...] peoples [...] who renew themselves according to the rhythm of global conflicts] (*Chronik* 151).

Change in the neighbourhood is described as a process of evolution and self-renewal; then, only at the very end, there is a suggestion of actively promoted change in the form of new initiatives (a residents' association) and even of institution-driven change ("ein 'Haus des Rechts'" [a "house of law", offering free legal advice]. But whether this will make any impact on the rhythm of change is to be doubted: "der schon so lange andauernde Rhythmus von Aufschwung und Niedergang wird sich erhalten" [the rhythm of boom and decline that has been lasting so long already will maintain itself] (*Chronik* 151).

Honigmann's narrative, then, should be understood as presenting what is merely a section of a rhythm of constant and ongoing change, with this rhythm being seen as the underlying structure constituting the neighbourhood. The fluidity implied here emphasises duration and the extension of experience over time, but allows for an openness of boundaries, constitution and trajectory/evolution of the neighbourhood. Linearity is further resisted by the fact that the appearance of the leitmotif of the "Straße des Anfangs" [street of beginning] in the last two lines of the text seems to feed right back into the book's beginning, where the motif is established in the very first two sentences. In these very last lines of the *Chronik*, book, other central figures of thought of the text are called up once more; it is worth quoting the sentence in full:

> Ich sitze auf meinem Sonnenplätzchen, auf dem Balkon, der zur Straße geht, in der manchmal Bäume, Hunde und Rabbiner fliegen, halb in Träumen und halb in Gedanken über die schon ziemlich lange Zeit, die ich hier habe vorbeiziehen sehen, und den kleinen Weltraum unserer Straße, die nach überallhin offen ist und von der so oft gesagt wird, ach ja, in der Straße haben wir am Anfang auch gewohnt.

> [I sit in my little place in the sun, on the balcony that faces the street through which trees, dogs and rabbis fly from time to time, half dreaming and half thinking about the rather long time that I've seen move past here, and about the small universe of our street that is open to all directions and of which it is so often said, oh yes, we used to live in this street too in the beginning.] (*Chronik* 152)

As if summarising her project in these lines, Honigmann firstly points to the position of the narrator as an observer, comfortably placed in the neighbourhood, but in a 'Randposition' [marginal position].[28] She secondly untethers her text from the notion of 'Chronik' as a fixed record of facts only, for instead of providing the precision of historical dates, her narrative configures both space and time as expanded and imprecise ("the rather long time" and "the small universe of our street"). Thirdly, she emphasises that the notion of belonging is compatible with the notion of openness and change: the neighbourhood engenders a sense of belonging ("our street"), but the structure of this neighbourhood is ever-changing and unbounded. Overall, the emphasis on time in flux, on motion and new beginnings supports the idea of openness as crucial characteristic of this neighbourhood, open even to the unreal, to objects defying the laws of nature. Referring back to the confident and relaxed statement "wenn hier Bäume fliegen, warum nicht auch Hunde" [if trees fly about here, why not dogs, too] made much earlier in the book (*Chronik* 34), Honigmann conjures up an image reminiscent of a Marc Chagall painting: of a chronicle of Jewish life, floating and untethered. This description, then, reminds us, in a very subtle way, of the context of Honigmann's oeuvre as a whole, in which the interest in narrating Jewish life has played an important role.[29] It also underlines the sense of freedom inherent in the possibility of change, which permeates *Chronik meiner Straße* just as much as *Das überirdische Licht*, in which, in a memorable passage, the narrator complains: "Wir hassen es, ewig DDR-Bürger bleiben zu müssen" [We hate having to continue being GDR citizens for ever] (*Licht* 100).

Barbara Mann, interpreting an article by Daniel and Jonathan Boyarin, has pointed to the particular importance of place-making, i.e. granting specific, local meaning to more abstract, undifferentiated space,[30] in texts by Jewish authors: "Jews are always a 'displaced' people", she argues, "and therefore conscious of the need to turn space into place."[31] And indeed, it is appropriate to see both of Honigmann's texts discussed here as acts of literary place-making. The resulting places, however, are not fixed or static. Rather than suggesting that they "allow displaced subjects to put down new roots in the diaspora", as Katja Garloff states in reference to *Chronik meiner Straße*,[32] I prefer to describe Honigmann's literary treatment of transnational neighbourhoods as "nomadic" place-making, an act of establishing a temporary *Vertrautheit* and an insistence on fluidity and change, rather than the sense of settled belonging implied by the concept of roots.

Notes

1. Hannerz, Ulf (1980): *Exploring the City: Enquiries Toward an Urban Anthropology*. New York: Columbia University Press, 99.
2. Ehrig, Stephan, Britta C. Jung, and Maria Roca Lizarazu (2020): Conference Report: Exploring the Transnational Neighbourhood. Integration, Community, and Co-Habitation, *Journal of Romance Studies* 20(1), 179–181, 181.
3. Honigmann uses this term herself, see Honigmann, Barbara (2006): 'Wenn mir die Leute vorwerfen, daß ich zuviel von mir spreche, so werfe ich ihnen vor, daß sie überhaupt nicht über sich selbst nachdenken' – Zürcher Poetikvorlesung (I): Über autobiographisches Schreiben. *Das Gesicht wiederfinden: Über Schreiben, Schriftsteller und Judentum*. Munich: Hanser Verlag, 31–60.
4. Honigmann, Barbara (2006): Eine 'ganz kleine Literatur' des Anvertrauens: Glückel von Hameln, Rahel von Varnhagen, Anne Frank. *Das Gesicht wiederfinden: Über Schreiben, Schriftsteller und Judentum*. Munich: Hanser Verlag, 7–29, 28. All translations from Honigmann's texts in this chapter are my own.
5. Deleuze, Gilles, and Félix Guattari (1986): *Kafka: Toward a Minor Literature*, translated by Dana Polan. Minneapolis: University of Minnesota Press, 17.
6. Honigmann, Barbara (2008): *Das überirdische Licht. Rückkehr nach New York*. Munich: Hanser Verlag, 9. *Das überirdische Licht* is henceforth cited in the text as *Licht*.
7. Honigmann, Barbara (2016): *Chronik meiner Straße. Roman*. Munich: dtv, 53. *Chronik meiner Straße* is henceforth cited in the text as *Chronik*.
8. The reference is to the Remarque Institute at New York University.
9. "[M]anchmal fürchte ich sogar, mich in meinem ledigen Leben in Manhattan ein bißchen aufzulösen" [sometimes I even fear that I might unravel a little in my unfettered life in Manhattan] (*Licht* 125).
10. His description of Manhattan as simultaneously island and sea, as fixed and in motion, strikes a chord with Honigmann's text, as the opening sentences, eerily evoking a pre-9/11 world, show: "To *see* Manhattan from the 107th floor of the World Trade Center. Below the wind-stirred haze, the urban island, a sea upon the sea rises on the crested swell of Wall Street, falls into the trough of Greenwich Village, flows into the renewed crests of midtown and the calm of Central Park, before breaking into distant whitecaps up beyond Harlem" (De Certeau 122).
11. De Certeau, Michel (1985): Practices of Space. *On Signs*, edited by Marshall Blonsky. Baltimore: Johns Hopkins University Press, 122–145, 129.
12. Consider in this context the city's description as "the symbolic capital of the diaspora", for instance (in this formulation) by Barbara Mann (130).
13. Honigmann, Barbara (1996): *Soharas Reise*. Berlin: Rowohlt.
14. Ahmed, Sara (2020): *Strange Encounters: Embodied Others in Post-Coloniality*. London: Routledge, 180.

15. Ibid., 8.
16. Ibid., 180.
17. Jeremiah, Emily (2012): *Nomadic Ethics in Contemporary Women's Writing in German: Strange Subjects*. London: Camden House, 177.
18. Honigmann, Barbara (1999): Selbstporträt als Mutter. *Damals, dann und danach*. Munich: Hanser Verlag, 83–88, 87.
19. The line is from Heym's poem 'Träumerei in Hellblau' [Reverie in Light Blue]. It does not appear in the final version of the poem, but is cited in an interim version in Heym, https://www.aphorismen.de/gedicht/143504.
20. Massey, Doreen (2005): *For Space*. London: Sage, 151. For further discussion of the concept of *throwntogetherness*, see Massey, chapter 13.
21. Garloff, Katja (2020): Diasporic Place-Making in Barbara Honigmann. *Rebuilding Jewish Life in Germany*, edited by Jay Howard Geller and Michael Meng. New Brunswick, NJ: Rutgers University Press, 166–180, 175.
22. Ibid.
23. Massey (2005), 151f.
24. Honigmann, Barbara (1999): Von meinem Urgroßvater, meinem Großvater, meinem Vater und von mir. *Damals, dann und danach*. Munich: Hanser Verlag, 39–55, 52.
25. Renneke, Petra (2012): *Im Schatten des Verstehens: Denken und Nicht-Wissen. Die Prosa Barbara Honigmanns*. Würzburg: Königshausen & Neumann, 56.
26. Cixous, Hélène (2005): My Algeriance, in other words: To Depart Not to Arrive from Algeria. *Stigmata. Escaping Texts*. London: Routledge, 126–141, 138.
27. Barbara Honigmann: Reading and Conversation with Robert Gillett, Institute of Modern Languages Research, University of London, 23 February 2017.
28. Honigmann, Barbara (2006): Eine 'ganz kleine Literatur' des Anvertrauens: Glückel von Hameln, Rahel von Varnhagen, Anne Frank. *Das Gesicht wiederfinden: Über Schreiben, Schriftsteller und Judentum*. Munich: Hanser Verlag, 7–29, 28.
29. For the close connection between Jewishness and motion, see Heuser, Andrea (2011): *Vom Anderen zum Gegenüber. "Jüdischkeit" in der deutschen Gegenwartsliteratur*. Böhlau, 315f. See also Honigmann, Barbara (2000): *Alles, alles Liebe!*. Hanser: "Ich finde es eigentlich gut, daß das Judentum keinen Ort hat und das Innere, wie Du es nennst, ausschließlich Handlung, also etwas Bewegtes und vielleicht Bewegendes ist" (130) [I actually like the fact that Jewishness is not associated with place and that the core, as you call it, is nothing but action, i.e. something that is in motion and perhaps something that is setting other things in motion].
30. Mann, Barbara (2012): *Space and Place in Jewish Studies*. New Brunswick, NJ: Rutgers University Press, 17f.
31. Ibid., 110.
32. Garloff (2020), 177.

Works Cited

Primary Literature

Honigmann, Barbara (1996): *Soharas Reise*. Berlin: Rowohlt.
Honigmann, Barbara (1999): Selbstporträt als Jüdin. *Damals, dann und danach*. Munich: Hanser Verlag, 11–18.
Honigmann, Barbara (1999): Selbstporträt als Mutter. *Damals, dann und danach*. Munich: Hanser Verlag, 83–88.
Honigmann, Barbara (1999): Von meinem Urgroßvater, meinem Großvater, meinem Vater und von mir. *Damals, dann und danach*. Munich: Hanser Verlag, 39–55.
Honigmann, Barbara (2000): *Alles, alles Liebe!*. Munich: Hanser Verlag.
Honigmann, Barbara (2006): Eine 'ganz kleine Literatur' des Anvertrauens: Glückel von Hameln, Rahel von Varnhagen, Anne Frank. *Das Gesicht wiederfinden: Über Schreiben, Schriftsteller und Judentum*. Munich: Hanser Verlag, 7–29.
Honigmann, Barbara (2006): 'Wenn mir die Leute vorwerfen, daß ich zuviel von mir spreche, so werfe ich ihnen vor, daß sie überhaupt nicht über sich selbst nachdenken' – Zürcher Poetikvorlesung (I): Über autobiographisches Schreiben. *Das Gesicht wiederfinden: Über Schreiben, Schriftsteller und Judentum*. Munich: Hanser Verlag, 31–60.
Honigmann, Barbara (2008): *Das überirdische Licht. Rückkehr nach New York*. Munich: Hanser Verlag.
Honigmann, Barbara (2016): *Chronik meiner Straße. Roman*. Munich: dtv.

Secondary Literature

Ahmed, Sara (2020): *Strange Encounters: Embodied Others in Post-Coloniality*. London: Routledge.
Cixous, Hélène (2005): My Algeriance, in other words: To Depart Not to Arrive from Algeria. *Stigmata. Escaping Texts*. London: Routledge, 126–141.
De Certeau, Michel (1985): Practices of Space. *On Signs*, edited by Marshall Blonsky. Baltimore: Johns Hopkins University Press, 122–145.
Deleuze, Gilles, and Félix Guattari (1986): *Kafka: Toward a Minor Literature*, translated by Dana Polan. Minneapolis: University of Minnesota Press.
Ehrig, Stephan, Britta C. Jung, and Maria Roca Lizarazu (2020): Conference Report: Exploring the Transnational Neighbourhood. Integration, Community, and Co-Habitation. *Journal of Romance Studies* 20(1). 179–181.
Garloff, Katja (2020): Diasporic Place-Making in Barbara Honigmann. *Rebuilding Jewish Life in Germany*, edited by Jay Howard Geller and Michael Meng. New Brunswick, NJ: Rutgers University Press, 166–180.

Hannerz, Ulf (1980): *Exploring the City: Enquiries Toward an Urban Anthropology.* New York: Columbia University Press.

Heuser, Andrea (2011): *Vom Anderen zum Gegenüber. "Jüdischkeit" in der deutschen Gegenwartsliteratur.* Cologne: Böhlau.

Heym, Georg (1964): Träumerei in Hellblau. *Dichtungen und Schriften: Gesamtausgabe,* vol. 1, edited by Karl Ludwig Schneider. Hamburg: Verlag Heinrich Ellermann. https://www.aphorismen.de/gedicht/143504. Accessed 29 June 2021.

Jeremiah, Emily (2012): *Nomadic Ethics in Contemporary Women's Writing in German: Strange Subjects.* London: Camden House.

Mann, Barbara (2012): *Space and Place in Jewish Studies.* New Brunswick, NJ: Rutgers University Press.

Massey, Doreen (2005): *For Space.* London: Sage.

Renneke, Petra (2012): *Im Schatten des Verstehens: Denken und Nicht-Wissen. Die Prosa Barbara Honigmanns.* Würzburg: Königshausen & Neumann.

Territories of Otherness

Genoa's Prè Neighbourhood as a Deviant Terrain and Exotic Counterspace in Ilja Leonard Pfeijffer's *La Superba* (2013)

BRITTA C. JUNG

Abstract

This chapter explores the depiction of Genoa's Prè neighbourhood as a deviant terrain and exotic counterspace in Ilja Leonard Pfeijffer's award-winning city novel *La Superba* (2013). As a whole, the novel presents the port city as a gateway to Europe and a migratory junction both in a spatial as well as a socio-historical sense, bringing together those who find themselves on the move (i.e. tourists, migrants, transmigrants and refugees). It explores their differences and commonalities within the city's deeply ingrained social structures and hierarchies by not only evoking the Mediterranean imaginary but also by framing Genoa as a multiterritorial Other that is alternately placed on the shores of both Europe and Africa, as well as in between. Yet, despite this geo-cultural shift which is (at least initially) positively connoted, the novel's Dutch narrator frames the historic neighbourhood of Prè through a colonial gaze, establishing it thereby as an exotic counterspace in which he not only satisfies his voyeuristic urges but also attempts to re-establish his own privileged status as a Northern European, male 'expat' and celebrated author. In other words, Prè comes to embody the deviant within the Other, and – in reference to the novel's blurring lines of the migratory experience – the place where the narrator's own journey ends as an emasculated, cross-dressing prostitute.

Introduction

Few contemporary Dutch writers divide opinion quite like Ilja Leonard Pfeijffer – a trained classicist whose doctoral research explored the work of Pindar of Thebes, an award-winning poet and novelist, and what could be termed a 'European public intellectual'.[1] Since his 1998 literary début, Pfeijffer has published numerous poetry collections, stage plays, essays, columns, travel accounts, stories, political satires and novels. Like the subject of his academic study, Pindar of Thebes, Pfeijffer's works are marked by an exuberance of language and matter, and littered with idiosyncrasies. Lauded by some critics as a literary genius, he is considered by others an antiquated stylist. His works challenge the casual reader not only in narratological but also in linguistic, epistemological and ethical terms. It therefore hardly comes as a surprise that "Pfeijffer's prose", as critic Alina Cohen notes, "shocks and disturbs, and the reader both rejects what he says and yearns to hear more."[2] Overall, Pfeijffer's work is perhaps best described as a transgressive practice, i.e. an overstepping of boundaries which leads – in its all-encompassing quality – to a subversion of the normative arrangements that our everyday life (and our understanding of it) is embedded in. This naturally also relates the way space/spatiality is configured and practised, both in relation to global and local contexts, as well as temporal ones. Pfeijffer's acclaimed city novel *La Superba* (2013) is a case in point.

Set in the Italian port city of Genoa, the author's adopted home, *La Superba* chronicles the urban experiences of Pfeijffer's narrating alter ego, who is variously referred to as Ilja, Leonard or Leonardo in the novel. A modern-day *flâneur*,[3] Ilja spends his days strolling through the city's labyrinthine structures, committing his observations, experiences and interactions to paper in pursuit of his next bestseller. The novel's plot wanders like its narrator, who embodies a transgressive spatial practice through his mobility as well as his writing. In his sketches and musings, Ilja introduces a myriad of individuals that inhabit the urban space, most notably the neighbourhoods of Molo, San Vincenzo, Maddalena and Prè, all of which are part of the city's Centro Est or Eastern Centre: Italian socialites, bartenders, waitresses, politicians and civil servants; American tourists, British 'expats' and other European 'luxury immigrants';[4] Romanian beggars, North African and Middle Eastern rose peddlers, Senegalese boat refugees; land- and slumlords, prostitutes, and countless others. What links these individuals in Ilja's notes and sketches is the space they share or, indeed, do not share.

The following chapter will, therefore, first explore the spatial configurations and practices in Pfeijffer's *La Superba*. It will illustrate how Genoa is configured as a counterspace to the narrator's uber-organised Dutch homeland, a multiterritorial Other that is alternately placed on the shores of Europe and Africa, as well as in between. This is then contrasted with the racialised configuration of the historic Prè neighbourhood that is not only the home to the marginalised migrant communities from Africa and the Middle East but also a place where prostitution and crime run rampant. The centrally located Prè constitutes an exotic space and 'deviant terrain'[5] within Genoa where Ilja not only satisfies his voyeuristic urges but also attempts to reaffirm his own privileged status as a Northern European expat and hypermasculine macho man as he slowly but steadily surrenders to the city's dark forces. Prè, in other words, manifests the deviant within Genoa's Otherness. In a final and concluding step, this chapter will examine to what extent Ilja's mobility and writing constitute a transgressive spatial practice that questions and subverts not only the normative arrangements of the various spaces within the city, but also the normative arrangements of Europeanness in the context of migration, particularly those that cast the picture of a renewed enlightened cosmopolitanism. However, in light of the theme of the present volume, a few words regarding the transnational neighbourhood are warranted first.

Defining the Transnational Neighbourhood: *La Superba*'s Spatial Imaginaries

Looking at the transformation of London's Docklands, Doreen Massey once noted that, "[w]hatever the abstract concept of place which people hold, there will always be differences, debates, even struggles, about how places are viewed. There will be differences within the place, and differences between those (or some of them) and some without."[6] Massey concluded that we need to move beyond the social construction of space by also incorporating the spatial construction of the social, i.e. the extent – following Wendy Wolford – to which the physical environment of a city like Genoa, or indeed its individual neighbourhoods, "is internalized, embodied, imagined, and remembered."[7] Employing the term 'spatial imaginaries', Wolford goes on to define the spatial construction of the social as "cognitive frameworks, both collective and individual, constituted through the lived experiences, perceptions, and conceptions of space itself."[8] It is these cognitive frameworks that Ilja, and by extension Pfeijffer's novel itself, seeks to explore, especially if we consider that the novel's titular character is in fact the city of Genoa, La Superba.[9]

Perhaps one of the most enduring characteristics of the Mediterranean imaginary are the sustained linkages and ongoing exchanges of its urban centres across borders.[10] Mediterranean cities such as Genoa have played a key role in connecting East and West as well North and South, acting as commercial and cultural intermediaries between them well into the early modern period. Through their sustained linkage and ongoing exchange, they are the historical precursors of what we would nowadays describe as transnational cities.[11] However, the development of long-distance seafaring devalued these commercial connections significantly, and Europe's base of power shifted north- and westward. The Mediterranean became part of the European periphery and Genoa a port of departure for millions of Italians looking for a better life in the Americas and elsewhere in the 19th and early 20th century. Concurrently, Italy and the Mediterranean witnessed the rise of mass tourism, with affluent travellers not only seeking out the cultural, artistic and historical heritage but also a type of premodern exoticism that was seen as decidedly different from the experience of modern urbanity, particularly in northern metropolises such as Paris, London and Berlin. More recently, as net emigration started to turn into net immigration in Italy in the 1990s due to both its geographic location and relative wealth as well as its high demand for a flexible workforce,[12] Italy and the Mediterranean have also come into focus as part of the European Union's external border management and migration policies that have turned the region – as critics and activists have posited – into "Europe's migrant graveyard".[13] Images of sunbathers and bedraggled migrants making their way ashore have added yet another layer to the way it is internalised, embodied, imagined and remembered.

Pfeijffer's *La Superba* charts this Mediterranean spatial imaginary by casting the port city of Genoa as a gateway to Europe and a migratory junction in both a spatial and a temporal sense. In other words, it brings together those who find themselves on the move: tourists, transmigrants, retirement migrants, forced migrants, refugees and asylum seekers, and undocumented migrants, as well as unskilled and skilled workers, and highly trained specialists that are part of today's globalised work culture, while also envisioning the historic experiences of 11th-century crusaders, 12th-century sea merchants and 19th-century Italian emigrants as they pass through the city. The novel explores their differences and commonalities within Genoa's deeply ingrained social structures and hierarchies, and asks whether distinctions such as race and class alter after crossing borders. Indeed, as the novel progresses, the lines between these groups seem to be increasingly blurred, with the migratory experience often boiling down to a maelstrom of a desire for a better life, hardship, disillusionment and shame – all of which are at the heart of the multitude of stories being told by Ilja and the other characters, to themselves, to each other, and to those who have been left behind.

As a result, Genoa and its neighbourhoods become "densely packed contact zones",[14] in which the ever-shifting paths of individuals in movement come together for a brief moment in time, only to pass and never to be repeated. And yet, by recounting and committing them to paper, Ilja transfixes them in time, thereby contrasting not only the multitude of seemingly ephemeral experiences of those thrown together by chance in the city's streets and cafés, but also the different experiences across centuries. Massey refers to this being set down "next to an unexpected neighbour" as *throwntogetherness*.[15] In Ilja's notes and city sketches, everybody becomes an unexpected neighbour to everybody else: socialites, bartenders, waitresses, politicians, civil servants, cruise ship and other tourists, expats, rose peddlers, boat refugees, slumlords, prostitutes, crusaders, sea merchants, and Italian emigrants – although not all neighbourhoods and public spaces are equally open to everybody, as we will see later on. Moreover, with the intention to redraft his notes into his next great novel, Ilja not only relies on and engages with existing cognitive frameworks on a personal level but seeks to actively partake in the shaping of the city's spatial imaginary on a larger scale.

As we encounter two novels within one, i.e. Pfeijffer's *La Superba* and Ilja's notes and sketches which form the basis of his intended novel, the chapter will henceforth explicitly distinguish between the two where necessary by either referring to Pfeijffer's *La Superba*/novel or Ilja's novel, notes and sketches.

'Africanising' Genoa: Configuring the City as a Multiterritorial Other

When Ilja is asked by a weary Rashid, a Moroccan technician turned rose peddler and an acquaintance of Ilja's, why he has left his home country and moved to Genoa, a seemingly insurmountable gap opens between them. While Rashid's migration to Europe is an economic endeavour and a calculated investment by his extended family who do expect a return on it, Ilja's migration is borne out of repleteness and boredom. To him the modern, largely man-made and hyper-constructed land- and cityscapes of his homeland and the Dutch desire for a well-regulated, smoothly running everyday life that accounts for the country's core concepts of straightforwardness, pragmatism and egalitarianism leave life with few to no surprises, stifling his creativity as an artist:

> Ik viel bij wijze van spreken al in slaap voordat ik naar bed ging en werd zelfs in de tussentijd niet wakker. Ik kende alles al. Ik kende het verhaal al. En uiteindelijk ben ik toch een kunstenaar. Ik heb input nodig. Inspiratie noemen ze dat, maar ik haat dat woord. De uitdaging om wakker te worden in een nieuwe stad waar niets vanzelf spreekt en waar ik het voorrecht heb om mezelf helemaal opnieuw uit te vinden. De uitdaging om wakker te worden. [...] Comfort is als een slaapliedje, een drug, een antidepressivum dat alle emoties afvlakt. Je ziet het ook aan de gezichten van de mensen in mijn vaderland. Ze hebben de weke uitdrukkingsloosheid van wie niets meer te bevechten heeft en daar niet speciaal tevreden over is omdat het normaal is geworden dat alles perfect functioneert. (50)

> [I fell asleep even before I went to bed, in a manner of speaking, and didn't even wake up in the meantime. I knew everything already. I knew the story already. And at the end of the day, I'm an artist. I need input. Inspiration is what they call it, but I hate the word. The challenge to wake up in a new city where nothing is obvious and where I have the freedom to reinvent myself anew. The challenge of waking up. [...] [C]omfort is like a lullaby, a drug, an antidepressant that numbs the emotions. You can see it on the faces of the people in my homeland. They have the limp expressionlessness of people who no longer have to fight for anything and aren't particularly pleased about it because it's normal for everything to function perfectly.] (53f.)

Rashid, who struggles to carve out a living for himself and to meet his family's expectations, leaves without a word – Ilja's lofty explanation a metaphorical slap in his face. After all, Rashid's life in Genoa is marked by marginalisation, discrimination and exploitation, with his occupation as a *rozenverkoper* [rose peddler] also outwardly marking his precarious economic and social status in the public sphere. As a side note, and in reference to the previously mentioned openness/non-openness of certain spaces to certain groups, I would like to point out that although Rashid is one of the most mobile characters in the novel, walking every day the 12 kilometres from his home in Prè to Nervi in the eastern periphery of Genoa and back to sell his roses, he often remains invisible to and/or ignored by those outside of Prè. Yet Rashid also feels alienated from large parts of the migrant community in his own neighbourhood, as he acknowledges later on, noting that Ilja is one of his few meaningful contacts and "[z]ijn enige vriend hier" [his only friend here] (71/80).

The juxtaposition of Ilja's perfunctory life in the Netherlands and an elusive, almost dream-like life in Genoa where he is wide awake is not only striking, but builds on a Northern ideological construct that relies on hegemonic, evolutionist notions of modernity, progress and what Arjun Appadurai would call trajectorism;[16] and frames the Mediterranean and the South more generally as a belated, imperfect, and not-yet North.[17] Indeed, Ilja perceives Genoa as a living and breathing thing, an indifferent organism that withstands the test of time (and humanity), simply chugging along: "Toen ik wakker werd, hoorde ik hoe de stad begonnen was met de dag te vermalen tussen haar eeuwenoude rotte tanden. Op verschillende plekken in de buurt werd er geboord in haar afbrokkelend gebit. Buren scholden elkaar uit door de open ramen" [When I woke up, I heard the city starting to chew the day between her ancient, rotten teeth. In different parts of the neighbourhood, her crumbling ivories were being drilled. Neighbours swore at each other through open windows] (16/10). This image is then amended shortly after, turning a zoomorphic city structure into a different form of organism altogether:

> Er zouden vandaag schepen arriveren met Nederlandse, Duitse en Deense toeristen op terugreis vanuit Sardinië of Corsica. Er arriveren tientallen keren per dag en de toeristen zullen voorzichtig en met tegenzin een middagje een klein weinig verdwalen in het labyrint. Veel verder dan de steegjes op een paar meter van Via San Lorenzo durven ze zelden te gaan. […] [Z]e zullen geen weet hebben van de donkere jungle die aan hun voeten ligt. (16f.)

> [Today ships will arrive with Dutch, German, and Danish tourists on their way back from Sardinia and Corsica. They arrive dozens of times a day, and the tourists

cautiously and reluctantly lose themselves a bit inside the labyrinth for an afternoon. They seldom dare venture much further than the alleys a few meters from the Via San Lorenzo [...], oblivious to the dark jungle lying at their feet.] (10f.)

While Ilja's portrayal of Genoa as a *donkere jungle* [dark jungle] does invoke the tired metaphor and literary trope of the urban jungle, its invocation is deliberate and goes further. On the one hand, it configures the city as a wilderness and exotic counterspace to Ilja's uber-organised Dutch homeland, i.e. as an antithesis to (Northern) European civilisation and modernity. On the other hand, it also 'Africanises' the city by evoking images of tropical rainforests and premodern savagery, and by extension the idea of natural selection and what Herbert Spencer – with recourse to Charles Darwin – once described as the "survival of the fittest".[18] Threatening and foreboding, not least through the qualifier *donkere*, the jungle calls to Ilja as a means to unleash his creative potential by becoming "[een] deel van deze wereld", "een gelukkig monster, samen met de duizend andere gelukkige monsters" [a part of this world; a happy monster, along with thousands of other happy monsters] (17/11). Indeed, the allure constitutes a well-established trope in the context of colonialist literature and is reminiscent of white European characters like Marlowe and Kurtz in Joseph Conrad's *Heart of Darkness* for whom, as Chinua Achebe noted in his 1975 Chancellor's Lecture at the University of Massachusetts Amherst, the jungle and Africa become a source of temptation.[19] Ultimately, Ilja's embrace of the wilderness in the pursuit of his art and a more meaningful life, his attempt to exoticise his experience like Kurtz and become one of the *gelukkige monsters* [happy monsters], or – to put it in colonialist terms – to 'go native', ends in financial, social and gender dislocation. This dislocation is also topographically marked as his mounting debts and the associated shame force him more and more out of Molo, i.e. the city's historic seat of power[20] and his initial geographical focus as a resident, into Prè's red-light district where he begins to prostitute himself (348/406).[21]

However, before being chewed up by the urban jungle, Ilja only marginally differs from the timid cruise ship tourists he so abhors. As a highly educated, well-known and white 'luxury migrant' with a European passport, Ilja can be confident that he will come out on top as 'one of the fittest' – and he moves through the city accordingly. In its essence, the attitude and habitus displayed by Ilja echo what Edward Said once noted in reference to Johnny Weissmuller's depiction of Tarzan, i.e. that despite being a resident of the jungle and representing the savage, untamed and wild, he is still a white master of it[22] – something Ilja himself readily acknowledges when conceptualising his new novel: "[Deze] zal moeten gaan concentreren op het grote actuele vraagstuk van de immigratie, waarbij ik mijn eigen geslaagde luxe-immigratie zal contrasteren met het betreurenswaardige lot van al die sloebers uit Marokko en Senegal" [[It] will have to focus on the big topical issue of immigration, whereby I will contrast my own successful expat lifestyle with the deplorable fate of all those poor fellows from Morocco and Senegal] (92f./107). I would like to point out that his somewhat condescending description of African migrants as *sloebers* [wretches] echoes Ilja's highly idiosyncratic (and contradictory) relationship with this part of Genoa's migrant community, which I will return to later on. This being said, in contrast to works like Conrad's *Heart of Darkness*, Ilja seems to make a concerted effort to give a voice to a myriad of individuals who inhabit the urban space, including those who are usually marginalised/invisible, like Rashid or his flatmate Djiby, who has just about survived the dangerous journey from Senegal, first through Mali, Niger and Libya and then across the Mediterranean Sea in a dinghy, and has since been granted a temporary residence permit by the Italian government – both in an effort to relieve the pressure on the overcrowded refugee camp in Lampedusa and as a result of geopolitical quarrels within the European Union (239ff./276ff.). Indeed, Pfeijffer's *La Superba* dedicates one of its five chapters, i.e. one of its shorter 'intermezzos', to Djiby's story (235ff./271ff.). Largely consisting of direct speech by Djiby, the chapter reduces Ilja to a stooge. This is a marked departure from what Achebe criticises as the dehumanising and de-individualised portrayal of Africans in colonialist literature.[23] To what extent this departure holds will have to be seen in the context of the configuration of Prè, which is – with only a few exceptions – the home to the migrant communities from Africa and the Middle East.[24]

Despite Ilja's configuration of Genoa as an exotic, 'Africanised' counterspace to his Northern European homeland and his alleged understanding of the inner workings of Genoese everyday life, he ultimately – and fatally – relies on the city's inherent Europeanness, i.e. that it is bound by the rule of law, the very foundation of the confidence that he will come out on top as 'one of the fittest'. This is a misconception Ilja is warned about early on by an acquaintance from Sardinia but pays no heed to: "Jij denkt dat dit Europa is, omdat je met EasyJet binnen anderhalf uur terug kunt zijn in jouw overzichtelijke vaderland. Je vergist je. Je bent in Genua. Dit is Afrika. Deze wereld is jou volslagen wezensvreemd" [You think this is Europe because you can get here on EasyJet within an hour and a half from your efficient fatherland. You're mistaken. You're in Genoa. This is Africa. This world is totally foreign to you] (84/97). It is noteworthy that Cinzia explicitly places Genoa in Africa,[25] while Ilja does not. Accordingly, his first encounter with, or rather his first observation of, the city's deeply ingrained, hidden social structures and hierarchies, most notably the mafia, leaves him "degelijk geschokt. Genua had mij altijd een beschaafde Noord-Italiaanse stad gebleken. Nou ja, beschaafd is misschien het verkeerde woord. Maar in elk geval noorderlijk" [genuinely shocked. Genoa had always seemed like a civilized northern Italian city to me. Well, civilized might be the wrong word. But in any case, northern] (177/202). Contrary to his previous configuration of Genoa's spatial imaginary, Ilja echoes here rather the Italian intellectual tradition of *meridionalismo* [Meridionalism], i.e. the internal differentiation between a 'civilised' north and a 'backward' south, which first emerged in the aftermath of the country's unification in 1870.[26] This misconception is soon corroborated through Ilja's own experience. A business venture with another artist from Northern Europe not only throws Ilja into financial turmoil as the two of them are defrauded by the powerful Parodi family, an implied mafia clan, it also turns him into a social pariah as he runs afoul the influential Fulvia, an eccentric woman with the right connections within the city's deeply ingrained structures and hierarchies. Or as Alfonso, one of Ilja's acquaintances, observes:

> Daarmee heb je een van de machtigste vrouwen van Genua tot je vijand gemaakt. Daarmee heb je een van mijn trouwste politieke bondgenoten en een van mijn beste persoonlijke vriendinnen tot je vijand gemaakt. Ik kan je niet langer helpen. Sterker nog, je bent nu officieel mijn vijand. Dit is geen Amsterdam of Berlijn. Dit is Genua. Ik wens je succes met je manier van leven. (231)

> [You've made an enemy of one of the most powerful women in Genoa. And you've made an enemy of my most faithful political allies and one of my very dearest friends. I can no longer help you. More than that, you are now my enemy. This isn't Amsterdam or Berlin. This is Genoa. Good luck living the way you do.] (267f.)[27]

Alfonso's parting sentences underline both Genoa's Otherness in relation to (Northern) European metropolises such as Amsterdam or Berlin (or Paris), and Ilja's inherent incompatibility with it as a Northerner. In other words, the previously mentioned assumption that he can move through the jungle as its (European) master is soundly rejected. Moreover, nothing short of mocking Ilja, Signor Parodi posits that Genoa is not even part of Italy itself, but its own distinct entity where outsiders – whether European or African – are merely tolerated and will always remain on the margins as foreigners:

> U gelooft in Europa en in de gedachte dat Italië een democratische rechtsstaat is en in de fantasie dat Genua deel uitmaakt van Italië. U gelooft in uw democratisch recht en in rechtsbescherming. [...] Hier bent u in Genua, waar mijn vrienden en vrienden van mijn vrienden al eeuwen de dienst uitmaken, en hoewel ik u nogmaals wil complimenteren met de wijze waarop u gepoogd hebt u onze manier van denken eigen te maken, zult u voor ons altijd een buitenstaander blijven. Erg-

er nog: een buitenlander. Wij kunnen uw aanwezigheid in onze stad tot op zekere hoogte tolereren en zelfs toejuichen in zoverre u zich uw eigen zaken houdt. Maar zodra u zich op ons terrein begeeft, bent u weinig meer dan de eerste Marokkaan of Senegalees. (228f.)

[You believe in Europe and in the idea that Italy is a democratic constitutional state and the fantasy that Genoa is part of Italy. You believe in your democratic rights and in the protection of law. [...] You are in Genoa, where my friends and friends of friends have been calling the shots for centuries, and although I'd like to compliment you once again on the way you attempted to adopt our way of thinking, you will always remain an outsider to us. Worse still, a foreigner. We can tolerate your presence in our city up to a certain degree, and even welcome it as long as you stick to your own business. But as soon as you start stepping into our territory, you're worth little more than your average Moroccan or Senegalese fellow.] (225f.)

Refuting the previously mentioned hegemonic, evolutionist notions of modernity, progress and trajectorism, Signor Parodi configures Genoa as a historical Other, i.e. one that does not follow a trajectory, a configuration that is mirrored in Ilja's transhistorical and translocal account of the migration experience by throwing together the (fictional) accounts of the migrants of today and those of 11th-century crusaders, 12th-century sea merchants and 19th-century Italian emigrants.

Deviant Terrain and Exotic Counterspace: Configuring Prè as the Deviant within Genoa's Otherness

Despite configuring Genoa as an exotic, 'Africanised' counterspace to his Northern European homeland, Ilja views and relies on the city's inherent Europeanness. In fact, unlike his Sardinian acquaintance Cinzia, Ilja himself never explicitly places Genoa in Africa. This is, however, not the case for the city as a whole. To the contrary, as an urban embodiment of intensifying transnational migration, Ilja configures Genoa's migrant neighbourhood Prè as distinctly African, and locates it accordingly when he notes that it is "tweehonderd meter [vanaf Via del Campo] naar Afrika" [two hundred meters from Via del Campo to Africa] (46/49). Drawing on Appadurai,[28] one could perhaps describe Ilja's Prè as a deterritorialised space within Genoa where the bonds not only between the geographic location of the neighbourhood and the people within it are loosened and reimagined, but also between Prè and the neighbouring Molo, San Vincenzo and Maddalena – with modern technology facilitating a transnational practice that closely ties the residents to their home countries. The continuous connection finds its visible expression not only in the countless internet cafés and phone shops that line the neighbourhood's streets, but also the numerous Western Union agents that are a constant reminder of the (crushing) financial responsibilities many migrants carry (46, 73 and 268/49, 82 and 311). As Ilja's portrayal of and his own engagement with the historic neighbourhood illustrates, the deterritorialisation and spatial reimagination of Prè not only open up the possibility for the (re)articulation of identities, but also revivifies "long-established colonial and Orientalist tropes."[29]

Following an early reference to Prè that signifies it as the place "waar Rashid woont met de rest van Afrika" [where Rashid lives along with the rest of Africa] (34/33), Ilja sketches a vivid, sensuous image of the neighbourhood during his first visit in the novel:

> Vanaf Via del Campo is het tweehonderd meter naar Afrika. Ik liep door de Porta dei Vacca, stak de weg over en was in Prè. Honderden internetpunten en belwinkels van nauwelijks een deur breed waren afgeladen met Kenianen en Senegalezen. Hun vrouwen verdienden intussen het geld door rinkelend klatergoud te verkopen op straat, telefoonhoesjes, papieren zakdoekjes, cd's, gootsteenonstoppers en handgesneden olifanten van tropisch hardhout. Ze zaten majestueus uitgewaaierd in traditionele gewaden. Talloze groentewinkeltjes hadden zich als mansbrede spelonken tussen de Phone-Center gedwongen. Ze hadden opschriften en prijslijsten in het Arabisch of in het Swahili. En op mysterieuze wijze was er nog ruimte over voor kapperszakken, gespecialiseerd in Afrikaans haar […]. Ik vermoedde dat je er ook de minnares van je man kon laten beheksen. Waarom zou het anders zo afgeladen vol zijn met opgewonden, gehavende negerinnen die niets kapperigs ondergingen? In een hoek achter de droogkappen vergaderden de dorpsoudsten over de ontstane situatie en de maatregelen die te nemen waren. Hier en daar werd iemands haar geknipt. Moslimbroeders slentereden gestreng over straat. Hoertjes stonden opvallend onzichtbaar in de steegjes. (47)

> [It's two hundred meters from Via del Campo to Africa. I walked through the Porta dei Vacca, crossed the road, and was all of a sudden in the Prè. Hundreds of internet cafés and call shops of barely a door's width across were packed with Kenyans and Senegalese. In the meantime, their wives were earning the money selling tinkling gilt items on the street – phone cases, paper handkerchiefs, CDs, rubber plungers, and elephants hand-carved from tropical hardwood. They sat there majestically spread in traditional robes. Numerous greengrocers had squeezed themselves in between the phone centres like narrow, man-sized caverns. They

had Arabic or Swahili lettering and price lists. And in some mysterious way, there was still space left for hairdresser's shops specializing in African hair [...]. I suspect you could also get a spell cast on your husband's mistress in there. Why else would they be so full of excited, shabby-looking black women, not having anything hairdresser-y done to them? In a corner behind the dryer hoods, the village elders gathered to discuss the situation that had arisen and the measures to be taken. Dotted around the place were a few people having their hair cut. Muslim brothers strolled sternly along the street. Prostitutes were conspicuously inconspicuous in the alleyways.] (49f.)

In addition to the visible markers of a lived transnational everyday practice, such as shops and the linguistic landscape, Ilja's spatial imaginary of Prè is permeated by the 'survival strategies' typically associated with the most marginalised and vulnerable migrant groups, i.e. economic migrants, refugees and/or undocumented immigrants. Having few financial resources left upon their arrival, and facing significant linguistic and bureaucratic barriers, Karen Jacobsen posits that the economic activities of these groups are often "based in the informal sector, oriented towards generating quick cash, and characterized by low financial risk" – with the selling of (cheap) consumer goods and services such as hairdressing being but two examples.[30] One might add that, given the red tape of the asylum process around labour and the general barriers illegal immigrants face, a lot of these activities can easily be done off the books too. The descriptor *gehavende* [shabby-looking] furthers the overall impoverished impression of the scene, marking a stark contrast to the rather fashionable and poised women in the cafés and bars in Maddalena or Molo. Indeed, given Ilja's often misogynistic attitude, as well as its combination with the descriptor *opgewonden* [excited] and the racist term *negerinnen* [negros, f.],[31] the portrayal of the women implies a barely concealed value judgement that places black (migrant) women at the lowest rung of the hierarchical/racialised order.

Returning for the moment to the question of the economic activities of Prè's residents, Rashid's rose peddling and Djiby's work by day for shopkeepers and assistance to the elderly in these neighbourhoods are examples of a transgressive spatial practice that expands these types of economic activities beyond Prè but simultaneously maintains the social order and hierarchy, as they are entirely "contingent upon the goodwill and cooperation of most of the local population."[32] Outside Prè, Rashid and Djiby remain tolerated guests at best. The resulting precariousness is also observed by Ilja, although he only alludes to it incidentally when he notes that "[s]oms *mocht* [Djiby] 's ochtends vroeg voor Oscar de tafeltjes, stoelen en parasols van de Gradisca buiten zetten" [[s]ometimes in the early mornings, Oscar *allowed* him to put out the Gradisca's tables, chairs, and umbrellas] (238/275).³³ Indeed, the modal verb *mocht* [was allowed to]³⁴ highlights not only the power imbalance between 'employer' and 'employee', but also that the latter needs to be grateful that he is even allowed to work for the former – underscoring once again how repressive migration laws and red tape remove agency and power from migrants like Djiby.

This being said, the economic activities observed and described by Ilja in relation to Prè, generate – as Jacobsen asserts – only "small, irregular sums of money" which "must be supplemented by other kinds of work – sometimes including high-risk activities, like prostitution or smuggling."³⁵ These more insidious economic activities become ever more apparent as the novel progresses. Not only does Moroccan technician turned rose peddler Rashid get increasingly involved in the drugs trade, a downward trajectory that ultimately ends in the Marassi Prison (108/126), but the women selling *rinkelend klatergoud* [tinkling gilt items] on the street also act – as Ilja supposes later on – as lookouts for their "zonen en neven, die dealen en allerlei andere louche zaakjes bedrijven" [sons and nephews, who deal drugs and get up to all kinds of other shady business] (235/272). While the remark carries once again a value judgement on the part of Ilja, it also underscores that Rashid's fate is by no means solely premised on the individual decisions taken but rather on structural problems both within the migrant community, i.e. the responsibility towards those at home who expect a return on their investment, and outside, in that migrants from these marginalised groups often tend to be locked out of opportunities for work and earning.

In addition to configuring Prè as a space populated by shabby-looking black women and dominated by the more informal economic activities, Ilja highlights the neighbourhood's Otherness in relation to the city as a whole as the migrants maintain their own cultural practices and values, and join and form communities within it. To Ilja and many other Genoese residents, Prè quite simply *is* Africa, and he encounters it with a colonialist mentality. It is a deviant territory within the counterspace, a *terra incognita* to be explored (and exploited), if you will, where black women wear traditional dress, village elders gather to discuss community affairs, Muslim Brothers 'patrol' the streets, and transactional sex is an everyday feature. The portrayal of the elderly as village elders is revealing in that it not only gives Prè an air of provincialism and primitivism but also suggests the existence of an alternate, non-state authority within the neighbourhood, i.e. the patriarchal elder council, that administers tribal law – with the presence of the Muslim Brotherhood alluding to yet another alternate, religiously oriented non-state authority.

Moreover, Ilja's assumption that the shops and streets double up as a place for services in the occult, witchcraft and sorcery reproduces a long tradition of spiritual Othering in Europe that has been, as Amber Murray outlines, "a central feature of the colonial production of knowledge", including Conrad's hugely successful (if controversial) *Heart of Darkness*, and "deeply enmeshed within both the production of racial hierarchies and the teleos [sic] of the 'civilising mission'".[36] Or as Peter Pels asserts, "Western images of Africa as a dark and occult continent functioned [...] as a way to contain African phenomena within the parameters of imperial, colonial, and neocolonial power and ideology."[37] This spiritual Othering not only contributes to Prè's configuration as a place of darkness, obscurity, danger and primitivism, it also racialises and genders it. On the one hand, it differentiates between migrants from Northern Africa and the Middle East, who predominantly practise one of the Abrahamic religions, and those from sub-Saharan regions, where traditional African religions and beliefs are (still) more widespread and infuse everyday life.[38] Although Ilja acknowledges that there are "witte en zwarte heksen, zij die helpen en zij die schaden" [white and black witches – those who help and those who cause damage] (235/272), the spiritual Otherness holds an unmistakably threatening quality, not least due to the fact that both types of witches look alike to the inexperienced eye of white Europeans. On the other hand, Ilja's portrayal places the practice of the occult, witchcraft and sorcery squarely in the female domain. Indeed, the previously described state of excitement of the women engaging with the occult not only echoes age-old ideas of female hysteria, i.e. a display of behavioural deviance, it also ties the practice of the occult explicitly to colonial visions about African savagery and libidinal excess.[39] Spiritual and sexual Otherness appear intrinsically entwined as Ilja hones in on infidelity as a reason for seeking such services and – in a second description of Prè – imagines the partner's virility and/or a sexual rival's limps as targets of it (235/271f.). The sexual Otherness of Prè is further confounded by both the neighbourhood's thriving commercial sex market and the widespread practice of cross-dressing within it.[40] In this context, for instance, Ania Loomba has pointed to the attribution of homosexuality, drugs and cross-dressing to Africans in Leo Africanus' *A Geographical History of Africa* (1600),[41] which was the authoritative work on Africa at the time and shaped the idea of the 'dark continent' for generations of Europeans to come, including Ilja's spatial imaginary of Prè.[42]

In combination with the aforementioned drug dealing and petty crime of the male youth, Prè is captured as deviant terrain that is outside the bounds of the normative Genoese/Italian/European imaginary and what Bridget Anderson calls the *community of value* – both in economic as well as behavioural, spiritual and sexual terms.[43] The underlying, thus far tantalising, threat of danger that goes hand in hand with the neighbourhood's exoticism becomes more concrete and unappealing as the sun sets, as tribalised gangs turn Prè into a warzone and the (uneasy) truce between the different migrant groups falls apart in their hands:

> Voetstappen klinken hol terwijl je wandelt tussen de loopgraven en ze klinken voor alle partijen even verdacht. De Senegalezen voeren oorlog tegen de Marokkanen, de Zuid-Amerikanen tegen de Senegalezen en de Marokkanen, de Marokkanen tegen iedereen. Ze gebruiken stenen en flessen als munitie. Soms gebruiken ze munitie als munitie. Het komt voor dat er doden vallen, al lees je daar zelden iets over in de krant omdat de slachtoffers illegaal zijn en officieel niet bestaan en omdat ze om verdere problemen te voorkomen door hun landgenoten zo snel mogelijk worden opgeruimd. Van de politie hebben ze sowieso niets te verwachten. Ze vereffenen die rekening wel op hun eigen manier. Dat je niet wordt geraakt in het spervuur, heb je uitsluitend te danken aan je blanke huid. Voor de oorlog tussen de immigranten ben je irrelevant. [...] Van de bendeleden mag je rustig onwetend voorbijsjokken door het niemandsland dat is gewapend op een manier waar jij geen weet van hebt. Maar in dat niemandsland zijn gauwdiefjes actief die het hebben voorzien op je wankele tred, je mobieltelefoon en de vijf euro die je nog in je broekzak hebt. De politie is hier geen partij. Zij mijden Via di Prè na zonsondergang omdat het er dan gewoonweg te gevaarlijk is. (236)

> [Footsteps echo hollowly as you walk between the trenches, sounding just as suspicious to everybody else. The Senegalese are at war with the Moroccans, the South Americans with the Senegalese and the Moroccans, and the / Moroccans with everyone. They use stones and bottles as ammunition. Sometimes they use ammunition as ammunition. There are sometimes fatalities, though you seldom read about them in the papers since the victims are illegals, and so officially don't exist, and to prevent further problems, are whisked away as quickly as possible by their fellow countrymen. The police are of no help. They settle scores in their own way. The only thing protecting you from being hit in the crossfire is your white skin. You're irrelevant in the war between immigrants. [...] [T]he gang members allow you, quietly and ignorantly, to trudge through a no-man's-land armed in ways you have no knowledge of. But there are pickpockets in no-man's-land and they set their sights on your unsteady walk, your mobile phone, and the five euros you have left in your trouser pocket. The police are no players here. They avoid Via di Prè after sunset because it's simply too dangerous.] (272f.)

Ilja's assertion of a no-go zone where Italian state authority is absent is deeply rooted in the political act of localising the so-called 'danger zones' of far-away, crisis-afflicted regions in European cities – framing those within it as a threat to the security and social harmony of the rest of the population.[44] This second portrayal of the Prè not only goes beyond the exoticism previously described by Ilja in that it turns the tantalising threat into concrete, physical danger, even though the European outsider remains by and large a non-entity in the neighbourhood's internal conflicts; it also lays bare the racialised/ethnicised tensions – and perceived hierarchy – between Prè's different migrant groups that has so far only been hinted at in words and deeds. For instance, despite sharing lodgings with Djiby, Rashid claims legal, social and moral superiority over those from sub-Saharan Africa, who he tends to homogenise and subsume under the label of 'illegal immigrants' (71/80).

Despite Ilja's intention to write a city novel on Genoa and to give voice to its residents and those passing through (although the absence of black female migrants is not only notable but rather telling), Prè is to him little more than the localised spectacle of the ghettos, favelas, barrios and townships that have in recent times – as Uli Linke and others have noted – become "tourist destinations" for affluent travellers to venture "into the urban netherworlds of dispossession."[45] The precarious living conditions described by Rashid and Djiby underscore this spatial configuration of Prè, with more than a dozen people sharing a damp, rat-infested two-bedroom apartment. Although Ilja's strolls through the neighbourhood cannot be classified as 'slum tourism' in the strictest sense, i.e. commercially organised sightseeing tours in areas of urban poverty,[46] they share certain attitudinal similarities in that they reinforce the racialisation of Genoa's spatial imaginary. This becomes particularly apparent during a visit of his German translator, Inge. On the second day of her visit, Ilja and Inge stroll through Molo, Maddalena, Porto Antico and Carignano before turning towards Prè, where Ilja is excited to share the sordid exoticism and deviance of the neighbourhood with his guest, noting: "Ik wilde haar Afrika laten zien. Ik wilde zien hoe exotisch zij in al haar kolossale blondheid zou afsteken tegen de duistere achtergrond van steegjes vol gevaar en grijzende witte tanden" [I wanted to show her Africa. I wanted to see how exotically she, in all her colossal blondness, would stand out against the dark background of alleyways filled with danger and grinning white teeth"] (97/112). The episode is particularly noteworthy, as Ilja thinks Prè a "memorable travel destination" for Inge and seemingly equates the neighbourhood with what Linke describes as a "living museum[...] and human zoo[...]".[47] Indeed, this attitudinal deindividualisation and dehumanisation finds an explicit expression in his reduction of the residents to a stereotypical body feature, i.e. their *grijzende witte tanden* [grinning white teeth]. On the other hand, it is not the local residents but Inge that is characterised as exotic due to her stereotypical Northern (European) appearance, highlighting once again Ilja's emotional and intellectual alienation from his homeland. Much to Ilja's delight, Inge reacts with the 'appropriate' mix of curiosity and fear, reaffirming not least of all Ilja's increasingly challenged hypermasculine machismo by seeking physical reassurance from him, "alsof [hij] een inheemse gids was die haar moest beschermen tegen de wilden" [as though [he] was a local guide who could protect her from the savages] (97/113).

Conclusion: Mobility and Writing as a Transgressive Spatial Practice?

Jacques Rancière posits that transgression recentres power relations by disturbing "the relationship between the visible, the sayable, and the thinkable", and making thereby tangible what has previously been excluded.[48] To a certain extent, this also applies to Ilja's mobility and writing as he moves through Genoa's neighbourhoods, giving voice to the city's residents, including vulnerable and marginalised migrants like Rashid and Djiby, with the latter's account of his journey across Northern Africa and the Mediterranean Sea being particularly haunting. Through Ilja's encounters *with* and his observations *about* them, the racialised relationship between Prè and the other neighbourhoods becomes apparent. Migrants like them may move through the city to pursue informal economic activities, yet – outside of Prè – they remain largely invisible to those around them. Indeed, exploitation is ripe among the neighbourhood's migrant communities due to the precarious legal, economic and social status of many of the residents and the continued financial responsibilities they carry towards those who they have left behind in their home countries – with both land-/slumlords, employers and local authorities as well as criminal kingpins and human traffickers taking advantage.

While Ilja's encounters and observations spell out the unbalanced power relation the residents of Prè often find themselves in, he also sheds light on the racialised/ethnicised tensions within the neighbourhood itself and thereby lays bare that Prè engenders communal togetherness along with differences and conflict. By giving Rashid and Djiby a prominent voice within his notes and city sketches, Ilja attempts a marked departure from the often dehumanising and de-individualised portrayal of Africans in European literature. Moreover, by highlighting the historical parallels to 11th-century crusaders and 19th-century Italian emigrants, Ilja underscores the shared experience migration engenders, and the Othering and marginalisation that often come with it. In doing so, Ilja seems to assert that migration processes and the discourses surrounding it are continuously shifting – yesteryear's destitute Italian emigrant is today's economic migrant from Morocco and Senegal. Yet, at the same time, Ilja exoticises Prè by revivifying age-old tropes of spiritual, sexual and – in lieu of the more insidious (economic) activities – moral Otherness. Despite a general openness towards individuals like Rashid and Djiby, and highlighting the inner-communal tensions, Prè remains by and large a homogenised Other, i.e. a deviant terrain and exotic space within the favourably 'Africanised', multiterritorial city.

In other words, Ilja configures Prè consciously and subconsciously as the deviant within the 'Africanised' European Otherness of Genoa.[49] On the one hand, his mobility and writing are a transgressive spatial practice that transcends geographic, social, cultural and temporal boundaries; on the other hand, they comply with established normative arrangements of Europeanness and Genoa's spatial imaginary. After all, Ilja remains an outsider, i.e. at least until his own failure and descent into prostitution, which is echoed in the shift of his geographic focus from Molo to Prè. Indeed, considerable parts of his notes and sketches about Prè, including the lengthy descriptions above, are based on mere assumptions, as he never identifies a source of his local 'knowledge;' and they could very well be exaggerations. This is particularly true with regard to his classification of Prè as a no-go zone that is ravaged by racialised/ethnicised gang violence and petty crime, as well as his portrayal of African femininity, sexuality and spirituality – not least since Prè's female voices are notably absent. Ilja's general misogyny notwithstanding, the usage of the racist term *negerinnen* [negroes, f.] in reference to black women further highlights Ilja's emotional and intellectual distance from this particular group. His treatment of Prè at times amounts to little more than a colonialist variation of 'slum tourism', a voyeuristic venture into Genoa's netherworlds of dispossession and racialised Otherness where he gets to reaffirm not only his own privileged existence as a Northerner but also his hypermasculine machismo that is increasingly challenged in his own sexual encounters. Ultimately, this reaffirmation proves to be only temporary – at least in part. Ilja becomes a part of Prè's precarious world yet maintains his inherent whiteness and the privileges it affords.

This narratological arc, i.e. the equation of Ilja's migratory experience with the experience of the most marginalised and vulnerable migrant groups, and more importantly groups who have historically found themselves at the receiving end of the colonial project, challenges not only our epistemological understanding of migration but warrants the question to what extent Pfeijffer's literary exploration can be considered ethical. After all, as already mentioned, Ilja has much greater agency in his migratory experience due to his privileged status as a successful white male European citizen than Rashid, and certainly Djiby, who face considerable barriers in legal, linguistic and socio-economic terms. His failure is first and foremost the result of his own choices, particularly his choice not to return to his home country in order to deal with his financial woes due to a misplaced feeling of shame and his superiority complex:

Te veel mensen weten dat ik met veel bombarie ben geëmigreerd om mij te laven aan la dolce vita italiana. Ik werd en wordt erom benijd. Om met hangende pootjes terug te keren, als de eerste de beste nitwit uit mijn favoriete televisieprogramma, *Een huis in de zon*, die de plaatselijke rioolverordening niet kan lezen en toe te geven dat het allemaal een beetjes anders is gelopen dan gehopt en dat het eerlijk gezegd nogal is tegengevallen, zou een enorme nederlaag zijn. (345)

[Too many people know that I emigrated with great fanfare to slake my thirst with la dolce vita italiana. I was and am envied for it. But to return home with my tail between my legs like the next nitwit on my favorite television programme, *A Place in the Sun*, who can't read the local sewer regulations, and to admit that it all went a little different than planned, and that, to be honest, it was rather disappointing, would be a huge loss of face.] (402f.)

Rashid and Djiby, on the other hand, and many of the other residents in Prè, carry heavy (financial) responsibilities towards those they have left behind in their home country. Moreover, despite giving them a voice and allowing them to tell their respective stories 'in their own words', it remains a mediated account. These are Ilja's notes and sketches; it is Pfeijffer's novel; and Ilja is – as several episodes indicate – conceptualised as an unreliable narrator.

Notes

1. Cf. Beeks, Sara (2019): Ilja Leonard Pfeijffer as a Luxury Immigrant: A European Public Intellectual and the 'Refugee Crisis'. *FKW: Zeitschrift für Geschlechterforschung und visuelle Kultur* 66, 101–116. Beeks defines Pfeijffer as such with recourse to Odile Heynders, who posits that literature is still a major drive of the public intellectual's activity, while "literature is a lively and complex negotiation of text, author, reader and society." Zooming then in on the literary intellectual in particular, Heynders notes that they are oftentimes male, "with a certain artistic prestige and writing career, who tr[y] to convince an audience beyond [their] main readers or followers, and in doing so deliberately us[e] various media platforms, styles and genres." Heynders, Odile (2016): *Writers as Public Intellectuals: Literature, Celebrity, Democracy*. Basingstoke: Palgrave Macmillan, 20 and 7.
2. Cohen, Alina (2016): Migration Gone Awry. *Los Angeles Review of Books* (25 March).
3. Ilja's framing as a modern-day *flâneur* builds on a long tradition of assuming a natural sympathy between the *flâneur* and the artist, more precisely progressive artists, which has been cemented – amongst others – by Balzac, Baudelaire and Benjamin. Cf. Buck

Morss, Susan (1989): The Flâneur's Object of Enquiry Is Modernity Itself. *The Dialectics of Seeing: Walter Benjamin and the Arcades Project*. Cambridge: MIT Press.
4. In a note to his Dutch editor, who is the fictive addressee of his musings and city sketches, he contrasts his "geslaagde luxe-immigratie [...] met het betreurenswaardige lot van al die sloebers uit Marokko en Senegal" [my own successful expat lifestyle with the deplorable fate of all those poor fellows from Morocco and Senegal]. Cf. Pfeijffer, Ilja Leonard (2017): *La Superba*. Amsterdam: De Arbeiderspers, 2nd ed., 92f. [*La Superba*, translated by Michele Hutchison. Dallas: Deep Vellum Publishing, 2016, 107]. All page references to the Dutch and English version are henceforth cited in the text, where necessary separated by a slash.
5. Jein, Gillian (2015): (De)Facing the Suburbs: Street Art and the Politics of Spatial Affect in the Paris Banlieues. *The DS Project: Image, Text, Space/Place, 1830–2015*, http://thedsproject.com/. Accessed 28 June 2021.
6. Massey, Doreen (1994): Double Articulation: A Place in the World. *Displacements: Cultural Identities in Question*, edited by Angelika Bammer. Bloomington: Indiana University Press, 110–121, 118f.
7. Wolford, Wendy (2004): This Land Is Ours Now: Spatial Imaginaries and the Struggle for Land in Brazil. *Annals of the Association of American Geographers* 94(2), 409–424, 410.
8. Ibid.
9. The city was first nicknamed 'La Superba', i.e. 'the proud one', by Francesco Petrarca who in 1358 wrote: "Vedrai una città regale, addossata ad una collina alpestre, superba per uomini e per mura, il cui solo aspetto la indica signora del mare" [You will see a royal city, leaning against an alpine hill, superb for men and for walls, whose appearance alone indicates the lady of the sea]. Quoted from Guglielmi, Laura (2019): *Le incredibili curiosità di Genova: Uno sguardo su più di mille anni di storia della Superba*. Rome: Newton Compton.
10. Cf. Matvejević, Predrag (1999): *Mediterranean: A Cultural Landscape*. Oakland: University of California Press.
11. Cf. Vertovec, Steven (2009): *Transnationalism*. New York: Routledge, 3; Kwak, Nancy, and A.K. Sandoval-Strausz (2017): *Making Cities Global: The Transnational Turn in Urban History*. Philadelphia: University of Pennsylvania Press.
12. Cf. Dainotto, Roberto M. (2006): The European-ness of Italy: Categories and Norms. *Annali d'Italianistica* 24, 19–39, 21.
13. So e.g. Alessandra Sciurba (President of Mediterranea Saving Humans) at a press conference in Tunis on 19 February 2020.
14. Ehrig, Stephan, Britta C. Jung, and Maria Roca Lizarazu (2020): Conference Report: Exploring the Transnational Neighbourhood. Integration, Community, and Co-Habitation. *Journal of Romance Studies* 20(1), 179–181, 179.
15. Massey, Doreen (2005): *For Space*. London: Sage, 300.

16. Appadurai, Arjun (2013): *The Future as a Cultural Fact: Essays on the Global Condition.* London: Verso.
17. Michel Huysseune, for instance, notes how Italy was increasingly interpreted "as the southern (and Catholic) Other, in opposition to northern (and Protestant) modernity" from the 18th century onwards – a view that was reinforced by linking Protestantism to the emergence of capitalism (Max Weber). Huysseune, Michel (2006): *Modernity and Secession: The Social Sciences and the Lega Nord in Italy.* New York and Oxford: Berghahn, 45.
18. Herbert Spencer first used the phrase in his *Principles of Biology* (1864), in which he drew parallels between his own economic theories and Darwin's biological ones: "This survival of the fittest, which I have here sought to express in mechanical terms, is that which Mr. Darwin has called 'natural selection', or the preservation of favoured races in the struggle for life." Spencer, Herbert (1864): *The Principles of Biology*, vol. 1. London and Edinburgh: Williams and Norgate, 444f. The idea of the "preservation of favoured races in the struggle for life" is – as we will see – particularly interesting in the racialised imaginary evoked by Pfeijffer's novel, which explores different types of migratory experiences.
19. Achebe, Chinua (2016): An Image of Africa: Racism in Conrad's 'Heart of Darkness'. *Massachusetts Review* 57(1), 14–27.
20. With the Cattedrale di San Lorenzo (Genoa Cathedral), the Palazzo Ducale (Doge's Palace), and the *palazzi* of the most eminent Genoese families, i.e. the city's religious and political seat of power, being located in Molo.
21. Ilja's descent into prostitution, particularly as a transvestite, marks not only the endpoint of a longer development within the narrator's hypersexualised exploration of the city that oscillates between reality and dream-like fantasy but is also part of the novel's general traversal of boundaries – with his gender identity and his once-privileged status as a revered writer from the European North being but two examples.
22. Said, Edward W. (2001): Jungle Calling. *Reflections on Exile: And Other Essays.* London: Granta Books, 327–336.
23. Achebe (2016).
24. One important exception is Samir, the successful Iranian owner of the Gloglo bar in Maddalena, who serves as a counter-image to the many struggling migrants, including Rashid and Djiby. It is, however, notable that Ilja does not dedicate much time to Samir's migratory experience in his musings (176f./200ff.).
25. Even more to the point is the seemingly homogenised continent of Africa, which is a marked contrast to a regionalised Italy and indeed Europe.
26. For a brief explanation of the *meridionalismo* and its key figures, cf. Huysseune (2006), 48ff. Although, it has to be pointed out that Ilja does immediately qualify the word *beschaafd* [civilised], implying a difference with the 'civilised' Northern Europe.

27. The last sentence of the translation is a literal translation and deviates from Hutchinson's translation, which reads: "Good luck living the dream."
28. Appadurai, Arjun (1995): The Production of Locality. *Counterworks: Managing the Diversity of Knowledge*, edited by Richard Fardon. London and New York: Routledge, 204–225; Appadurai, Arjun (1996): *Modernity at Large: Cultural Dimensions of Globalization*. Minneapolis: University of Minnesota Press.
29. Graham, Stephen (2006): Cities and the 'War on Terror'. *International Journal of Urban and Regional Research* 30(2), 255–276, 256. Cf. also Thomas, Deborah A., and Kamari Maxine Clarke (2006): Introduction. *Globalization and Race: Transformations in the Cultural Production of Blackness*, edited by Kamari Maxine Clarke and Deborah A. Thomas. Durham: Duke University Press, 1–34, 27.
30. Jacobsen, Karen (2005): *The Economic Life of Refugees*. Bloomfield: Kumarian Press, 11.
31. It is noteworthy that Hutchison's English translation opts to replace the racist term with the more neutral term "black women".
32. Jacobsen (2005), 16.
33. The emphasised verb *allow* is a slightly more literal translation and deviates from Hutchinson's translation, which reads: "Oscar had him put out the Gradisca's tables, chairs, and umbrellas."
34. It has to be noted that Hutchison's translation changes the passive voice to an active one, with Pfeijffer's original (passive sentence) structure drawing even more attention to Djiby's disempowered and marginalised position.
35. Jacobsen (2005), 11.
36. Murray, Amber (2017): Decolonising the Imagined Geographies of 'Witchcraft'. *Third World Thematics* 2, 157–179, 158.
37. Pels, Peter (1998): The Magic of Africa. Reflections on a Western Commonplace. *African Studies Review* 41(3), 193–209, 194.
38. Cf. Muzzanganda Lugira, Aloysius (2009): *African Traditional Religion*. New York: Chelsea House Publishers, 11f.
39. Loomba, Ania (2015): *Colonialism/Postcolonialism*. London: Routledge, 153–163.
40. Indeed, it is important to note that human trafficking from sub-Saharan Africa to Europe for the purpose of forced labour and sexual exploitation is a flourishing business. Among European countries, Italy reports a particularly high share of migrant sex workers, of whom about half originate from Africa. Cf. e.g. TAMPEP (2009): *Sexwork in Europe: A Mapping of the Prostitution Scene in 25 European Countries*. Amsterdam: TAMPEP International Foundation.
41. Africanus' account was first written in Arabic, then in Tuscan and published around 1530. It was subsequently translated into French and Latin for the erudite in 1556.
42. Loomba (2015), 157. Cf. also Spronk, Rachel, and Thomas Hendriks, eds. (2020): *Readings in Sexualities from Africa*. Bloomington: Indiana University Press. Cf. also Robert

Connell's notion of the hegemonic masculinity that refers to a culturally exalted form of masculinity that is linked to institutional power and envisions – as Judy Root Aulett et al. note – 'masculine' men usually as "white; from elite from elite schools; with professional, managerial, or political careers; citizens of nations of the Global North; and heterosexual." Root Aulett, Judy, Judith Wittner, and Kristin Blakeley (2009): *Gendered Worlds*. New York and Oxford: Oxford University Press, 5.

43. Anderson, Bridget (2013): *Us and Them? The Dangerous Politics of Immigration Control*. Oxford: Oxford University Press, 2ff.
44. Andersson, Ruben (2019): *No Go World: How Fear Is Redrawing Our Maps and Infecting Our Politics*. Oakland: University of California Press, 15.
45. Linke, Uli (2013): Racializing Cities, Naturalizing Space: The Seductive Appeal of Iconicities of Dispossession. *Antipode* 46(5), 1222–1239, 1223. Cf. also Freire-Medeiros, Bianca (2013): *Touring Poverty*. New York: Routledge; Frenzel, Fabian, Ko Koens, and Malte Steinbrink, eds. (2017): *Slum Tourism: Poverty, Power and Ethics*. London: Routledge.
46. Linke (2013), 1224.
47. Ibid., 1223.
48. Rancière, Jacques (2006): *The Politics of Aesthetics: The Distribution of the Sensible*. London: Continuum, 65.
49. Cf. Spivak, Gayatri Chakravorty (1988): Can the Subaltern Speak? *Marxism and the Interpretation of Culture*, edited by Cary Nelson and Lawrence Grossberg. Urbana: University of Illinois Press, 271–313.

Works Cited

Primary Literature

Pfeijffer, Ilja Leonard (2016): *La Superba*, translated by Michele Hutchison. Dallas: Deep Vellum Publishing.

Pfeijffer, Ilja Leonard (2017): *La Superba*. Amsterdam: De Arbeiderspers, 2nd ed.

Secondary Literature

Achebe, Chinua (2016): An Image of Africa. Racism in Conrad's 'Heart of Darkness'. *Massachusetts Review* 57(1), 14–27.

Anderson, Bridget (2013): *Us and Them? The Dangerous Politics of Immigration Control*. Oxford: Oxford University Press.

Andersson, Ruben (2019): *No Go World: How Fear Is Redrawing Our Maps and Infecting Our Politics*. Oakland: University of California Press.

Appadurai, Arjun (1995): The Production of Locality. *Counterworks: Managing the Diversity of Knowledge*, edited by Richard Fardon. London and New York: Routledge, 204–225.

Appadurai, Arjun (1996): *Modernity at Large: Cultural Dimensions of Globalization*. Minneapolis and London: University of Minnesota Press.

Appadurai, Arjun (2013): *The Future as a Cultural Fact: Essays on the Global Condition*. London: Verso.

Beeks, Sara (2019): Ilja Leonard Pfeijffer as a Luxury Immigrant: A European Public Intellectual and the 'Refugee Crisis'. *FKW: Zeitschrift für Geschlechterforschung und visuelle Kultur* 66, 101–116.

Buck Morss, Susan (1989): The Flâneur's Object of Enquiry Is Modernity Itself. *The Dialectics of Seeing: Walter Benjamin and the Arcades Project*. Cambridge: MIT Press.

Cohen, Alina (2016): Migration Gone Awry. *Los Angeles Review of Books* (25 March).

Dainotto, Roberto M. (2006): The European-ness of Italy: Categories and Norms. *Annali d'Italianistica* 24, 19–39.

Ehrig, Stephan, Britta C. Jung, and Maria Roca Lizarazu (2020): Conference Report: Exploring the Transnational Neighbourhood. Integration, Community, and Co-Habitation. *Journal of Romance Studies* 20(1), 179–181.

Freire-Medeiros, Bianca (2013): *Touring Poverty*. New York: Routledge.

Frenzel, Fabian, Ko Koens, and Malte Steinbrink, eds. (2017): *Slum Tourism: Poverty, Power and Ethics*. London: Routledge.

Graham, Stephen (2006): Cities and the 'War on Terror'. *International Journal of Urban and Regional Research* 30(2), 255–276.

Guglielmi, Laura (2019): *Le incredibili curiosità di Genova: Uno sguardo su più di mille anni di storia della Superba*. Rome: Newton Compton.

Heynders, Odile (2016): *Writers as Public Intellectuals: Literature, Celebrity, Democracy*. Basingstoke: Palgrave Macmillan.

Huysseune, Michel (2006): *Modernity and Secession: The Social Sciences and the Lega Nord in Italy*. New York and Oxford: Berghahn.

Jacobsen, Karen (2005): *The Economic Life of Refugees*. Bloomfield: Kumarian Press.

Jein, Gillian (2015): (De)Facing the Suburbs: Street Art and the Politics of Spatial Affect in the Paris Banlieues. *The DS Project: Image, Text, Space/Place, 1830–2015*, http://thedsproject.com/. Accessed 28 June 2021.

Kwak, Nancy, and A.K. Sandoval-Strausz (2017): *Making Cities Global: The Transnational Turn in Urban History*. Philadelphia: University of Pennsylvania Press.

Linke, Uli (2013): Racializing Cities, Naturalizing Space: The Seductive Appeal of Iconicities of Dispossession. *Antipode* 46(5), 1222–1239.

Loomba, Ania (2015): *Colonialism/Postcolonialism*. London: Routledge.

Massey, Doreen (1994): Double Articulation: A Place in the World. *Displacements: Cultural Identities in Question*, edited by Angelika Bammer. Bloomington: Indiana University Press, 110–121.

Massey, Doreen (2005): *For Space*. London: Sage.

Matvejević, Predrag (1999): *Mediterranean: A Cultural Landscape*. Oakland: University of California Press.

Murray, Amber (2017): Decolonising the Imagined Geographies of 'Witchcraft'. *Third World Thematics* 2, 157–179.

Muzzanganda Lugira, Aloysius (2009): *African Traditional Religion*. New York: Chelsea House Publishers.

Pels, Peter (1998): The Magic of Africa. Reflections on a Western Commonplace. *African Studies Review* 41(3), 193–209.

Rancière, Jacques (2006): *The Politics of Aesthetics: The Distribution of the Sensible*. London: Continuum.

Root Aulett, Judy, Judith Wittner, and Kristin Blakeley (2009): *Gendered Worlds*. New York and Oxford: Oxford University Press.

Said, Edward (2001): Jungle Calling. *Reflections on Exile. And Other Essays*. London: Granta Books, 327–336.

Spencer, Herbert (1864): *The Principles of Biology*, vol. 1. London and Edinburgh: Williams and Norgate.

Spivak, Gayatri Chakravorty (1988): Can the Subaltern Speak? *Marxism and the Interpretation of Culture*, edited by Cary Nelson and Lawrence Grossberg. Urbana: University of Illinois Press, 271–313.

Spronk, Rachel, and Thomas Hendriks, eds. (2020): *Readings in Sexualities from Africa*. Bloomington: Indiana University Press.

TAMPEP (2009): *Sexwork in Europe: A Mapping of the Prostitution Scene in 25 European Countries*. Amsterdam: TAMPEP International Foundation.

Thomas, Deborah A., and Kamari Maxine Clarke (2006): Introduction. *Globalization and Race: Transformations in the Cultural Production of Blackness*, edited by Kamari Maxine Clarke and Deborah A. Thomas. Durham: Duke University Press, 1–34.

Vertovec, Steven (2009): *Transnationalism*. New York: Routledge.

Wolford, Wendy (2004): This Land Is Ours Now: Spatial Imaginaries and the Struggle for Land in Brazil. *Annals of the Association of American Geographers* 94(2), 409–424.

"Your Allah can't see you here"

Moscow's Subterranean Spaces and Dissimulated Life in Svetlana Alexievich's *Vremya sekond khend* (2013)

EMMA CROWLEY

Abstract
This chapter explores how Svetlana Alexievich's polyphonic interpellation of urban Moscow in *Vremya sekond khend* [*Secondhand Time*] interrogates the intertwining of the Soviet past and the post-Soviet neighbourhood, focalising the oft-forgotten imperialist legacies of Soviet modernity and the particular transnationalism that it has produced. Alexievich excavates the difficulties of making a "cultural and psychic place of one's own"[1] in an urban environment that is spatially structured around the projection of a resurgent and ethnically singular 'new Russia'. Her work's approach to testimonial literature functions as an aesthetic counterpoint to the vertical, hierarchical space that reproduces the logic of socialist imperialism in the present day. This rift between the city's visual imaginary and the concealed, or rather subterranean, informal economy of Tajiki and Uzbeki migrant labour underscores the dissimulated life of Moscow's migrant labour force. Here, the transnational neighbourhood is not so much a space of connection as a stifled multiplicity in which barriers mark out linguistic, ethnic and economic difference, where secret knocks allow for secret welcomes and violence frequently emerges as evidence of the city's accumulated histories. *Secondhand Time* is a critical riposte to the patriarchal and nationalist currents of affect in the former Soviet Union, interrogating how spatial coordinates of belonging are mapped onto residual structures of Soviet statecraft and exposing, through an aesthetics of correlation, the links between that which is in plain sight and that which has been concealed.

Introduction

Towards the end of Svetlana Alexievich's 2013 work, *Vremya sekond khend* [*Secondhand Time*], the author interviews Gafkhar Dzhurayeva, director of Moscow's Tajikistan Foundation, about her experience of supporting Tajik migrants who have moved from the economically struggling Central Asian Republic to Russia's capital. Alexievich listens quietly as Dzhurayeva recounts a litany of stories of Tajik suffering, abuse and poverty in an openly hostile and xenophobic environment. Exasperated by her own recollection of these accounts, Dzhurayeva directs her frustration at Alexievich, whose curiosity about the world of Moscow's migrants betrays the author's ignorance of the brutal reality of everyday life for the Tajik community.

> Znayete, kto ya? Ya rabotayu alkhimikom… U nas obshchestvennyy fond deneg net, vlasti net, yest' tol'ko khoroshiye lyudi. Nashi pomoshchniki. Pomogayem, spasayem bezzashchitnykh. Zhelayemyy rezul'tat poluchayetsya iz nichego: iz nervov, iz intuitsii, iz vostochnoy lesti, iz russkoy zhalosti, iz takikh prostykh slov, kak 'moy dorogoy', 'moy ty khoroshiy', 'ya znala, chto ty nastoyashchiy muzhchina, ty obyazatel'no pomozhesh' zhenshchine'. Rebyata, govoryu ya sadistam v pogonakh, ya v vas veryu. Veryu, chto vy lyudi (8712).

> [Do you know what I am? I'm an alchemist…We run a non-profit – no money, no power, just good people, our helpers. We aid and rescue the defenceless. Our results materialise out of nothing: just nerve, intuition, Eastern flattery, Russian pity, and simple words like 'my dear', 'my good man', 'I knew you were a real man and wouldn't fail to help a woman in need.' 'Boys,' I say to the sadists in uniform, 'I have faith in you. I know that you're human.'][2] (579)

Dzhurayeva's exasperation captures the conflict at the centre of *Vremya sekond khend*, and Alexievich's oeuvre more broadly, between the author's ideal of an essential 'humanity' or 'soul' of the post-Soviet people and a social system predicated upon corruption and latent violence. "I'm piecing together the history of 'domestic', 'interior' socialism", Alexievich writes in her introduction to *Vremya sekond khend*, "[a]s it existed in a person's soul" (36). This chapter will explore how Alexievich's representation of the Central Asian migrant community underscores this conflict between Alexievich's affective search for the 'soul' and a brutal social system, while interrogating the intertwining of the Soviet past and the post-Soviet neighbourhood, in turn focalising the oft-forgotten imperialist legacies of Soviet modernity and the particular transnationalism that it has produced.[3]

In her exposition of the disjuncture between 'Moscow Apartments' and 'Moscow Basements', Alexievich creates an image of a vertically divided city that is spatially structured around the projection of a resurgent and nationalist 'new Russia'. Here, the transnational neighbourhood is not so much a space of connection as a stifled multiplicity in which barriers mark out linguistic, ethnic and economic differences, where secret knocks allow for secret welcomes and violence frequently emerges as evidence of the city's accumulated histories. In the city that Alexievich presents for her reader, a rift between the urban visual imaginary and the concealed, or rather subterranean, informal economy of migrant labour underscores the dissimulated life of Moscow's migrant labour force in the period prior to the 2014 Crimean crisis, when the city was rebuilding itself under the rubric of Sergey Sobyanin's mayoral administration. I use 'dissimulated' here to refer to the split nature of Moscow's urban life at the time of Alexievich's compilation of this text – the burgeoning 'megacity' that functioned as a beacon of neoliberal revivalism, and the public secret of a concealed and reviled Central Asian migrant community. Alexievich's interviews of Tajik migrants depict a demographic that are largely absent from the city's visual commons at this time, their home lives – that communal intimacy between a city's citizens that frequently characterises the transnational neighbourhood – are hidden, removed from view. Indeed, in contrast to the other transnational neighbourhoods explored in this collection, Moscow's makeup as a post-socialist city has impacted the social spatial composition of its Central Asian communities, which are scattered across the territory of Moscow's 12 districts (*okrugs*) in fragmented pockets instead of accumulating within specific enclaves or designated areas such as the banlieues of Paris and Lyon, or Berlin's Neukölln neighbourhood. Transnationalism in this context is not so much "a co-existing heterogeneity" as an underground phenomenon where informal practices of regulation and control function to separate the 'silenced lives' of casual migrant labourers from a prosperous new 'comfort class' of citizens.[4]

Similar to other post-socialist and post-Soviet urban centres, the majority of Moscow's housing was developed under a centrally planned economic model, limiting the individual's ability to choose where to live.[5] Socio-spatial differentiation did exist in the Soviet era, but it was, and is, distinct to that of similarly sized capitalist cities in which segregation based on class has been more pronounced. In Soviet Moscow, the barriers between social strata were generally not too rigid and so families of different social status could live side by side as neighbours. There is now an increasing trend towards the establishment of 'economical' neighbourhoods located at the city's peripheries, where poor quality housing seems only fit, one commentator notes, for overnight stays.[6] However, this process of social spatial segregation is slowly developing and has been further hindered by the spread of Covid-19. At the time of Alexievich's interviews, both official and unofficial migrant residences were located seemingly at random, frequently close to, or even within, construction sites and other spaces of employment. This is due partly, as Ilya Gashnitsky, Maria Gunko and others have documented, to the absence of a housing scheme for migrants in the Russian capital and the informality of Russia's migration regime, which, as we will see, deliberately reinforces conditions of ambiguity and illegibility.

Moscow Inc.'s Migration History

The extracts of *Vremya sekond khend* I look at in this chapter present a particular moment in the transformation of Moscow's urban landscape in the wake of the 2008 economic crash and prior to the 2014 Crimean crisis. This was a period of transition for the city as it welcomed the leadership of its new mayor, Sergey Sobyanin, in 2010, following the 18-year administration of Yury Luzhkov. Luzhkov, notorious for his self-propagated image as chief of Moscow's large-scale urban regeneration programme in the late 1990s and early 2000s, nicknamed 'Moscow Inc.', had been damaged by the fallout from the 2008 global economic downturn. Relying heavily on a system of patronage with real estate businesses, Luzhkov's administration oversaw "the mass conversion of the city centre from residential to commercial purposes",[7] ushering in a construction boom in the early 2000s while heading a mayoral regime that sought to combine the benefits of capitalism and socialism.[8] In the wake of the 2008 crash, however, the challenges that had begun to plague Luzhkov's administration, including severe air pollution, traffic problems and a chaotic city image, combined with the collapse of the property companies that had driven Moscow Inc., brought an end to this era of commercial construction and real estate speculation.[9] Thus, in 2010, then President Medvedev introduced the close ally of Vladimir Putin, Sergey Sobyanin, as Moscow's new mayor. Sobyanin began his role as mayor at a time when Moscow, so long the political and cultural heartland of both the Russian Federation and the former Soviet Union, had begun to turn its back on what had become known as 'the Putin Consensus'.[10] Waves of anti-corruption protests in addition to growing dissent at the chaotic and heavily commercialised infrastructure of the Russian capital, not to mention high unemployment figures and the growing impoverishment of Russia's provincial centres, triggered a drive by Sobyanin and his administration to reorganise the city's landscape, including the redesign of public space and the expedited gentrification of the city's outer reaches. This political manoeuvre, aimed, as Mirjam Büdenbender and Daniela Zupan note, at "facilitating continuous commodification" and nullifying the political dissent of the Moscow bourgeoisie,[11] importantly also included a shift in the city's attitude to its migrant population and their function as the invisible workforce propping up the city's economy.

Moscow has always been a city of migrants, from its advent as a royal stronghold of the Rus in the 12th century to its consolidation as a seasonal destination for provincial labourers in the early 19th century.[12] During Soviet times, however, the extension of Moscow's administrative power to encompass the 15 Soviet republics sweeping from Central Asia to the Balkans marked the beginning of a new relationship between Muscovites and the city's migrant population – a relationship based on the slogan, '*Druzhba Narodov*' or 'Friendship of the Peoples', and rooted in a communist ideology that promoted egalitarian fraternity among all citizens. Azeris, Kazakhs, Uzbeks and Tajiks were welcomed into the universities and onto the construction sites of the burgeoning union, creating new kinship networks while seeking to become incorporated into the Soviet project as '*svoi*', or 'Us', rather than '*chuzhie*', or 'Other'. And yet, as Jeff Sahadeo writes,

> Even as common Soviet citizenship and cultural knowledge positioned them as insiders, ethnic migrants from the Caucasus, Central Asia, and the Asian RSFSR were considered 'Black,' among various epithets, differentiating them from peoples of European or Slavic appearance just as, across Europe, as Philomena Essed and others have argued, whiteness, Eurocentrism, and resistance to cultural diversity grew alongside increased migration in the late twentieth century.[13]

Although the term 'race' was largely avoided by Soviet officials, researchers like Sahadeo and Eric Weitz have maintained that Soviet policy racialised difference in the USSR, "endowing each nation with characteristics, from appearance to culture and ways of life."[14] For many ethnic Russians and Ukrainians living and working in the metropolitan hubs of the Soviet Union, their Central Asian brothers were labelled black, or *chernye*, and grouped together by racial and orientalist epithets that described them as backwards, 'eastern' and underdeveloped in comparison to an ostensibly white, advanced, European Russian population. Magazines like *Moscow: A Capital for Everyone* extolled the admirable friendship of the peoples in the 1970s and 1980s, and yet, as Sahadeo has pointed out, "only Slavs or Balts [...] smiled for photos in the magazine's pages."[15]

The presence of Central Asian migrants in Moscow is thus rooted in the history of Soviet Socialism and the Communist Party's imperialist expansion into Central Asia, the Caucasus and Eastern Europe. As Tamar Koplatadze argues in her article 'Theorising Russian Postcolonial Studies' the Russo-Soviet domination of the republics of Central Asia and the Caucasus, in particular, may be closely aligned with models of Western colonisation due to the implementation of cultural, economic and political domination, a settler population, and the expropriation of resources for the benefit of a core metropolitan centre.[16] While this is not to infer that the imperialism of the Soviet Union can be neatly mapped onto Western-derived models of postcolonial critique, an analysis of the imperialist policies of the Soviet Union aids in an explanation of the specific cultural, political and economic relations that connect Central Asia and Russia, and for the purpose of this essay, the high numbers of Central Asian migrants in Moscow and their racialisation as 'Other' in this urban space. When the Soviet Union collapsed in 1991, the support systems of social welfare and wage-levelling that had been critical in stabilising the fragile economies of the Union's border republics went with it.[17] The structural imbalances between the economic cores of St Petersburg and Moscow, and peripheral regions in Central Asia and the Caucasus had consolidated the unevenness of Soviet modernity and, in the wake of its dissolution, a combination of economic desolation and inter-ethnic conflict devastated communities in Baku, Osh and Gorno-Badakhshan. Consequently, migration rates from Central Asia and the Caucasus to a relatively economically prosperous Moscow rose throughout the 1990s, exacerbated by the ever-increasing economic disparity of the post-Soviet era. By 2005 a Kyrgyz schoolteacher with a double teaching load would still be earning five to six times less than he would as an unskilled labourer on a Moscow building site.[18] By 2012 it was estimated that out of the 12 million migrants living in Russia, more than a third were from Central Asia, working principally in jobs that Russians would reject, such as municipal labour, office cleaning, and manual kitchen labour.[19] Moreover, such a figure excludes the significant number of *nelegaly*, or illegal migrant labourers, who are integral to Moscow's political economy of migrant illegalisation and who exist, as Madeleine Reeves has described, in a space of uncertainty, dependent on irregular housing and employment, subject to the increasingly international trend for cheap, tractable, casual and often potentially deportable labour.[20]

It is roughly at this juncture in Moscow's post-Soviet history, as Sobyanin took up his new role as mayor in 2010, that Alexievich compiled her interviews with Gafkhar Dzhurayeva and the city's Tajik communities. *Vremya sekond khend* is a huge text, encompassing hundreds of different voices, edited and whittled down from years of interviewing across the length and breadth of the former Soviet Union.[21] In it Alexievich attempts to reckon with the curious ways in which the past, that is, the looming spectre of the USSR, has been refashioned through the perspective of contemporary Russophone society. More precisely, her critique is fixed upon the authoritarian figures of Vladimir Putin and Aleksandr Lukashenko and how their respective regimes have reshaped the imperialist fervour and masculinist dogma of the Stalinist era. As always, she tells this story, so to speak, 'from below', augmenting the voices of people she encounters on train journeys and at beer stands, former rank-and-file members of the Communist Party, student activists in Belarus, fellow writers whose family were imprisoned in the gulags, Russian-speaking immigrant communities in Chicago, and Tajik migrants in Moscow.

My work on Alexievich is interested in how the affective force of what she terms her 'novel of voices' translates for the reader the political complexities and ambiguities of the post-Soviet landscape on a world literary stage. The tension between intimacy and objectivity that Alexievich creates in her portrayal of Tajik everyday life in Moscow and her re-presentation of Tajik subjectivities depends upon a vertical arrangement of urban space that pointedly draws upon the historical hypocrisies of the Soviet era. This chapter thus seeks to capture how Alexievich's formal and stylistic approach to writing (and re-writing) Russo-Soviet history, presents the anguish, violence and tensions of this time as they are expressed in the transnational, urban setting. It also wonders how Alexievich's polyphonic style of writing, which tends to glance broadly at feelings of ideological malaise and disillusion across the former Soviet Union, generalises the binarisation of integration in Moscow neighbourhoods by focusing on the disjunctions between Tajiks and ethnic Russians – is this a deliberate ploy in order to shoehorn these vignettes into the author's creative vision, or a pragmatic representation of a divided city?

From Moscow's Apartments to Moscow's Basements

Mid-conversation, Gafkhar Dzhurayeva breaks off her interview with Alexievich to answer an urgent message. As Alexievich waits, she recalls conversations she has had with residents of Moscow apartments, commencing a contrapuntal narration of the city's social attitudes towards economic migration. This interruption of analepsis, which takes the reader back in time to previous interviews Alexievich has conducted, serves to contextualise Dzhurayeva's story, and the stories of the Tajik migrants that follow, within a broader societal view of contemporary Moscow and its migrant workforce. The voices that Alexievich here recalls are anonymous and condensed, layered one atop the other in a deliberate juxtaposition of opposing views but returning repeatedly to the underlying difference between 'us' and 'them', each voice trailing off into ellipses as if dissolving into a background murmur that crowds Alexievich's thoughts as she sits and waits for Dzhurayeva to return.

> Eto moy rodnoy gorod. Moya stolitsa. A oni priyekhali syuda so svoim shariatom. Na Kurban-Bayram rezhut u menya pod oknami baranov. A chto ne na Krasnoy ploshchadi? Kriki bednykh zhivotnykh, krov' khleshchet… Vyydesh' v gorod: tam… i tam… krasnyye luzhi na asfal'te… YA idu s rebenkom: 'Mama, chto eto?' V etot den' gorod 'cherneyet'. Uzhe ne nash gorod. Ikh sotni tysyach iz podvalov vyvalivayet… Politseyskiye v steny vzhimayutsya ot strakha… (8784)

> [This is my hometown. My capital. And they've showed up here with their Sharia law. On Kurban Bayram, they slaughter their sheep right under my windows. Why not on Red Square then? The cries of the poor animals, their blood gushing

everywhere...You go outside, and here, and there...you see red puddles all over the pavement. I'm out walking with my kid: 'Mama, what is that?' That day, the city goes dark. It stops being our city. They pour out of the basements by the hundreds of thousands... The policemen press themselves against the walls in terror....] (584)

Ya druzhu s tadzhikom. Yego zovut Said. Krasivyy kak bog! U sebya doma on byl vrachom, zdes' na stroyke rabotayet. Vlyublena v nego po ushi. Chto delat'? Kogda vstrechayemsya, gulyayem s nim po parkam ili uyezzhayem kuda-nibud' za gorod, chtoby nikogo iz moikh znakomykh ne vstretit'. Boyus' roditeley. Otets predupredil: 'Uvizhu s chernomazym, pristrelyu oboikh'. Kto moy otets? Muzykant... okonchil konservatoriyu... (8793)

[I'm dating a Tajik. His name is Said. He's as beautiful as a god! At home, he was a doctor; here, he's a construction worker. I'm head over heels for him. What do I do? We go walking in the parks or get out of the city altogether so that we don't run into anyone who knows me. I'm afraid of my parents finding out. My father warned me, 'If I see you with a darkie, I'll shoot you both.' What does my father do? He's a musician...he graduated from the conservatory...] (584)

U nas ryadom stroyka. Khachi shnyryayut, kak krysy. Iz-za nikh v magazin vecherom strashno vyyti. Za deshevyy mobil'nik mogut ubit'... (8784)

[There's a construction site next door. Khachi scuttling about like rats. Because of them, I'm scared of walking home from the shop at night. They could kill you for a cheap mobile phone...] (584)

The technique of counterpoint illuminates the relational quality of divergent and opposing voices, creating a dialogic structure that – as Mikhail Bakhtin has written – can reveal distinct forces at play in the structure of a novel, or the 'novel of voices' in this case. Such a composition can also invoke a paratactic style, to borrow from the literary critic Edward Said, which places together words or phrases independently, that is, in a neighbourly manner, without coordinating them or subordinating them through the use of conjunctions.[22] For Said, parataxis as a literary device invites comparison while maintaining an ambiguous distance from the meaning of relation. A paratactical style may thus allow a writer to explore controversial or oppositional ideas and concepts without having to firmly place themselves in one camp or another, inviting the reader, rather, to take up the issue of textual meaning while leaving the author at a more ambiguous distance. Read in this light, Alexievich's paratactical positioning of her narrative subjects enables the author to distance herself from their story in order to place them within the longer *durée* of the rise and fall of *Homo sovieticus*, obscuring her position as curator of these vignettes and bearer of an aesthetic and artistic vision.

In order to meet directly with the Tajik community she has learned of through Dzhurayeva, Alexievich accompanies an anonymous friend and journalist to the basement of an imposing *Stalinka*, or Stalin-era apartment building in central Moscow. Before entering, the author pauses and looks up, taking time to note for the reader the particular history of these buildings in Moscow and their resonance today,

> Vybrali dom 'stalinku' v samom tsentre Moskvy. Stroilis' eti doma pri Staline dlya bol'shevistskoy elity, potomu i zovut ikh 'stalinkami', oni i seychas v tsene. Stalinskiy ampir: lepnina na fasadakh, barel'yefy, kolonny, vysota potolkov v kvartirakh tri-chetyre metra. Potomki byvshikh vozhdey obedneli, syuda pereyezzhayut 'novyye russkiye'. Vo dvore stoyat 'bentli', 'ferrari'. Na pervom etazhe goryat ognyami vitriny dorogikh butikov. (8867)

> [We chose a building – a Stalinka right in the centre of Moscow. These buildings are called Stalinkas because they went up during Stalin's time, built to house the Bolshevik party elite. And they're still upscale today. Stalinist imperial style: elaborate mouldings on the facades, bas-reliefs, columns, three-to-four-metre ceilings. As the descendants of the country's former leaders have gone down in the world, the 'new Russians' have been taking their places. The courtyard is full of Bentleys and Ferraris. On the street level, the lights are on in the windows of swanky boutiques.] (589)

Today the Stalinka is, as Alexievich notes, a symbol of material wealth and success in the 'new Russia'. This symbolism mirrors their past prestige as totems of Stalin's vainglorious drive to build a new and beautiful Moscow in the aftermath of the shockingly angular and brutalist creations of the revolutionary avant-garde and their utopic cityscapes. In her book *Moscow, The Fourth Rome*, Katerina Clark describes how

> [this] turn to beauty [in the 1930s] meant a reaction against avant-gardism and a return to conventional tastes, but the foregrounding of the beautiful was also tied to a system that cut across discursive boundaries. It is arguably the point at which the ideological or political met the literary, the artistic, and the architectural.[23]

Stalin's first Five-Year Plan, from 1928 to 1932, was intended to rapidly industrialise and collectivise the Soviet Union, thus providing the foundations for a

Figure 1: *Palace of the Soviets*, winning design by Boris Iofan following submission to competition for creation of the Palace of the Soviets in 1933 © Shchusev State Museum of Architecture.

radically new society and attracting specialists from abroad, including Le Corbusier, Hannes Meyer, Ernst May and Albert Khan, to invest in what appeared as a revolutionary opportunity to change the course of human life. A grand, socialist cityscape was designed to be worthy of this dream. Such planning on the part of the Communist Party was a clear interpretation, Clark argues, of the metaphoric use of architecture in Marx and Engel's work *The German Ideology*, where the authors use the relationship between base and superstructure as a model for the relationship between all elements of society – "the redesigned Moscow was to be a dazzling capital whose glory reflected on the regime that erected it, and was to provide the core of its symbolic system, an exemplum for the new (Stalinist) sociopolitical and cultural order."[24] Nothing was more emblematic of this urban vision than the proposed Palace of the Soviets, an enormous structure intended to replace the demolished Cathedral of Christ the Saviour on the banks of the Moskva river (Figure 1). The neo-classical design conceived by the Soviet architect Boris Iofan was described by an official Communist Party pamphlet (distributed to workers alarmed at the intensive labour and cost to be dedicated to the planned structure) as colossal: "On this round earth there will be no building that is taller and larger than the Palace of the Soviets."[25]

Alexievich then, as she gazes up at the *Stalinka*, is highlighting the aesthetico-political tradition of Soviet ideology and, more pointedly, the skywards thrust of this building, the height of these elevated ceilings, the grandeur of these columns – as a paean to the vertical manifestation of this superstructure – and the endemic denigration of their base, concealed below. Such a vertical impression of space, Stephen Graham argues, is critical to understanding the multilevel volume of the world's major cities and how such invisible, three-dimensional architectures and geographies signify the integration of the world's economic peripheries into dominant, urban modes of production, exchange and extraction.[26] "[S]truggles over the right to the city", Graham writes,

> [t]o living space, to resources, to security, to privacy, to mobility, to food and water, to justice – and, even, given the loitering power of killer drones and bombers across large parts of the earth, to the right to live rather than to die – are increasingly shaped across vertical as well as horizontal geographies of power. Making these central to our understandings of the contemporary world is pivotal because, as geographer Gavin Bridge argues, 'adding height and depth to the horizontal plane magnifies the possibilities of relative location, affording additional means of control.'[27]

A volumetric comprehension of Moscow's social spatial makeup can thus attend to the ways in which Alexievich presents the city's migrant labour force in relation to the economic and ideological infrastructure of post-Soviet Moscow. In juxtaposing her documentation of conversations that have taken place with Russians in 'Moscow Apartments' with the interviews she conducts with Tajik migrants in 'Moscow Basements', Alexievich reproduces a top-down cartography that situates the Tajik population as a figurative and literal 'underclass'.

And so down Alexievich and her guide descend into the basements of this Moscow building, down into what the author describes as "a completely different world" (589). "Dolgo petlyayem mezhdu rzhavykh trub i zaplesnevelykh sten" [We spend a long time winding among rusted pipes and mould-infested walls] (8885/589), Alexievich writes, "vremya ot vremeni dorogu nam peregorazhivayut zheleznyye krashenyye dveri, na nikh visyat zamki i stoyat plomby, no vse eto fiktsiya. Uslovnyy stuk i prokhodi" [[f]rom time to time our path is obstructed by painted metal doors studded with locks and seals, but that's just for show. If you know the secret knock, you're in] (8885/589). Within these "infested walls" reside the migrant communities Alexievich has come to interview – "Dlinnyy osveshchennyy koridor: po obe storony komnaty steny iz fanery, vmesto dverey raznotsvetnyye shtory. Moskovskoye podzemel'ye podeleno mezhdu tadzhikami i uzbekami" [A long, well-lit corridor is lined with rooms on either side: their walls are made of plywood, they have multicoloured blinds for doors. Moscow's underground world is divided between the Tajiks and the Uzbeks] (8885/589). As with her other interviewees, Alexievich seeks out the intimacy of the domestic here in which to apprehend an iteration of the post-Soviet 'soul' for her work. Akin to James Ferguson and Akhil Gupta's concept of *place-making* then, which refers to the process by which spatial meanings are localised to constitute a 'place', Alexievich underscores the intertwining of domesticity and place in her work as a means of capturing not only the transterritorial but also the transtemporal connections between home and away, the Soviet past and the post-Soviet present.[28] Down in this cramped and mildewed space she gathers another shard of her vast chronicle of the history of "domestic", "indoor socialism" (36).

After she has been invited into one of the many rooms by a resident who recognises her guide, Alexievich's voice disappears from the text, replaced by fragments of the testimonies she has recorded. These polyphonic voices are anonymous and brief. They last only so long as to leave an impression upon the reader, a hint as to the life of the narrator, and the difficulties they have encountered in their role as disposable labour for the citizens of Moscow. One voice, for example, recounts a racial attack on the metro:

Ko mne podoshli v elektrichke troye… Ya s raboty yekhal. 'Ty chto tut delayesh'?' 'Domoy yedu'. 'Gde tvoy dom? Kto tebya syuda zval?' Nachali bit'. Bili i krichali: 'Rossiya dlya russkikh! Slava Rossii!'. 'Rebyata, za chto? Allakh vse vidit'. 'Tvoy Allakh tut tebya ne vidit. U nas svoy Bog'. Zuby vybili… rebro slomali… Polnyy vagon lyudey, i odna tol'ko devushka zastupilas': 'Ostav'te yego! On vas ne trogal'. 'Ty chego? Khacha b'yem'. (8903)

[Three guys came up to me on the commuter rail….I was heading home from work. 'What are you doing here?' 'I'm going home.' 'Where's your home? Who asked you to come here?' They started beating me up. Pummelling me, screaming, 'Russia for Russians! Glory to Russia!' 'Why are you doing this? Allah sees everything.' 'Your Allah can't see you here. We have our own God.' They knocked my teeth out….broke one of my ribs…A train car full of people and only one girl stood up for me. 'Leave him alone! He didn't do anything to you.' 'What's your problem? We're beating a *khach*'.] (590)

Others describe the chilling coldness of their treatment by employers, Moscow's police force and would-be neighbours:

> Moy drug tozhe prosil u khozyaina deneg za rabotu. Politsiya potom yego dolgo iskala. Otkopali v lesu… Mama grob poluchila iz Rossii… (8931)
>
> [My friend wanted to know when his boss was going to pay him. It took the police a long time to find his body afterwards. They'd buried it in the forest....His mother received a coffin from Russia.] (592)
>
> Vygonyat nas… Kto Moskvu otstraivat' budet? Dvory podmetat'? Russkiye za te den'gi, chto nam platyat, pakhat' ne stanut. (8931)
>
> [If they kick us out, who's going to build Moscow? Who'll sweep the courtyards? Russians would never work for this kind of money.] (592)
>
> Uzhe pyat' let ya v Moskve, i so mnoy ni razu nikto ne pozdorovalsya. Russkim nuzhny 'chernyye', chtoby oni mogli chuvstvovat' sebya 'belymi', smotret' na kogo-to sverkhu vniz (8949).
>
> [I've lived in Moscow for five years, and not once has anyone said hello to me on the street. Russians need 'blacks' so they can feel 'white'. So they have someone to look down on.] (593)

Layered one atop another in Alexievich's densely packed text, these Tajik narrators literally crowd out the page as if jostling for space in a manner analogous to the cramped conditions of the basement commune Alexievich recreates for the reader. Tonally, they come across as uninhibited and frank, willing to divulge their experiences of abuse and loneliness to this invited stranger. This compression and fragmentation of the text creates a horizontal positioning of testimonies alongside each other, which appears as a typographical opposition to the verticality of the social spatial system they live within, placing the Tajik migrants beside, rather than below, their Russian neighbours – their voices articulating for a reading public the concealed quarters of dissimulated life in the post-Soviet sphere.

As Alexievich passes through the basements she remarks, "Kommuna" [It's a commune], taking note of the detritus of life that has amassed in the darkened corners and gaps of these low-ceilinged rooms:

Zakhodim v komnatu: u vkhoda gora obuvi, detskiye kolyaski. V uglu plita, gazovyy ballon, k nim pritisnuty stoly i stul'ya, perekochevavshiye syuda s blizhayshikh pomoyek. Vse ostal'noye prostranstvo zanimayut dvukh"yarusnyye samodel'nyye krovati. (8892)

[There's a heap of shoes in the doorway next to a number of prams. In the corner, a stove, a gas tank, and tables and chairs dragged here from nearby dumpsters, all packed tightly into the small common space. The rest of the room is taken up by homemade bunk beds.] (589)

Alexievich's impression of the crowded basement room recalls the memories of communal apartments that populate so many of the narratives of *Vremya sekond khend*, in which residents, as one narrator remembers, were "surrounded by many, many other bodies; other eyes" (589). The cultural historian Svetlana Boym describes how, as a symbol of the original revolution, the communal apartment was a site of memory and of contradictions in the USSR – "an attempt to practice utopian ideologies and to destroy bourgeois banality" that became an institution of social control and a breeding ground for police informants.[29] In Alexievich's representation of this basement home, the memory of the *kommunalka* takes on a second-hand countenance that inserts itself into the broader theme of her work, creating a dialectical relationship between submerged socialist forms and present-day communities that gestures towards, but does not declare, the irony of the communal apartment becoming once more the site of societal breakage and neighbourly subterfuge in Moscow. Her writing thus frames the living conditions of the Tajik community within a form of nostalgia that is attentive to the residues of collective formations in contemporary post-socialist society, what Boym has elsewhere characterised as 'reflective' nostalgia – an exploration of longing and belonging that tends to dwell in the contradictions of (Soviet) modernity.[30]

When Alexievich exits the basement residence after sharing a meal of pilaf with her Tajik hosts, she looks once more up at the buildings around her and reflects: "Iz podzemel'ya podnimayemsya naverkh. Teper' ya smotryu na Moskvu drugimi glazami yeye krasota kazhetsya mne kholodnoy i trevozhnoy. Moskva, tebe vse ravno lyubyat tebya ili net?" [We ascend from the underground. I look at Moscow with new eyes – its beauty now seems cold and uneasy. Moscow, do you care whether people like you or not?] (8946/594). Her personification of the city appeals to a nostalgic vision of an inclusive, Soviet Moscow, an egalitarian city that, as Weitz, Sahadeo and others have argued, never actually existed. Moreover, the idea that the issue at hand is a problem of appreciation, or disillusionment – that Moscow is simply *unlikeable* – reveals the dissociation between Alexievich's affective interpretation of the post-Soviet condition, and the real conditions of precarity and violence continuously reproduced by the city's infrastructure of informal migrant labour. Russia is a country, as Vladimir Malakhov puts it, with zero, "pro-immigrant opinion makers",[31] and a slew of openly xenophobic pundits whose racist rhetoric feeds into an ethno-nationalist populism that subtends Putin's appeal. Madeleine Reeves's ethnographic research on legal illegality or the 'clean fake' documentation of Kyrgyz migrants in Moscow has analysed how a "complex and contradictory" system of overlapping regional and federal legislation, a structure of pay and rewards for those policing illegal migration, and a policy of 'open borders' directly controverted by "a cripplingly restrictive quota system for employment" has forced the majority Central Asian migrant population in the city into a "space of uncertainty".[32] Most impactful, argues Reeves, has been the marketisation of work permits and residency registrations negotiated by an abundance of intermediaries (*posredniki*) both "inside and outside the state" – a network of middlemen variously connected to Russian state apparatuses whose control of migrant documentation into and out of Russia has created a political economy of migration illegalisation that maintains migrant workers in a vulnerable and deportable state of exception.[33]

This state of exception or 'uncertainty' is precisely what Alexievich encounters when she descends into the Moscow basement to interview migrants and hear their brutal stories of abuse. Basements became a focal point of Russia's migrant narrative because of the difficulties migrants faced, and continue to face, in obtaining and maintaining a residency registration and work permit. Managed by utility companies who were also frequently the employers of these migrants, the empty basements of Moscow's apartment blocks became convenient sources of hot water boilers, electricity and ample space for sleeping berths.[34] During the chaotic administration of Mayor Luzhkov, and as Moscow's in-migration numbers grew, stories of overcrowded, 'infested', and 'rotten' basements 'teeming' with migrants were shared across social media and in popular news sources. Basements became a signifier of the migrant 'problem' and although they were not the only form of residency for the migrant workforce, the popularity of this image of subterranean hideouts, often framed as parasitically living off of the water and electricity of neighbours above ground, accords with how spatial 'lowness' has become so widely culturally synonymous with assumptions of inferiority, danger, and disease. The "widespread and unthinking use" of vertical metaphors, writes Graham,

> works powerfully to stipulate and demarcate political and social power in ways that effectively overlap with the human experience of material and geographical verticalities. Vertical and other spatial metaphors literally work to constitute and reconstitute social power: they both derive directly from the physical and

phenomenological experience of social life and actively influence how people perceive and shape the social and political world.³⁵

Indeed, in the case of Moscow, the preoccupation with illegal basement dwellings corresponds to the social, cultural and political concealment of Central Asian life in the capital. The claims of migrants that "we can't be seen" (*bizmoskvada koronboibuz*) or "we live silently" (*tynch jashabiyz*) expresses a social dissimulation that is confirmed in representations of hidden basement occupations, aligning the experience of living underground with the retraction of power, agency and, ultimately, humanity.³⁶

By 2013, when Alexievich first published *Vremya sekond khend*, basements were no longer the principal residency option for Moscow's Central Asian community. As demands for migrant housing grew, provisional dormitories were constructed in building sites, warehouses and within dilapidated mobile homes. The media, both local and international, began to take notice of the escalating cases of xenophobic violence and the incremental rise in apperception of the dire living conditions of migrants, spurred by several horrific incidents, including a fire in Moscow's Khachalovsky market that killed 17 Tajik and Uzbek migrants in April 2012, and a fire at an underground parking garage in Moscow in January 2009 that killed 12 Tajik migrants. At the same time, Muscovite vigilantes, both men and women, began 'outing' the basement homes of migrant communities, often filming themselves as they broke into the cloistered accommodation and posting these videos to YouTube or personal blogs.³⁷ As they carelessly pick their way through the clothes, food cupboards, and toiletries of workers living in these makeshift homes, these 'vigilantes' appear defiant, indignantly zooming in on the morass of cables that expose how migrant workers have been co-opting the building's electricity supply for their own use.³⁸ Such videos accompanied an increasing number of media articles in the Russian media reporting crimes carried out by individuals described as having a 'Central Asian appearance', and mirrored videos created and uploaded by Russia's Federal Migration Service (FMS), showing FMS raids on basement and dormitory dwellings. In 2012 Putin published an essay in a popular daily newspaper, *Nevisimaya Gazeta*, that called for more stringent measures to be taken by the municipal police against illegal labour migration, as well as "criminal and all kinds of grey schemes".³⁹ This essay and a concurrent speech delivered to the board of the FMS marked an ongoing shift in the government's attitudes towards the political economy of migrant management, legal and illegal. In Putin's words, "civilized conditions for labour migration" had to be enforced, and he reserved particular ire for the spread of new forms of residencies nicknamed 'rubber apartments' (*rezinovye kyvartiry*), so called because of their flexible ability to house multiple sleeping spaces in an area of only a few square feet.⁴⁰

Conclusion

Alexievich's description of her descent into the Moscow basements and the crowded intimacy of these subterranean rooms reveals a desire to engage with the place-making habits of her subjects as she is brought into their domestic space. By focalising the sharp spatial divisions between communities in present-day Moscow – the verticality of the bourgeois Muscovites and the subterranean dwellings of migrant labourers – Alexievich foregrounds the asymmetrical production of post-Soviet society. Reading against the grain of her nostalgia for a lost Soviet 'fraternity', Alexievich's polyphonic texts highlight how this entrenchment of dependency is contiguous with the spatial orderings that undergirded the racialised coloniality of the Soviet socialist system. Her practice of collectivising anonymous voices thus testifies in part to the diverse and spatially variant experiences of the collapse of the USSR, suggesting both the erasure of cultural identity under the USSR and the systemic verticality of tiered citizenship as a historical legacy in the post-Soviet sphere. However, Alexievich's positioning of these stories within her broader creative project – the encyclopaedia of the 'Red Man' or *Homo sovieticus* – frames these narratives within a reflexive nostalgia that fails to capture the reproduction of precarity and the negotiation of the dialectic of legality and illegality that Central Asian migrants must navigate on a daily basis in contemporary Moscow. Her vision of transnationalism is thus tempered by her resolute application of the 'post-Soviet' frame in her work, obfuscating the complexities of cultural heterogeneity and the differing degrees of isolation and integration that different 'post-Soviet' communities experience, both as part of a diaspora within Moscow, and in their home countries.

Notes

1. Smith and Katz (1993), 69.
2. Alexievich, Svetlana (2020): *Vremya sekond khend*. Vremya: Kindle edition, 8712 [*Secondhand Time*, translated by Bela Shayevich. London: Fitzcarraldo, 2015, 579]. All page references to the Russian and English version are henceforth cited in the text, where necessary separated by a slash.
3. Conventionally, the term 'transnational' refers to the crossing of international borders where those borders in question are of the nation-state. However, due to the multinational make-up of the Soviet Union, as Lewis H. Siegelbaum and Leslie Page Moch write, "crossing borders defined as national did not mean leaving the country". This distinction may have caused some scholars to question the application of transnational frames of analysis to the Soviet Union during the rise of transnational studies in the

1990s. However, as Siegelbaum and Moch explain, the application of transnational analysis to both the Soviet Union and post-Soviet contexts draws productive attention to the "internationalist and mobilizational" dimensions of the Soviet Union, while also providing a vital framework for post-Soviet migration from Central Asia to Russia. The utilisation of transnational frameworks within Soviet, post-Soviet and Russian studies has increased rapidly in recent years, with some notable publications including: Moch, Leslie Page, and Lewis H. Siegelbaum (2016): Transnationalism in One Country? Seeing and Not Seeing Cross-Border Migration Within the Soviet Union. *Slavic Review* 75(4), 970–986; Byford, Andy, Connor Doak, and Stephen Hutchings (2020): *Transnational Russian Studies*. Liverpool: Liverpool University Press; Turaeva, Rano, and Rustamjon Urinboyev (2021): *Labour, Mobility and Informal Practices in Russia, Central Asia and Eastern Europe*. London: Routledge.

4. Massey, Doreen (2005): *For Space*. London: Sage, 9; Reeves, Madeleine (2017): Living From the Nerves: Deportability, Indeterminacy and the 'Feel' of Law in Migrant Moscow. *Affective States: Entanglements, Suspensions and Suspicions*, edited by Mateusz Laszczkowski and Madeleine Reeves. New York and Oxford: Berghan Books, 235–269, 242; Büdenbender, Mirjam, and Daniela Zupan (2017): The Evolution of Neoliberal Urbanism in Moscow, 1992–2015. *Antipode* 49(2), 294–313, 308.
5. Gunko, Maria, and Ilya Kashnitsky (2016): Spatial Variation of In-Migration to Moscow: Testing the Effect of the Housing Market. *Cities* 59, 30–39, 31.
6. Ibid.
7. Büdenbender and Zupan (2017), 301.
8. Ibid., 300.
9. Ibid.
10. That is, the agreement among Russian elites that the rule of Putin is required in order to maintain their prosperity and peace within Russia.
11. Büdenbender and Zupan (2017), 303.
12. Merridale, Catherine (2014): *The Red Fortress: The Secret Heart of Russia's History*. London: Penguin, 200.
13. Sahadeo, Jeff (2012): Soviet 'Blacks' and Place-Making in Leningrad and Moscow. *Slavic Review* 71(2), 331–358, 338.
14. Sahadeo, Jeff (2007): Druzhba Narodov or Second-Class Citizenship? Soviet Asian Migrants in a Post-Colonial World. *Central Asian Survey* 26(4), 559–579, 560; Weitz, Eric D. (2002): Racial Politics without the Concept of Race: Reevaluating Soviet Ethnic and National Purges. *Slavic Review* 61(1), 1–29, 3.
15. Sahadeo (2007), 559.
16. Koplatadze, Tamar (2019): Theorising Russian Postcolonial Studies. *Postcolonial Studies* 22, 469–489, 478. For more on this see also Carey, Henry F., and Rafal Raciborski (2004): Postcolonialism: A Valid Paradigm for the Former Sovietized States and Yugoslavia? *East European Politics and Societies* 18(2), 191–235, 200; Todorova, Ma-

ria (2010): Balkanism and Postcolonialism, or on the Beauty of the Airplane View. In *Marx's Shadow: Knowledge, Power, and Intellectuals in Eastern Europe and Russia*, edited by Costica Bradatan and Serguei Alex Oushakine. Lanham: The Rowman & Littlefield Publishing Group, 179; Riabczuk, Mykoła (2013): Colonialism in Another Way: On the Applicability of Postcolonial Methodology for the Study of Postcommunist Europe. *Porownania*, 13, 47–59, 56; Fieldhouse, David Kenneth (1966): *The Colonial Empires: A Comparative Survey from the Eighteenth Century*. New York: Delacorte Press, 339.

17. Reeves, Madeleine (2013): Clean Fake: Authenticating Documents and Persons in Migrant Moscow. *American Ethnologist* 40(3), 508–524, 513.
18. Ibid.
19. Estimates of the number of migrants in Moscow vary enormously depending on whether they are inclusive of undocumented migrants. As Madeleine Reeves has noted, some estimates assume that one in 10 migrants are 'illegal', while in 2012 the Russian Federal Migration Service put the number of migrants illegally resident in Russia at 3.5 million. Those numbers are now assumed to have gone down significantly due to the impact of Covid-19 on unemployment figures. Cf. Russia Lost 5M Migrants During Pandemic, *The Moscow Times* (16 December 2020).
20. Reeves (2013), 510; De Genova, Nicholas (2005): Migrant Illegality and Deportability in Everyday Life. *Annual Review of Anthropology* 31, 419–447; De Genova, Nicholas (2005): *Working on the Boundaries: Race, Space and "Illegality" in Mexican Chicago*. Durham, NC: Duke University Press.
21. In one interview, Alexievich comments that it took her over 20 years to create *Vremya sekond khend*, Alexievich, Svetlana (2013): Svoboda – eto to, chto my ne umeyem [Freedom is what we cannot do]. *Ogonyok* 34 (2 September), https://www.kommersant.ru/doc/2264009. Accessed 8 January 2021.
22. I am here indebted to Keya Ganguly's discussion of parataxis in Edward Said's work in her chapter, 'Exile as a Political Aesthetic', in the edited collection *After Said: Postcolonial Literary Studies in the Twenty-First Century*, edited by Bashir Abu-Manneh. Cambridge: Cambridge University Press, 2018, 69–86. See also Said, Edward W. (2003): Introduction to the Fiftieth Anniversary Edition. Mimesis: The Representation of Reality in Western Literature, by Eric Auerbach, translated by W. R. Trask. Princeton, NJ: Princeton University Press, ix-xxxii.
23. Clark, Katerina (2011): *Moscow, The Fourth Rome: Stalinism, Cosmopolitanism, and the Evolution of Soviet Culture, 1931–1941*. Cambridge, MA: Harvard University Press, 106.
24. Ibid., 84.
25. Zubovich, Katherine (2010): *Moscow Monumental: Soviet Skyscrapers and Urban Life in Stalin's Capital*. Princeton, NJ: Princeton University Press, 26.
26. Graham, Stephen (2018): *Vertical: The City from Satellites to Bunkers*. London and New York: Verso, 5.

27. Ibid., 6.
28. Ferguson, James, and Akhil Gupta (1992): Beyond 'Culture': Space, Identity, and the Politics of Difference. *Cultural Anthropology* 7, 6–23.
29. Boym, Svetlana (1994): *Common Places: Mythologies of Everyday Life in Russia*. Cambridge, MA: Harvard University Press, 123.
30. Boym, Svetlana (2001): *The Future of Nostalgia*. New York: Basic Books, xvii–xix.
31. Malakhov, Vladimir (2019): Why Tajiks Are (Not) Like Arabs: Central Asian Migration into Russia Against the Background of Maghreb Migration into France. *Nationalities Papers* 47(2), 310–324, 315.
32. Reeves (2013), 509.
33. Ibid., 511.
34. Demintseva, Ekaterina (2017): Labour Migrants in Post-Soviet Moscow: Patterns of Settlement. *Journal of Ethnic and Migration Studies* 43(15), 2556–2572, 2562.
35. Graham (2018), 15.
36. Reeves (2017), 236.
37. Roth, Andrew (2013): Russian Youth Group with a Mission: Sniffing Out Illegal Migrants. *The New York Times* (3 September).
38. Ibid.
39. Putin, Vladimir (2012a): Rossiya: natsional'nyy vopros [Russia: The National Question]. *Nevisimaya Gazeta* (23 January).
40. Putin, Vladimir (2012b): Rossiya ne dolzhna byt' stranoi, kuda mozhno v'ekhat kto ugodna, kak ugodna i kuda ugodna [Russia Must Not be a Country Where Anyone Can Enter Anyhow and Anywhere]. Address to the Collegium of the Federal Migration Service (26 January).

Works Cited

Primary Literature

Alexievich, Svetlana (2015): *Secondhand Time*, translated by Bela Shayevich. London: Fitzcarraldo.

Alexievich, Svetlana (2020): Vremya sekond khend. Moscow: Vremya Kindle edition.

Secondary Literature

Alexievich, Svetlana (2013): Svoboda – eto to, chto my ne umeyem [Freedom is what we cannot do]. *Ogonyok* 34 (2 September 2013), https://www.kommersant.ru/doc/2264009. Accessed 8 January 2021.

Anonymous (2009): Tajik Workers Lived at Moscow Garage in Which They Perished. *Radio Free Europe* (13 January), https://www.rferl.org/a/Seven_Dead_In_Fire_In_Moscow_Underground_Car_Park/1369470.html. Accessed 9 January 2021.

Anonymous (2011): Palace of the Soviets. *Russia Trek* (29 July), https://russiatrek.org/blog/history/moscow-palace-of-soviets-soviet-architectural-giant/. Accessed 9 July 2021.

Anonymous (2012): Arestovan arendator zdaniya na rynke, gde sgoreli 17 chelovek [The arrest of the tenant of the market building, in which 17 people were burned]. *Izvestia* (5 April), https://iz.ru/news/521054. Accessed 9 January 2021.

Anonymous (2012): Fire at Moscow Market Kills 17. *Radio Free Europe* (3 April), https://www.rferl.org/a/moscow_market_fire_kills_12/24535617.html. Accessed 9 January 2021.

Anonymous (2020): Russia Lost 5M Migrants During Pandemic, *The Moscow Times* (16 December).

Bakhtin, M.M. (1981): *The Dialogic Imagination: Four Essays by M. M. Bakhtin*, translated by Caryl Emerson and Michael Holquist. Austin: University of Texas Press.

Boym, Svetlana (1994): *Common Places: Mythologies of Everyday Life in Russia*. Cambridge, MA: Harvard University Press.

Boym, Svetlana (2001): *The Future of Nostalgia*. New York: Basic Books.

Büdenbender, Mirjam, and Daniela Zupan (2017): The Evolution of Neoliberal Urbanism in Moscow, 1992–2015. *Antipode* 49(2), 294–313.

Byford, Andy, Connor Doak, and Stephen Hutchings (2020): *Transnational Russian Studies*. Liverpool: Liverpool University Press.

Carey, Henry F., and Rafal Raciborski (2004): Postcolonialism: A Valid Paradigm for the Former Sovietized States and Yugoslavia? *East European Politics and Societies* 18(2), 191–235.

Clark, Katerina (2011): *Moscow, The Fourth Rome: Stalinism, Cosmopolitanism, and the Evolution of Soviet Culture, 1931–1941*. Cambridge, MA: Harvard University Press.

De Genova, Nicholas (2005): Migrant Illegality and Deportability in Everyday Life. *Annual Review of Anthropology* 31, 419–447.

De Genova, Nicholas (2005): *Working on the Boundaries: Race, Space and "Illegality" in Mexican Chicago*. Durham, NC: Duke University Press.

Demintseva, Ekaterina (2017): Labour Migrants in Post-Soviet Moscow: Patterns of Settlement. *Journal of Ethnic and Migration Studies* 43(15), 2556–2572.

Ferguson, James, and Akhil Gupta (1992): Beyond 'Culture': Space, Identity, and the Politics of Difference. *Cultural Anthropology* 7, 6-23.

Fieldhouse, David Kenneth (1966): *The Colonial Empires: A Comparative Survey from the Eighteenth Century*. New York: Delacorte Press.

Ganguly, Keya (2018): Exile as a Political Aesthetic. *After Said: Postcolonial Literary Studies in the Twenty-First Century*, edited by Bashir Abu-Manneh. Cambridge, MA: Cambridge University Press, 69–86.

Graham, Stephen (2018): *Vertical: The City from Satellites to Bunkers*. London and New York: Verso.

Gunko, Maria, and Ilya Kashnitsky (2016): Spatial Variation of In-Migration to Moscow: Testing the Effect of the Housing Market. *Cities* 59, 30–39.

Koplatadze, Tamar (2019): Theorising Russian Postcolonial Studies. *Postcolonial Studies* 22, 469–489.

Malakhov, Vladimir (2019): Why Tajiks Are (Not) Like Arabs: Central Asian Migration into Russia Against the Background of Maghreb Migration into France. *Nationalities Papers* 47(2), 310–324.

Massey, Doreen (2005): *For Space*. London: Sage.

Merridale, Catherine (2014): *The Red Fortress: The Secret Heart of Russia's History*. London: Penguin.

Moch, Leslie Page, and Lewis H. Siegelbaum (2016): Transnationalism in One Country? Seeing and Not Seeing Cross-Border Migration Within the Soviet Union. *Slavic Review* 75(4), 970–986.

Putin, Vladimir (2012a): Rossiya: natsional'nyy vopros [Russia: The National Question]. *Nevisimaya Gazeta* (23 January), https://www.ng.ru/politics/2012-01-23/1_national.html. Accessed 9 January 2021.

Putin, Vladimir (2012b): Rossiya ne dolzhna byt' stranoi, kuda mozhno v'ekhat kto ugodna, kak ugodna i kuda ugodna [Russia Must Not be a Country Where Anyone Can Enter Anyhow and Anywhere]. Address to the Collegium of the Federal Migration Service (26 January), http://archive.government.ru/docs/17877/. Accessed 9 January 2021.

Reeves, Madeleine (2013): Clean Fake: Authenticating Documents and Persons in Migrant Moscow. *American Ethnologist* 40(3), 508–524.

Reeves, Madeleine (2017): Living From the Nerves: Deportability, Indeterminacy and the 'Feel' of Law in Migrant Moscow. *Affective States: Entanglements, Suspensions and Suspicions*, edited by Mateusz Laszczkowski and Madeleine Reeves. New York and Oxford: Berghan Books, 235–269.

Riabczuk, Mykoła (2013): Colonialism in Another Way: On the Applicability of Postcolonial Methodology for the Study of Postcommunist Europe. *Porownania* 13, 47–59.

Roth, Andrew (2013): Russian Youth Group with a Mission: Sniffing Out Illegal Migrants. *The New York Times* (3 September).

Said, Edward W. (2003): Introduction to the Fiftieth Anniversary Edition. *Mimesis: The Representation of Reality in Western Literature*, by Eric Auerbach, translated by W.R. Trask. Princeton, NJ: Princeton University Press, ix-xxxii.

Todorova, Maria (2010): Balkanism and Postcolonialism, or on the Beauty of the Airplane View. *In Marx's Shadow: Knowledge, Power, and Intellectuals in Eastern Europe and Russia*, edited by Costica Bradatan and Serguei Alex Oushakine. Lanham: The Rowman & Littlefield Publishing Group.

Turaeva, Rano, and Rustamjon Urinboyev (2021): *Labour, Mobility and Informal Practices in Russia, Central Asia and Eastern Europe*. London: Routledge.

Sahadeo, Jeff (2007): *Druzhba Narodov* or second-class citizenship? Soviet Asian migrants in a post-colonial world. *Central Asian Survey* 26(4), 559–579.

Sahadeo, Jeff (2012): Soviet 'Blacks' and Place-Making in Leningrad and Moscow. *Slavic Review* 71(2), 331–358.

Weitz, Eric D. (2002): Racial Politics without the Concept of Race: Reevaluating Soviet Ethnic and National Purges. *Slavic Review* 61(1), 1–29.

Zubovich, Katherine (2010): *Moscow Monumental: Soviet Skyscrapers and Urban Life in Stalin's Capital*. Princeton, NJ: Princeton University Press.

Transnational Neighbourhood and Theatrical Practices

The Concept of Home, Negotiating Strangeness and Familiarity, and the Experience of Migrant Communities in North Essex

MARY MAZZILLI

Abstract

By placing theatrical and related ethnographic practices at the centre of the debate around migration, this chapter contends that in the experience of migrant communities, at the local level of urban microcosms, a transnational neighbourhood exemplifies negotiations between strangeness and familiarity, where the concept of strangeness defines the figure of the migrant as the stranger, and familiarity as part of the process whereby the migrant attempts to make their country of destination into their own home. This chapter will argue that theatrical practices, operating at a local/micro level, are best placed to facilitate the process of a transnational/transcultural neighbourhood, because the performative space as a communal place can transform strangeness, a condition affecting much of the migrant experience, into familiarity. This will be documented by critically assessing the project *Human Side of Migration*, which has involved migrant communities (Syrian, Polish, Filipino and Chinese) from the North Essex region, in the research process that informed the writing of *Priority Seating*, a new stage play, which uses verbatim and non-verbatim techniques and styles.

Introduction

In response to the Brexit referendum, the *Human Side of Migration*[1] has involved migrant communities (Syrian, Polish, Filipino and Chinese) from the North Essex region, in the research process that informed the writing of *Priority Seating*, a new stage play, which uses verbatim and non-verbatim techniques and styles. By placing theatrical and related ethnographic practices at the centre of the debate around migration, this chapter contends that in the experience of migrant communities, at the local level of urban microcosms, a transnational neighbourhood exemplifies negotiations between strangeness and familiarity, where the concept of strangeness defines the figure of the migrant as the stranger, and familiarity as part of the process whereby the migrant attempts to make their country of destination into their own home. This chapter will argue that theatrical practices, operating at a local/micro level, are best placed to facilitate the process of a transnational/transcultural neighbourhood, because the performative space as a communal place can transform strangeness, a condition affecting much of the migrant experience, into familiarity. This will be documented by critically assessing the experience of researching, interviewing migrant communities in the North Essex area, writing the play, and the play itself within the context of ethnographic/verbatim theatrical practices.

Contextualising the project within the field of theatre, as will be explained later on, this project follows the footsteps of many theatrical projects that have investigated issues related to migration by using ethnography and verbatim theatre. However, in this regard, I can claim some originality: unlike many theatrical projects that normally follow the experiences of one migrant group at a time, mine dealt with different migrant groups and their relations at one given time. It is in the interaction between theory and practice where I believe this chapter makes the most unique contribution, first by taking recourse to emerging new definitions of home and home-making. Secondly, in the spirit of this edited volume, this chapter demonstrates how the positioning of the transnational neighbourhood as a microcosm allows for a nuanced understanding of the migrant experience, which refutes the binary discourse of strangeness/familiarity and articulates a discourse of interconnectivity among migrant communities. At a theoretical level, this investigation of the specific North Essex reality as transitional urban network will reflect to what extent the transnational neighbourhood can be equated with the concept of home, i.e. to what extent it equates to the "close interaction, indeed con-formation, of (the ideas of) home and community".[2] Home is, here, considered as an affect that has the capacity to be experienced as polycentric, thus, as attached to a point of origin as well as a destination. Through the lens of this definition of a polycentric notion of home and as connected to the idea of community, the transnational neighbourhood implies the interconnectivity among communities, and the co-habitation of different communities. By relating theory and practice, where ethnographic practices are considered at the centre of the debate around migration, this chapter will be divided into three different sections (plus a conclusion) plunging in and out of theory while explaining the project, its process, and outcomes. The first section introduces how the project came about and its context. The second section, divided into three subsections, will present the theoretical context, the strangeness/familiarity and the transnational neighbourhood as it equates with the notion of home as affect, i.e. (2.1) in relation to migration studies, (2.2) in relation to theatre and in particular, (2.3) the role played by space in theatre. The third section, subdivided into four subsections, will present the project and the play, bringing in the theory by critically assessing (3.1) the research process prior and during the writing of the play, (3.2) the play itself, (3.3) the ethnographic/verbatim approach of the project, and (3.4) commenting on the outcome of this project and the play.

1. About the Project: The Beginning

Before going into the details of the theoretical framework, I will talk about how the project came about, which will reveal its partial auto-ethnographic nature. The *Human Side of Migration* was conceived in the aftermath and in response to the UK's Brexit vote in June 2016, which had led me to question my own identity as an Italian migrant, who has lived her entire adult life away from her country of origin. Having made the UK my home as an adult and tried to assimilate to the British culture, the outcome of the referendum had suddenly made me aware of my own strangeness, as a European non-British passport holder. At this point, I became very much aware of my own dichotomy, between strangeness and familiarity, between feeling at home and feeling displaced. The referendum also coincided with my relocation to North Essex, to Colchester, a well-renowned pro-Brexit region. To my surprise, however, I noticed how multicultural North Essex is, with many migrant communities being settled in the area. By proxy, dealing with my own personal questions of identity, I decided to explore the migrant experience of others, surveying the experience of other first-generation migrants from this area. Originally, this project aimed to give a platform to marginalised communities, reduce their feelings of alienation, and encourage dialogue between those communities and other sections of society. By liaising with existing local migrant communities in the North Essex region, in particular the local Chinese, Polish, Syrian and Filipino communities, an intensive period of research over two months saw the following activities take place: testimonial gathering through interviews with members of each community (30 people were interviewed), followed by in-depth interviews with selected members from each community (10 in total), and one theatre workshop, involving University of Essex graduates who worked with selected members of each community (20 participants in total).

The interviews enabled the members of the migrant community to talk about their stories and their current situation, reflecting on the meaning of home and the process of home-making. The material of the in-depth interviews informed the initial writing of monologues created from the transcripts of the interviews, based on four characters, who conversely were based on the four groups that were interviewed. These were shared in the workshop, which saw the participation of a core group of interviewees, who were invited to respond to the material. Their responses informed the further writing of the play, which was then rehearsed and workshopped with professional actors and presented as a staged reading at Mercury Theatre on 17 November 2017. The reading was then followed by an open discussion on the night, led by a panel made up of local councillors, representatives of each community, sociologists and LiFTs[3] researchers. In June 2018, one focus group comprising the core group of interviewees assessed the impact of their participation in the project on their sense of belonging, on the perception of home and homemaking. Themes that emerged during the interviews confirmed the duality I was experiencing between strangeness and familiarity but also the fluidity between the two. As will be further explored later on, the people I interviewed experienced both, but not all the time. Another element that emerged was the question of intercommunity relations, which inadvertently became a central concern of the play and affected the participating interviewees the most.

In the two years that followed, until the beginning of 2020, further research was carried out on the question of home and home-making, which looked into Sanja Bahun's edited volume *Thinking Home* and her forthcoming publication *Modernism and Home*. The concept of home and home as affect, which will be discussed at length later on, informed subsequent activities, which saw the theatrical experience being used as an educational tool to affect young people's understanding of migration and home. The educational material, combining the theoretical premises of Bahun's study and extracts from the play, was used to enable young people to understand experiences of migration, home and cultural identity; workshops were delivered to 150 pupils aged 6–13 at six schools in North Essex and Suffolk, which had either a strong interest in the performing arts and/or a highly ethnically diverse student population.

Unlike many other theatre projects, which focus on the representation of one community at a time,[4] this project brought together different migrant communities and, very importantly, also included European migrant communities, which are underrepresented in theatre and in the creative industries. As mentioned above, one of the main impacts of the process leading to the writing of the play, and the staged reading itself, for instance, as recounted in responses given by the core interviewees, was that this project highlighted the need to create interaction among communities. The interviewees recognised that the different communities do not often interact with one another and realised that this needs to happen. The project intentionally did not explore the interaction between migrants and the host country but focused on presenting the experience of people coming from different countries in one space, thus representing the tapestry of a microcosm made up of interconnecting cultures.

2. Strangeness/Familiarity

2.1. Relation to Migration Studies

Having outlined the general premises of this project, this chapter will now explore and analyse its theoretical premises and context, concerning the tension of strangeness/familiarity as connected to the migrant experience, the concept of home as equated with the transnational neighbourhood and how these relate to the theatrical medium and in particular the question of space and place. Strangeness is a condition that is typical of the migrant experience. Graziella Parati talks about the location of strangeness, thus defining strangeness not only as a condition but also as spatial entity:

> The location of 'strangeness' resides both in the country where their migration originated and where their migration took them. The location of 'strangeness' resides both in the destination culture that they inhabit and in the attempt to re-inscribe their selves within the pre-migration familiar context. Strangeness becomes a marker for the changes in both who and what they are.[5]

The spatial (and temporal) dimension of migration has been part of conventional accounts of the migration experience, as Vince Marotta explains:

> In this bounded view, the migration experience comes to signify processes that challenge and disrupt the container model of society and its institutional and symbolic tools – citizenship and belonging. From a conventional perspective, for a migrant experience to reveal and distinguish itself from other experiences, it has to satisfy several preconditions: it has to have a spatial and a temporal dimension and must occur within a nation-state system.[6]

Hence, Marotta points not only to the disruptive nature of the migration experience but also to the spatial dimension that contains it. This is not merely a physical space but is part of the geopolitically constructed nation-state system, which also extends to any idea of a 'transnational' migrant experience, affected by a prior existence of a nation-state system.[7] It is, however, beyond the nation-state system that we find the root of strangeness as part of a phenomenological process.

As cited in Marotta's article, which surveys major trends in the conceptualisation of the migrant experience, Alfred Schutz's phenomenology of the stranger has been adopted by many studies on migration as it "speaks directly to the nature of experience and its relation to knowledge construction."[8] The stranger, for Schutz,

> is the cultural other who attempts to assimilate into the host group; however, strangers find it difficult to assimilate because they do not share the taken-for-granted basic assumptions or world-view of host members.[9]

Whilst emphasising assimilation as playing an important part in the strangers' experience, Schutz also defines this experience as a disruption that forces migrants to question their worldview:

> immigrants have gone through a disruptive phenomenon; the stranger's previous self has been transformed through a self-reflective process of inquiry in which they reinterpret and rewrite past horizons and thus expand their knowledge base. Yet, when the stranger finally incorporates the host's scheme of meaning, expression and interpretation, the host's lifeworld becomes the lifeworld of the stranger.[10]

In this process of assimilation, according to Schutz, the passage from their lifeworld to that of the host country indicates that their condition of strangeness changes to one of familiarity, only when they leave behind their own lifeworld and adopt that of the host country. This means that in this process of assimilation, to some extent, to overcome their condition of strangeness, migrants need to reject their relation to their country of origin, which describes the passage from strangeness to familiarity as one of loss and rejection. This definition of the migrant experience, unlike Parati's, not only disregards the migrants' relationship to their country of origin but also places the life of migrants on a polarity between familiarity and strangeness, with any locality in between being one of self-questioning and disruption. The latter denies the possibility that the place in between strangeness and familiarity can be a positive one and also does not account for the migrants' attempt to make a home for themselves without totally leaving behind their attachment to their country and culture of origin.

In this regard, I find it useful to connect the migrant experience to an understanding of home and home-making. Such an understanding is provided by the interrelationship between home and community as presented by the edited volume *Thinking Home* by Sanja Bahun and Bojana Petric. This volume focuses on the connection between home and community, the "close interaction, indeed co-formation [of], (the ideas of) home and community"[11] and proposes the notion of home as an affect, which has the capacity to be experienced as polycentric, thus, as attached to a point of origin as well as of destination. The emotional dimension of home and home-making considers home "as it interacts with human values and human rights in various communities."[12] Such a definition, applied to the migrant experience context, helps position it in a transnational neighbourhood, more fluid than as accounted for in the strangeness/familiarity binary.

In a forthcoming publication, Bahun goes into more detail about the definition of home as affect, first of all by defining affect as being "described as an embodied emotive response forged out of the subject's everyday relationship with the world; a mental processing of reality which excites pleasurable or unpleasurable sensations and feeds our 'moods' in environment". Most importantly, by reflecting on the concept of "affective atmosphere", as elaborated by Lauren Berlant, Bahun states that affect operates "as a discourse and a behavioural practice that interprets and produces that world itself – 'a form of social action' that creates effects in reality."[13] The fact that affect can create and influence change and as a social dimension applies well to the connection home and community. Quoting Mary Douglas' notion of home, Bahun defines it as "a specific space and deep time through an affective experience" and embedded in a community of individuals.[14] In other words, affect as a mental process, behavioural practice and social action creates interactive relations between home and community, between individual and collective, and due to their emotive nature as an "act of imagination"[15] such interactions, albeit unstable and unpredictable, are also fluid, polycentric and multidirectional.

Applied to the migrant experience, in their building up a sense of home, while assimilating the host culture, this describes the potential for migrants to form multidimensional emotional ties not only with the host community, but also with the many communities in the host country and with communities in their country of origin, thus generating further and extended communities that live and develop beyond national boundaries and geographies. This devalues strangeness and familiarity as categorical attributes to the migrant experience and proposes a continuous interaction between the two. Equating this with the transnational neighbourhood and the key focal points of spatiality, temporality and agency, i.e. beyond the binary of strangeness and familiarity, migrants can be considered to have a strong agency in determining the negotiations of both spatial and temporal realities of home and belonging, which are not stable but subject to continuous transformations. Thus, there could be possible periods where one prevails over the other, or both can coexist at the same time, mirroring the emotional complexities of human nature and the dynamic interaction between individuals and communities, all of which constitute most transnational neighbourhoods. It is through the lens of this definition of home that, in the spirit of this edited volume and the fluidity and openness of its definition, this adds another dimension to the transnational neighbourhood, further stressing the interconnectivity among communities, and the co-habitation of different communities.

2.2. Familiarity and Strangeness in Theatre

As we move on and consider theatrical practices, I consider the interconnection between strangeness and the familiar to be at the heart of tragedy, as we can see them clearly being played out in the definition of the tragic hero. I focus here on tragedy as a genre, and the tragic hero in particular, because even though I worked within the practices of verbatim theatre, in experimenting with genres, and in writing the play *Priority Seating* in particular, I consider its characters to be "tragic heroes" according to Paul Hammond's definitions of the "unhomely". In *The Strangeness of Tragedy*, talking about the tragic hero, Hammond refers to Freud's definition of the uncanny and reflects on how the *heimlich* [familiar, homely] and *unheimlich* [uncanny, strange] share "overlapping semantic fields, so that *heimlich* means both 'what is familiar and agreeable' and 'what is concealed and kept out of sight', and in this latter sense 'inaccessible to knowledge, hidden and dangerous' – and therefore *unheimlich*."[16] Most importantly, he explains that a better rendering of *unheimlich* is not the uncanny but "unhomely":

> The *unheimlich* describes the condition of being displaced; one's grasp of 'home' (*Heimat*) is undone, as the distinction between home and foreign is elided; one becomes divided or multiplied, as events seem to be repeated and time no longer seems to follow its normal course: man is no longer at home in the world.[17]

Hammond connects the notion of *unhomely* to that of the tragic hero, which is not only an abstract condition but one that encapsulates the essence of home and belonging, of losing one's own sense of origin and destination. However, I would argue that the above quote does not fully equate *unhomely* with strangeness but presents it as a condition whereby the distinction between strangeness and the familiar is blurred by a sense of multiplicity and divisions. Conversely, like the migrant, the tragic hero can experience simultaneously strangeness and familiarity and the tension between the two in a continuous process of self-questioning and self-discovery.

Even though Hammond emphasises strangeness as the condition of the tragic hero, he also attributes a spatial connotation to the notions of homely/unhomely.

> The space which we think of as home – and by space here I mean both geographical space and conceptual space, both the literal hearth and that framework of familiar assumptions which holds ourselves in place – such a space is labile; we

discover that our home ground is *unheimlich*, that a foreignness haunts the familiar. Tragic protagonists are displaced from their *heimlich* spaces, and find their identities fissured or multiplied.[18]

It is in this spatial connotation, resonating with Parati's locality of the migration experience, that again we find the connection with a multidimensional, polycentric notion of home (identity), which, again, in my view blurs the boundaries between strangeness and familiarity. Such a spatial connotation is relevant when we consider theatrical practices as inherently being space-bound, as will become clear later when referring to Chris Goode's notion of space in theatre.

In theatre and tragedy in particular, as mentioned above, strangeness and familiarity are at the heart of theatrical practices and the theorisation on the function of theatre, on whether it represents or does not represent reality. At two opposite poles of the theatrical tradition are Aristotle and, millennia later, German playwright and director Bertolt Brecht. Aristotle advocated the idea of mimesis, imitation of reality, thus suggesting that theatre should aim for familiarity on stage.[19] Brecht's *Verfremdungseffekt* [distancing/alienation effect], on the other hand, pushed for a process of defamiliarisation on stage, encouraging the audience's critical distance towards what was represented on stage.[20] Generally, Brecht's notion of theatre has affected much of experimental modern and contemporary theatrical practices. Vicki Angelaki, talking about the theatre of contemporary British playwright Martin Crimp, refers to the practice of "making strange" as part of producing theatrical innovation in terms of experimental forms of playwriting, whereby the familiar is rendered unfamiliar in the process of deconstructing reality and fiction on stage.[21]

Mimesis and defamiliarisation (or making strange) in theatre are not totally opposite practices. For instance, mimesis in tragedy does not mean that what we see on stage is real; mimesis implies imitation, which in turn implies fictionalisation. Furthermore, strangeness as a condition of the tragic hero could appear at odds with Aristotle's idea of mimesis, but as such it can be explained as a necessary transformational phase that not only changes the hero's life on stage but also the audience's perception of reality, through a process of "making strange" at an aesthetic and dramaturgical level. The idea of catharsis, of purification, is the product of this process of defamiliarisation, of rendering the familiar strange. In this regard, Aristotle's idea of tragedy shares some similarities with Brecht's theatre.

Notions of strangeness and familiarity can also be equated with the reality/non-reality tension in theatre. Closer to this project and the writing of the play, I cannot but discuss strangeness and familiarity equated with the reality/non-reality tension in connection with verbatim theatre, whose "claim for veracity"[22] has been questioned by scholars and theatre practitioners. This will be discussed later on in reference to the research and writing process of this project, which embraced veracity (familiarity) but, in a similar vein to Martin Crimp, also welcomed experimentation, thus strangeness, here intended as "strange making" on an aesthetic and dramaturgical level.

2.3. Space and Place in Theatre

Going back to the notion of home as a spatial concept and the migrant experience as locality, when we talk about theatre, one cannot avoid referring to the connection between theatre and space, i.e. the performative space. Famous theatre-maker Peter Sellars talks about theatre as connecting communities, with the potential to create shared spaces: "The act of making theater is the act of recognizing, affirming, extending, imagining, and re-affirming a community or, possibly, communities. Metaphorically at first, and then literally and tangibly, theater is the creation of newly shared space on Earth."[23] In *The Forest and the Field*, Chris Goode references the objection by poet Keston Sutherland in his rehearsal that "[p]eople don't live in spaces […] [t]hey live in places",[24] suggesting the idea that any performance space is also a place, with a context. Goode refers to John Cage's famous composition from 1952, 4'33", which demonstrates that not even the emptiest of spaces are devoid of total silence, but are inhabited by background sounds. By focusing on the notion of places rather than spaces in theatre, unlike Peter Brook's idea of 'Empty Space',[25] Goode highlights how the performative space is never a neutral space.

Connecting to the concept of home as affect, this definition of space as an inhabited space full of noises, connotations and pre-meanings – the assumption that as there is no silence, there is no no-meaning – suggests that home or homes are places rather than spaces full of connotations even before we start to inhabit them. Furthermore, if home is a place created by the interaction of communities and people, home is never devoid of meaning. Thus, equating with the idea of place, transnational neighbourhoods are inhabited places formed by the migrant experiences that simultaneously produce familiarity from strangeness, and strangeness from familiarity. This occurs in their attempt to make a home for themselves, by filling their new homes with meanings, while having to negotiate with the pre-existing meanings of those spaces, thus continuously negotiating between strangeness and familiarity. These meanings and connections are created by the microcosm of communities of individuals, not only by the macrocosm of the social, cultural structures and by and large the political structures of the nation-system. Thus, transnational neighbourhoods imply connections between communities at the micro level of communities rather than at the macro level of cultural and national systems, where a sense of home as affect is formed and informs much of the migrant experience. Working at a micro level, theatre further empowers this microcosm of interactions, creating a shared place, a common ground facilitating the polycentric and multidimensional discourses and interactions among communities.

3. The Human Side of Migration

3.1. The Research Process

The project exploited the potentiality of theatre as a catalyst for interaction by employing an ethnographic approach, collecting and exploring real life experiences through a process of audio-recorded face-to-face verbal interviews. The initial sets of interviews were carried out mainly in groups and offered me a general sense of the migrant experience in each community group. These were followed by in-depth interviews with individuals. Some of them ended up forming the core group of participants, who followed through the full process. Such an approach varied, though, according to the accessibility to individual community groups. For instance, accessibility to the Chinese, Filipino and Syrian communities was facilitated by existing organisations, such as Refugee Action Colchester, Colchester Chinese Organization and the Catholic Parish of St Helena and St James the Less. Furthermore, these three groups seemed eager to participate and easy to reach. For the Polish community, even when contacted through the parish, reluctance to participate meant that I only had two interviews with two different individuals. The paucity of Polish interviewees did not greatly affect the outcome of the project, since my intention was not to give a representative portrayal of the migrant experience but to create a sharing opportunity. In fact, the stories that were selected for the play were those from individuals who were most eager to share, because they believed in the process and also felt the need to interconnect with others from other communities.

Coincidentally, the stories selected were unique and distinctive, and even though all of them were from first-generation migrants, they represented different waves of migration. The Chinese interviewees had moved from Hong Kong to the UK in the 1950s. The Filipino interviewee had moved in the last 20 years, the Polish interviewee in the last 10 years, with the Syrian interviewee being the most recent. Even though they had experienced some form or another of discrimination, most of them had made the UK their home and were settled in the urban community. This was not the case of the Polish experience, whose responses, possibly affected by the Brexit vote, reported accounts of serious discrimination. Similarly, the Syrian refugees expressed uncertainty about their future and talked about the trauma of having to flee their country of origin, which affected how they felt about their settling in the UK.

As for the question on the notion of home (Do you miss your country of origin? What does home mean to you?), such differences were also reflected in the answers. One of the main Chinese respondents, who migrated to the region in 1950s, felt settled but ambivalent about his country of origin, in between nostalgia and forgetfulness:

> Because I was basically bought up, I spent my teens in Hong Kong, I'm still very nostalgic of Hong Kong. It doesn't mean I want to go back and live there, but I always regard Hong Kong as part of my life. But increasingly, I've found that I have less of an affiliation with Hong Kong than I do with I think Colchester. For me, it's also a bit different. My children are born here. My grandchildren are here. This is very much my root now. I regard my present home as my home. Hong Kong is a place that I have a lot of history with. I would never forget about Hong Kong.

The main Filipino respondents (wife and husband) expressed a more ambivalent feeling towards the UK as the host country and a stronger attachment to their country of origin:

> I still think that I'm an immigrant. Because I'm a foreigner, because of my colour, or whatever race for me. I still think I'm from the other country. Sometimes I just stop thinking that I'm an immigrant here because we already received our nationality. It's like you've been accepted in a family community, but if you're experiencing things like racism and other things, it will come back again that you're just an immigrant.

In one of their final comments both husband and wife said, "Yeah, of course. There's no place like home", referring to their country of origin.

Whilst expressing anger towards the UK as their host country, interestingly, the main Polish respondent also expressed quite ambivalent feelings towards their country of origin:

> The thing is, when I go home… I don't travel a lot home. I can see the sadness of the people that's on the street. I can see development. My home place is completely different than it was 13 years ago. But I can see the sadness and those people are not really happy.

The main Syrian respondent also avoided directly expressing a sense of attachment towards either the host country or the country of origin. Possibly as a reaction to the destruction of their home and the experience of war and conflict, they expressed a need to look forward to the future without defining what the future might bring:

> I can't tell you about the future. I think different now. Home is home. My child is my future. The most important thing is not to be stubborn, what you think is right might not be later on. Now I feel much better. I can't describe what it is like but even if you go through darkness, people need to move on to see beyond. You need to push and go on.

It is quite telling that the Syrian respondent equates the future with their current family, their son; their sense of home is connected to affects, to family relations – in this case not the family they left behind but their present family, their offspring, who in their minds represent the future and the future is what matters to them.

The ethnographic research did not aim to paint a macro-level picture of the migrant experience and as such the above responses cannot be taken as representative of all migrant experiences, not even of those living in North Essex. However, in attempting to draw a general picture, the experiences of the selected individuals are not dissimilar to those I interviewed in group sessions. As a general rule, with the exception of the Polish respondents, at the beginning of the interview process most of them said that they felt settled in the host country, yet when digging deeper, talking about some rare yet still quite vivid incidents of discrimination, they expressed some unease about their sense of belonging. An important aspect that transpired was their ability to experience home as an affect and multiple homes, through the multiple connections to several communities (work-related community, their children's school, local organisations, connection with their country of origin, etc.). All these elements were integrated in the writing of the play. Before going into detail about the artistic choices, which will explain how the original interviews were integrated into the script, I will talk, first, about the play and the draft presented at the staged reading, and then will discuss the context of the ethnographic approach and verbatim theatre.

3.2. Priority Seating

The play presents four characters on an imaginary train back to the UK (possibly the Eurostar from France). On this train, there is only one seat and an inanimate/non-speaking character is sitting in it. The premise of the play, and one of the connotative thematic layers, is that the non-speaking inanimate character is the only character occupying the only seat in the carriage. As given away in the title, the dystopian setting of the play is that the world of the play represented here is one where priority rights (access to seating in the train) are given only to those with privileges, due to the lack of resources. The latter equates migration with a society that is unequal in the attempt to symbolically articulate the fact that hatred against migrants is, in some cases, caused by situations where resources are deemed to be scarce. The social backdrop is clearly presented by having the inanimate/non-speaking character on stage sitting in the only seat in the carriage and by a voiceover in the first scene of the play, a loudspeaker announcement explaining the priority system with absurdist humour. This setting plays an important part in creating conflict among the four characters and dramatic tension, as, with the exception of John Carlo, everyone (we have a heavily pregnant woman, a physically disabled woman and a frail elderly man) is in need of a seat yet is denied this during the journey; thus, the lack of seating becomes a point of contention.

Besides the fictional setting, each character, to the greatest possible extent, has been moulded by proxy on individual respondents, while representing the four migrant groups. Saya is a Syrian pregnant woman who is the odd-one-out as she has lived in the UK for the least amount of time, thus representing a new migrant and the refugee experience. Echoing the Polish respondents' discontent, Agusia, a Polish woman who has lived in the UK for 10 years, is really unhappy about her situation and suffers from a physical disability, used as a marker of her displacement. Cheon, an elderly Chinese man who moved to the UK from Hong Kong in the 1950s and who is married to an English woman with children and grandchildren, represents one of the earliest post-war migration waves. John Carlo, a Filipino man who is married with three children, works as a carer/nurse and has lived in the UK for over 20 years, is the only one without any particular physical condition that would make the impossibility of sitting down during the journey really unbearable.

In terms of the basic plot, the train is stalled, and the characters start talking about their experiences as migrants. They debate why they cannot sit in the only seat, but as they begin to realise the train cannot move forward, they start blaming one another. Agusia thinks that Saya is the reason why they are not allowed back into the UK. The men try to defend Saya, but they become more and more frustrated with the situation. Cheon tries to dispose of the inanimate/non-speaking character, but the train seemingly derails. Expressing satisfaction with his situation as a migrant at the beginning, John Carlo also becomes increasingly upset and tells stories of how he has been discriminated against on the basis of his skin colour and by the authorities. At the end, there is some sort of reconciliation between Agusia and Saya, as Agusia realises that she has only projected her anger about the situation onto Saya. The play ends with the characters left in limbo, and the question remains whether they reach their destination.

3.3. Verbatim Theatre and Ethnographic Approach

As mentioned above, I chose an ethnographic research approach working within the genre of verbatim theatre and documentary theatre, while also embracing experimentation on an aesthetic and dramaturgical level. An ethnographic approach is often used in theatre-making, sometimes with the intervention of the ethnographer;[26] and like in the case of this project, with the involvement of the writer themselves. Generally, what is produced on stage are verbatim accounts of the words used by interviewees themselves, not merely a version of their stories:

> Ethnographic theatre is, in its simplest terms, theatre that uses actual voices and real stories to create a play, either through the research of the writer or through the involvement of participants in the actual script [...] Verbatim theatre is often linked with ethnographic theatre. In verbatim theatre, participants of a community are interviewed and their actual words are used in the script.[27]

The scope of verbatim theatre is to represent authentic truthful stories on stage, thus voicing the experiences of the people and community they are trying to represent. However, scholars and theatre-practitioners have questioned the authenticity of this process:

> By acknowledging that the very process of transposition of reality onto the stage will throw up its own limitations and potential accusations on the grounds of 'manipulation of facts', it is possibly more honest to once again seek to stay faithful to the language of theatre which renders the real-life story into a metaphorical framework, rather than to maintain a claim to complete authenticity. [...] [W]hat is much more important is for the theatre artist/interviewer to engage epistemically on a number of levels with what is being related to them both verbally and non-verbally by their interviewee so that they can find an appropriate theatrical translation for it.[28]

It is in agreement with this view that as an ethnographer/writer I was an active listener and observer, and created a relationship with the respondents. It is in this vein that I created a fictional framework, and it is in this framework I inserted their stories, while slightly changing them and sometimes moving away from their exact wording. Having created a relationship with the respondents, I managed to involve them in the writing process, where I could check directly with them whether the slight changes made to their stories and the fictional framework were still close enough to their versions of facts, thus avoiding misrepresentations and enabling their stories to be heard in all their complexities and nuances. This sort of process was possible because, thanks to the ethnographic approach and in the theatrical workshop, a shared common place was created where experiences were exchanged and my role was one not only of a distant observer but of an invested participant with my own experience of migration, who was looking for common ground with others with similar experiences to understand my own. To some extent, even if not using my own experience, there was an element of auto-ethnography that helped me connect to the interviewees and made it easy to find "an appropriate theatrical translation for" their experiences that worked at a dramatic level while respecting their veracity. Going back to the tension between strangeness and familiarity, one could argue that at the artistic and creative level the process of research and writing of the play exemplified the fluidity of familiarity and strangeness also on an aesthetic and dramaturgical level, thus (to use Angelaki's terms) "making their stories strange", while still allowing them to recognise them as their own and thus retain a sense of familiarity.

In the theatrical context, this is not the first and only play to deal with migration, but as I said at the beginning of the chapter, there are very few plays that connect different migrant communities. One play that comes close to *Priority Seating*, in terms of the variety of the migrant experience, is *The Container* (2007) by Clare Bayley, a play about refugees (two Afghans, two Somalis and a Turkish Kurd) stuck in a big container crossing Europe, which was staged in a container at the Young Vic in 2009 and in 2007 at the Edinburgh Fringe. However, the focus in this play is on the refugee experience, and even though the writer talked a lot to refugees (Hoby[29]), it is not a verbatim play.

In a similar way, Ros Horin's *Through the Wire* (2005), a verbatim Australian play about the detention of asylum seekers in Australia, deals with migrants from different countries, but mainly from Iran and Iraq, and like Bayley's play explores the condition of imprisonment, of forced detention, where migrants are on their journey of migration or have been stopped from pursuing it. Attracting much press coverage and also controversially failing to secure funding from the Australian government, this play is an interesting example of how theatrical and narrative strategies can manipulate verbatim theatre to great dramatic and to some extent political effect. Wake talks how it "blurs the boundary between theatre and reality through a series of textual, paratextual and performance strategies",[30] these being the ring-composition narrative[31] and the characters talking into microphones with their images projected onto the backdrop of the stage through a live feed.

Moving away from plays about migration, Owen Sheers' *Pink Mist* (2012) is a verse-drama about three young soldiers from Bristol who are deployed to Afghanistan. Not strictly verbatim, Sheers employed an ethnographic approach by interviewing soldiers and their families, which as material for the play was included alongside the medieval Welsh poem *Y Gododdin* in a lyrical dramatic composition.

These examples of verbatim and pseudo-verbatim theatre show very clearly that testimonial material can be often re-imagined through theatrical strategies for dramatic effect whilst still fulfilling, to different extents, the aim of giving voice to the voiceless, and above all of enabling audience to identify (familiarity) with realities other than their own (strangeness) through the theatrical shared place. In the case of *Through the Wire*, for instance, "realist aesthetic facilitated [audiences'] identification with asylum seekers".[32] In the case of *Priority Seating*, the main fictional element added to the verbatim account was the use of an absurdist situation as backdrop to the play: a train that cannot reach its destination in an unequal society and the presence of an inanimate mannequin/non-speaking character. The setting was inspired by Jean-Paul Sartre's *Huis Clos* (*No Exit*, 1944), an existentialist play about three unrelated deceased characters that are destined to argue, for eternity, about their own condition behind closed doors (in French legal terms *huis clos* means behind closed doors), which exemplifies an existential sense of entrapment. Furthermore, additionally some re-writing was needed in the dialogical exchanges between the characters (all the testimonials were gathered individually from each respondent). Sartre's play, which represents three characters at odds with one another, led me to add and create conflict, especially, between the two female characters, Agusia and Saya. This deviates slightly from the strictly verbatim/documentary model and is part of the formal experimentation of this play.

3.4. Comments on the Play

Going into more detail about the main artistic choices, I will explain how strangeness/familiarity tensions and home as an affect with a polycentric nature are articulated in the play. The play follows a two-act structure, which is used to create a journey, a progression, which works at both an aesthetic and a narrative level between reality and the theatrical, between verbatim and non-verbatim, between the use of long monologic speeches, dialogical exchanges, and in Act 2 a totally scripted poetic interlude. Inspired to some extent by Horin's play, which shifts between reality and the theatrical (the stories of the people she interviewed and the manipulation of these stories for the theatrical spectacle), in *Priority Seating* the first act presents the characters in the realistic setting of a train carriage (absence of seats and the presence of the inanimate/non-speaking character already hint at the oddity of the situation) and they are engaged in long monologist expositions about their experiences of migration. Developing the conflicts that had started to emerge in the first act and in the attempt to remove the inanimate/non-speaking character from the only seat, the second act presents more clearly a dystopian world, with the setting being gradually destroyed till the final derailment of the train. Stylistically, in the second act more dialogic interactions take place and the absurdist setting is more prominent. It is in these dialogic interactions that I as a writer had to intervene, create and add to the testimonials gathered during the research period. Thus, this means that in the second act more creative interventions had to be applied and were less close to the verbatim accounts. In scene 3 of Act 2, all characters are engaged in a slow dance accompanied by a poetic interlude. In this regard, the transition between the two acts marks a passage from familiarity to strangeness. However, such a passage is never fully complete, as much of the text and the stories from the respondents' account are still recognisable even in Act 2.

The strangeness/familiarity tension is part of the symbolic journey of the characters: at the beginning, most of the characters are familiar with this journey; they have taken this train many times. But then the train stalling makes the journey more and more strange to them. The strangeness between the characters creates conflict, as we see Agusia accusing Saya, the outsider, of being the reason why the train stalls. It is then, through the process of sharing their accounts, of finding their common ground, that familiarity is experienced, as they also realise that they are involved in the same situation together. The recognition that they are all in it together is the core message of the play and the main outcome of the project. The common shared space facilitated by the ethnographic and theatrical experience had created a meeting place for intercommunity relations. In the end, through the theatrical workshop, the staged reading and the follow-up focus group, the different participants interacted together, started to share thoughts and ideas and found common ground. It is no coincidence that one of the main impacts of the project was that the participants realised that more connections among the different migrant communities in the urban setting of North Essex were needed. To some extent, the play's narrative mirrors this process: in the same way that the respondents had found common ground throughout the process, the characters also realise that despite their differences, they all share similar experiences and are in the same situation together. The sameness and similarities among migrant experiences were also part of Horin's play, which, however, focused mainly on the refugee experience and did not show much conflict between the characters. Thus, I can claim that this project goes further than Horin's.

Conclusion

By bearing in mind the parallel characters of the play and the migrant inter-community relations, one can also draw conclusions about the translational neighbourhood as equated with the concept of home and home-making when considering the question of place and agency. Similarly to Bayley's container, it is important to notice that the space, the setting of a moving train, is not a fixed place; similarly to both Bayley's container and Horin's detention camp, the train in *Priority Seating* also exemplifies a condition of entrapment, a condition that, unlike in Bayley's and Horin's plays, the characters only become aware of later on. The in-betweenness and the moving nature of the setting are at odds with the fixed urban place, the microcosm of the research process. This is also at odds with the respondents' situation, which in most cases, having made North Essex their new home, fluctuates between familiarity and strangeness. Furthermore, beyond its apparent liminality, the train is not an empty space but is a place with pre-established connotations, exemplified by the inanimate/non-speaking character sitting in the only seat in the carriage, whose meaning is expanded by the voiceover referring to priority privileges. The latter is challenged literally and allegorically by the characters, whose needs/wants are to recreate a sense of comfort, make this place their own, make themselves at home.

Beyond the destruction of the place, the disappearance of the inanimate/non-speaking character and the dismantling of the only seat can also be interpreted as the characters' ability to take over the space by deconstructing its own premise as a place, which at the beginning was marked by control and inequality. Even though they cannot escape this situation of entrapment, they find a way to establish their own sense of home and belonging, where home, understood as an affect, is the place created by personal and emotive experience. Despite the characters complaining that they could have taken advantage of the fact that the inanimate/non-speaking character had gone in scene 9 of Act 2, conversely, by not taking the seat, they did not submit to the pre-imposed condition where comfort is only possible by sitting on a given chair. The fact that they end up sitting on the floor means that they chose to create comfort for themselves, on their own terms. Going back to the parallel characters of the play and the migrant intercommunity relations, through the second act and the ending, the theatrical experience still ends up mirroring the respondents' experience of home, which fluctuates between familiarity and strangeness, is pluridimensional and above all is connected to a community of individuals. The characters in the play not only find common ground but also create a sense of community.

Thus, while the train signifies a reclaimed and almost atemporal transnational place (a space that transcends national borders and also is not tied to specific temporal conditions) symbolising the migrant experience and the agency of migrant communities in their never-ending journey of resilience, of continuous adapting and responding to constraints, the project has given migrant communities agency and a common place to explore their common grounds. This is thanks to the power of the theatrical experience, which can create a shared space for interconnecting communities. It is through this process that one can see the potential of transnational neighbourhoods as a discourse that is fluid and polycentric and can also empower migrants beyond the binary of strangeness and familiarity. Furthermore, by focusing on one microcosm – such as the North Essex region as a transitional urban network, a place on the margins, away from the main cosmopolitan centres – such a discourse can overcome binaries and allow for a more nuanced understanding of the migrant experience not as a monolithic entity but as a meeting of individuals and communities. The positive responses to the reading and to the following educational activities, forming a 2021 REF Impact case study, have explored this further and with future plans for a full production and regional tour of the play, which has been re-written since, the hope is to continue building positive discourses around transnational neighbourhoods and the notion of home, now more important than ever in a post-Covid-19 and post-Brexit society.

Notes

1. This project was awarded with the Arts Council Grant of the Arts (England) and ESRC Impact Acceleration Account 2017.
2. Bahun, Sanja, and Bojana Petric (2018): Homing in on Home. *Thinking Home: Interdisciplinary Dialogues,* edited by Sanja Bahun and Bojana Petric. London: Bloomsbury Academic, 14–22, 14.
3. The Department of Literature, Theatre and Film Studies.
4. In a recent publication, Cox, Emma (2014) *Theatre and Migration*. Basingstoke: Palgrave Macmillan, examples are given of theatre pieces that deal with diverse migrant groups but focus only on the refugees and asylum seekers.
5. Parati, Graziella (2013): *Migration Italy: The Art of Talking Back in a Destination Culture*. Toronto: University of Toronto Press, 129.
6. Marotta, Vince (2020): The 'Migrant Experience': An Analytical Discussion. *European Journal of Social Theory* 23(4), 591–610, 597.
7. Ibid.
8. Ibid., 600.
9. Marotta, Vince (2012): Theories of Strangers: Introduction. *Journal of Intercultural Studies* 33(6), 585–590, 585.
10. Marotta (2020), 602.
11. Bahun and Petric (2018), 14.
12. Ibid.
13. Bahun, Sanja (forthcoming 2022): *Modernism and Home*, 12.
14. Ibid., 14f.
15. Ibid.

16. Hammond, Paul (2009): *The Strangeness of Tragedy.* Oxford: Oxford University Press, 5.
17. Ibid., 6.
18. Ibid., 6f.
19. Aristotle & Kenny, A. (2020) Poetics. Oxford: Oxford University Press.
20. Brecht, Bertolt (1964): *Brecht on Theatre: The Development of an Aesthetic*, translated by John Willet. London: Methuen Drama.
21. Angelaki, Vicky (2012): *The Plays of Martin Crimp: Making Theatre Strange.* Basingstoke: Palgrave Macmillan.
22. Hammond, Will, and Dan Steward, eds. (2008): *Verbatim, Verbatim : Contemporary Documentary Theatre.* London: Oberon, 6.
23. Cox, Emma (2014): *Theatre and Migration.* Basingstoke: Palgrave Macmillan. Kindle edition, 117.
24. Goode, Chris (2015): *The Forest and the Field: Changing Theatre in a Changing World.* London: Oberon, 51.
25. Peter Brooks' *The Empty Space* (1968); this also contradicts Michel de Certeau's idea that "space is a practiced place." Cox (2014), 154.
26. Summerskill, Clare (2020): *Creating Verbatim Theatre from Oral Histories.* New York and Abingdon: Routledge, 12.
27. Wiltshire, Kim (2015): *Writing for the Theatre.* London: Palgrave Macmillan, 158.
28. Radosavljevic, Duška (2013): *Theatre-Making: Interplay Between Text and Performance in the 21st Century.* London: Palgrave Macmillan, 137.
29. Horby, Hermione (2009): The Container – Young Vic. TheObserver.co.uk (19 July).
30. Wake, Caroline (2013): To Witness Mimesis: The Politics, Ethics, and Aesthetics of Testimonial Theatre in Through the Wire. *Modern Drama* 56(1), 102–125, 107.
31. Whereby the first and final scenes both portray a particular element (event, object, person, phrase, etc.), the second and second-last scenes both depict another element, the third and third-last scenes yet another element, and so on, all the way into the narrative's centre. Ibid., 107.
32. Ibid., 118.

Works Cited

Primary Literature

Bayley, Claire (2007): *The Container (NHB Modern Plays).* London: Nick Hern Books.
Horin, Ros (2004): *Through the Wire.* Unpublished manuscript.
Mazzilli, Mary (2017): *Priority Seating.* Script available from the HEI on request. Link to the reading of the full play, https://www.youtube.com/watch?v=cOhhOt-p8F4&feature=youtu.be. Accessed 7 July 2021.

Sartre, Jean-Paul (1989): *No Exit and Three Other Plays*. New York: Vintage International.
Sheers, Owen (2013): *Pink Mist*. London: Faber & Faber.

Secondary Literature

Angelaki, Vicky (2012): *The Plays of Martin Crimp: Making Theatre Strange*. Basingstoke: Palgrave Macmillan.
Aristotle & Kenny, A. (2020) Poetics. Oxford: Oxford University Press.
Bahun, Sanja (forthcoming 2022): *Modernism and Home*.
Bahun, Sanja, and Bojana Petric (2018): Homing in on Home. *Thinking Home: Interdisciplinary Dialogues*, edited by Sanja Bahun and Bojana Petric. London: Bloomsbury Academic, 14–22.
Brecht, Bertolt (1964): *Brecht on Theatre: The Development of an Aesthetic,* translated by John Willet. London: Methuen Drama.
Brooks, Peter (2008): *The Empty Space*. New York: Penguin.
Cox, Emma (2014): *Theatre and Migration*, with a foreword by Peter Sellars. Basingstoke: Palgrave Macmillan. Kindle edition.
Goode, Chris (2015): *The Forest and the Field: Changing Theatre in a Changing World*. London: Oberon.
Hammond, Paul (2009): *The Strangeness of Tragedy*. Oxford: Oxford University Press.
Hammond, Will, and Dan Steward, eds. (2008): *Verbatim, Verbatim : Contemporary Documentary Theatre*. London: Oberon.
Horby, Hermione (2009): The Container – Young Vic. TheObserver.co.uk (19 July).
Marotta, Vince (2012): Theories of Strangers: Introduction. *Journal of Intercultural Studies* 33(6), 585–590.
Marotta, Vince (2020): The 'Migrant Experience': An Analytical Discussion. *European Journal of Social Theory* 23(4), 591–610.
Parati, Graziella (2013): *Migration Italy: The Art of Talking Back in a Destination Culture*. Toronto: University of Toronto Press.
Radosavljevic, Duška (2013): *Theatre-Making: Interplay Between Text and Performance in the 21st Century*. London: Palgrave Macmillan.
Summerskill, Clare (2020): *Creating Verbatim Theatre from Oral Histories*. New York and Abingdon: Routledge.
Wake, Caroline (2013): To Witness Mimesis: The Politics, Ethics, and Aesthetics of Testimonial Theatre in Through the Wire. *Modern Drama* 56(1), 102–125.
Wiltshire, Kim (2015): *Writing for the Theatre*. London: Palgrave Macmillan.

About the Authors

Daniela Bohórquez Sheinin is a PhD candidate in History at the University of Michigan, US. She specialises in urban, cultural and oral history. Her dissertation, *Staging Neighborhood: Making Queens in the Construction of New York's Last Great Park*, details the complex histories of material, ethnic, social and political neighbourhood change around Flushing Meadows–Corona Park in 20th-century Queens, New York. Her work has appeared in the *Journal of Transnational American Studies* and the *Gotham Center for New York City History Blog*, and she was co-founder and first host of the historical podcast *Reverb Effect*.

Emma Crowley is a Lecturer with the English Department at the University of Bristol, UK. Her research to-date has focused on the intersection of world literature and legacies of the global Cold War, focusing on the relation between literary form, politics and economies of fiction. She also researches the possibilities of decolonial theory as praxis, literary activism and genre fiction. Her work is interdisciplinary and multilingual, and she is committed to breaking down the boundaries between the teaching and research of English literature and other disciplines.

Stephan Ehrig is a Lecturer in German at the University of Glasgow, UK, working on the literary and cinematic responses to the post-war GDR modernist built environment. He has published on 19th-century German literature and theatre and on East German literature, theatre and film. His first monograph, *Der dialektische Kleist* (Transcript, 2018), offers the first in-depth reception history of Heinrich von Kleist's works in literature and theatre of the GDR. His co-edited volume, *The GDR Today. New Interdisciplinary Approaches to East German History, Memory and Culture* (Peter Lang, 2018), pursues similar interests by featuring innovative research on the GDR which challenges established frameworks and concepts.

Anne Fuchs held Professorships of Modern German Literature and Culture at University College Dublin, the University of St Andrews, and the University of Warwick. She is the co-founder of the UCD Humanities Institute and assumed its Directorship in October 2016. Her research interests include memory studies (in particular German politics of memory since 1945), German literature in the 20th and 21st centuries, German-Jewish literature, modernism, the cultural history of walking, and time and temporality in the digital era. Recent publications include *Precarious Times* (Cornell University Press, 2019), *Ästhetische Eigenzeit in Contemporary Literature and Culture* (special issue of *Oxford German Studies*, co-edited with Ines Detmer, 2017), and *Time in German Literature and Culture, 1900–2015: Between Acceleration and Slowness* (Palgrave Macmillan, 2016, co-edited with J.J. Long). In 2009, she was elected a member of the Royal Irish Academy (MRIA); in 2014, she was elected a Fellow of the British Academy (FBA).

Christina Horvath is a Reader in French Literature and Politics at the University of Bath, UK. Her research addresses urban representations in literature and film, with emphasis on artistic expressions of advanced marginality such as contemporary French 'banlieue narratives' and favela literature in Brazil. She has published widely on contemporary French and Francophone literature, banlieues and postcolonial legacies in France. Since 2013, she has been working on the conceptualisation and testing of 'Co-Creation', defined as an arts-based method to promote social justice in disadvantaged urban areas.

Britta C. Jung is a Lecturer in German Studies and Applied Linguistics at Maynooth University, and a former Irish Research Council Postdoctoral Fellow at the UCD Humanities Institute, University College Dublin, Ireland. Her publications include *Komplexe Lebenswelten – Multidirektionale Erinnerungsdiskurse: Jugendliteratur zum Nationalsozialismus, Zweiten Weltkrieg und Holocaust im Spiegel des postmemorialen Wandels* (Vandenhoeck & Ruprecht, 2018), several peer-reviewed articles on contemporary German and Dutch literature, and a bilingual volume on Central European Border Spaces (Vandenhoeck & Ruprecht, 2021, co-edited with Sabine Egger and Stefan Hajduk). Her current research project examines how literary texts by authors from a migrant and non-migrant background respond to prevailing normative concepts such as national identity, heritage and community.

Emilio Maceda Rodríguez is a full-time Professor of the School of Sciences for Human Development of the Autonomous University of Tlaxcala, Mexico. He is a member of the academic body Vulnerability, Human Development and Public Policies, UTALx-225. He holds a PhD in Regional Development from El Colegio de Tlaxcala A.C., and Bachelor's and Master's degrees in History from the Benemérita Universidad Autónoma de Puebla. He is currently directing the project 'Families and Care in Migration Contexts'. He is a founding member of the *Pequeñas y Pequeños Universitarios* Program of the Autonomous University of Tlaxcala. His lines of research include international migration, migrant families and care, transnational religious practices, nostalgia market, transnational migrant entrepreneurs, and virtual and digital ethnography.

Anna Marta Marini is a PhD fellow at the Instituto Franklin, Universidad de Alcalá, Spain, where her main research project (in collaboration with the CISAN–UNAM) delves into the representations of border crossing and the 'other side' in US popular culture. Her main research interests are: critical discourse analysis related to violence, discrimination and state repression; the representation of borderlands and Mexican American heritage; and the re/construction of identity and otherness in film and comics, particularly in the horror and (weird) western genres. She is currently the president of the PopMeC Association for US Popular Culture Studies.

Mary Mazzilli is a Senior Lecturer in Drama and Literature at the University of Essex, UK, and co-director of the Centre for Theatre Research. She has an expertise in both Chinese and British drama and theatre. She is also a playwright and her plays have been staged in the UK and China. Before joining Essex in 2016, Mary was a Lecturer in Theatre Theory and Contemporary Practice at Goldsmiths in the Theatre and Performance Department (2015–2016). In 2012–2014, she was a Postdoctoral Fellow at Nanyang Technological University, Singapore. For several years, she has been a Research Associate at SOAS, University of London, where she lectured in Chinese Theatre and Cinema. In addition to theatre, she has a strong expertise in literature (world, comparative literature and women's writing). Her monograph *Gao Xingjian's Post-Exile Plays: Transnationalism and Postdramatic Theatre* (Bloomsbury, 2019) has attracted excellent reviews.

Maria Roca Lizarazu is a Postdoctoral Researcher in Creative Futures at the Moore Institute, NUI Galway, Ireland. Her publications include *Renegotiating Postmemory: The Holocaust in Contemporary German-language Jewish Literature* (Camden House, 2020) as well as several peer-reviewed articles on contemporary German-Jewish literature and culture, particularly the works of Maxim Biller, Max Czollek, Eva and Robert Menasse, Katja Petrowskaja, Sasha Marianna Salzmann and Benjamin Stein. Her current research project examines literary encounters with difference and diversity in contemporary, post-migrant Germany.

Gad Schaffer is a Lecturer in the Departments of Multidisciplinary Studies and Galilee Studies at Tel-Hai College, Israel. He is also the academic head of the Historical Cartography Research Institute at Tel-Hai College, which promotes research using historical maps and aerials from the 19th century onward using new technologies of mapping. Schaffer is a historical geographer, and has published widely on landscape changes in the Land of Israel from the 19th century to the present, based on historical maps, aerial and satellite imagery, and the use of Geographic Information Systems (GIS). His research interests are landscapes, land use/land cover changes, cartography, cultural landscapes, urban and agricultural landscapes, and GIS.

Godela Weiss-Sussex is a Professor of Modern German Literature at the Institute of Modern Languages Research, University of London, UK. She is also a Fellow in German at King's College, Cambridge. Her main research interests lie in the culture and literature of the 20th and 21st centuries in the following areas: women's writing, the works of German-Jewish writers produced in Germany and in exile, multi- and translingualism, concepts of *Heimat* and belonging, and minor and minority literatures. Recent publications include *Rethinking Minor Literatures: Contemporary Jewish Womens' Writing in Germany and Austria* (special issue of *Modern Languages Open*, co-edited with Maria Roca Lizarazu, 2020) and *Women Writing Heimat in Imperial and Weimar Germany* (special issue of *German Life and Letters*, co-edited with Caroline Bland and Catherine Smale, 2019).

Naomi Wells is a Lecturer in Modern Languages with Digital Humanities at the Institute of Modern Languages Research, School of Advanced Study, University of London, UK. She previously worked as a researcher on two large UK Arts and Humanities Research Council funded projects: 'Transnationalizing Modern Languages: Mobility, Identity and Translation in Modern Italian Cultures' and 'Cross-Language Dynamics: Reshaping Community'. Her previous publications have focused on migration and multilingualism in Spanish- and Italian-speaking contexts, with her current research exploring the role of digital media and technologies in relation to diasporic cultures and communities. She is also joint Editor of the Digital Modern Languages section of the *Modern Languages Open* journal.

www.ingramcontent.com/pod-product-compliance
Ingram Content Group UK Ltd.
Pitfield, Milton Keynes, MK11 3LW, UK
UKHW021847140426
5217IPUK00022B/1634